ANXIOUS DAYS
AND TEARFUL NIGHTS

ANXIOUS DAYS AND TEARFUL NIGHTS

Canadian War Wives during the Great War

MARTHA HANNA

Carleton Library Series 252

McGill-Queen's University Press
Montreal & Kingston • London • Chicago

© McGill-Queen's University Press 2020

ISBN 978-0-2280-0366-3 (cloth)
ISBN 978-0-2280-0367-0 (paper)
ISBN 978-0-2280-0459-2 (ePDF)
ISBN 978-0-2280-0460-8 (ePUB)

Legal deposit third quarter 2020
Bibliothèque nationale du Québec

Printed in Canada on acid-free paper that is 100% ancient forest free
(100% post-consumer recycled), processed chlorine free

This book has been published with the help of a grant from the Canadian Federation
for the Humanities and Social Sciences, through the Awards to Scholarly Publications
Program, using funds provided by the Social Sciences and Humanities Research Council
of Canada.

Funded by the   Financé par le
Government   gouvernement   Canada   Canada Council   Conseil des arts
of Canada   du Canada   for the Arts   du Canada

We acknowledge the support of the Canada Council for the Arts.

Nous remercions le Conseil des arts du Canada de son soutien.

Library and Archives Canada Cataloguing in Publication

Title: Anxious days and tearful nights : Canadian war wives during the Great War /
    Martha Hanna.

Names: Hanna, Martha, 1955– author.

Series: Carleton library series ; 252.

Description: Series statement: Carleton library series ; 252 | Includes bibliographical
    references and index.

Identifiers: Canadiana (print) 20200264567 | Canadiana (ebook) 2020026656x |
    ISBN 9780228003670 (softcover) | ISBN 9780228003663 (hardcover) |
    ISBN 9780228004592 (PDF) | ISBN 9780228004608 (ePUB)

Subjects: LCSH: Military spouses – Canada – History – 20th century. | LCSH: World War,
    1914–1918 – Women – Canada. | LCSH: Military spouses – Canada – Psychology –
    History – 20th century. | LCSH: Military spouses – Canada – Social life and
    customs – 20th century. | LCSH: World War, 1914–1918 – Canada.

Classification: LCC FC557 .H36 2020 | DDC 940.3086/550971–dc23

This book was designed and typeset by Peggy & Co. Design in 10.5/13 Sabon.

For my mother,
Patricia Frances Barber
With love

Contents

Acknowledgments

This book began with a question: How did their distance from the fighting front of war affect the experience of civilians – war wives in particular – of the First World War? Having devoted the best part of two decades to exploring how the war shaped the everyday lives of men and women on the French home front; having discovered that regular and honest communication between French soldiers and their wives gave civilians an often unsettling knowledge of the war, I wanted to know whether this was unique to France. Were civilians several thousand kilometres from the battlefields of northern France and Belgium not only protected from but also unaware of the true character of the war? To explore this question, I turned to Canada and, after many trips to archives in Ottawa, supplemented by briefer forays into archives in Toronto and Winnipeg, I discovered that distance from the European battlefields mattered, but in a different way than I had originally imagined.

My exploratory expeditions would not have been possible without the help of dedicated archivists and editors, and the hospitality of family. Carol Reid and Shannyn Johnson at the Canadian War Museum's Centre for Historical Research offered invaluable assistance as I searched for the correspondence of Canadian soldiers and, more recently, the illustrations included in this book. Many archivists at Library and Archives Canada worked diligently to guarantee that the boxes I needed arrived at my desk with exemplary promptness, and the always friendly Legionnaire staff added warmth to wintry trips to Ottawa. In Winnipeg, Rachel Mills at the Archives of Manitoba helped secure my access to the Edith Rogers papers. I don't know whom to thank for undertaking the remarkable digitization project that has made available the service records of all men serving in the Canadian Expeditionary Force, but this book could not have been written without their labours. Nor, indeed, could the database created for this book, which builds upon these service records, have been created without the excellent efforts of my research assistant, Michael Rupert. Sarah Luginbill deserves recognition – and thanks – for preparing the index. As I considered the evidence I had unearthed in these trips into the archives and assessed its significance, I benefited enormously from the insights of my esteemed colleague and good friend Barbara Engel, with whom I shared many a pleasant lunch and probing conversation about the lot of Canada's war wives. Kyla Madden and Jane McWhinney, my editors at MQUP, also prompted me to think carefully about the story that emerges from these archival sources.

The women whose experiences of the Great War are told here discovered during the course of that war the singular importance of family. I, too, have been reminded on many occasions while researching this book how greatly I have come to rely on – and appreciate – the encouragement, hospitality, and intellectual conversation my family has provided over many years. To Josh and Cheryl, whose Ottawa home became my home-away-from-home during my many research trips: thank you for the great meals, the warm welcome, and your patience as I recounted tales of stories found in the archives. Earl, of course, contributed little to our post-dinner conversations beyond an occasional, contented purr, but he always made me feel that he had accepted me as family. To Kate, who graciously opened her Toronto house to me, and to Peter, who offered insights into the sometimes-arcane nature of the law: thank you for indulging my curious passion for the First World War. To Tristan, who at my request explored the divorce records buried in Senate proceedings, my thanks and gratitude. And to Doug, Brenda, Bryan, and Grace: Winnipeg's blustery days were warmer thanks to your friendly hospitality. Bob, Beth, and Jerren have lived with this book and my intermittent anxieties about whether I could do justice to these women's experiences, and have always offered their unreserved reassurances. No one, however, has shaped this project and my passion for it more directly than my mother. For those of us who are three – or even four – generations removed from the men and women of the Great War, their lives are (at best) subjects of historical interest. For my mother, who was born ten years after the Battle of the Somme took the life of her grandfather, the war and the pall of bereavement it inevitably wove shaped her childhood and, in many ways, made her the resilient, devoted, and accomplished woman she would become. This book is dedicated to her.

Troops embarking from Victoria, British Columbia, 1914. CWM 20000013-018_2.
George Metcalf Archival Collection, Canadian War Museum.

Maggie Ormsby, Margaret Ormsby, and Hugh Ormsby [1916]. "April 9, 1916,
My dear Maggie … I was very pleased indeed to get the photo of my darlings."
CWM 20000013-012, Maggie Ormsby and the Children, George Metcalf Archival
Collection, Canadian War Museum.

Lawrence Browning Rogers [1915]. cwm 20040015-003, Portrait of Lawrence Browning Rogers, George Metcalf Archival Collection, Canadian War Museum.

"G'Bye Mary, the Patriotic Fund Will Care for You." Patriotic Fund Poster. Library and Archives Canada, Acc. No. 1983-28-576.

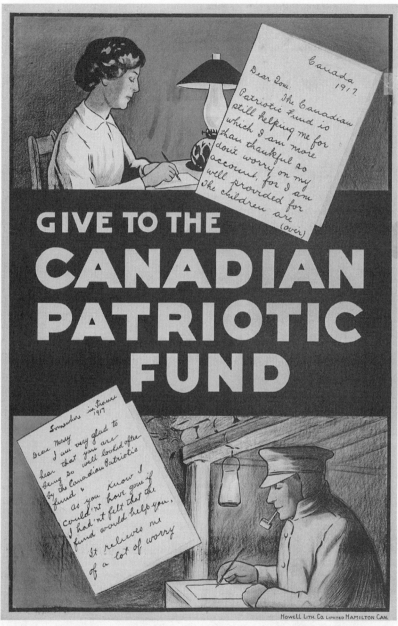

"Give to the Canadian Patriotic Fund." Canadian Patriotic Fund canvassing, 1917.
Library and Archives Canada, Acc. No. 1983-28-581.

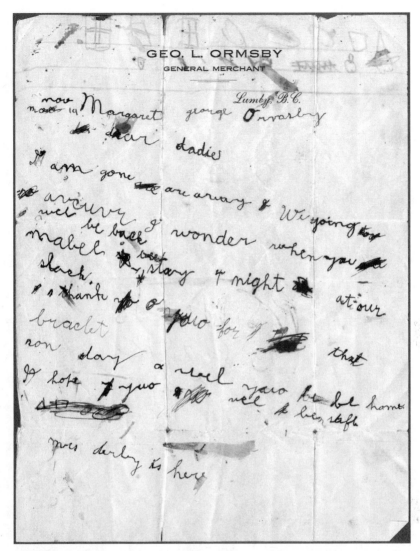

Margaret Ormsby to her father, George Ormsby: "November 19 [1915] We going to Vancouver I wonder when you wil be back." CWM 20000013-001, Fonds of Sgt. Ormsby, George Metcalf Archival Collection, Canadian War Museum.

Postcard from Lawrence Rogers to his son, Howard Rogers, September 1915: "I've come here to dodge the girls." CWM 20040015-016, George Metcalf Archival Collection, Canadian War Museum.

Postcard from Lawrence Rogers to May Rogers [ca 1917]: "Cheer up, we ain't the first that's had to do it." cwm 20040015-017. George Metcalf Archival Collection, Canadian War Museum.

George Ormsby, Maggie Ormsby, Margaret Ormsby, and Hugh Ormsby, 1918. CWM 20000013-011, Ormsby Family Portrait, George Metcalf Archival Collection, Canadian War Museum.

ANXIOUS DAYS
AND TEARFUL NIGHTS

Introduction

Montreal. 14 May 1915. The *Megantic* is about to set sail for Liverpool, the men aboard bound for war. Ted Clarke is in a hurry. Before the ship weighs anchor, he needs to send his wife and children a postcard. Much to his regret, he had not been able to say goodbye in person when the troop train pulled out of the Oshawa station for Montreal. And now, before leaving Canada for good, he must do so. He assures Frances that he will write as soon as he arrives in England, but in the meantime, she should keep a close eye on the papers for an announcement that the *Megantic* has safely crossed the Atlantic. He surely knows (and shares) her anxiety, for only a week earlier, a torpedo fired from a German submarine had sunk the ocean liner *Lusitania*. Twelve hundred perished. Knowing all too well that in the spring of 1915 ocean travel is a hazardous enterprise, Clarke seeks solace in faith: "God bless you all," he prays.[1] After that, silence.

Although it is almost certain that Ted Clarke did write to his wife and children upon arriving in England and following his deployment to France, perhaps expressing his worries and almost certainly conveying his affection – as so many other married Canadian soldiers did – no trace of further correspondence remains. If Frances confided in him her concerns about the family budget or bemoaned the high cost of living, as other Canadian wives did; if she commented on the riches earned by those who stayed home or indulged in wishful thoughts about the prospects for prosperity when the war was won, these resentments and reflections also elude us. Frances Clarke's experience of the Great War remains an almost total mystery.

It is, however, possible to construct a plausible picture of her life, her ordinary travails and her extraordinary anxieties by building a composite portrait of Canada's war wives. Drawing upon the extant correspondence of married Canadian soldiers, the traces of their wives' daily lives now safeguarded in national and provincial archives, and the fragmentary evidence of these women's economic resources and peripatetic routines preserved in their husbands' military service records, *Anxious Days and Tearful Nights* asks the question: What was it like to be a Canadian war wife during the Great War? And, moreover, how can a deeper understanding of these women's lives illuminate, in ways not yet fully clear, the disruptive and often tragic effects of that now-distant war?

There were almost ninety thousand women like Frances Clarke in Canada during the First World War.[2] Or, to be more precise, somewhat like her. She was thirty years old when she arrived in Canada from England in February 1914, accompanied by five children and bound for Oshawa, where she would reunite with her husband and oldest daughter. Of course, not every war wife had so many children, and many were much younger, perhaps newlyweds who had hastened to the altar shortly before or just after their husbands enlisted. But women like Frances Clarke from the ranks of the labouring classes, with several young children at home and emotional ties to the "Old Country," were in the majority among Canada's war wives.

Many lived in southern Ontario, the heart of Canadian recruitment.[3] In the newly incorporated Toronto neighbourhood of Earlscourt, so heavily populated by British immigrants as to be known colloquially as "Little Britain," British-born married men enlisted in large numbers. In 1916, when recruitment was most vigorous, the *Toronto Daily Star* reported that of the 1,457 men who had enlisted from Earlscourt (only ninety-four of whom were Canadian-born) fully two-thirds of the total cohort were married, many with three or more children at home.[4] An analysis of married soldiers from Manitoba, which boasted the highest rate of voluntary enlistment in Canada, reveals a similar pattern: in a province populated largely by recent immigrants, British-born recruits were, not surprisingly, a strong presence and, as was the case in Toronto, many had several children to support. Although southern Ontario and Manitoba led the way in military recruitment, enlistment included married men – British- and Canadian-born – from across the nation.[5]

The core documentation upon which this book is built consists of the wartime correspondence of men both born in Canada and recently arrived from Britain. Among the Canadian-born were Frank Maheux, a lumberjack who struggled to make a living in the woods north of Ottawa, and Laurie Rogers, a gentleman farmer in the Eastern Townships; and typical of the recent immigrants were Henry Hillyer, an employee of the Westmount municipal authorities, Will Mayse, a Baptist minister in Manitoba, and George Ormsby, who settled with his wife and two children in Vernon, British Columbia. As with the men, the war wives were both Canadian-born and recent immigrants. Angeline Maheux, for instance, was a member of the Odawa First Nation whose mother and two brothers lived on the reserve at Maniwaki.[6] Betty Mayse and Margaret Ormsby were born in Ontario, later moving with their parents out west, where they met and married their husbands. Among the British immigrants were May Timmins, who had arrived in Canada as a newlywed with her husband, George, in 1905. Perhaps May even crossed paths with Frances Clarke, comparing ideas about child-rearing and complaints about the price of coal, for they lived only a few blocks apart in Oshawa, Ontario.

Historians of Canada during the Great War have mined the wartime correspondence of Maheux, Rogers, and Ormsby to great effect. Because these married men wrote at considerable length and because their wives preserved the letters they so eagerly received, historians such as Tim Cook and Desmond Morton have been able to extract from this epistolary archive a deep and nuanced portrait of the front-line experiences, aspirations, anxieties, and innermost thoughts of these and many other Canadian soldiers.[7] Our knowledge of the war is infinitely richer for their efforts. *Anxious Days and Tearful Nights* uses these records for a different purpose: to unearth and understand the much less familiar lives of Canada's war wives. A close reading of the letters their husbands sent home allows us to distill the collective experiences of Canadian war wives and discover how distance and long-term separation defined their wartime lives and distinguished them in critical ways from their contemporaries in Europe.

Distance from the fighting lines mattered in two ways. Canadian civilians were largely insulated from the radically disruptive material deprivation that came to characterize everyday life in wartime Europe. This is not to say that material conditions in Canada – the price of food, the availability of heating fuel, the cost of rent – remained untouched by wartime inflation; but such material stresses never proved so destabilizing as to prompt women to protest the very legitimacy of the state, as they did in Berlin and Vienna, Moscow and Petrograd. But if distance offered a degree of protection from the most adverse material consequences of the war, it is reasonable to surmise that it intensified the psychological stresses caused by the war. The vast distance that separated Canada from the battlefront made it almost impossible for married men to go home on leave, denying married couples in Canada a most important source of solace enjoyed by European soldiers and their wives. Distance also delayed and disrupted communication between husbands and wives, preventing the quick and regular exchange of letters seen in many European countries, particularly in France, where a letter from the front would usually reach its recipient within three days. Canadian wives often waited three weeks or more for reassuring letters in their husband's hand.

Separated from their husbands for years on end, unable to reunite even briefly during leave, subjected to the lengthy silences occasioned by erratic trans-Atlantic postal services, and compelled to manage the family home and cope alone with the anxiety that inevitably accompanied the illnesses of young children, Canadian war wives shared with their European sisters most of the anxieties of wartime separation but little of the occasional respite. When Arthur Meighen astutely observed in 1917 that Canadian women whose menfolk were fighting in France knew only days filled with anxiety, and nights with tears, he did more than make a rhetorical point in the conscription debate. He acknowledged the psychological stresses occasioned by wartime separation.[8] We have long known that the war frayed the nerves of the men who fought it, giving rise in the most anguished cases to the disorder then identified as shell shock.[9] We have not fully appreciated that civilians also endured the psychological effects of war. War wives and war widows did not directly suffer shell shock – whose shattered victims have become a metaphor for the war itself – but they suffered often-debilitating nervous strain nonetheless. To study the experiences of Canadian war wives is, therefore, to shed light on how the Great War transformed the lives of women who, although protected from war's most grievous material consequences, were by no means immune to or untouched by its distressing emotional effects.

❧

For decades, popular memory all but ignored the women whose husbands went off to war in 1914. In part, this is because the iconic soldier of the First World War was – and largely continues to be – the young, unmarried man barely out of school who, the story goes, enlisted with great enthusiasm only to become deeply disillusioned by the unanticipated horrors of front-line combat. His equally iconic female counterpart remains the young, unmarried woman who, according to her family circumstances, social status, and education, contributed to the war effort as a volunteer nurse or stenographer, munitions worker or tram driver. Yet this concentration on the young and the unmarried has overlooked a stark reality of military service (and its consequences for family life) during the First World War: married men constituted a significant proportion of all European armies and a non-trivial presence in the Canadian Expeditionary Force (CEF). In

France, where conscription placed eight million men in uniform – fully 20 percent of the national population and 60 percent of the active adult population – perhaps as many as five million were married.[10] Conscription mobilized a somewhat smaller percentage of the adult male German population, but at least one-third of all German soldiers (and likely more) were married: in Bavaria, where German archival records are the most complete, married men accounted for more than half of all conscripts. A similar pattern obtains for the army of the Habsburg Empire. The military service of married men in Austria was so common that "of the 25,616 Viennese men who had died in service between 1914 and 1918, about 70 percent were married."[11] Even in Russia, where conscription reforms enacted in 1912 had exempted from military service "the only son or sole able-bodied male worker of a household," married men still served in significant numbers: by 1916, 44 percent of all peasant households in Moscow province had seen all their male workers – including many married men – drafted into military service.[12] Britain did not introduce conscription until 1916, initially exempting married men but ultimately requiring the enlistment of all able-bodied males of military age except those who served in civilian jobs deemed essential to the war effort. By the end of the war, more than 1.5 million married British men had seen military service.[13]

The extensive mobilization of married men in Europe has spurred historians to analyze how the Great War affected the wives who remained at home. Three interrelated topics of inquiry – and three important conclusions – characterize this scholarship. First, the vast scale of wartime mobilization, which transformed millions of men in each combatant nation from civilian breadwinners to soldiers, meant that many war wives had to work; others chose to do so, and yet others – especially in the Central Powers – found it almost impossible to do so: their lives were too burdened by the demands of everyday life to make waged labour, whether in factories or in public employment, a viable possibility. Second, the material hardships created by four years of war so profoundly plagued civilian life in central and eastern Europe as to propel soldiers' wives in Germany, Austria, and Russia into the public sphere of political protest. Finally, wives in all the European nations where literacy was well established became regular (albeit, often noticeably ungrammatical) correspondents.

Many of the European war wives who had no choice but to work following their husbands' mobilization were peasant women. In villages from the French slopes of the Pyrenees to the Russian steppes, these women – no strangers to hard work – now took on the back-breaking tasks that had previously been deemed "men's work." They managed the family farm; hired labour if and when they could; and seeded, ploughed, and reaped the fields when they could not. Their labour went, for the most part, unappreciated. In France, where more than half of the men drafted into the army were peasants, wives and parents went into the fields to maintain the family patrimony as best they could. Memorialized in fiction and film as *les gardiennes*, French peasant women successfully brought in the harvest of 1914, earning the approbation of city folks, but when in subsequent years crop yields declined precipitously these same women became objects of scorn and derision, criticized as lazy, self-indulgent, and indifferent to the suffering of those who could not grow their own food. Italian women seem to have been more successful than their French counterparts at maintaining their family farms; Alison Belzer notes that "despite the absence of over 3 million male workers, Italy's national agricultural output remained constant during the war."[14] And Russian peasant women, long accustomed to managing their farms when husbands left their native villages in search of work, continued to toil and till the land. In the judgment of at least one scholar, during the war years these women "saved the farms of the peasantry from total collapse."[15]

Numerous though they were, the soldiers' wives of rural Europe are not the women most readily identified with the disruptive effects of the war on economic production, family life, and established gender roles. The women who captured the public imagination during the war by virtue of their apparently incongruous place in public life – the women who became the face of home-front mobilization – were those who found work in munitions factories, as tram conductors, as bank clerks and office staff. War wives certainly placed themselves in the ranks of these untraditional workers. Historian Peggy Bette has shown that in France, "the post offices recruited 11,000 (to replace their 18,000 mobilized men), the education sector hired 12,000, amounting to half the mobilized teachers (30,000) and the Parisian tramways hired 5,000. Wives, daughters, and sisters now commonly filled in for employees who had been mobilized."[16] European armies hired women as clerical staff, often giving priority to the female kin of men who had been killed or disabled while in uniform. By January 1917, more than 100,000 French women were civilian employees of the army.[17]

The same ruthless calculus that persuaded military commanders to place women in temporary office positions also informed factory managers' much more visible decisions to hire women as munitions workers. Too many men were needed at the front to sustain the traditional practices of assigning only men to the non-combatant duties of a modern army or the heavy labour of a modern factory. Starting in 1915, when it became evident that the relentless war required the equally relentless production of munitions, large numbers of women, some of whom were war wives, went to work in munitions factories: by the end of the war, half a million French women were so employed, twice that number in Britain. In both Britain and France, war wives were sometimes able to combine munitions work with their domestic responsibilities because in France and, to a lesser extent, Britain, munitions factories provided on-site childcare facilities; and as of 1917, the French state required these factories to provide nursing rooms for new mothers.[18] Russia's war wives – known as *soldatki* – also found jobs in the vastly expanding war-industries sector. Barbara Alpern Engel observes that "between 1914 and 1917, the percentage of women in Russia's industrial labour force rose from 26.6 to 43.2 percent." As would become evident in February 1917, when soldiers of the Petrograd garrison refused to fire on striking women workers, "a sizable proportion of [those] married women workers must have been soldiers' wives."[19]

The challenges of combining factory labour with family life were more acute in Germany and Austria-Hungary, where war wives (along with other married women) had to dedicate hours on end to the search for ever scarcer food supplies. War wives in Germany discovered that there was little incentive to working outside the home, whatever pressure or inducements the state might bring to bear. State-financed allowances for the families of mobilized men were by no means extravagant, but, as Ute Daniel has demonstrated, "if the difference between family allowance and earnings was not very great and if, in addition, part of that difference had to be spent on transport, increased wear and tear on clothes, and child minders ... then it made little sense economically for women to go out to work."[20] In Austria, too, it is not clear that war wives were a significant presence in the substantial ranks of munitions workers. Indeed, the Austrian state actively discouraged soldiers' wives from seeking or holding jobs outside the home by threatening to cancel or reduce their separation allowances: "many women complained that when they sought outside employment to 'supplement the supplement' they were denied state funds altogether."[21]

Confronted with the insuperable difficulties of everyday life, many war wives in Germany, the Habsburg Empire, and Russia became anti-war wives. Some protested in private, urging their menfolk to secure permission to return home or, if need be, to desert.[22] Tara Zahra writes of a young Czech girl who begged her father to desert: "We are here alone without our father, and perhaps we will soon be without a mother as well, as our mother doesn't want to and cannot support us ... Every day she goes without breakfast, and at lunch we have only black coffee. At night she comes home totally exhausted and cries from hunger, and we cry with her."[23] A similarly afflicted peasant woman in a small German village complained to her husband: "They take the breadwinner away from the children and let them starve to death, they are crying for bread the whole day long … I have to stand in the street all day long and wait for hours until I get a few things to eat."[24] When the breadwinner could not return home, the most desperate of war wives contemplated suicide. Maureen Healy describes the tragic plight of an Austrian war widow who in 1917 threatened to kill herself and her two children because she could no longer put enough food on the table to support them.[25] Such private lamentations sometimes gave rise to public protest. By early 1918, women in Berlin did not hesitate to denounce the war and the deprivation it had wrought. As Belinda Davis has noted, "they shouted 'Enough with the murder at the front, down with the war! We don't want to starve any longer!'"[26] Women in Vienna were equally disillusioned and equally critical of the monarchy's failure to secure even the most basic necessities for its citizens. War wives were not alone in undermining the legitimacy of monarchical authority, but they certainly contributed to the process. Nowhere was this more evident than in Russia. From 1916 onward, Russia's *soldatki* emerged as a visible and disruptive force: they rioted to secure foodstuffs, stole what they could not afford to purchase, challenged the authority of Tsarist officials, called for an end to the war, and contributed in very direct ways to the downfall of autocracy in 1917.[27]

So many war wives in the most hard-pressed European nations wrote to their husbands to complain about the miseries of life on the home front that the authorities denounced letters of this type as fundamentally unpatriotic. But women paid no heed to such criticism and continued to send their *Jammerbriefe* (moaning letters) to the front. By dint of necessity, for millions of men and wives separated by the demands of military service, marriage became "marriage by correspondence."[28] And the available evidence strongly suggests that husbands and wives depended upon – in fact, demanded – a postal service capable of delivering a letter within a matter of days, not weeks; that they used regular correspondence not only to complain, to commiserate, to lament the hardships of everyday life but also to express love and affection; and that the intrusion of censors – often thought to be an insurmountable obstacle to frank and uninhibited conversation – never fully prevented soldiers from writing about the war or their wives from writing about the hardships of life at home. Married couples separated by military service wrote with extraordinary frequency, often daily, generating millions upon millions of letters.

Although only a tiny fraction of European war wives' letters has
survived, those that do exist make clear that, because husbands were
willing to express in their letters home something of the brutal character
of the war, their wives were not as unaware of or indifferent to the
horrors of the front lines as popular opinion has long believed. Nor
were husbands in uniform unaware of or unmoved by the difficulties
that plagued the everyday lives of their wives at home. Married soldiers
worried when their children fell ill; fretted when their wives were worn
down by endless work; grew angry when they feared their families
were going hungry. More than anything, however, their letters revealed
how much they longed for leave. Far from feeling alienated from the
home front, these men yearned to be reunited with those they loved.
Any rupture in the established routines of correspondence gave rise
to a soldier's fear that his wife had abandoned him; any extended and
unexpected silences prompted a wife to fear that her husband had been
killed. Regular correspondence, made possible by a mostly efficient
postal system, was the very glue that held wartime marriages together.

Anxious Days and Tearful Nights examines and highlights how the
collective – and quite varied – experiences of Canada's war wives both
resemble and differ from those of their European counterparts. Canadian
war wives did not, in the main, move into paid employment during
the war; they did not riot in the streets to overthrow the established
government; and in the letters they wrote to their husbands they did
not indulge in erotic reveries of what would happen in the precious days
when their husbands came home on leave (however much they might
have wished for such happy occasions). Leave was unimaginable; radical
political protest (at least from the ranks of war wives) so exceptional as to
be almost unknown; and waged labour for married women acceptable
only in the most desperate circumstances.

This is not to say that Canadian war wives had an easy time of it
or that they passively accepted a life of penury as their inevitable lot.
Far from it. Nancy Christie has shown that working-class war wives,
organized in Soldiers' Wives Leagues, actively (and successfully) lobbied
the federal government in 1915, demanding that their husbands assign a
substantial portion of their military pay to their dependents at home.[29]
Two years later, chapters of the Great War Next-of-Kin Association,
formed by working-class war wives in defence of their economic interests, demanded (and secured) an increase in the Separation Allowances
funded by the federal government.[30] Balancing an often-inadequate

budget was just one of the persistent challenges that Canada's war wives faced. Like war wives in Europe, for as long as their husbands were away, they also had to manage all household chores, adapt to life as a single parent, and care for children when they fell ill. Even more than European war wives, who had to contend with the unusually cold winters of 1916–17 and 1917–18, they had to prepare for winters in years of high prices and aggravating coal shortages. They had to establish strategies for coping, which often meant moving in with parents for the duration and sometimes meant relocating to Britain. And they had to come to terms with a mail system that was slow, irregular, and frustratingly susceptible to lengthy and unexplained silences.

To understand why Canadian war wives did not flock in large numbers to paid employment during the war, we must turn to the insights and evidence adduced by a generation of historians who have explored both the history of Canada's war and the history of Canadian working-class women in the early twentieth century. Three conclusions emerge from this scholarship. Military mobilization in Canada did not create a manpower shortage so severe as to require the extensive employment of *married* women in untraditional fields; the Canadian government, supported by public philanthropy and prodded by war wives themselves, provided the financial support deemed sufficient to meet their basic needs; and social and cultural norms continued to look askance at the prospect of married women – especially married women with young children – working outside the home. In a nation where the demand for married women's paid labour was much less pressing than it was in Europe and where soldiers' wives were, in the main, more adequately supported by the state, the ideology of domesticity could (and did) remain well entrenched.[31]

Canada mobilized 619,636 men, of whom 424,592 served overseas. This deployment without doubt made a significant contribution to the war effort, but it was much less disruptive to the rural and urban economies of the nation than the more extensive mobilization of men in Europe. Whereas in France mobilization placed 20 percent of the entire nation in uniform, the Canadian Expeditionary Force represented approximately 8 percent of Canada's national population. And mobilization in Canada drew much more extensively from urban workers than rural populations. Unlike in Europe, where peasants constituted a notable proportion of all enlisted men, only 20 percent of the Canadian force were farmers or farmhands.[32] There were, of course, soldiers' wives who found themselves – like the *gardiennes* of wartime France – in charge of family farms in Canada. One Alberta woman earned the acclamation of her neighbours when she and her adult daughter proved more adept at running the farm, bringing in the crops, and paying off the family debts than her rather dissolute husband had ever been.[33] Her energetic enterprise was perhaps exceptional, but not unique. Nellie McClung writes of encountering a recently widowed war wife who was resolved to keep her farm afloat: she drove "a mower [and] swung her team around the edge of the meadow with a grace and skill that called forth our admiration."[34] But in the main, Canada's war wives were city folk, and fewer opportunities to work for wages presented themselves in Canada's wartime economy than was the case in Europe.

At the beginning of the war, when Canada was still suffering the effects of a serious economic recession, many of the men who enlisted were unemployed. They were not, therefore, vacating jobs that would then have to be filled by women.[35] Indeed, as the unemployment crisis persisted into the first year of the war, many employers opted to lay off their female staff so as to create positions for unemployed married men. When the demand for female labour to replace enlisted men did arise in 1916, war wives remained vastly under-represented in the ranks of female war workers. It is possible that war wives in Paris, Ontario, for instance, where the employment of married women in the Penman Woollen Mill was a well-established practice, continued to work outside the home during the war. The mill stayed busy filling orders for the Army and experienced women workers were essential to its success. But this was exceptional: as Joy Parr has stressed, Paris was "not a typical manufacturing community."[36] The CEF did hire a veritable battalion of clerical workers, including some war wives, to manage the array of records generated by an army of more than half a million men. Much of this work was done in Britain, giving unexpected job opportunities to the educated and childless wives of Canadian soldiers who chose to follow their husbands to Europe for the duration of the war.

In Canada, where clerical work, once undertaken almost exclusively by men, did become "feminized" – historians speak of the war effecting a "pink collar revolution" – positions as stenographers, bank tellers, and clerks fell almost entirely to educated single women.[37] Banks, for example, hired single women to replace their employees who went to war, but, as Barbara Wilson has observed, bank managers were unimpressed with the results: "ten months after [women] were first employed as clerks and tellers, bank officials concluded that [they] were temperamentally unsuited to the banking business."[38] Married women were not even considered for such positions. Other enterprises often encountered organized resistance from unions who opposed management's efforts to hire women. Whereas women tram conductors became a recognized sight in every major European capital – in Germany almost three thousand war wives were employed as streetcar operators by 1915, stepping into jobs once occupied by their now-mobilized husbands[39] – in Canada they remained a rare and much remarked upon novelty. Linda Kealey has noted that in Vancouver "street railway workers … at the end of 1916 publicly asserted that they would not oppose the introduction of women conductors, as long as they became union members and were given equal pay for equal work."[40] The Vancouver streetcar companies must have balked at such conditions, for the first female conductors were hired not on the west coast but in Kingston in October 1917. Ultimately, Kingston hired twelve "conductorettes" (or "etties" as they were often called), all of whom appear to have been young unmarried women. In Halifax, the Nova Scotia Tramways Company had twenty women on its payroll by early 1918, but when the streetcar company in Toronto tried to follow suit, its male employees went on strike.[41]

Nor were munitions factories a site of substantial employment for Canada's war wives. Concentrated in southern Ontario, Montreal, and to a much lesser extent in the Maritimes, munitions factories probably hired no more than eleven thousand women, of whom perhaps a quarter (or approximately 2,600) were married.[42] Some of these married women were war wives for, as Kori Street has demonstrated, munitions factories sometimes recruited war wives and soldiers' sisters as a demonstration of patriotic loyalty to men in uniform. And, although these war wives were not as radicalized as the *soldatki* of Petrograd, whose strike in February 1917 sparked the first Russian Revolution, neither were they entirely complacent: when the Toronto munitions industry proposed extending the working day to fourteen hours, six days a week, war wives were among the women who threatened to strike. It is likely that most of the war wives who found work in these factories did not have young children at home: unlike the case in France or Britain, where the need for female labour was acute, comparable factories in Canada did not provide on-site childcare facilities.[43] In Canada's west, war-related work was thin on the ground and often not open to women. Although a handful of women found work in munitions factories in Victoria and Vancouver, opportunities elsewhere were limited. Nancy Christie notes that in both Moose Jaw and Winnipeg munitions manufacturers insisted on hiring only married men.[44] If fewer than three thousand married women found jobs in Canada's munitions factories, and if only a fraction of them were war wives, the presence of war wives in this quintessentially wartime workforce would have been modest, to say the least.

In *Fight or Pay*, the definitive history of a uniquely Canadian experiment in family support during the Great War, Desmond Morton hints at the reason that war wives were a much less noticeable presence in the labour force than was the case in Europe. As recipients of assistance from the Canadian Patriotic Fund (CPF), they were expected, if at all possible, to remain at home as the principal caregivers of their children. Whereas most combatant nations provided financial support in the form of separation allowances to the wives and children of men serving under arms, only in Canada were these state-funded allowances then supplemented by grants sustained (at least at first) by the private contributions of ordinary citizens.[45] The CPF (and its independently managed Manitoba affiliate) raised funds to provide soldiers' dependents with a combined monthly income deemed sufficient to cover the necessities of life. This income became so critical to married men's calculations that recruiters had to be careful what they promised: there was no guarantee that a married soldier's family would receive "the patriotic" because, it was stressed, each case had to be reviewed on its merits. Nonetheless, the Patriotic Fund provided supplemental support to thousands of families and disbursed more than forty million dollars over the course of the war.[46] In 1915 an Ontario wife with three children at home would receive approximately $37 a month: $20 in Separation Allowance and the balance from the CPF. If her husband was diligent – and military service records suggest that most were – starting in May 1915 she would also receive an additional $15 a month in Assigned Pay.[47] Fifty-two dollars a month was no king's ransom, but it was probably adequate in 1915 and comparable in many instances to the wages an unskilled labouring husband would have brought home. Two years later, however, war-generated inflation seriously eroded the purchasing power of these allowances, adding financial stress to the lives of women already facing a life marked by persistent anxiety.

When war wives' associations called upon the state to increase the rates of compensation provided to soldiers' dependents, they inserted themselves into the arena of public protest. But even the most progressive chapters did not question the fundamental belief that married women – especially married women with children – should not have to work outside the home.[48] On this point, they would have agreed with the male dignitaries and middle-class matrons who created and managed the Patriotic Fund. The responsibility of the Canadian government and the Patriotic Fund was clear: a soldier's family should be fully supported in his absence, and his wife should remain at home. Married women without children were eligible for only a small monthly stipend from the Patriotic Fund: they might have been expected to support themselves through paid employment, although it is impossible to know how many did so. Young brides who married on the eve of their husbands' enlistment were not initially eligible for any support from the fund. The CPF had little interest in subsidizing marriages that were, in the words of its executive secretary, "contracted in moments of irresponsibility."[49] Soldiers' wives with young children at home were, by contrast, to be spared the burden of waged labour. With one significant exception. When some patrons of the Fund complained in late 1916 and early 1917 that they could no longer find good household help, the CPF granted women who worked outside the home the same level of support as previously granted only to women who stayed at home.[50]

There was much about the Patriotic Fund to raise the hackles of respectable war wives of the working classes: recipients were subjected to monthly visits from often-patronizing women of the middle classes, who were especially alert to any signs of extravagant spending, slovenly housekeeping, or immoral behaviour on the part of their clients.[51] Surviving records from the Manitoba Patriotic Fund reveal, however, that the Patriotic provided invaluable assistance to Canada's war wives. When Ottawa was slow to process applications for Separation Allowances (as was common in the early years of the war) or when husbands failed to assign a portion of their pay to their dependents at home, the fund provided emergency grants to women who otherwise would have faced immediate destitution. When children (or their mothers) fell ill and had to be hospitalized, it often paid the medical bills. When coal became exorbitantly expensive, it negotiated bulk purchases at manageable prices. And when war wives found life in Canada too much to bear, it paid their fares home to Britain.[52] Life was hard for Canada's war wives; it would have been even harder had it not been for the Patriotic Fund.

The ideology that informed the enterprise, the fundraising efforts, and the advertising campaigns of the Canadian Patriotic Fund was well rooted in early twentieth-century Canadian life: a wife, almost everyone agreed, should devote herself exclusively to her domestic responsibilities. If she did not – whether by choice or by necessity – all manner of mayhem might ensue. Infants abandoned to the inadequate attention of strangers or older siblings could fall prey to life-threatening injury; older children might be tempted into delinquency. Such anxieties, which predated 1914, became particularly acute during the war in Canada as in Europe, when war wives became in effect, albeit not in law, "single parents."[53] In the absence of a stern but loving father, the presence at home of a caring but vigilant mother became ever more necessary, for the well-being of the family and the moral welfare of the nation depended upon it. Patriotic Fund allowances thus offered invaluable assurance to men contemplating enlistment that their families would be well cared for. They also implicitly preserved men's stature as breadwinners of their household. Since a wife's total monthly income – funded by the federal government, her husband's military pay, and the contributions of civic-minded Canadian civilians – was directly tied to and dependent upon her husband's military service, these allowances held the promise that a soldier's wife need not work, that his children would be cared for when ill and protected from the spectre of delinquency, and that, his absence from the family home notwithstanding, he would remain, in truth, the family breadwinner.[54]

The prevalent belief that husbands should provide an income and wives should remain at home was not unique to Canada. Deborah Thom has argued, for instance, that "the assumption of the male breadwinner and the female homemaker remained unchallenged" in wartime Europe. Yet in Britain at least, the war gave rise to a "temporary shift from deploring women's need to work as a required but undesirable supplement to male breadwinners to celebrating waged work as constructive for families, desirable for the nation, and healthy for women."[55] Because Canada was less buffeted by the strains of war than its European allies and because a war wife's income – derived from federally funded Separation Allowances, soldiers' Assigned Pay, and Patriotic Fund allowances – gave her a more comfortable standard of living than was the case in Europe, the presumption of a male breadwinner and female homemaker proved even more resilient, notwithstanding popular memory of the war as a watershed moment of transformation for women. Joan Sangster has made the important observation that, because Canadian women gained the right to vote in 1918, thus securing a right long demanded and long denied, the Great War lives in collective memory as an important and transformative juncture in the lives of Canadian women.[56] Indeed, this narrative would suggest that the war effected a transformation in the status of women comparable to and parallel with the equally estimable transformation in the status of the country itself, from "colony to nation."

Historians of Canadian women have subjected this parallel narrative of liberation and self-realization to critical scrutiny, emphasizing that whatever transformations the war might have wrought were neither seismic nor permanent. If, as optimists fervently hoped, the postwar era was to usher in "a New Day" for Canada's women, that day, as Veronica Strong-Boag has firmly established, did not dawn in quite the way many advocates of women's rights had anticipated.[57] Securing the right to vote was certainly a major accomplishment, but the view that a woman's primary place was in the home would persist well into the 1950s. A dozen "etties" taking tickets on Kingston's streetcars could not by themselves undermine the domestic ideology that had prevailed since the late nineteenth century. And insofar as Canada's war wives were, in the main, both able and expected to remain at home, they did little to unsettle that ideology. Far from functioning as a moment of rupture and disorientation, the First World War in fact reaffirmed the gendered order of early twentieth-century Canada.

∽⊱⊰∾

In a now iconic poster of the Great War a young girl sitting on her father's knee asks him: "What did you do in the war, Daddy?" The poster, produced in Britain in 1914, was meant to shame young and still-unmarried men into volunteering: could they bear to think of a day in the distant future when they would have to admit to their children that they had chosen to stay at home rather than fight? What kind of a man would so shirk his duty to home and hearth? But, in thinking about the thousands of married men in Canada who chose to enlist, another question comes to mind: "Why did you go to war, Daddy?" What kind of husband and father would voluntarily leave his wife and children to fight in a distant war? Chapter 1 explores why married men in Canada did so. Unlike their European counterparts, who were either subject to compulsory military service from the first days of the war or, as was the case in Britain, upon the extension of conscription to married men in the spring of 1916, married men in Canada were rarely conscripted. The Military Service Act of 1917 first compelled the enlistment of unmarried men and childless widowers, between twenty and thirty-four years of age; had the war lingered into 1919, it is probable that married men, placed in Class 2, would also have been conscripted. But for Canada's married men, military service was almost always a voluntary act. Chapter 1 analyzes the ebb and flow of their enlistment, from the initial rush to the colours in August and September 1914, to the lull of mid-1915, and into the more systematic enlistment campaigns of early 1916. A close analysis of national recruitment archives and the newspapers of Toronto and Winnipeg (two cities with particularly robust recruitment records) makes clear that in the last months of 1915, when local communities assumed responsibility for filling newly formed battalions, the tenor and intensity of recruitment initiatives changed substantively. Posters, movies, and recruitment rallies all spoke indirectly, but nonetheless persuasively, to married men, emphasizing the danger that would befall their families should Germany defeat Britain and thus leave Canada vulnerable to invasion.

The married men who carefully weighed the advantages and disadvantages of enlistment often delayed their decisions until early 1916, when (not incidentally) the fundraising drives of the Patriotic Fund were as insistent as they were ubiquitous. Reassured that their families would be well taken care of, married men who might otherwise have stayed in civvies succumbed to the relentless drumbeat of patriotic urgency. They could not have known that they would enter the trenches of the Western Front in time for the major campaigns of 1917: Vimy, Hill 70, and Passchendaele. Nor could their wives have fully apprehended what it would mean for their menfolk to serve in such conditions, despite newspaper accounts of major battles, letters published in local newspapers, and long casualty lists.[58] The innocence of the untested soldier would soon give way to experience, however, and the vague impressions of his wife yield to haunting and harrowing (albeit imperfect) understanding. Canadian wives would soon comprehend something of the horror of war because their husbands wrote about it in the letters they sent home.

Chapter 2 analyzes the wartime correspondence of married soldiers to determine what they were willing (and able) to write about and why they felt it necessary to share some of their most distressing experiences with their wives at home. Most of these married couples were literate and, in the main, competent letter writers. Whether born and raised in Canada or recent arrivals, they had become accustomed in their civilian lives to writing and receiving letters. Nothing, however, could quite have prepared them for the unprecedented and indispensable role that letter writing would assume in their wartime lives. The extant correspondence of Canadian soldiers reveals that, even though many letters were circumspect and cautious, it was possible to circumvent the censors and write from time to time of the misery, the horror, and the existential anxiety of front-line combat. Indeed, the letters often took on a confessional tone, allowing men in uniform to unburden themselves of their dark thoughts and moments of despair. These letters show that Canadian war wives were not as ignorant of those horrors as postwar memory has maintained and scholarly interpretation often insisted.[59]

Very few letters written by Canadian war wives have survived. It was of course easier for a wife to preserve her husband's letters than for him to protect cherished correspondence from home. Some letters, stored in damp, mud-encrusted knapsacks, were reduced to illegible mush; others were burned, in accordance with military orders. Yet others were destroyed along with the men to whom they had been written. It is difficult, therefore, to speak comprehensively about the character and content of Canadian war wives' correspondence. It is clear, however, that wives were for the most part regular and faithful correspondents. They did not write as often as their counterparts in Europe – it was not unusual for women in France, for instance, to write every day – but many tried to send a letter at least once and sometimes twice a week. They knew that few things mattered more to men in uniform than the daily mail call, and few days were more demoralizing than a day without word from home. As George Timmins observed from overseas – and many of his comrades would have agreed – "Don't forget your two [letters] a week as they are about all I care about now Of course its very nice to have a letter from anybody but its your letters that count."[60]

Even though the paucity of letters from the home front – and, especially, of letters written by war wives – constitutes a regrettable lacuna in the historical record of the First World War, a close reading of married soldiers' correspondence tells us much about the tenor of those two-way exchanges and their recurrent themes. Building upon this correspondence (supplemented by other archival records), chapter 3 constructs a collective portrait of the daily lives, persistent challenges, and coping strategies of Canada's war wives. Like their husbands, they hoped their letters would be a source of comfort and consolation, of reassurance and affection. But the letters were acts of confession too, giving voice to the daily concerns of women determined to maintain the family home, balance the household budget, assume the duties of a "single parent," care for children who were all too susceptible to sickness, and cope with loneliness, anxiety, and sometimes paralyzing fear.

Historians of the First World War have become attentive to the "coping strategies" that front-line soldiers developed for enduring the hardships and hell of combat.[61] We have paid less attention to the comparable strategies of women on the home front. *Anxious Days and Tearful Nights* investigates ways in which Canada's war wives became adept at coping with and accommodating themselves to the financial, material, and psychological stresses of war. Some of their strategies would have been familiar to married women of the nineteenth century who, by virtue of circumstance, had to live alone, often for months on end. In the years before Confederation, it was not uncommon for wives, ordinarily of the middle or more affluent classes, to live apart from husbands who travelled for work, served in the provincial or (after 1867) federal legislature, or enlisted for military service.[62] The wives of lumberjacks and fishermen also became accustomed to living alone and managing the family home.[63] Women in these circumstances proved adept managers of the home, the family budget, and sometimes the family business. As the scholarship on "single" women in pre-1914 Canada makes clear, these women often relied upon and contributed to networks of "interdependence" – of kin and community – which provided company and consolation, financial and familial support.[64] This was also true of war wives, many of whom became ever more reliant on kinship networks, often moving great distances to be close to parents or in-laws. A database created for this project, based on the service records of almost three hundred married Manitoba soldiers, shows that war wives moved often, some many times. Some sought out more affordable accommodation in a city they already knew and in neighbourhoods populated by other war wives; others moved great distances to live with parents in another province; yet others relocated to Britain.

Chapter 4 examines why a significant number of Canadian war wives decided to move to – or, in many cases, return to – "the Old Country" for the duration of the war. The more generous allowances granted to officers' wives made it possible for the privileged few to live in London or along the Kentish coast. Some, like the recently married Edna Tompkins, found work in the London payroll offices of the CEF; others gave their time to various charitable and philanthropic enterprises. Life in Britain made it possible for them to be on hand when their husbands were granted leave or were convalescing from wounds. These women were the exception, however. Most of the war wives who relocated were, like their husbands, British-born and chose to return to their hometowns or villages where they could live with or near their extended family. Some settled comfortably, while others struggled to find affordable accommodation that would tolerate fractious children. Archival records document some of the challenges these women faced and the pressure placed on them by British and Canadian authorities in 1917 to return to Canada. However much they might have hoped that life in wartime Britain would ease the burdens of single parenthood, many war wives discovered that temporary resettlement was no simple solution to the problem of wartime separation.

One all-powerful thought sustained (most) husbands and wives separated by war: *après la guerre* family life would resume, marital affection would flourish, and life would return to normal. For some married couples, this was certainly true. However, as chapter 5 reveals, postwar life was often fraught: returning veterans, eager to reassume their role as the family breadwinner, had such ambitions thwarted by the worldwide recession of the early 1920s; war widows had to accustom themselves to the emotional and financial reality that their husbands were never coming home. In yet other cases, couples survived the war, but their marriage did not. By 1919 Canadians, like their European allies, were particularly concerned – indeed, convinced – that the war had created a "crisis of marriage," the most incontrovertible evidence of which was an epidemic of divorce. Newspaper stories, prominent citizens in Parliament and public life, and returning veterans all feared that unfaithful wives, having betrayed their husbands, had dealt the institution of marriage a critical blow. The significant increase in divorce petitions appeared to give substance to these suspicions. Chapter 6 examines the extent of and evidence for this widespread anxiety, while also demonstrating that war wives, often painted as the villains of marital disintegration, were perhaps more frequently its unwitting victims. When men far from home betrayed their marriage vows, entered into bigamous marriages, or simply refused to return home to their Canadian families – when marital desertion was at least as pervasive as divorce – war wives had to come to terms with the economic and emotional effects of broken marriages. Deserted wives were ineligible for the pensions that offered war widows a modicum of economic security; and unlike divorced women, were unable to remarry (at least, legally). Manitoba's deserted war wives could seek financial support from the Soldiers' Deserted Wives Fund; those in British Columbia qualified for the newly created Mothers' Allowances. In all other provinces, a deserted war wife had to eke out a living on wages barely sufficient to support a young single woman.

⁂

By exploring the question "What was it like to be a soldier's wife in Canada during the First World War?" *Anxious Days and Tearful Nights* broadens our understanding of the transformative and often traumatic effects of the First World War on the lives of women whose very ordinary existence far from the battlefields of northern France has been largely consigned to the shadows of historical memory. Complementing rather than duplicating existing scholarship on women's work, family life, and the war, it reveals how married couples separated by wartime service used correspondence to maintain both the routine and the affection of domestic life; how wives with young children adapted to and coped with the quotidian challenges of what we today would call "single parenthood"; and when and for what reasons Canada's war wives chose to relocate to Britain. It highlights the ways in which these women's experiences of marital separation brought on by the war resembled and differed from those of their European counterparts. And it concludes that, more than anything else, the life of a war wife – especially a war wife separated from her husband for years on end – was marked and marred by unrelieved psychological stress. War wives had to manage the family home, care for children susceptible to a panoply of potentially fatal diseases, live on budgets ill-adjusted to the inflationary effects of wartime society, and cope with their own illnesses. And all the while they were aware that their husbands were in imminent and inescapable danger. They knew this not just because the newspapers routinely tallied the casualties inflicted on local regiments, but because their husbands – overcoming their own understandable reticence – told them so. Unable to enjoy even the least respite confident that their husbands were safely removed from the killing fields of the Western Front, Canada's war wives led lives overshadowed by anxious days and tear-filled nights.

PART ONE

Off to War

"Daddy, why did you go to war?"
Recruitment and Enlistment

When Jack Howe arrived at Valcartier in September 1914, resolved to join the ranks of the newly formed Canadian Expeditionary Force, he would have found himself in familiar company. Among the volunteers who answered the call to enlist in August 1914, recently arrived British-born immigrants outnumbered native-born Canadian men. Indeed, of the thirty thousand Canadian men who had enlisted by the end of September, 60 percent were, like Howe, native-born Britons.[1] By the end of the year, fully 70 percent of all Canadian men who had signed up for overseas service were native to the British Isles. Born in Somerset, England, in 1875, Howe and his wife, Ellen, had uprooted their five children and settled in Toronto, where they no doubt hoped to make a better life for themselves. But a tradition of military service – Howe had served for four years in the Royal Marine Light Infantry – combined with a desire to provide for his family and a strong familial connection to the "Old Country" prompted him to enlist. He embarked at Quebec in late September, crossed the Atlantic in early October, and first caught sight of "the Land of Old England" eleven days later.[2] Even though many of the men who sailed with him shared his emotional attachment to England, most were much younger than Howe and few were married. This, at least, is what the casualty figures from their first engagement with the enemy would suggest. When the German army sent wafts of poison gas into the allied front lines at Ypres in the late afternoon of 22 April 1915, eighteen thousand Canadians were in the front lines. Over the course of the next three and a half days, at least 1,374 Canadian troops died in the Second Battle of Ypres. Only 103 of these men were married.[3] Jack Howe was one.

The voluntary enlistment of married men in the CEF started slowly. Military authorities did not actively discourage married men from enlisting, but the presumption prevailed in August 1914 (and would persist for many months to come) that for Canada at least this would be – and indeed should be – a single-man's war. The "General Instructions and Conditions of Enlistment" issued in mid-August 1914, stated quite clearly: "Preference will be given to unmarried men who have previously served or who have undergone some form of military training."[4] To make it even more apparent that single men were preferred, any married man presenting himself to a recruiting officer during the first year of the war had to demonstrate that he had already secured his wife's permission to enlist. Many of them did not and, as Desmond Morton has vividly demonstrated, married men who showed up at a recruiting office without having first won their wives' consent caused no end of problems for Sam Hughes, the minister of the militia, who was beset by correspondence from angry wives demanding that their husbands be sent home at once.[5]

Married men would enlist in greater numbers as the war dragged on and the search for able-bodied soldiers intensified. Yet the preponderance of unmarried men in the ranks of the CEF continued, making it markedly different from the large conscript armies of Europe, where married men were required by law to serve; and different even from the British Expeditionary Force, which, having relied on volunteers through the end of 1915, had the following year introduced conscription for single and, subsequently, married men. When Canada imposed conscription in 1917, it initially drafted only unmarried men and widowers without dependent children. Had the war lasted into 1919 (or even into 1920, as some military planners anticipated), married men would no doubt have also been subject to conscription. But such extreme expedients were never needed and almost all the married men who served in the CEF did so voluntarily. Why they chose to enlist – and why they were more likely to enlist in early 1916 than at any other point in the war – is the story to be told here.

⟨⟩

In the earliest months of the war, several factors emerged – and often converged – to encourage married men to enlist. Some were purely practical; for men like Jack Howe, it was unemployment and a desire to provide their family with a steady income. Others were more emotional; for men with parents, siblings, sometimes a wife and children in the "Old Country," defending the mother country was certainly a powerful motive. Other men were moved by idealistic outrage: the German invasion of Belgium in the earliest weeks of the war had endangered civilians, caused an exodus of bedraggled refugees, and shown all too clearly the brutal face of German militarism.

The economic recession of 1913–14, which affected urban Ontario and the agricultural west with particular severity, cost many men their jobs, bringing hardship to married and single men alike. Recently arrived immigrants would have been unduly hard hit. Migration had sent more than a million British citizens to Canada in the decade and a half before the Great War, and when immigration peaked in 1913, more than 400,000 immigrants – of whom approximately 40 percent were British-born – settled in Canada. But jobs did not await them all. When factory jobs in central Canada were scarce, employers did not hesitate to specify that "British need not apply." Further west, on the prairies, where immigrants had flocked by the thousands in the decade or more before the war, a perfect storm of economic misery – a drought that reduced the need for agricultural labourers, the end of railway construction, and the closing down of public-sector jobs – sent men in large numbers to the recruiting offices.[6] The Army promised a private $1.10 per day, a sergeant, $1.50, and a lieutenant, $2.60.[7] A private's wages compared poorly with what a skilled labourer might have earned in peacetime, but when skilled labourers lost their jobs or found only intermittent employment, as was often the case in 1914, the "King's shilling" looked very attractive indeed. One Winnipeg man, married with two children, had earned $60 a month when fully employed, but when he was laid off in the fall of 1914, the family struggled to meet even their most basic expenses. A trip to the recruiting office in December guaranteed him a regular income and his family an escape from penury.[8]

Jack Howe was certainly aware of the economic security to be gained from enlisting in the CEF. From the few letters he wrote to his wife, it is unclear whether he had been unemployed in the summer of 1914, although there are hints that he had been recently laid off. What is perfectly clear is that he took comfort in his belief that his enlistment would provide Ellen and their children with an income adequate to their needs. "I have been told by the Officer that all Wife's & Family will be looked after well & be lots better off then those with their Husband's that is in Toronto." For as long as Howe was in uniform, Ellen would receive a monthly Separation Allowance of $20 funded directly by the federal government, $20 a month in Assigned Pay, and a supplemental allowance of $19 – determined by family need and the number of children in a household – from the Canadian Patriotic Fund. The authorities did not yet require soldiers to allocate at least half of their monthly pay to their dependents – that stipulation would take effect only in May, 1915 – and so Howe's decision to provide Ellen with $20 in Assigned Pay was made of his own volition: "I have left the money out of my pay to look after [the children] & you contenfortable with what you will get of the government I am giving my life on a chance for all you conforts."[9] An additional $20 a month would not have purchased an abundance of "conforts," but Howe rightly understood that his willingness to contribute two-thirds of his pay packet to the family purse would give Ellen a small, but real, margin of financial security. In 1915 Toronto, income provided by the Separation Allowance and Canadian Patriotic Fund grant barely covered the most basic expenses of a working-class family.[10] Assigned Pay, if regularly received, would lift a family out of penury and into the ranks of modest self-sufficiency. Ellen Howe learned the value of this extra $20 the hard way. Her husband, killed in the Second Battle of Ypres in April 1915, was at first listed as "missing in action." It was only in February 1916 that the military authorities officially confirmed that he had been killed in action. When a man's death remained unconfirmed – and the possibility still existed that he might have been taken prisoner – his designated dependents continued to receive both his Separation Allowance and Assigned Pay. After six months, however, Assigned Pay distributions ceased. This had very real consequences for Ellen Howe and her three school-age children: from September 1915 through February 1916, they were forced to live on a very meagre income of $39 a month.[11]

For the many British-born recruits who enlisted in 1914, close ties to Britain were also among the reasons that persuaded them of the benefits of military service. In the heyday of pre-war immigration, some British-born immigrants had settled in Canada as members of an extended family; others as married couples determined to make a new life for themselves. Many were single men, leaving parents (and sometimes fiancées) in Britain until they could establish themselves. Yet others were married men who travelled to Canada alone, intent on making a home and amassing the savings needed to bring their families over. Because long-settled Canadians feared that the British were intentionally encouraging the emigration to Canada of their indigent and work-shy, the Canadian government had taken steps starting in 1908 to inhibit the settlement in Canada of the very poor and (for other reasons entirely) those deemed racially undesirable. Upon arrival in Canada, a British-born immigrant had to demonstrate that he had sufficient funds to cover transportation costs to his final destination and an additional "$50 if arriving in the winter, and $25 if landing at other times of the year."[12] For some of the married men who had ventured to Canada on their own, the economic crisis of 1913–14 made it difficult to save such sums; dreams of family reunification were temporarily thwarted. The outbreak of war gave these men an opportunity to reunite with wives and children still living in Britain.

Sam Hughes's insistence that married men secure the written permission of their wives before enlisting would have presented men whose wives remained in Britain with a real logistical hurdle: how could they obtain the documentation required in order to attest? A well-organized couple could certainly have exchanged the correspondence needed to expedite a husband's enlistment, and several couples clearly did so. Ernest Hawley had a wife still in Scotland when he presented himself for service at Valcartier in late September. John Larkin and Edward Lawlor had wives waiting for them in England. Each of these men identified themselves as married when they enlisted and presumably came up with the requisite paperwork to satisfy the recruiters.[13] For other couples, delays, hesitations, and communication difficulties may well have complicated (and perhaps cooled) a man's patriotic impulse. Presenting oneself as single, as Frederick Bryant did when he enlisted at Valcartier, was, all things considered, a much simpler option. Perhaps Bryant really was unmarried in September 1914 and married soon after his arrival in England; for there were many men in the first waves of Canadian enlistment who found themselves in such a situation. It is doubtful that Bryant was of that number. It is more likely that his wife, Beatrice, was alive, well, and still living in Britain. When in December 1914 she submitted the papers needed to prove that, as the wife of a Canadian soldier, she was eligible to receive a Separation Allowance, her application was approved, and her Separation Allowance backdated to August 1914. So, too, with Catherine Graham in Dundee, Scotland, whose husband, Charles, enlisted in the very earliest weeks of the war. Born in Glasgow in 1872, he also told the recruiting officers at Valcartier that he was unmarried. Subsequent developments showed this to be a convenient fiction. A member of the First Contingent, he arrived in France in time to participate in the Second Battle of Ypres, where he was seriously wounded. Not only did he suffer the long-term effects of exposure to gas but he was buried alive for twenty-four hours before being rescued and sent back to England to recover. Judged medically unfit for future service, he was discharged in July 1916 and returned to Canada, where he settled in London, Ontario. At that point he sought the assistance of the Canadian Department of Militia and Defence: would it be possible to secure the passage of his wife and four children, aged six to sixteen, who had remained in Scotland when he had immigrated to Canada? At first the authorities were unsympathetic:

"There is absolutely no arrangement or understanding of any kind by which the Canadian Government undertakes to bring to this country the wives and families of soldiers, unless such wives and families have been previously domiciled in Canada."[14] It is not clear who decided that, in light of wartime complexities, such a policy was unduly harsh, but by the end of 1916, Graham and his family were reunited in London, Ontario. His brutal experiences of combat notwithstanding, his enthusiasm for the war effort had not ebbed and in 1917 he re-enlisted.

Unlike Charles Graham, Frederick Bryant, and Joseph Bolton, all of whom desperately wanted to be reunited with their wives and children, William Didsbury, who also identified himself upon enlistment at Valcartier as unmarried, seems to have had no desire to reconnect with his wife – or even acknowledge her existence. When he enlisted, he designated his mother, Margaret, who lived in Winnipeg, as his next of kin and recipient of his Separation Allowance. After his death in April 1915, a tussle developed as to who should receive his pension. His mother appeared the obvious beneficiary, but when it became evident that Didsbury had left a widow, Sarah, and child, both living in Sheffield, the widow's claim (temporarily) prevailed. Ultimately, however, Sarah's right to a widow's pension was denied on the grounds that she had not been supported by her husband at the time of his enlistment. The final adjudication held that only her child was entitled to an orphan's pension. This bureaucratic wrangling strongly suggests that, before moving to Canada, William had abandoned but not formally divorced his English wife. Unlike others who had then remarried in Canada – only to have their bigamous relationships exposed when both wives sought a Separation Allowance or a widow's pension – William Didsbury appears to have preferred the single life.

The initial recruitment rush soon ebbed. In August and September 1914, thirty thousand men enlisted; in October slightly more than five thousand. Once winter set in and job prospects dimmed again, enlistment revived somewhat. Frank Maheux and George Ormsby were two of more than thirteen thousand men who signed attestation papers in November 1914. Maheux would have preferred to enlist sooner; he had been thinking of nothing else since first hearing of the outbreak of war in August 1914. Knowing full well, however, that his long-suffering wife would have objected, he bided his time. He had done things in the past, he would freely admit, that had strained their marriage and justly earned her opprobrium. Whiskey was usually to blame. But volunteering for overseas service was something else entirely. And thus, when Maheux went to Ottawa in October 1914, he did so on the sly. As he admitted afterwards: "I didn't tell you that I was going ... for the reason; that I know that if I tell you you would not let me go." Who could have blamed her? Isolated in a small, remote logging village sixty miles north of Ottawa, with six children underfoot (the youngest still a babe in arms), and a precariously balanced family budget at the best of times, how was she supposed to cope if her husband was thousands of miles away fighting in France? Surely, Frank reckoned, discretion was a precondition of valour. But he dreaded his neighbours' scorn as much as he feared his wife's disapproval. Had he presented himself to the recruiting sergeants at Valcartier, he might well have been judged medically unfit. His hearing was, he had to admit, "a problem," and the examining doctors employed at Valcartier were rigorous in their attention to medical infirmities. At least five thousand men who tried to enlist in August and September 1914 failed the medical examination.[15] Maheux could not have contemplated the shame of returning home, rejected for active service, knowing that "every body had laugh at me." Manly pride and marital prudence thus prompted him to wait until the initial enlistment rush subsided and only then report to the recruiting office in Ottawa (where, perhaps, the doctors were less punctilious). Once the deed was done, he could confide in Angeline.[16]

Like Maheux, George Ormsby was in his thirties, married with children and uncertain economic prospects. Unlike Maheux, Ormsby was an immigrant with strong family ties to Ireland, where he had been born in 1879. Arriving in Canada at the turn of the century, he first tried his hand as a lumberman in the interior of British Columbia, where he met and married Margaret McArthur in 1907. By 1914 they were shopkeepers in Lumby, British Columbia, with aspirations to own a ranch in the fruit-rich Okanagan Valley. But the merchant's life, selling dry-goods and groceries, could not in Ormsby's mind compare to the lure of military service. As he explained to a still-skeptical Maggie months after he had left Canada, he firmly believed he was born to be a soldier: "As far back as I can remember I longed for the life and my whole soul was in Britains battles."[17] This argument would also have made sense to Maheux, who confessed to a similar taste for military life. Fearing that his Angeline would have little patience for such romantic nonsense and knowing that as a married man his first responsibility was to provide for his family, he initially framed his decision to enlist in terms that other married men struggling to support their families would have understood: in uniform Maheux would guarantee his family a more regular and robust income than he had ever earned as a lumberjack. He calculated that instead of the $22 a month he customarily (and sometimes erratically) earned hewing lumber, his family could now count on $25 from the Patriotic Fund and $20 in Separation Allowance. He would contribute an additional $15 in

Assigned Pay. But he could not deny that he also longed for the soldier's life. Having served in the Boer War, he had acquired a competency in English – the language in which he and Angeline would subsequently communicate – and a lingering fondness for soldiering: "When a man is soldier once it is the same like sickness all summer I had that in my mind." He knew well the hardship and danger that awaited every man in uniform. Yet he was not afraid of either. Fatalism guided his path, convinced as he was that, just as he had come through the South African war without a scratch, he would survive this new conflict, too. If his time were to come, it could come just as easily in the backwoods of Quebec as in the trenches of France. Or so he told himself.[18]

Although financial calculations were important attractions to enlistment, more abstract motives – honour and duty, manliness and familial affection – also mattered. James Evans, born in Wales and a resident of Manitoba when he enlisted in 1914, had served in the Boer War and entered the CEF as a captain. He was married and had several children, all of whom he would miss dearly but, as he explained in March 1915 shortly after having arrived in England, he had a higher motivation: "I miss you & the kiddies more than I can tell, at the same time I still feel that I could not have done anything else, as the old saying goes, 'I could not love thee dear so much loved I not honour more.'"[19] Not every soldier could summon up such a well-turned phrase to explain why he had chosen to enlist. Many found refuge in the less poetic – though much repeated – axiom that he simply wanted to "do his bit." This, at least, was how Laurie Rogers explained his decision to enlist in February 1915.

Laurie Rogers was as eager as Maheux to enlist but knew better than to do so without first securing the permission of his wife, May. Whether it was to avoid the unseemliness of being turned away by the recruiting officers or to make his case for enlistment as persuasive as possible, Rogers did not rush to the recruiting office in the first months of the war. Instead, he worked over the winter of 1914–15 to put his house in order and persuade May that duty compelled him to enlist, no matter how hard the consequences or how high the price asked of all of them. In his late thirties and the father of two, Rogers had struggled to find his true vocation in life. A man of some education and a middle-class upbringing – his father had been a major and had grown up in the English-speaking society of late nineteenth-century Montreal – he had tried his hand at many pursuits but feared that he had failed at all of them. He and May, his wife of thirteen years, had only recently taken up farming in Quebec's Eastern Townships, in the town of East Farnham. That, too, was a struggle, made no easier by neighbours with a penchant for mean-spirited gossip and smug self-satisfaction. Rogers thus looked upon the outbreak of war as a new opportunity, in which he could serve his country and prove to his intimidating father-in-law and his overly critical neighbours that he was not an abject failure after all. Once he had put the farm in order, guaranteeing that May and the children would be able to fend for themselves come spring, he made his way to the nearby town of Sweetsburg in February 1915 and enlisted for overseas service. By June 1915 he was in training camp at Valcartier, battling hunger and homesickness during the day and worries about his family's well-being at night: "I have too much time to think and it gives me the Blue Devils when I lay awake and think of you dear and the kiddies, but then I feel it was my duty and when a man feels that it is a strong pull to do right."[20]

Members of the much battered, battle-tested First Contingent and men of the Second Contingent, including Ormsby, Maheux, and Rogers, who arrived in Britain in the spring and summer of 1915, found in Europe yet further reasons to justify their enlistment. Exposure to the plight of Belgian refugees prompted them to reflect more deeply on why they had chosen to leave the comfort of home and the company of a wife and children for the miserable life of a soldier. It was only after Jack Howe arrived in Belgium and witnessed the dire plight of refugee families who had fled the onslaught of the German Army at the beginning of the war; it was only when he heard dreadful rumours of atrocities inflicted on civilians (some true and others grossly exaggerated), that he framed his enlistment and the cause for which he was fighting in broad, idealistic terms. He had enlisted not just to provide Ellen and their children with a reliable income but to defend the innocent and to guarantee that his own family would not suffer as Belgian and French families had suffered during the invasion of 1914: "The Germans was awful when they first came through last October with the women killing them if they did not do what they wanted very old people could only just walk along ... I tell you it but it hit lots of us fellows pretty hard to think what could happen to your own while you were away fighting they are crowded up in barns sleeping any where some of them have not seen or heard of their husband since the war began & do not know if they are alive prisoners & dead nor do not know where to find them I often thing how thankful it is not our homes & towns."[21]

Canadian soldiers arriving in the south of England in the first six months of 1915 were also well acquainted with tales of German barbarism. Forced to drill in the mud and rain of Salisbury Plain, subjected to the avaricious instincts of local merchants who assumed that Canadian troops had money to burn, and increasingly homesick, these men nevertheless did not regret their decision to enlist. If anything, they became more convinced than ever of the rightness of their decision and the righteousness of their cause. Frank Maheux, who would spend much of the war worrying about his family's food supply, was heartbroken by stories of Belgian suffering: "I see on the paper here that if the United States don't gives lost [lots] food, they are giving lost [lots] all ready, they be 10000 dying from starvation it is very sad that war for them poor people now."[22] Laurie Rogers was equally moved by the ordeals (of civilians and soldiers alike) recounted by men returning from the front lines: "It was "[my] duty," he explained to May, "to come over here and do my bit whatever it is, and although my heart is very sore at being away and no telling for how long, if it came to the same place in my life again I would feel it my duty not only to England but to myself and you to enlist again. If you were here and could see all the poor fellows who are back from the front and here some of the tales they have to tell you would have to put on men's clothes and get into it too."[23]

Even more inflammatory than stories of displaced Belgian families were accounts of German atrocities – some recent, some dating to the first days of the war – that circulated widely by the spring of 1915. Maheux arrived in England only days after a German submarine had sent the *Lusitania* and more than a thousand passengers (including at least a hundred Canadians) to a watery grave; he could not help but note: "I hear a vessal with 1500 person went down to the bottom, they got blown up by a submarine."[24] The sinking of the *Lusitania* also enraged George Ormsby: "What a cowardly act, our chaps and in fact the whole army is furious – I am afraid there will be very few prisoners taken by our boys. An act like this makes us all the more determined to crush the brutes and for my part I will never quit while I am able to strike a blow."[25] Tales of atrocities against Canadian soldiers were also widespread in the spring and summer of 1915, the most famous (or infamous) of which was the story of the crucified Canadians. Maheux told his wife a story he had heard of how English and French soldiers, recapturing a trench held only days earlier by the Canadians, came across "6 Canadians killed in a barn they were nailed with a bayonette in each hand to the barn and it what marked in English (That show you Canadians to stop in Canada.)." Apocryphal though it was, the story of the crucified Canadians enflamed the blood and intensified the fighting ardour of men like Maheux, who resolved that no German prisoners would be taken alive on his watch.[26]

Long before these letters arrived in Canada, Canadian civilians – or, at least, those who regularly read a newspaper – were well aware that a German submarine had torpedoed the *Lusitania*, were more than convinced that German troops had crucified Canadian soldiers, and were suitably outraged by accounts of German depravity against innocent women and children. Such stories, which dominated the Canadian press in May and June of 1915, converged to create a veritable catalogue of German frightfulness in the weeks following the attack on the *Lusitania*. Even though initial reports, filed within hours of the attack on 7 May 1915, were hopeful – the *Toronto Daily Star* reassured its readers that "the passengers of the *Lusitania* are believed to be safe"[27] – it quickly became evident that such optimism was profoundly misplaced. By 10 May, Torontonians could read heart-warming accounts of gallant men giving their lifebelts to women and heart-rending stories of mothers burying their infants at sea.[28] It soon became clear that more than a hundred Canadians had drowned when the ship went down. Some were the prominent citizens one might expect to find on a luxury liner; others were babes in arms and newlyweds on their honeymoon. All, it seemed self-evident, were victims of German barbarism, and Canadians were as enraged – and in some instances, moved to violence – as their British brethren.[29]

The sinking of the *Lusitania* was not the only evidence of "Teutonic Savagery" to accost the sensibilities of Canadian citizens in the spring of 1915. On 11 May, the *Star* summarized two "eye-witness accounts" of the crucifixion of a Canadian soldier by German troops, who (allegedly) bayonetted him to a tree and then shot him repeatedly. One report was relayed from a dying Canadian who swore he had seen the body; the other report came from men recovering from their wounds in hospitals near Paris, "all firmly of the belief that a Canadian soldier had been crucified."[30] A month later, a convalescent Canadian soldier, addressing a recruiting rally in Winnipeg, relayed a similar story of two wounded Canadian soldiers taken prisoner and crucified by their German captors. And like Maheux and the *Toronto Daily Star* before him (which had almost gleefully reported that a "tearing passion" had overtaken Canadian troops bent on revenge for the killing of their wounded comrades), Captain Rogers reassured his audience that "the Canadians later exacted a terrible revenge."[31]

These accounts served to confirm suspicions, widespread in Britain, France, and Canada by May 1915, that in its treatment of soldiers and civilians alike the German Army was criminally indifferent to international law and common decency. This, after all, was the conclusion already reached in late April 1915 when the Germans used poison gas at Ypres, and it was reaffirmed only weeks later when the famous (and subsequently infamous) Bryce Report laid bare a catalogue of German offences against French and Belgian civilians committed in the first weeks of the war. Widely believed during the war, and subsequently dismissed out of hand as inflammatory propaganda, the Bryce Report

drew on the testimony of civilians and soldiers to paint a damning
portrait of German brutality – villages destroyed, civilians used as human
shields, rampant pillage and sexual violence. Much that was contained
in the Bryce Report did in fact happen, but its accounts of women
mutilated and babies with amputated hands were, in most cases, wild
exaggerations.[32] Nonetheless, these tales of "outrages" committed against
women and children resonated powerfully and reappeared frequently
in public discourse in the weeks and months following the release of
the report. When on 12 May 1915 the *Toronto Daily Star* summarized the
key arguments and evidence of the Bryce Report, at the very same time
that it was tallying the dead from the *Lusitania* and relaying accounts
of crucified Canadian soldiers, it minced no words: "How Foe Makes
War on Civilians, Babes Crucified, Adults Tortured."[33]

Did such stories actively spur men still in Canada to enlist? Community
leaders, whether in the press, in pulpits, or at recruiting rallies, certainly
hoped they would. Oft-repeated references to German atrocities
informed discussions about why Canadian men should volunteer
for the war in terms that would have spoken with particular force to
married men. Accounts of Canadian casualties sustained in the Second
Battle of Ypres, which included both the notorious German gas attack
of 22 April and the subsequent and much-heralded counter-offensive by
Canadian troops at the nearby village of St Julien, would have stirred
the blood of single and married men alike, prompting a noticeable
increase in enlistment. Rumours of crucified Canadians might have
done the same. Reports of the sinking of the *Lusitania*, however, spoke
in a different register, for visions of innocent women and children
destroyed by a ruthless – indeed, even Satanic – enemy appealed directly
to men's familial affections. Immediately after the *Lusitania* disaster,
Toronto preachers castigated the leaders of Germany as "a band of men
who are the very incarnation of the spirit of anti-Christ" and called on
"every man to do his part in order that this thing should be done away
with."[34] Only days after reporting on German troops' vicious treatment
of Canadian wounded, the *Manitoba Free Press* reprinted an article
first published in the *New York Post* entitled "The *Lusitania* Horror
and the German Mind." The torpedoing of the passenger ship was
not, the author contended, some tragic mishap but, like the massacre
of Belgian innocents and the destruction of the historic library at
Louvain, the inevitable result of Germany's warped and malevolent
Kultur.[35] Similar arguments recurred through the remaining months of

1915, reinforced by references to new atrocities, including the bombing of British coastal towns and the execution in October 1915 of Edith Cavell, the British nurse condemned to death in occupied Belgium for providing assistance to Allied soldiers.

The war against *Kultur*, waged with indefatigable zeal in all Allied nations, offered an ideological justification for the Great War. In Canada it would become part and parcel of an increasingly elaborate and sophisticated campaign of recruitment. And embedded in the *Kultur* argument was the suggestion that a married man had an obligation to defend his family from the dastardly Hun. It is possible that this argument contributed to a noticeable, albeit not dramatic, increase in enlistment evident in some regions of Canada in the summer of 1915. Toronto, which prided itself on its patriotic resolve, enlisted more than sixteen thousand men between the beginning of June and the end of September 1915, and more than two thousand in the last two weeks of July alone. Military District 10, which comprised Manitoba, Saskatchewan, and parts of northern Ontario, recruited almost 9,500 men. All told, enlistment across the nation increased from 37,858 at the beginning of June to 105,426 as of 2 October 1915.[36] Many of these new recruits were single men, but married men – and especially those who were British-born – were also receptive to these rallying cries. A sample of married men who enlisted in Manitoba reveals a spike in enlistment in June and July 1915, confirmed by evidence from the Manitoba Patriotic Fund, which had 1,559 cases on its registers in March 1915, and 3,017 in September.[37] In Toronto one newspaper report showed that of seventy-one recruits documented in mid-September, thirty were married. Only seven of these thirty were born in Canada.[38]

Improvements in recruitment evident in the summer of 1915 were temporary, however, and were not sufficient to allay the concerns of the Ministry of the Militia and Defence. Ottawa was not yet ready to ask women to "put on men's clothes" (as Laurie Rogers had suggested in jest), but it was certainly concerned about Canada's capacity to field an ever-larger fighting force. The Second Battle of Ypres had made it abundantly clear that the war would not be quickly won, and that casualties, on a scale heretofore unimaginable, would have to be replaced by men not yet in uniform. Prospects for future recruitment were far from reassuring. Some regions continued to "do their bit," Toronto and the Canadian west, in particular.[39] By contrast, recruitment was stalling in the Maritimes and lethargic in Quebec.[40] Various explanations emerged as to why Canadian men, especially Canadian-born men, were slow to enlist. Authorities in Ottawa, convinced that recruitment officers responsible for drumming up enlistments were falling down on the job, took steps to remove the ineffective ones from their positions. Recruitment officers and other local worthies, not surprisingly, suggested other explanations for the modest results of late 1915. Civilian jobs were now plentiful; Canadian-born men were not yet persuaded that this was their war; and accounts of impoverished disabled soldiers and war widows barely able to support themselves did nothing to encourage new recruits.

By the late summer of 1915, the economic impulse to enlistment, so evident in August and September 1914, had all but disappeared. A bumper crop on the Prairies created jobs for the many men who had stumbled through the winter of 1914–15, sometimes sustained only by the financial support of the Patriotic Fund; and industrial production, now focused on munitions manufacturing, revived in central and eastern Canada. In the spring of 1915, the British Expeditionary Force had suffered a series of embarrassing defeats which the British press attributed to an inadequate supply of munitions. The "shell scandal" that ensued gave rise to the creation of the Ministry of Munitions under the stewardship of David Lloyd George. When he announced in June 1915 that "for the moment we have more than plenty of men for the equipment available ... we want the workshops to equip them with weapons," his words echoed from Manchester (where they were delivered) to the Maritimes, and beyond.[41] In August 1915 Ottawa circulated a memorandum to all military districts, informing commanding officers that "no men who are at present engaged in the manufacture of munitions should be allowed to enlist, but it should be pointed out to them that they are serving the country as well by carrying on their present employment and helping towards a successful issue of the war in another way."[42] Coal miners and machinists were in especially high demand. In the industrial towns of Nova Scotia, for instance, it was reported: "The fact is that men are in such demand at the industries here that they do not readily answer the call to enlist."[43] So, too, in Ontario, where munitions factories offered a decent living without the dangers of armed combat. Patriotism could be practised as readily on the home front as on the Western Front.

Although the able-bodied men of Truro and New Glasgow, Peterborough and Belleville could support themselves well by working in mines and munitions factories, there was reason to believe that in other regions economic uncertainty might still induce men to volunteer. In the rural communities of eastern Ontario and Nova Scotia, agricultural labour kept men fully occupied through early October, but once the harvest season was over, it was thought that men might be willing to respond to the recruiters' message. In late October, the commanding officer of the 3rd Military Division (which covered most of eastern

Ontario and the Ottawa Valley), perhaps stung by suggestions that his recruiting officers were not doing their job, argued: "Harvesting operations are without doubt, greatly retarding recruiting, and the general opinion would appear to be that immediately harvesting is completed, recruiting will be much brisker."[44] The vagaries of seasonal employment created similar prospects along the banks of the St Lawrence. One recruitment officer observed that, as the logging shanties that dotted the north shore of the river closed down for the winter, many recruits might be found in the remote hamlets along the Gulf of St Lawrence. Acknowledging that the men of this region were "difficult to convince," he suggested that "recruiting might be successful in that part of the country [only if they were] to send a man of that place who knows everybody and every village."[45]

Another impediment to voluntary enlistment in 1915 was that many Canadians, especially those who were native-born, did not yet see Britain's war as Canada's war. Writing in June 1915, the president of Dalhousie University was perturbed by newspaper reports that "the call for volunteers for the overseas service has met with an inadequate response of late in this part of Canada" and feared that the local population failed to understand "the very serious nature of the conflict in which we are engaged, and ... the necessity and not only the duty of everyone who can to go to the front."[46] In the rural hinterlands of Quebec, local mayors and priests did little to encourage the eligible young men in their midst to enlist. Perhaps it was because they were reading newspaper reports indicating that recruitment in Britain was already declining noticeably? If the young men of Britain, whose homes and families lay within the direct line of aerial assault – attacks on coastal towns in England had occurred as early as December 1914 and London fell victim to Zeppelin raids starting in May 1915 – were unwilling to enlist, why should the hard-working men of northern Quebec shoulder the burden of combat?[47] Francophones were not the only skeptics. In Montreal the Citizens' Recruiting Association distributed a pamphlet to English-speaking residents of Quebec, entitled "The Questions of a Hesitating Canadian and the Answers of a Canadian who Believes that this is 'Our War.'" Arguing that the Royal Navy was all that protected Canada from a German invasion and that a British defeat would inevitably expose Canada to the tyrannical rule of German militarism, the pamphlet appealed directly to the honour and manhood of Canada's reluctant warriors: "By fighting Germany in France and Flanders we are fighting her just as truly as though her soldiers were on our soil, our towns threatened with the fate that befell Louvain and Ypres, and our wives and daughters with the fate, worse than death, that befell so many of

Belgium's wives and daughters. The Canadian who says the War does not concern him because it is being fought in France does not understand the situation. He is like a man who does not concern himself when the house next door is on fire."[48]

Whereas a robust economy and a pervasive doubt that this was "Canada's war" affected married and unmarried men alike, married men could point to other arguments and circumstances, unique to them, that further discouraged their enlistment. Why should a married man enlist when everyone from the British prime minister to authorities in Ottawa and local recruiters agreed that this was above all a single-man's war? If single men were reluctant to enlist, why should married men fill the ranks in their stead? And if they did enlist, what guarantees existed that their families would be well supported in the event of their death or disability? Too many stories of bureaucratic incompetence and government parsimony in the issuance of pensions had appeared in the press for a married man to be assured that his family would be well cared for.

In Canada as in Britain, attitudes toward the enlistment of married men were ambivalent and debates about the military responsibilities of married men highly fraught. Attuned to developments in Britain, which by late 1915 was in the midst of a national campaign to identify all men eligible for military service, Canadian newspaper readers were fully cognizant of Britain's "Derby Scheme," which encouraged married men to attest (indicate their willingness to serve), at the same time promising that they would be called up only after all single men had been recruited or conscripted. When addressing the House of Commons in November 1915, Prime Minister Asquith pledged (in words that would then be repeated on posters distributed across Britain) that "the obligation of the married man to serve ought not to be enforced or held to be binding upon him unless – I hope by voluntary effort, but if needed in the last resort by other means – the unmarried men are dealt with." Married men, he promised, would not be "called upon to serve until the young unmarried men have been summoned to the colours."[49] Thus reassured that their turn had not yet come, fully a third of all age-eligible married men in Britain refused to attest when canvassed by the Derby Scheme.[50] The expectation that they would be called to serve only in the most exceptional circumstances remained a powerful political talking point in Britain throughout the spring of 1916, when necessity finally compelled the conscription of all men, married and single, not employed in protected occupations.

Canadians aware of these ongoing debates could reasonably have concluded that if many married men in Britain felt no compunction to serve; if the British ultimately drafted married men only with great reluctance (and in the face of considerable opposition), surely married men in Canada, responsible for the financial well-being of wife and child, had no moral obligation to volunteer. And they certainly had no obligation to enlist while there were still unmarried men oblivious to their duty.[51] The Citizens' Recruiting Association of Montreal tackled this argument head on: to the married man who asked why he "should go to the front when so many unmarried men are shirking their duty?" the pamphleteer responded sympathetically: "Yours is a difficult position. The unmarried man, without responsibilities, should go first. But if he shirks his duty, and the State continues to depend for its salvation upon the system of voluntary recruiting, your duty becomes all the more imperative. The War must be won. The State must be saved." To soften the blow, the recruiters reminded married men that "the Canadian who leaves his family behind is not leaving them destitute."[52] Separation allowances, Assigned Pay, and support from the Patriotic Fund guaranteed that a married man's dependents would be adequately provided for. And therein lay the rub: the military service of married men came with a significant price tag.

Because the federal budget had to fund Separation Allowances for soldiers' wives and pensions to soldiers' widows and orphans, advocates of conscription, which would first draw single men to the ranks, argued that Canada could scarcely afford the cost of married men's enlistment. A letter originally published in the Montreal *Financial Times* and then reprinted in the *Toronto Daily Star* made this point explicitly. T. Kelly Dickinson called for the conscription of unmarried men, whom he criticized for loitering at skating rinks and hanging around movie houses while married men rushed to the colours, "with a view to acting fairly with married men, and at the same time relieving in part the enormous financial obligation imposed on the country by the raising of an army of half a million men." He feared that the "cost of maintaining the families of these men [was] well nigh prohibitive."[53] Lt. Col. B.H. Brown knew exactly what those costs were: "A battalion in camp in which there are 1,000 married men costs $650 more per day to maintain than a battalion in which there are 1,000 unmarried men. This increased cost for a month is $20,000 and for a year is $240,000." He could not help but conclude that "in the interests of efficiency and economy it is desirable that single men be enlisted first."[54]

All in all, there were many legitimate reasons for married men not to enlist in the last months of 1915: jobs were plentiful; political discourse in Britain and Canada recognized that married men should not be called upon until all eligible single men had stepped forward; and the enlistment of a married man cost his nation dearly. For the married man contemplating enlistment at this time, there was an additional reason to hesitate: would the government really honour its economic pledge to the men who served and the families they left behind? In the early months of the war, wives often waited weeks, sometimes months, for their first Separation Allowance cheque. Angeline Maheux received her first cheque in mid-December, two months after Frank had made his way to the recruiting office in Ottawa and, as was customary, she received her Assigned Pay only after he arrived in Europe. Margaret Ormsby also complained that she did not receive her monthly stipends regularly, prompting George to reply: "I cannot understand why your remittance money does not come regularly. You should receive $40 for the month of March which would not reach you until about the 20th of April. I have signed off 20.00 per month for you from March 1st I do hope you wont run short."[55]

Given the scope of the enterprise, delays of this sort were no doubt inevitable; but they were nonetheless frustrating, especially for families living on the edge of poverty. What was perhaps understandable in late 1914 or early 1915, as the bureaucratic apparatus necessary to support a nation at war ground into action, became more irksome as the war moved into its second year. When the *Toronto Daily Star* acknowledged in September 1915 that wives were still encountering delays in receiving their Separation Allowances, it placed the blame on husbands who had failed to fill out the proper paperwork or had taken their marriage certificate with them when they left home. It was important, the *Star* noted, that wives hold onto the certificate in order to support their applications.[56] Military authorities suspected that delays might also have been due to bureaucratic bungling. In October 1915, the Paymaster of the 3rd Military Division, headquartered in Kingston, issued instructions to all recruiting officers in his division: "Immediately a recruit is enlisted and sworn in, if he is either a married man, widower, or sole support of widowed mother, a separation allowance card [is] to be made out and forwarded same day to Divisional Paymaster. The Divisional Paymaster is to be given authority to pay these Separation Allowances until such time as the man is drafted to a Battalion."[57] Weeks later, however, a new national policy designed to save money specified that, effective 1 November 1915, wives would not receive their Separation Allowance until their husbands had been assigned to a battalion, often a month or more after enlistment. As one officer sagely observed, this new policy "may slacken recruiting for a time."[58]

Penny-pinching policies when applied to pensions for disabled soldiers and war widows were even more inimical to enlistment. As soldiers wounded and disabled at the Second Battle of Ypres returned to Canada in the fall of 1915 and as war wives were transformed into war widows, stories emerged of paltry pensions, inadequate job-training programs, and serious lapses in providing for destitute families. The *Toronto Daily Star* was especially vigilant in bringing these stories to light, giving particular attention to the sorry plight of disabled men unable to support their families and war widows struggling to get by on pennies a day. In early October, the *Star* wrote of the difficulties encountered by men medically discharged from the army. Although many of these men would have been unmarried, the *Star* focused its attention most sharply on family men with wives and children to support. Following a soldier's discharge, all financial assistance to his family – Separation Allowances, Assigned Pay, and Patriotic Fund support – ceased. Yet jobs suitable for the medically discharged, several of whom spoke of having "shattered nerves," were either difficult to find or poorly paid. Rarely was a man in such circumstances able to support his family.[59] Military authorities knew that such stories were anathema to recruiting; the commanding officer of the 34th Battery training in Kingston noted only days later that "failure to properly take care of returned injured will injuriously effect recruiting." He observed that this was "already noticeable in Toronto."[60]

Tragic stories – of veterans returning to wives and infants so ill as to require hospitalization; of a shell-shocked soldier forced to support his wife and two children on an annual stipend of $192 (when the cost of living in Toronto was at least $60 a month); of widows like Ellen Howe being denied a pension for many months until their husband's death had been confirmed – all eroded confidence in the will and capacity of the Canadian government to provide adequately for those most grievously affected by the war.[61] Pension reform was clearly in order. The Toronto and York Patriotic Fund made the case only days before Christmas, when it observed that a monthly stipend of $22, the pension granted a totally disabled veteran, was completely inadequate to meet the cost of living in wartime Toronto. Even though a married man received a supplement of $11 a month, a family man with three children to support could count on only $50 a month.[62] When penury was the inevitable price a disabled soldier paid for his patriotic service, what married man would enlist? Militia officers were forced to conclude: "The present pensions provisions are one of the most serious obstacles to enlistment that exists."[63]

By the time George Timmins enlisted in March 1916, Canada was in the throes of a recruitment campaign unprecedented in scope, intensity, or psychological acumen. And although unmarried men continued to be the recruiters' primary focus, married men like Timmins were neither exempt from nor indifferent to their pleas. English-born immigrants who had arrived in Canada in 1905, George and May Timmins were well settled in Oshawa by the time he attested. Having weighed his competing responsibilities to home and nation, his was not a rash or hasty decision, nor one prompted by unemployment. As he noted a year later, sitting in a muddy, miserable trench in northern France, "we considered all sides of the question before my enlistment."[64] Could he in fairness leave his wife to shoulder the responsibility of managing the family home and caring for three children, the youngest not yet two? No one, surely, would think less of him if he opted to stay home, where he had a steady job and a family to support. Family tradition suggests that he waited until the baby, born in 1914, could toddle around on her own. And his own letters reveal that neither he nor May believed he would be away from home for as much as two years: "Do you remember how we used to talk over the possibilities of my being away a long period? We used to gasp almost at the idea of being apart two years, but always agreed that that would be the very extreme. What a rude awakening."[65] These considerations would certainly have played an important part in his decision to enlist – May would not be left alone for very long and the baby would probably be out of diapers and sleeping through the night. But it is also possible that his decision was influenced by the ever more insistent messages that came to dominate the recruitment campaign of early 1916. He and May would have noticed that Prime Minister Borden's New Year's pledge to muster half a million men for the ongoing war coincided with a more energetic, more organized, and more professional strategy of recruitment designed to persuade men to enlist and, just as important, incite women to urge them on.

Some of the methods deployed in the service of national recruitment were well established but, by early 1916, of doubtful efficacy; others were thoroughly modern and psychologically astute. Public lectures, long a staple of recruiting rallies and usually delivered by prominent local citizens or returned soldiers who could speak directly about the character of combat on the Western Front, were now complemented by eye-catching posters, patriotic movies, and systematic canvassing of neighbourhoods and workplaces.[66] As had been the case in the first year of the war, unmarried men remained the primary targets of these new recruitment efforts. By early 1916 it was evident, however, that single men were not enlisting in the numbers needed to meet

Borden's pledge. Whatever the costs – to family life and the national budget – married men would also need to be called up. The character of national recruiting thus shifted to include married men. In posters and movie palaces, public rallies and door-to-door canvassing, military recruiters increasingly subjected married men to the siren call of duty; and they did so by emphasizing the threat a German victory would pose to the virtue of women, the well-being of children, and the tranquility of family life. Alluded to in posters, decried in pamphlets, and depicted with memorable ferocity in movies, the enemy's gross mistreatment of women and children became a recurrent theme in the recruitment rhetoric of 1916 Canada.

Although recruiters initially placed great confidence in the persuasive power of a rousing patriotic lecture, such talks were increasingly ineffective, especially when pitched to single men. Recruiting rallies in the Maritimes to mark the first anniversary of the war had had disappointing results: well-attended meetings in New Glasgow and Stellarton, for example, garnered only three recruits.[67] Three months later, military officials in Ontario were similarly stymied, forced to concede that "the holding of public meetings does not seem to in any way stimulate recruiting ... as a general rule, the men who should be got at do not attend these meetings."[68] Nor, alas, did they go to church. In early 1916, clergymen in Toronto and Winnipeg complained that the patriotic pitch delivered from a Sunday pulpit had become so commonplace – and so grating on the ears of the men to whom it was directed – that young men were simply absenting themselves from church.[69] They weren't staying away from work, but recruiting rallies held in factories and other places of work also produced meagre results. In early February 1916, a series of visits to Toronto factories had minimal success: three British-born men (two of whom were married) at the A.R. Clarke leather company; one man (out of an audience of two hundred) at another; and five, including three married men, at a third factory. Disgusted by the reluctance of single men to sign up, the recruiter attempted to shame them into enlistment. Noting that six hundred of the eight hundred men in his battalion were married, he exhorted the crowd: "Why, in Heaven's name, the married men should join and the single men hold back is more than I can understand. That ought to get under the skin of every one of you. You know it isn't right to let the married men go and the single stay at home. It is a damnable thing and it ought to make every single Canadian blush with shame."[70]

When potential recruits stayed away from church and turned a deaf ear to lectures delivered at work, recruiters hoped for better results from pleas made in the picture palaces of major (and minor) cities across Canada. Protests from pious citizens who complained that such exercises thus sullied the Sabbath did not deter recruiters: they knew that young men were more likely to be found at the movies on Sunday evening than in the pews on Sunday morning.[71] In Toronto, a rally held at the Loews Theatre, which featured lurid tales of atrocities against civilians, including "the outraging of women" and the crucifixion of a sixteen-year-old girl nailed to the door of her own cottage, garnered fifteen recruits. A similar event at the La Plaza Theatre, at which the recruiter argued that "the best memorial [the men of Toronto] could give Edith Cavell was to offer themselves in the service of the King and country" saw twenty-five men step forward. A month later, similar events in Winnipeg featured convalescent veterans of the Second Battle of Ypres who provided eye-witness commentary on the war on the Western Front and urged every able-bodied man in attendance to enlist "without delay."[72] And in New Brunswick local military authorities worked with the managers of movie theatres "to have, each evening, five minutes of 'war talk.' Soldiers would be taught "to deliver these five-minute addresses and the oc of the Detachment should arrange to have a new man each night take his place before the audience and deliver a five-minute 'spiel.'"[73]

   No one went to the movies just to listen to a "five-minute spiel." They went to be entertained by the best that modern cinematic technology could offer. Documentaries detailing the life of an enlisted man, lantern slide shows capturing images of the lovely English countryside, and feature films imported from Hollywood regaled audiences with stirring patriotic messages, a nostalgic vision of the "Old Country," and dystopian tales of German invasion. A travelogue, sponsored by the *Toronto Daily Star* and screened at Massey Hall in late February, offered a pitch-perfect appeal to any British-born immigrant not yet in uniform. A photo montage juxtaposed images of elegant English country homes and bucolic villages, which almost reduced the "Old Country" folk to tears, with photographs of the last voyage of the *Lusitania*. The *Star* was confident that travelogues such as this would "affect recruiting in Toronto for the better."[74] In mid-March, when Manitoba was at the high point of its recruiting campaign, the Walker Theatre screened a documentary detailing the lives of Canadian soldiers, from their departure from Victoria to their arrival in England and participation in the Second Battle of Ypres. Mixing the amusing and the mundane with the heroic and the hair-raising, the film, which ran for a full week with two screenings each day, was further enlivened by the illuminating and entertaining commentary of Sergeant Fred Wells, "an unassuming sort of hero" who had been wounded at Ypres, where he lost an arm and was taken prisoner by the Germans. Repatriated in a prisoner exchange, he was back in Canada with his "dry humour" intact and eager to urge his compatriots to do their bit.[75]

While travelogues tugged at the heart-strings of British-born men not yet in uniform and documentaries urged young men to join those who were already doing their duty, a movie conjuring images of a German invasion of North America would perhaps prompt the still-hesitant Canadian-born to see the war as an immediate threat to home and family. *Battle Cry of Peace* was just such a film. First released in August 1915 in the United States, where it played to large and enthusiastic audiences eager to embrace the "preparedness" campaign of many would-be interventionists,[76] it found equally appreciative audiences when screened in Canada in the spring of 1916. Described with the hyperbole befitting a Hollywood blockbuster as "the most noteworthy achievement in the history of motion pictures," *Battle Cry of Peace* imagined scenes of an America devastated by a German invasion: the "bombardment of New York," "Washington Reduced to Ruins," "the execution of American civilians." These and other scenes of unimaginable misery were "arousing a nation to the sufferings of Belgium and the perils at its gates."[77] When would-be movie-goers in Toronto first saw advertisements for the film in early March, they were promised that it portrayed the "diabolical treatment of women and children, and the other incidents that this war has shown follow invasion by a ruthless foe."[78] A week later, as the film began its engagement at the Strand movie theatre, similar rhetoric reminded the citizens of Toronto that all events depicted in the film – including "American women … compelled to self-destruction in order to save themselves from dishonour" – were based on incidents suffered by the citizens of Belgium. Torontonians responded with rapt enthusiasm. Originally scheduled for a one-week run, *Battle Cry of Peace* enjoyed such a "prodigious success" that it was extended into a second week.[79] And at the end of March, the 204th Battalion sponsored a free screening of the film for all men not yet in uniform, urging them to "see what might happen to Canada if men do not rise to the defence of their homes."[80]

By late March 1916 Canadians were primed to believe that a German invasion, and all the moral and physical devastation it would bring in its wake, was a very real possibility. Rumours to the effect that German agents were responsible for the fire that destroyed the Parliament buildings in Ottawa in early February became immediate grist for the recruiters' mill: "Today you're not fighting for any English-man's home," one recruiter proclaimed, "you're fighting for your Canadian homes. What happened at Ottawa last night? That might happen tomorrow in Toronto, with our Parliament Buildings, our City Hall. That ought to tell you just how close the war is getting home to you, for there is not a doubt that the burning of the Parliament Buildings was the work of the devilish Hun."[81] Newspaper accounts published at the end of March of a German plot to dynamite bridges and railways in Canada only intensified the anxiety and consolidated the conviction that Canada was indeed vulnerable to invasion.[82] *Battle Cry of Peace* thus presented Canadian audiences with a scenario more plausible than fantastical. Following its extended Toronto run, the film moved westward, screening in Winnipeg in early April and subsequently in Regina.[83] In early May the film returned to Toronto, where it ran at Massey Hall for an additional week. All who had not yet seen "the most tremendously realistic and gripping war drama photographed" were urged to do so: "See it and think of your dear ones."[84]

Even those who could not afford a ticket to the movies might well have seen similar images of Germanic brutality in the posters that came to dominate recruiting in late 1915 and, even more so, in early 1916. Many recruitment officers in the summer of 1915 had called on Ottawa to follow Britain's lead and produce (or import) its own eye-catching, multicoloured posters. Unlike the visually arresting posters produced in Britain by the Parliamentary Recruiting Committee,[85] the only posters used in Canada before the summer of 1915 were simple blood-red sheets of paper that placarded public spaces and provided information on rates of pay, determined by rank, and emphasized that a soldier's dependents would receive a Separation Allowance and a portion of his assigned pay. More informational than inspirational, these "red posters" seemed to be doing little to swell the ranks of the CEF. In late June 1915, therefore, Ottawa authorized the production of two distinctive posters – "Heroes of St. Julien and Festubert" and "The Gem of Liberty" – both of which were designed and printed in Canada and were available in English and French. Starting in early August, the posters arrived by the hundreds in recruiting offices and railway stations across Canada.[86] Both posters gave pride of place to a Canadian soldier, flanked by the Union Jack and (more subtly) sprigs of maple leaves. Neither targeted married men explicitly, although married men – like their single compatriots – might well have been inspired to emulate the Canadian heroes who had held their ground at St Julien in the face of poison gas, massive losses, and unsuccessful counterattacks.[87]

The expectation that Canadian men – and, specifically, married men – should go to war to protect their families from the horrors that had befallen Belgian civilians became more explicit in posters that circulated in 1916. Whether manufactured in Canada or imported, with suitable textual tweaks, from Britain, these posters emphasized the familial responsibilities of Canada's menfolk. Recruiters in Montreal, for example, urged men to join the 73rd Royal Highlanders by reminding them: "Mothers, Wives and Sweethearts expect you to protect them. You may do so with the 73rd Royal Highlanders of Canada."[88] A poster targeted directly at Québécois men imagined what the "Hun" would do if he ever set foot in Canada. Accompanying the visual image of a young woman and child, shot dead on a snow-covered street in a village laid waste by German soldiers, was the injunction: "CANADIENS C'EST LE MOMENT D'AGIR. N'ATTENDEZ PAS QUE LES BOCHES VIENNENT METTRE TOUT A FEU ET A SANG AU CANADA. CANADIENS SOYEZ HOMMES! NE RESTEZ PAS EN ARRIÈRE. ENROLEZ-VOUS DANS NOS REGIMENTS CANADIENS-FRANÇAIS."[89]

Women, too, were targeted by posters and other public pleas that reminded Canadians of the outrages inflicted on women and children by marauding Germans.[90] An argument frequently repeated in late 1915 and early 1916 in flyers, pamphlets, and at recruiting rallies was that they also had to play their part, by sacrificing the men in their lives for the greater good of defending civilization, hearth, and home. In October 1915 the Citizens' Recruiting Association of Montreal produced a pamphlet, twenty thousand copies of which were distributed to English-speaking households in Quebec, urging mothers and wives to give their menfolk to the war effort: "Was the ravishment of Belgium no concern of yours? Do you care nothing if the babies of other Scarboroughs are done to death by German bombs? Will you do nothing, risk nothing, to put an end to the massacre of the innocent on other Lusitanias? When you recall these unspeakable atrocities perpetrated on non-combatants, on mothers, maidens and infants, by the Germans, can you say to your boy 'Don't go'?"[91] Two months later, when the city of Toronto launched a recruitment campaign with the goal of filling eleven new battalions, women riding the city's streetcars were accosted by soldiers in uniform distributing a flyer calling upon them to encourage their menfolk to enlist. Although the flyer was directed primarily toward mothers – who were roundly criticized across Canada for selfishly keeping their sons at home – wives were by no means exempt. Mothers, sisters, girlfriends, and wives: all were urged: "Make your son, your husband, your lover, your brother join now while he yet retains the remnants of honour."[92] This message also infused the efforts of the Women's Emergency Corps, which convened in Toronto for the first time in January 1916, dedicated to the cause of robust recruitment. Women were to assume one of two tasks: if they were in a position to do so, they were to take up paid employment for the duration of the war, thus freeing young men to volunteer for overseas service; and all women were expected "to persuade the men in their family to enlist."[93] Single women were to impress upon their sweethearts their patriotic responsibilities; mothers were to overcome their natural instincts and let their sons sign up; and, as a battalion commander speaking to a recruiting rally in February 1916 made clear, married women were to "allow their husbands or dependents to enlist."[94]

The poster "To the Women of Canada," which duplicated almost verbatim a British poster produced in 1915, made a similar argument. Printed in both French and English, it alluded to the atrocities inflicted on Belgian women and children – "You have read what the Germans have done in Belgium. Have you thought what they would do if they invaded this country?" – and urged Canadian women to remember that "the safety of your home and children depends on our getting more men NOW." Women, moreover, should not let private sentiment stand in the way of public duty. If one wifely word of reservation was enough to keep a man from doing what he knew he ought to do, one word of encouragement was often all he needed to steel his resolve. Women, therefore, should realize that "the one word 'Go' from you may send another man to fight for King and Country." To make it clear that wives were as critical as mothers in this enterprise of national importance, the poster concluded: "When the war is over and someone asks your husband or your son what he did in the Great War, is he to hang his head because you would not let him go? Won't you help and send a man to enlist today?"[95]

One question remained unanswered: Who would support a soldier's family in his absence? For men who had enlisted in the early months of the war the prospect of a reliable and respectable income, sufficient to support a wife and children, had often proved a powerful inducement to enlist. By late 1915, however, jobs were plentiful and men had little economic incentive to enlist. If this was true of unmarried men, a fully employed married man would have had even less reason to leave home for the now well-known, frequently documented horrors of front-line service. At the very least, he would have to know that his family would not suffer economically if he decided to enlist. But a household income dependent entirely on a soldier's Assigned Pay and his wife's Separation Allowance was not enough to maintain a wife and two children in early 1916.[96] Could a married man responsibly subject his loved ones – those he was honour-bound to provide for – to a life of abject poverty? He could fulfill his duty to his nation only if he knew that in so doing he was not compromising his equally compelling duty to those he loved. For families of modest means and no savings to fall back on, the supplement offered by the Canadian Patriotic Fund might make all the difference to a man's calculations. Posters and pamphlets alluding to – and in some instances, citing without authorization precise promises of – the generosity of the fund thus became ever more prevalent in the recruiting campaigns of late 1915 and early 1916. So common, in fact, that the CPF protested in February 1916 to the Department of Militia and Defence, demanding that recruiting literature no longer contain "definite statements as to the figures of the allowances to be made from the Canadian Patriotic Fund." Ottawa immediately ordered recruiting officers across the nation to cease and desist: henceforth "anything in the nature of a guarantee for a fixed sum for allowance is to be avoided."[97]

Although recruiting officers could no longer promise a married man that his family would receive a supplemental allowance from the CPF, provincial fundraising campaigns, which coincided with the recruitment efforts of early 1916, reminded potential recruits of the fund's existence and its generosity. Posters and advertisements for these pledge drives were ostensibly directed at donors but, when read in conjunction with newspaper accounts detailing the successes of these annual campaigns, they also offered a married man considering enlistment reassurance that his family would be well taken care of. One poster, printed in Hamilton, captured a farewell scene of a Canadian soldier, his wife, and their infant child. As the soldier holds the baby in his arms, he turns to bid his wife goodbye: "G'Bye Mary – THE PATRIOTIC FUND WILL CARE FOR YOU."[98] When the Toronto and York Patriotic Fund successfully concluded its annual campaign in late January, having raised well over two million dollars, it congratulated those who had donated and reassured those who were contemplating enlistment: "Toronto is resolved that the wives and children or other dependents of every soldier, now or to be, will not suffer because the breadwinner has become a fighter in the great cause."[99]

When the Manitoba Patriotic Fund, which operated independently of the national organization, launched its annual campaign in early April, it knew that recruiters in the province were desperate for new volunteers. Like its counterparts in Hamilton, Kingston, Regina, and other cities, the Citizens' Recruiting League of Winnipeg had recently conducted a city-wide canvass, first of homes and subsequently of businesses, to identify all eligible unmarried men.[100] Although Manitoba men had enlisted in significant numbers since the earliest days of the war, soldiers who went door to door, asking residents and neighbours to identify unmarried men residing on their street, discovered that there were probably four thousand single men in Winnipeg not yet in uniform. Even if every one of these men were to enlist – and only half would ultimately do so voluntarily – many more men had to be found: the city battalions needed to recruit sixteen thousand men if they were to sail for France at full strength. The *Manitoba Free Press* could not help but conclude: "Married men will have to be called out."[101] The fundraising campaign of the Manitoba Patriotic Fund could help make that happen. Large advertisements appeared daily in the city newspapers, urging Winnipeggers to give generously to this most worthy cause. The advertisements encouraged those who could not enlist to give, attempted to shame those who would not, and prodded those who were still contemplating a life of combat. One advertisement, timed to coincide with the screenings at the Walker Theatre of *Battle Cry of Peace*, was especially noteworthy. Contrasting the vibrant, growing cityscape of 1916 Winnipeg with scenes of the city gutted by fire and destroyed by bombs, the advertisement played on the fears of invasion that had been circulating since February 1916: "If you want never to see Winnipeg as it is pictured above, then answer the second appeal of the Manitoba Patriotic fund."[102]

❧

More than 100,000 Canadian men, married and single, enlisted in the first four months of 1916, almost 34,000 in March alone.[103] This rate of recruitment far exceeded any other period during the war, including the early rush of August and September 1914. In Toronto, which had contributed more than 20 percent of all enlistees through December 1915, recruitment continued to be brisk: 3,157 men attested in February; 2,981 in March.[104] So, too, in Military District 10, comprising Manitoba and Saskatchewan, where Winnipeg continued to lead the way. The *Manitoba Free Press* proudly reported that 54,000 men from these two prairie provinces had enlisted since August 1914, of whom fully one third – 18,432 – had signed up in the first three months of 1916. The recruitment drive for Military District 10, which started in earnest in March 1916, saw four thousand men enlist in the first two weeks, more than half of whom were Winnipeg men.[105] Many of these new recruits were single men, but married men – especially but not only the British-born – also heeded the clarion call. In Toronto, the *Daily Star* reported recruitment returns, albeit on an irregular basis. Whether to applaud the patriotism of those who did enlist, or to shame those who did not, the paper made a point of identifying the recruits' marital status and whether they were British- or Canadian-born. In January 1916, it reported that in a cohort of 127 recent recruits only ten of the fifty-one Canadian-born men were married, but fully one half of the seventy British-born enlistees were married. Two months later, Canadian-born enlistments had improved – twenty-eight of the fifty-three men in this sample were born in Canada – but married men continued to be more evident in the ranks of the British-born: fourteen of twenty-five English-born men were married.[106] In the Earlscourt neighbourhood of northwest Toronto, popularly known at the time as "Little Britain," 914 of the 1,457 men who enlisted between August 1914 and April 1916 were married, the great majority British-born.[107] In Manitoba, where British immigration in the decade before the war had swelled the population, a sample of the married men who enlisted in 1916 reveals a similar preponderance of recent immigrants. Most of these men were in their mid-thirties when they enlisted and fully three-fourths had been born in the British Isles.

The Canadian Patriotic Fund and its Manitoba counterpart knew well that married men were enlisting in significant numbers. At the end of December 1915, the CPF had disbursed $565,306 to wives and dependents of volunteers in the CEF or reservists called to the colours in the allied armies of France, Britain, Belgium, and Italy. By May 1916, it was distributing $803,574 to needy dependents and by July, over a million dollars. Manitoba experienced a similarly substantial surge in families securing support from the fund. As early as September 1914, there were 409 Manitoba families on the books of the Patriotic Fund; by June 1915 that number had quadrupled to 1,720. But the most significant increases occurred in 1916. At the beginning of April 1916, when the Patriotic Fund launched its annual appeal, over five thousand Manitoba families were registered with the Patriotic Fund; two months later there were 6,345.[108]

Some of the men who responded to the recruitment campaign of 1916 were no doubt cajoled, shamed, or otherwise "induced" into enlistment; others were temporarily inspired by drink and soon regretted their decision. This, at least, was the argument put forth by the National Manufacturing Company of Brockville when they sought to recover munitions labourers from their firm who enlisted in the early months of 1916. Although some of these men insisted that their enlistment was in no way coerced, Bertram Fraser, a married man and employee of the firm, did think better of his decision and was allowed to return to civilian life.[109] But only coal miners, munitions workers, and the substantial number of men who failed their medical examination had the luxury of changing their minds.[110] All other enlistees were in uniform for "the duration of the war, plus six months." Presumably, many of these men – and perhaps the married men more than most – had, like George Timmins, thought carefully about their decision, and enlisted in a sober and resolute frame of mind. It is impossible to know precisely what finally prodded them to enlist: a poster or a movie; a lingering affection for the Old Country, or anxiety about an enemy assault on Canadian shores; manly pride or a determination to defend women and children? Reassured at least that their wives and children would be well cared for, most left their homes with a heavy heart, knowing that for the duration of the war their marriages would be sustained – and their family life conducted – by correspondence alone.

"Trenches are not good places to write letters"
Marriage by Correspondence

Laurie Rogers was surely correct when he observed: "A husband or a wife thousands of miles away is no fun."[1] Because wartime marriage was fraught with the heartache of separation, the intensification of economic hardship, and persistent anxiety about the well-being of wives and children or the survival of husbands, married couples quickly learned that letter writing would have to become an integral and indispensable facet of family life. However rudimentary their letter-writing skills – spelling mistakes were commonplace, punctuation often cursory – they had no choice but to practise marriage by correspondence. Everyone realized that regular correspondence was a most imperfect instrument of family communication – perhaps even more so for Canadian families than for their British and French allies. Soldiers of all nations lamented any delay in mail delivery, fearing that their wives had forgotten them, but mail sent from Canada to the front lines moved excruciatingly slowly and it was not uncommon for days – sometimes weeks – to go by with no letters from home.

Wives suffered similarly from lapses in and interruptions to letter writing, especially in the early months of 1917. When Germany resumed unrestricted submarine warfare, sending hundreds of ships to the bottom of the Atlantic, the delivery of mail from or to Canada was infuriatingly erratic and unreliable. Censorship, more overbearing in the British and Canadian expeditionary forces than in the French army, also proved a constant source of irritation, frequently impeding full and frank communication. Nonetheless, Canadian men in uniform – like their British and French allies – depended on letters from home to sustain their morale, to maintain contact with those they most loved, and to be reassured that they, too, were still loved. In turn, and often at the urging of their wives, they struggled to describe in their letters home something of their experiences in the front lines, conveying to the home front more of the horrors of combat than was once believed. Although wives could not know in a visceral, immediate way what it was like to serve on the Western Front, many came to understand that it was pretty damned awful.

✧

The generation of men who went to war in 1914 and the anxious women they left behind grew up in an age of almost universal literacy and growing access to and reliance on postal services.[2] These men and women thus had both the skills and the infrastructure needed to practise marriage by correspondence. This is not to say that they found it easy. Even though primary education had been compulsory in England and parts of Canada since the 1870s, letter writing was an acquired skill with established protocols. For men and women of the middle and professional classes, the ability to write a well-phrased letter was an essential aspect of bourgeois respectability. But for children of the working classes, whether schooled in Britain or Canada, letter writing was a more uncertain accomplishment. Many of the married men who enlisted in the CEF had attended school in Britain, where the art of letter writing was introduced only in the last year of the elementary curriculum; children who left school before then would have been only vaguely familiar with the finer points of epistolary etiquette.[3] Access to the letter-writing manuals that proliferated in Europe and North America in the nineteenth century would have taught them that a well-formed letter required adherence to certain protocols: many writers felt they had to apologize for writing in pencil rather than pen, or for letters filled with spelling errors. And almost everyone knew and relied to some extent upon the formulaic phrases that by tradition opened and closed a properly written letter.[4] Writing a letter was much more complex than simply jotting down whatever ideas, impressions, and sentiments came to mind.

However imperfect their mastery of written English, however halting their command of letter-writing protocols, British and Canadian households had by the beginning of the twentieth century come increasingly to rely upon letter writing to stay in touch with distant family members, engage in commerce, and order goods from the mail order catalogues that were becoming a beguiling feature of modern life. In British households touched by the waves of emigration characteristic of the years before the Great War, family members who struck out on their own exchanged letters with those they had left behind in the Old Country – begging for money, bragging of recent triumphs, or simply

offering reassurance that they were still alive.⁵ Men like John Samuel
Whitlock, who enlisted in Saskatoon and whose wife and children still
lived in Birmingham, or John Farmer, whose wife and seven youngest
children remained in England while he tried to make a life for them all
in British Columbia, would have been well trained in the art of marriage
by correspondence long before either one enlisted in 1916.⁶ Even those
who lived only a few miles away from family and friends would have
made use of the illustrated postcards that proliferated in Canada and
Britain in the decades before the Great War.⁷ From the 1890s onward,
the affordable, attractive, and all-purpose "penny" postcard became the
preferred – and sometimes only – means for people of modest means to
stay in touch. As Edith Hall, a young English girl of the working class,
recalled, her family sent and received postcards almost daily:

> Just prior to the Great War of 1914 when I was about six years old,
> postcards with the then half-penny postage were sent between
> my relations each day. My grandmother would send us a card *each
> evening* which we received by first delivery the next morning. She
> would then receive our reply card the *same evening*. If one lived in
> the same town as one's correspondent, an early morning post card
> would be delivered at twelve mid-day the same day and a reply
> card, if sent immediately, would be received the same afternoon.⁸

Perhaps families in Canada's largest cities were equally accustomed
to the daily exchange of postcards, which were spoken of colloquially
as "the poor man's telephone."⁹ Toronto was certainly a hive of letter-
writing energy by the early twentieth century, when almost half a million
pieces of mail were delivered in the city every week.¹⁰

Recently arrived immigrants, whether living in Canada's largest cities
or smallest rural outposts, relied on the mail to stay in touch with family
in Europe. Long-established Canadians were also regular clients of the
postal network. Men and women of the comfortable classes had become
accustomed since at least the early nineteenth century to writing to one
another when work, political campaigning, or (occasionally) military
service took them far from home.¹¹ By the end of the century, letter
writing was no longer an enterprise exclusive to Canada's prosperous
classes. A newly expanded postal service, which in 1891 boasted over
eight thousand post offices and by 1911 more than thirteen thousand,
made it possible for families to keep in touch with neighbours and
distant kin. Out-migration from eastern and central Canada made it
necessary. When young (and not so young) Canadians ventured south
into the United States in search of employment, or west to the Prairies

in search of economic independence, the postal system allowed them to maintain contact with parents, wives, and children still residing in the Maritimes, Quebec, and Ontario.

Ready access to a post office, ideally no more than four kilometres from the family home, also gave most rural Canadians, like their urban counterparts, the capacity to participate in the commercial culture of modern life: placing orders with mail order catalogues and opening post office savings accounts.[12] They could not expect overnight delivery, of course; nor could their correspondents count on an immediate response to a recently delivered letter. In Lumby, British Columbia, for example, where George and Maggie Ormsby settled before the war, locals complained that "the mail transport came and went so quickly that 'ranchers living some distance from the office [could not] answer an important letter for three days from the time of receiving it.'"[13] These inconveniences notwithstanding, only the most remote communities lacked regular access to the national mail.

Although many Canadian couples were by 1914 familiar enough with the rudiments of letter writing, were accustomed to receiving mail order packages, and were, as a consequence, reliant in one way or another on regular postal service, nothing in their civilian lives quite prepared them for the particularities of wartime correspondence. Writing a letter in the comfort of one's home offered scant preparation for writing from a water-logged trench, especially when under the watchful eye of a military censor. As William Coleman, a captain in the CEF, observed: "trenches are not good places to write letters."[14] They were, however, excellent places to receive and marvel over packages sent from home. Like the distribution of letters, the shipment of packages was an enormous enterprise that at times threatened the efficient functioning of every nation's military postal system. In the weeks leading up to Christmas and New Year's, French postal authorities sorted upwards of 600,000 packages each day.[15] The British also sent parcels, though in more modest numbers. British families prepared sixty thousand parcels a day (and 4.5 million in December 1916), soon overwhelming the vast sorting facility built in Regent's Park in 1915.[16] Parcels from England and France usually arrived at the Western Front within a week. Those shipped from Canada could take two months or more.

This meant that every parcel had to be sturdily wrapped and filled only with items that would survive weeks of unrefrigerated transit. Canadian families prepared boxes of fruitcake, fudge, maple sugar – and socks. Hundreds and hundreds of pairs of socks. Henry Hillyer's packages included toiletries, tobacco, and, on one occasion, a fruitcake that arrived in France somewhat the worse for wear: "The lid had evidently been removed and replaced although the cake was whole and tasted very nice indeed."[17] Not all baked goods fared even that well, as Laurie Rogers and Frank Maheux discovered to their regret. In anticipation of his first Christmas away from home, Maheux had his heart set on a *tourtière*, and his mother and wife both obliged. As one can well imagine, the results were profoundly disappointing. His mother's parcel arrived in time for Christmas, but when he opened it he discovered that "every thing was moulded and green I suppose the box got wet I never was so sorry in my life, I had to throw them away."[18] Angeline's parcel fared only slightly better: "The meat pie was the same as the one my mother sent me all molded, to long coming, but the rest was all right I am surprised they charged you so much in the mail for a small box like that."[19] When Laurie Rogers received a parcel of homemade raisin cakes he framed his thanks as tactfully (and honestly) as possible: "Those raisin cakes keep fine and even if they are a little bit stale they are from home." A few weeks later another parcel arrived, this time in excellent condition: "Dear May ... Since we arrived here the parcel of eats arrived and believe me we four enjoyed them. Everything was in fine condition nothing smashed or squashed ... It is awfully good of you to go to so much trouble in baking and making candy when you are so busy but if you only knew how much we think of the things from home you would feel highly complimented."[20]

Parcels offered much more than relief from the monotonous rations sent up the line. Tangible reminders of familial affection, they were also essential to maintaining camaraderie at the front. Although every parcel contained something for the exclusive enjoyment of the recipient – cookies made by young children, family photographs to wear close to one's heart – it was understood that men would share most of their temporary bounty. One Canadian soldier noted: "Most boys get parcels very often indeed, and naturally your own crowd all share up alike. Last night, one of us got a cake, chocolate, café au lait, etc., and sitting round the old brazier we were quite happy for a time."[21] Soldiers certainly appreciated the parcels they received from home, but they also worried that their families spent money they could ill afford to provide them with packages. In the fall of 1917, Laurie Rogers implored May – whose packages included homemade cookies, maple sugar, and, most famously, a teddy bear made by his young daughter – to conserve her strength and her savings: "Now dear girl I don't want you to send me cake and candy for two reasons first it gives you a lot of extra work and secondly everything is so expensive I know you will go without yourselves just to be sure that I get something and I don't want that. Don't think dear girl that I don't appreciate the trouble that you go to for I do and also enjoy the cake and fudge but I wont have you and the kiddies doing without for me."[22]

⟪∘⟫

A soldier in the trenches could have lived, grudgingly perhaps, without parcels, but neither he nor his wife could have contemplated a life without being in touch. Obstacles to regular correspondence were, however, legion. As an officer, William Coleman would at least have had access to something resembling a desk. Enlisted men lacked even that modest luxury. Writing from "a hole under the ground" in late 1916, Frank Maheux confessed that with only a flickering candle to light his page, he could "hardley see that the reason I can hadly folling the lines, you talk about rats it is a fright they jumped over you, I never see the like and they are big buggars."[23] Even so, such miserable conditions did not make letter writing impossible; it was not uncommon for French soldiers, for example, to write home every day from the front lines, because they were confident that their letters would – under most circumstances – be delivered in no more than three days. Canadian soldiers, by contrast, realizing that their letters would not be delivered for several weeks, were more likely to write only once or twice a week, often waiting until they were in reserve positions before putting pen to paper. Uncomfortable conditions, intrusive censorship, and infuriating disruptions in delivery all made marriage by correspondence especially trying for husbands and wives alike.

Canadian couples separated by war and the width of the Atlantic Ocean reluctantly became used to the fact that mail moved with nerve-fraying slowness and irregularity. Under ideal conditions, a letter from Canada would cross the Atlantic in about a week, be sorted in London and then redirected to the appropriate unit on the front lines. If all went without a hitch – if snow did not delay the trains in Canada, if a soldier had not been wounded or assigned to a new unit, if the "mailman" in the trenches was not hit by shellfire – a letter from Toronto or Montreal would be delivered within two weeks; letters from the west coast would, of course, take longer. William Coleman, who kept meticulous records of letters sent and received, noted in the summer of 1916 that his wife's most recent letter from Toronto had taken "just fourteen days." This was a vast improvement on conditions earlier that year, when he had sometimes waited a full month for her letters. He had noted on 21 March 1916, for instance, that his wife's most recent letter, sent on 21 February, reached him "somewhere in Belgium" exactly a month later. "This letter has been the longest on the way of any, but as I think I mentioned in my last letter we had no Canadian mail whatever for over two weeks."[24] Laurie Rogers suffered the same delays, observing in April 1916 that he had "received three letters from [his wife] dated 'Feb. 20 and 27 and March 16' all in a bunch the first I had had in five weeks owing to the mail having been held up for some reason or other. My but it was a great relief to get them and the kiddies [letters] to find out you were all well."[25]

By late 1916 the improvements of the summer months were long past. The onset of wintry weather in the north Atlantic delayed ship passages, sometimes doubling the time it took to cross the ocean. Disruptions and delays in mail delivery became even more frequent as of February 1917, on account of the German navy's resumption of unrestricted submarine warfare. From February through the end of April, submarines sank at least 500,000 tons of Allied shipping each month. As one scholar of the naval war has noted, in one two-week period "seventy-eight British ships were sunk and the overall tonnage lost in these two weeks, if prorated over a year, would have amounted to half of the merchant marine at the disposal of the Allies. Estimates of a vessel's chances of surviving a round trip between the United Kingdom and a destination beyond Gibraltar were, for this period, about one in four."[26] When the *Laconia* sailed from New York in mid-February 1917 and was torpedoed a few days later, thirteen passengers perished, and more than a million pounds of silver and at least five thousand bags of Canadian mail went to the bottom.[27]

When soldiers were deprived of letters, some concluded that their wives no longer cared for them. David McLean grew increasingly irritated in the early months of 1917 when he went for weeks without a letter from his wife. At first he thought she was simply indifferent to his plight: "Well I haven't got any letters from you tonight yet Mr. Grant gets his all right but none for me so after this I will just write to you when you write to me. I suppose you people over in Canada have such a fine time you never think of those that are out here putting up with all those hardships for them but never mind after the war things will be different. We will look after ourselves first so goodbye." By late March, however, with the arrival of letters long delayed in transit, his mood improved somewhat: "I received four letters from you yesterday, one dated Feb. 15th, 16th, 26th and Mar. 1st. It has been a month and two days since I received your last letter it being dated Jan. 29th so I don't know if you wrote one between that one and Feb. 16th. If you did I did not receive it."[28] Laurie Rogers, by temperament a more congenial fellow than McLean, was less inclined to blame his wife for the long delays that plagued mail delivery in early 1917. When the Valentine's Day card he expected had still not arrived by mid-March, he speculated that "the big Fishes in the sea are enjoying it or else the Mermaids have it posted on a rock."[29]

Mail service from France to Canada was even more erratic and annoyingly slow: correspondence from England or France usually took at least a month to reach Canadian destinations and, because mail boats sailed only once a week, letters often arrived in bunches rather than at regular intervals. William Coleman, knowing that his wife, Della, was eager to receive word from him as often as possible and frustrated by the delays in service in early 1916, went to great lengths to expedite the delivery of his letters. Ordinarily, letters written by enlisted men were censored on the front lines and then all letters, whether written by officers or enlisted men, were again subject to random censorship review at the base camp, before being shipped to England to await the next scheduled mail boat to Canada. Coleman discovered a further cause for delay: "Mail via [the] purely Canadian route is usually seven or eight days between boats, and this I understand was the way all our mail from the front has been going." This meant that a letter destined for Canada could be delayed in France, where it was subject to censorship, and then again in England, while awaiting the next boat for Halifax, Saint John, or Quebec. If Coleman could circumvent the established process by first sending a letter to England with a fellow officer heading to London on leave, and then having it mailed by way of the United States, he hoped that his letters would arrive in Toronto more quickly. His plan, he well knew, was strictly illegal. Under no circumstances were men returning to England on leave allowed to carry personal correspondence with them; to ensure compliance, rank and file troops were usually searched as they boarded ships at the Channel ports. Because officers were not subject to such indignities, Coleman could ask a fellow officer travelling to England on leave to take a letter with him: "As long as leave is on I can send over a letter every week to be posted in England. This of course is against orders, but if I give it to an officer, and the letter is censored before it goes I do not think any harm can come to me." Once the compliant smuggler arrived in England, Coleman's letter could be stamped, submitted to the civilian mail service and marked "via New York."[30] This, he hoped, would bring the letter to Della's door within two weeks.

Rank and file soldiers had few such expedients available to them. Ordinarily, their wives had to wait until the mail wended its way from France to London, from Liverpool to the Maritimes (in winter) and Quebec or Montreal (when the St Lawrence was ice-free). Waiting for letters thus became the national obsession of wives (and parents) living on the edge of nervous breakdown. They would scan the newspapers hopefully for announcements of ships arriving in Halifax or Quebec, bringing home wounded and convalescent soldiers; this they knew would mean the arrival of mail bags, too. At the height of the submarine warfare campaign of early 1917, when many of the married men who had enlisted in 1916 were either in England or had recently arrived in France, mail delivery to Canada was especially unreliable. Lettie McLean remarked (and, given the rather testy tone of the surviving correspondence, probably complained) that she was "not getting letters regular" from her husband, to which he responded (equally testily): "Well I have wrote a great many more than I have received from you but there is times when in the trenches that the conditions are such that I can't write and you are lucky that you get as many as you do for I wish you could see the holes we crawl into and sleep."[31] In a much more understanding voice, William Mayse observed from Seaford, England: "My Dear Betty ... we are getting our mail anyway, though as far as I know there has been none lost so far – you are not getting my letters at all regular, I am writing at least twice a week you seem to be getting them all-together."[32]

Never fully resigned to the inefficiencies of the mail system, Canadian women naturally feared that a long, unexplained silence could signify only one thing: that their loved one had been killed or seriously wounded. Husbands did their best to reassure their wives that, whatever happened, they would be notified in private before anything appeared in the local paper. If a man was killed, his wife would receive an official telegram; if he was wounded, he would do what he could to send word home; and if he was fortunate enough to survive an especially bloody battle, he would send a telegram (if possible) or a field postcard (commonly spoken of as a "whiz-bang") to reassure his wife that all was well. George Ormsby, shortly after arriving in France, told his wife, Maggie, "I don't see that anything would be gained by cabling you if I am wounded I will be well looked after. I might however cable you after some heavy engagement just to let you know I am alright." A year later, however, after he was seriously wounded at the Somme and evacuated to a hospital in England, a family friend and "shirt-tail relative" in London sent a wire to Vancouver, alerting his wife to his condition: "Of course you will know by this time that Mrs Ormsby was the sender of the 'cable.' It was her idea to sign my name so that you would know I was not so seriously hurt that I could not cable; what a good angel she has been."[33] Several months later, William Mayse, while awaiting deployment to France, reassured his wife, Betty, that he and a friend were "arranging to send a joint cablegram, letting you & his people know when we cross over to France, we are expecting to go together, & we will send the cable to his father he has a business in the city, & as soon as he receives it, he will phone you & also let you know our address."[34]

❦

As soon as Canadian troops arrived in Europe, their letters were subject to military censorship. And because the CEF operated formally under the jurisdiction of the British Expeditionary Force, the system of censorship that obtained in the British ranks also applied to Canadian overseas forces. Unlike the French Army, in which censorship of letters occurred at a base several miles from the front lines, in the British Expeditionary Force and, hence also in the CEF, mail was censored first at the company level. Junior officers were allowed to censor their own letters (or have a friend do so for them), as Stuart Tompkins noted in a letter to his new bride: "As for my letters I censor them myself or get an officer to censor them which means that I assume responsibility that there is nothing military in them. Of course I must be careful just the same, indeed you yourself will admit that I am pretty guarded."[35] Knowing that the privilege of privacy was not extended to the men under his command, Tompkins was anxious not to abuse that privilege: "I certainly do not feel … that I can take liberties. I put my name on the outside of the envelope, if it means anything it means I have censored it … It is not playing the game to insert information which the men are not allowed to give."[36] And the men were not, in principle, allowed to say much. All letters written by rank and file soldiers had to be read and (if appropriate) censored by their company's junior officers, a task that the officers found laborious and their men found insulting.

The very possibility that a censor might take offence at a word, a phrase, or an entire paragraph in a soldier's letter had a chilling effect. Soldiers could only guess what might pass the censor without difficulty and what might be excised. And so they usually erred on the side of caution. In early April 1916, Laurie Rogers wrote: "If you find my letters kinds of a jumble it is so the censor will pass them I try not to write anything that they can take offence at but what I might think of they might have other ideas about."[37] He returned to this theme a few months later, after a particularly rough rotation in the front lines: "It is hard to write letters these days as there are so many things I may not put in a letter or the censor will cut them out or destroy the letter altogether. I would like to tell you a lot of things but must not so will try and save

them up until peace is declared."[38] Henry Hillyer offered a similar excuse
in a letter to his wife, Jennie, in November 1916: "There are lots of news I
could write and tell you I suppose the censor would score it all out and
incidentally crime the sender." One thing he knew for certain, however:
"We are not allowed to state where we are and yet the papers publish it
because I've seen it myself."[39]

Soldiers were allowed to tell their families which battalion they
were assigned to. Indeed, they had to, for letters could not be properly
sorted otherwise. Censorship prohibited them, however, from identifying where they were on the front lines. This was the most frequently
repeated injunction of military censors in all armies on the Western
Front. And it was also one of the rules soldiers did their best to circumvent. Recognizing that their families were anxious to know exactly where
they were at the front (and thus whether they were temporarily exposed
to or protected from danger), most soldiers tried to send this information
home one way or another. One hapless soldier in the Princess Patricia's
Canadian Light Infantry faced a court-martial for having written the
word "Vimy" in one of his letters.[40] More circumspect correspondents
offered broad hints that a wife familiar with newspaper accounts could
easily decipher. Laurie Rogers, having mentioned in a previous letter
that he had been "[u]p where the Princess Pats lost so many at the first
of the war," congratulated his wife for correctly concluding that he and
his company were at Ypres: "Your guess as to where I am is very good
and quite correct. That town must at one time have been a very beautiful
place but if you can remember the pictures of San Francisco after the
Earth Quake and then multiply it by two it will give you a small idea
of what the place looks like now."[41] Subsequently, he invented a private
code to convey his whereabouts to his brother-in-law, "so," he wrote to
May, "if you get it from him let me know and I will carry it on with you
too."[42] It is not clear that they ever made use of it, but it surely was not
as complex and impenetrable as the code Jack Ellis invented:

> The code works on my [service] number 675928. You start reading
> my letter and you take the 6th word (not including 'My Own
> Darling Kitty') now from that you take the first letter. Then from
> the 6th word you'll count 7, then take the first letter of that word.
> Then from that count 5 words and take the first letter again and
> so on till you have the whole number then start over again all
> through the letter. Now if you see one kiss only at the end of the
> letter look for something and pick out the letters as I explained, if
> I put 2 kisses instead of taking the letter take the whole word …
> Do you understand me dearest?"[43]

A much less convoluted and hence more universal code had a soldier place dots under a succession of letters, thus spelling out his location on the front.[44]

For some married soldiers, censorship offered a convenient excuse for not talking about the war or more private matters. George Ormsby, who was less than ardent in his letters home, excused his emotional reticence on the grounds that his letters had to be read by his commanding officer: "No doubt all my letters must seem cold and formal but you will understand that every letter has to be censored by own officers and of course one cannot be too loving under the circumstances."[45] Most, however, deeply resented the fact that a censor was required to review their private mail. As a junior officer, Stuart Tompkins would learn that he could call upon his fellow officers to "censor" his letters (without actually having read them), but he didn't know this in May 1916 as he prepared to sail from Canada: "from now on all correspondence is to be censored, so I suppose I cannot tell you that I love you eh!" As soon as his battalion arrived in England, they were warned again that censors would be watching closely for militarily sensitive information conveyed in letters home. This was a regulation Tompkins could readily obey. He was, he admitted, "not anxious to tell details of military interest and [would] do [his] part to prevent such becoming known. Still one hardly appreciates having one's personal letter perused by the jealous censor." Once in France, however, he discovered that he had the liberty to "write again and say things that need saying pretty often, that I love you more than ever. My heart goes out to you dearest at all times and I long for your words of encouragement and cheer. Believe me the mail is mighty welcome in the trenches, particularly when it comes from one who means so much to you."[46]

Enlisted men, who knew that every letter had to be submitted to and read by a junior officer, were often more constrained in what they said and more resentful of the censors' intrusive presence. George Timmins apologized to his wife for letters that were, he feared, "as unemotional as a schoolboys essay on horticulture," explaining "that its not the lack of love on my part, but fear of the eye of the — censor." Henry Hillyer was equally put out that the censor had the right to read his intimate correspondence. While his company was preparing to embark for France, he warned Jennie that his next letter would be "scrutinized by Mr. Walker first and then the Official Censor afterwards so I shall be wary of saying too many nice things to you so you will have to read between the lines." A month later he returned to this complaint: "You know my love, it is not very edifying to know that when one has expressed one's sentiments on paper to one's nearest and dearest that a third party has to peruse them."

He recognized that the censor was "not to blame" and "only acting under orders"; he even acknowledged that "this censorship is very necessary as with such a large body of troops here there are bound to be some very indiscreet persons sending military information unwitting." But Hillyer found the intrusion irksome nonetheless: "I for one feel a strong aversion to opening up and writing you a nice affectionate lover like letter and having it read thoroughly by a person who is in daily contact with myself."[47] As Desmond Morton has observed, "Part of a soldier's humiliation was the knowledge that his officers read every word of his personal letters and, as mess waiters knew, sometimes joked about them with brother officers."[48]

Canadian troops (like their British counterparts) could enjoy a temporary respite from the overbearing censorship of the front lines by using much coveted, albeit irregularly distributed green envelopes. First issued in the spring of 1915, these envelopes were imprinted with the assurance that "correspondence in this envelope need not be censored Regimentally," and with the warning that "the Contents are liable to examination at the Base." Captain Frederick Corfield, a career officer in the British Expeditionary Force, thought the men in his company would appreciate the new envelopes: "he can say things ... he doesn't want the officer who censors here to know." Nonetheless, Corfield quickly lost his enthusiasm for the envelopes: "I shan't use any more of those sort of envelopes as I think there's more chance of them being opened, crowds have been that I know of."[49] As an officer, Corfield didn't need to confide his innermost thoughts to a letter in a green envelope: he could simply ask a friend to certify that his letters had been duly censored. By contrast, enlisted men, whether in the BEF or the CEF, who wished to speak frankly about the war or lovingly to their wives, had no choice but to rely on green envelopes, knowing that even these letters were not entirely protected from censorship. George Ormsby feared that letters sent in green envelopes were more likely to be delayed than letters dispatched through regular channels. The several letters he had sent Maggie during the last month, he told her in June 1915, "were enclosed in green envelopes, and I have reason to think that these letters have been held up."[50] Perhaps his suspicions were warranted, but other evidence suggests that green-envelope letters were rarely intercepted by censors behind the lines and thus moved with uncommon speed through the postal system. When George Eastman sent his wife, Henrietta, a series of letters in green envelopes, starting in August 1915, she kept careful account of how long it took them to arrive in Toronto: two weeks was not unusual, and none took longer than three.[51]

Green envelopes were, however, more a privilege than a right, and soldiers were never sure when, and for what reason, their distribution might be interrupted or discontinued. It was standard practice to review closely all mail sent in advance of or during major battles, and thus it was not surprising that green envelopes were suspended during the Battle of the Somme, from July 1916, when the British and French armies first launched their assault, until October, when Canadian participation in the battle culminated at Courcelette.[52] Military necessity thus interrupted the distribution of green envelopes, as did any identifiable misuse of the system by individual soldiers. George Ormsby's initial reservations notwithstanding, he appreciated the opportunity to write home under cover of a green envelope – on one occasion sending Maggie undeveloped film of the front lines – and thus regretted any reduction in the allocation of green envelopes. In the fall of 1915 he groused: "We used to be allowed four green envelopes all summer but it is now cut down to one per week. So many of the boys took advantage of them and wrote home about their petty squabbles how such an officer treats his men, etc. and making complaints all around that the privilege was partly withdrawn and may be withdrawn altogether so then every letter we write home will have to be censored by our officer."[53] Several months later, unaware that the German Army was about to attack the Canadian lines at Mount Sorrel and thus severely disrupt all mail service, he promised that "when I get a green envelope I am going to write you a good long letter, you see we get only one green envelope every three weeks although we are supposed to get one every week." This time, he did not blame disgruntled colleagues who divulged more than they should have; he suspected rather that "the Govt. are beginning to practice economy at last."[54] Green envelopes remained in short supply for the rest of the year. It was only in November 1916 that Canadian soldiers were once again able to take advantage of the relative privacy they offered.

What did married Canadian soldiers say in the letters they sent home in those coveted green envelopes? Although nearly all regretted not being able to speak lovingly to their wives in letters subject to regulation censorship, rarely were they overly effusive even in letters protected by a green envelope. In this regard, they were much more reticent than French soldiers and their wives, whose letters were often openly affectionate and occasionally explicitly erotic. When Paul Pireaud feared that the war and a newborn child would cool their passion, his wife, Marie, promised that "not even a baby would prevent us from caressing each other as we did before."[55] And the pseudonymous Armandine wrote letters that must have stirred her husband's ardour: while anticipating her husband's next leave, she promised: "In my arms you will feel that you are in seventh heaven. I will know how to arouse you, electrify you, make you crazy with love. I will know how to possess you and make you possess me."[56] Nothing comparable appears in the letters Canadian couples exchanged during the war.

In the green envelope letters George Eastman sent home between August and November 1915, he frequently admitted that he was homesick, but only cautiously confessed his love. In August 1915, for example, he devoted much of his "green envelope" letter to thanking his wife for the parcel she had recently sent, assuring her that everything was much appreciated. The avowal of love that closed the letter was as timid as it was true: "Never mind Dear girl the longer the separation the happier will be the meeting. I hope it may be soon as I am lonesome for my Girls and you bet we will all be glad to get back ... I wish we were coming out for good – and then I could get home to my Girls. I don't think I will leave them again ... I will close for this time Keep lots of love for self and Ethel. By by your loving Hubby, Geo." In a subsequent letter, marked by a more introspective mood, he regretted that (in his judgment) he had not been "very good company sometimes," but he wanted Henrietta to know: "[I have] always loved you both no matter what way I felt." He did not regret signing up – admitting in fact that he loved the life of a soldier – but he also loved his "Girls and home": "When I get back I will always love my Girls more than ever before ... Give my love to all and Keep lots for your own dear self and Babe You know I love both so much." If he missed the erotic pleasures of home he could not bring himself to say so: the most he would allow was that he would "be home some day and then my Girl can attend to my feet I think I have cut my toe nails once since I left home."[57]

Eastman's letters leave no doubt of his affection, but there is little in his green envelope letters that would have raised the eyebrows of a regimental censor. Yet even his most bashful expressions of affection were, in his mind at least, too private to be read by anyone but his wife. Thus, when writing to acknowledge receipt of a photograph Henrietta had sent in advance of his Christmas parcel, he once again confided his most intimate thoughts to a green envelope: "My Dearest Wife and Daughter I just rec'd your dear letter and the Dear Faces that I love so much. Oh my love how nice you and Ethel look to me I kissed those Faces that I love I can not keep them in my pocket I have to be looking at them all the time how nice you have Ethels Hair done and your own done up the way I loved to see you how did you know how to do it it is just lovely and you look sweet I think that is all the Xmas present I want."[58] George Timmins was equally delighted by the family photographs he received from home and was quick to show them off; but in his avowals of love he was as shy as George Eastman. In November 1916, he confessed: "I have tried to write letters since I have been in France but somehow they have always seemed unsatisfactory to me on accounts of the thoughts of the censors having to read them." Once the green envelopes were available again, he resolved to "take a chance and call you all the nicest things I can think of just for once, expecting you to understand when I don't (as I am awfully shy about anybody else reading my love letters) that I am just as much in love with my wife as ever I was, whether I can write about it or not." Having promised to call May all the "nicest things he could think of," he quickly changed the topic and described the dangers of shellfire when in a reserve billet, and the misery of mud compounded by artillery bombardments in the front lines.[59]

That Canadian soldiers found it easier to talk of war than of love is perhaps not surprising: war surrounded them, and love was very far away. And, however much they might have wanted to protect their loved ones from the brutal facts of war, they also found it necessary to unburden themselves to those who cared the most. A close reading of letters written between late 1915 and the summer of 1917 – an eighteen-month period when the married men who had enlisted in the CEF between August 1914 and May 1916 were repeatedly exposed to combat – reveals how often they took advantage of their green envelopes (and, more rarely, leave in London) to describe in spine-chilling detail the dangers and miseries of the front; to confess their war-weariness; and to admit that, whatever the newspapers might be saying to the contrary, they did not always feel like heroes. Canadian soldiers shared with their wives enough of the character of front-line combat to give the women more than a glimpse of its horrors. It was not their intent to alarm their wives or shock them out of the complacency they often ascribed to other civilians. Rather, letter writing came to function as a form of psychological release, a "writing cure" that allowed for reflection and confession. Married soldiers did not confess to sins that would have put their marriages in jeopardy – no accounts here of being admitted to hospital for the treatment of venereal disease; nor did they sprinkle their letters with the rough and rude language of the trenches, where four-letter words

constituted a soldier's *argot*.[60] Indeed, even the mildest oath included
in a letter home called for an apology. Laurie Rogers, trying to describe
one especially "hot" day in February 1916, noted that "the noise was a
regular inferno and 'without cussing' it was just as near Hell as I want to
get to."[61] But if these men were, at least in their letters, always virtuous,
well-spoken husbands, they were not always valiant heroes, whatever
the daily papers proudly proclaimed. Even though they never ceased to
believe in the war, they suffered remorse, despondency, and resentment
that the burden of fighting it was not evenly shared. They were nearly
always homesick – especially at Christmas – and frequently disgusted by
the character of the war and the sacrifices it exacted. But they were also
resolute: war was hell, but unconditional victory was non-negotiable.

In November 1915 George Eastman took advantage of the green
envelopes to tell his wife of a particularly memorable and by no means
reassuring episode in an otherwise very ordinary tour of duty in the
trenches. A member of the First Contingent and survivor of the Second
Battle of Ypres, in the aftermath of which he had been briefly hospitalized, Eastman was resigned to the fatalistic optimism that, as Tim Cook
has demonstrated, was fundamental to psychic survival on the Western
Front.[62] In August 1915, following his return to the trenches, he tried
to reassure his wife that he had every hope of surviving the war: "If I
am to go why I must but I have been very lucky so far and I hope to
be until the end of the war."[63] He had little idea how soon his fatalism
would be put to the test of action. Writing on 3 November 1915, he spoke
plainly enough:

> Now dear Girl I want to tell you that I was so very near killed I
> will explain it all to you I was on sentry in the Trench and my feet
> got so cold I got down from where I was watching the Germans
> Trench to walk up and down to warm them and I was thinking of
> you and wishing I was home and as I turned to walk back I saw a
> German Bomb coming over the Trench it was dropping right in
> the Trench where there was 2 or 3 of the boys so I just jumped and
> caught it and threw it over the Trench it exploded right on top
> of the Trench but no one was hit. I believe that my Girls prayers
> helped me to do it as it saved my own life as well.[64]

Henrietta Eastman probably found little comfort in this tale of uncommon bravery. But her husband hoped she would be pleased to learn
that he had been recommended for the Distinguished Conduct Medal,
which he pointed out with justifiable pride was "the second highest
Honour in the British Army." Some of his comrades went so far as to

suggest that he should have been recommended for the Victoria Cross, and in a subsequent letter he indicated that his commanding officer went to London precisely to plead that case. But Eastman was happy enough with the DCM, especially (though he did not say as much to Henrietta) because it erased the field punishment to which he had been subjected for having been "drunk and absent from billets" only weeks earlier.[65]

George Eastman's luck did not hold. He was killed on 13 June 1916 in the last days of the Battle of Mount Sorrel. Those who survived the battle, including George Ormsby, Laurie Rogers, and Frank Maheux, wrote of it in their letters home with an unapologetic candour that probably would never have passed the censors. Rogers wrote from the quiet comfort of a London hotel room, where he was on leave in late June; his letter, sent through the civilian mails, would not have been subject to censorship. Ormsby and Maheux, however, wrote while still in France, probably taking advantage of the last green envelopes issued before the opening days of the Battle of the Somme. The letters they sent home, replete as they were with horrifying descriptions of combat, certainly suggest as much.

The Battle of Mount Sorrel has faded from popular memory of the Great War, eclipsed by the two enormous (and enormously costly) battles of 1916: Verdun and the Somme. For the men of the CEF who faced the German barrage unleashed on 2 June 1916, however, it was a battle unlike anything they had ever seen. The usually taciturn George Ormsby wrote at some length of its unprecedented ferocity, avowing that "the gun fire was the worst that has ever been experienced on the British front and only at Verdun has it been equaled." Describing his own survival as a miracle, he wrote that Canada had lost heavily, especially in the first two days of the battle: "There was a bad break made in our lines on Friday evening and over 9000 Germans advanced. Previous to this our boys of the Princess Pats, C.M.R.'s etc had been wiped out so the Germans had it all their own way until we arrived on the scene at daylight the following morning." Ormsby's own battalion helped recover ground lost on 2 and 3 June, but at significant cost. He wrote of seeing "our boys go over the crest of the hill running for all they were worth and as they poured along in an irresistible charge they were mown down in hundreds. But they actually chased Fritz right back into the trenches and followed him in but of course none of them ever came back as they were out numbered 50 to 1." Among the survivors were victims of shell shock and life-threatening wounds. One young man known to George and Maggie was temporarily out of his mind: "poor chap he seems to have had a dreadful shock – he is out of his head at times and is quite sensible at others but he attributes his pain to some disease, says he has been in Hosp. three weeks and has not been in any battle, when as a matter of fact I know that a week ago he was out in billets and was in the best of health as I was talking to him then. Further the Corporal told me he was picked up in the trenches unconscious so I know he was in there." Ormsby felt nothing but compassion for this young man, whom he judged a fine soldier who would be fully recovered "after a few months rest." Nothing could save young Percy Whitlow, however: this "young sergt who first drilled us at Lumby was hit and had his arm blown off he probably is dead."[66]

Laurie Rogers, recuperating in London, confessed that he felt lucky to have emerged unscathed from the battle.

> We were three nights and two days in it and were so badly cut up that we had to be withdrawn. Thank God I came through with a whole skin, but there was a time when I did not think there would be one man left. It has been said that the Bombardment we have just come through was the worst since the war began so you will immagine what it must have been like. The ground just shook like a jelly and the explosions were so heavy at times that I was lifted right off the ground ... I went into the front line with 75 men and two officers and there was only one officer and twelve of us left to march out, of course they were not all killed some were wounded some shell shocked.[67]

Rogers's description of Mount Sorrel, chilling as it is, nonetheless pales in comparison with that of Frank Maheux, whose written English was as evocative as it was unlettered:

> It is a fright, it is like a butchery, my dear wife, it is not war, their no name for it, the night before I was defending a Bridge with 5 mens, the Germans throw us 10 or 11 big trench mortars killed 3 of my camarades, and wounded another one on the leg ... and the worse dear wife it was all them corpses around us, and we could'n beried them on a/c the Germans had killed every one of us ... they was hands feets mens cut in pieces, by them big trench mortars ... I see poor fellows legs cut off, trying to pull themselves to some place of shelter against the shells, but only to die I saw to much Angelique.[68]

Letters like these made it clear to wives at home that the Battle of Mount Sorrel, which cost Canada almost eight thousand casualties, was dreadful in ways barely hinted at in the elevated, redemptive discourse of

Canada's national newspapers.[69] The Somme was even more atrocious. Although the Newfoundland Regiment participated in the very opening stages of the battle – the seven hundred casualties they suffered on 1 July 1916 forever commemorated at the distinctive Beaumont-Hamel memorial – the CEF entered the battle only in mid-September. This final stage of a battle that was supposed to win the war was marked by the first use of tanks, a technological breakthrough designed to give Allied troops a tactical advantage in their assault on the German lines. But when the tanks became mired in the mud, the infantry, "clustered near them like chicks around a mother hen," were easy targets for the German guns.[70] Frank Maheux witnessed this first-hand, and six weeks later sent home a photograph of a tank accompanied by a tart analysis of its tactical value. Indifferent to (or unaware of) the psychological effect these lumbering monsters had on the German troops who first watched their advance across No Man's Land, Maheux acknowledged that the tanks were impressive to look at – as large as an airplane, he attested – but feared that they made little positive difference on the battlefield: they "got blew by shells or stuck in shell holes we had to leave them behind all around the machine you see smoke that guns firing."[71]

The lack of green envelopes did not prevent Maheux from describing the horror of the Somme in two letters written in late September. It was, he avowed, "the worst fighting here since the war started." He found some comfort in knowing that the Canadian Corps had taken "all kinds of prisonners," but acknowledged the heavy price: "God we lost heavy, all my camarades killed or wounded we are only a few left but all the same we gain what we were after, we are in rest dear wife it is worse than hell, the ground is coverd for miles with dead corpses all over and your Frank past all true that without a scratch, pray for me dear wife, I need it very bad." Nor did he hesitate to confess that he had avenged the death of a good friend: "I was caught in one place with a chum of mine he was killed beside me when I saw he was killed I saw red, we were the same like in a butchery, the Germans when they saw they were beaten they put up their hands up but dear wife it was to late."[72] A few days later, still haunted by the scenes he had witnessed (and the "butchery" to which he had contributed), he reflected once more on the aftermath of battle: "How glad I'll be when this war will be done, you can['t] believe how it is after the big charge we made on the Germans, the Germans trench were [covered] with dead all over the ground, see some poor lads of ours wounded trying to crawled to some shell holes only to die there it was like a butchery in some places."[73]

Laurie Rogers was also at the Somme, and from his vantage point as a stretcher-bearer assigned to an advanced aid post, he too bore witness to the battle's grim aftermath. His letters were not as blunt in their description of pitched battle as Maheux's, but they did not disguise his dismay that the territorial gains of battle were so inconsequential and the human costs so devastating. Having served in a first aid post since May 1916, he had seen more of the grotesqueries of war than he cared to contemplate, and May Rogers had more than an inkling of the demoralizing duties of a stretcher-bearer in the front lines. A week before finding himself in the thick of battle at Mount Sorrel, Laurie had confessed to her that an artillery bombardment could unnerve even the most seasoned soldier: "You cannot tell how small a man feels when the big shells are breaking all over the place and the scream of them is terrible then a fellow begins to think what a small atom he is and on how slender a thread his life hangs or what little things might change the whole course of things." He spoke of an "officer [who had been] buried under his dug out," and although his men saved him from suffocation, he died two days later "after he was blown to bits." Laurie, by no means an insensitive man, laconically noted: "it must have been his fate." This distressing episode was as nothing, though, when compared to the death of a much-admired commanding officer: "We lost our Major and I don't think I ever felt so bad about anything as I did about that for you know I have been with him ever since Sherbrooke days. I had to pick him up in a blanket and sew it up and get him out of the trench and I am not ashamed to say that I cried while doing the job. The getting of him from the place where he was killed to where I could attend to him was just as messy a job as I want to go through again."[74]

Such stories would have done nothing to set May Rogers's mind at ease, knowing as she did that from mid-September through early October her husband's regiment was in the thick of battle at the Somme. Initially, he wrote only in phrases that would have passed the most punctilious censor. The regiment had taken part "in the big drive that has just come off and covered ourselves with glory altho we lost a lot of men … It was simply wonderfull to see some of the fellows going across the 42nd went over just as if they were on parade so did the 60th our fellows were also great and there cannot be too much praise given to them." And unlike Maheux, who made no apology for bayonetting German soldiers attempting to surrender, Rogers gave medical attention to wounded German prisoners. Some, he wrote, were "big fellows but some were only boys of 16 it is terrible to think of mere kids being knocked about in that way."[75] It was only after the battle was over that he wrote more openly – admitting that his company had been "in the big scrap on Sept. 15 and also in the one when Courcelette was taken"[76] – and more despondently. His company had suffered serious casualties in the first push: "Out of five officers who went in with my company only one came out with us, two were killed the others were buried in their dug out and had to go out perfectly deaf and I am affraid they will never hear again." Courcelette was, if anything, even worse. It was certainly more demoralizing:

> We have just come through another awful experience and there are very few of us left, hardly any of the old boys. Our fellows went over and took a German trench and held it for fifteen hours beating off three counter attacks of the enemy then for lack of supports and amunition had to let it go again. As usual someone blundered and we just got Hell instead of support. One officer that I dressed simply cried with rage and disappointment and some of the men were doing the same thing, believe me it was awfully discouraging to have to give it up after all the work we had in getting it.[77]

Caring for the wounded through three weeks of pitched battle and under relentless enemy shell fire was, he observed laconically, "hard on the nerves." There was little a first-aid post could do to save the grievously wounded or alleviate their suffering: "Some of the poor fellows had been lying in the open for three or four days so were in a pretty bad way and altho I have handled hundreds of wounded men it dose not get any easier to see the poor fellows suffering and altho we do all we can to help them there is still a lot we cannot do in the advanced aid post."[78]

The allied offensive at the Somme petered out by early November, when relentless rain made the ground impassable. Troops now hunkered down for what would be the coldest winter of the war. Confronting the cold, the chronic ailments that afflicted all front-line soldiers in the winter, and the drear recognition that the Somme had not won the war, a collective funk – which French soldiers dubbed *cafard* – settled over the front lines. So many had sacrificed so much for so little that such thoughts were almost inevitable. Frank Maheux had certainly had his fill of war. Bone-tired, soaked to the skin, and profoundly homesick, he could scarcely stomach the prospect of another winter in the water-logged trenches of northern France: "It rains and rains water over your boots our closes all wet, no place for rest, it is hell of a place I am wet true ... when I think we will have to past another winter them countrys France and Belgium I wouldn give a cent for it." More than anything, however, he was haunted by the brutality of the Somme and his role in it. He confided to Angeline that he had "lots of Germans on [his] conscience." He recognized that they did "the same to us, so the stronger wins," but he found little comfort in that bitter truth. He also feared that

Canadian civilians far from the killing fields failed to understand what the war was really like: "You people, you know it is war but God if you really knew how it is you would be mad."[79] When Angeline expressed her dismay that her brother, who was struck by shrapnel in October, had been wounded, Frank could not bring himself to utter mere platitudes: "You say in your last letter that you hardly believe Sam is wounded poor wife if you see the way it is here they are not by hundreds but by thousands, some loose their legs or arms and to many their lives you people in Canada don't understand what it is war if you were here only one day you will see how it is going."[80] Through the litany of letters he dispatched in the last months of 1916, he tried his best to convey this harsh reality.

If Maheux feared that Angeline, through no fault of her own, underestimated the horror of the war, others believed that their wives overestimated the heroism of men in uniform. A stretcher-bearer from Ottawa (identified only as R.A.L. when his letters were published in 1918) confessed to his wife: "'Heroics' are dead here, a charge is not the wonderful, glorious thing we were told it was. I have even begun to wonder if it ever was, or if the poets and historians and 'Press agents' of those days have been just kidding us." Like front-line combatants of all nations who were repulsed by the jingoistic rhetoric of their national newspapers, he confessed: "To read of 'Our splendid Canadians' makes us ill. We are just fed up, longing for the end, but seldom mentioning it, and hoping – when we think of it – that when we do get it – it will be an easy one, or something final. Our main effort is to think and talk as little of the war as possible."[81] Even the men who had earned the accolades given to heroes resisted the label, preferring to acknowledge their weaknesses rather than crow about their accomplishments. When Laurie Rogers wrote home to explain the circumstances under which he had received the Military Medal – providing medical aid while under direct shellfire – he denied that he had done anything heroic: "Don't think I am terribly brave for I feel that I should not get this medal I can be just as much affraid as anyone else but you see it was my duty to stay and dress the wounded and also by my example to try and cheer the others up and I tried to do what my duty called for and altho not wishing for anything like it again if the same thing were put up to me I would try and carry on as a man should." At first reluctant to have his story recounted in the local newspaper, he ultimately relented. He was pleased to know that May and the children were proud of him, and he was human enough to enjoy showing up his mean-spirited neighbours who had often insinuated that he would never amount to much. Nonetheless, he implored May not to "make any Hero out of that Medal business for as I told you before I am far from feeling one and sometimes wonder if I can keep the yellow streak under cover. You know we all have a yellow streak only some have a big one and some a small one but it is there all the same but some can hide it while the other poor fellow is caught with the goods on him."[82]

By November 1916, when green envelopes were distributed once again, more recently enlisted married men who had still been in training camps when the First and Second Contingents had endured the horrors of Mount Sorrel and the hell of the Somme had their turn to experience the dangers of war first-hand. Men like George Timmins – who enlisted in Toronto in March 1916, completed basic training in England over the summer, and arrived in France in the final days of the Somme – judged himself a hardened soldier by late 1916, familiar with the close calls and persistent discomforts of front-line service. As he recounted to his May in a series of green-envelope letters mailed in November and December, even the mundane tasks of war were fraught with danger and discomfort. On one occasion while in reserve, he and two other men went "to get coal and were just coming back when a shell dropped just behind us." That persuaded them to "hasten [their] footsteps considerable." When they moved into the front lines, life became even more perilous. The enemy aimed "snipers, machine guns, trench mortars, big shells, etc." into their trenches and the weather was abysmal:

Its been wet this last week and the mud is over our knees, in fact up to our thighs in places. I used to think that the mud tales were exaggerated, but now I see its as true as the scripture. Us gang only go out nights to hold the advanced posts and believe me its some job getting there in the dark. It sounds impossible for men to travel with sticky mud to their thighs with rubber boots right to the top of their legs and strapped on, but we do it everytime we go out on duty.[83]

When Timmins returned to this theme in a subsequent letter, hoping to give May a sense of his tasks as a "bomber" assigned to lob hand grenades into enemy trenches, he asked her to "just imagine kiddo 6 hours laying down in mud and water about 35 yds from Fritz. You dare not move around to get warmed up as that would attract to much attention." The men in his squad were "armed to the teeth," each one carrying "6 or more bombs besides rifle and ammunition." Realizing that a housewife in Oshawa had little experience of bombing raids on the Western Front, he asked May to entertain a thought experiment: "Just try sitting on the arm chair with a paper and a bottle of beer and everything that spells comfort, try it for 6 hours, don't move only slowly so that the darkness will swallow each move and see how you like it. Then imagine doing the same in oozy mud with a nice steady, cold rain falling on you." He confessed that it was "hard to be optimistic in those circumstances, but as soon as its over & your through for probably 24 hours (if things are quiet) you are in the best of spirits especially if the rum's up." Rum did nothing, however, to dispel the gloom of a Christmas without mail from home and exposed to an enemy bombardment. As he contemplated the dawn of 1917, Timmins was in a blue funk. He apologized for "wasting" his green envelope letters with tales of artillery bombardments, rat- . infested trenches, and bombing raids, when he could have been speaking of love, but as he explained, it was "the only chance I shall ever get of sending news at all, as ordinary letters are more apt to be censored than one with a green envelope."[84]

The despondency and weariness that front-line troops experienced in late 1916 should not be mistaken for defeatism. Men like Laurie Rogers, who confessed that he was "not much stuck on being back at the front," continued to believe in the cause they were fighting for. In mid-December, when German politicians held out the prospect of a negotiated peace, Canadian troops would have none of it. George Ormsby, who was grievously wounded at the Somme and spent the rest of 1916 recuperating in England, expressed from his hospital bed on Christmas Eve the hope that he would not have to take any further part in the war. But he had no doubts about the justice of the cause for which he had almost died or the importance of unconditional victory. If need be, he wrote, it would be his "duty to [return to the front lines] if the cursed Huns persist in their terms. Complete defeat and submission to us is the only thing that will ever make me relinquish the fight."[85] Laurie Rogers thought the same way: "We are all hearty sick of the game but not so sick that we cannot sit up and give a little more medicine, in fact when it comes to a show down we are right there with bells on and a brick in each hand." A negotiated peace was to him not an option: "There is no chance of peace until Fritzie is licked and properly licked at that I don't think there is a man over here that dose not wish for peace but not until we have properly finished the job and that is not yet. But we intend to do it and make a very good job while we are at it."[86]

Resolute and stoic determination, rather than martial enthusiasm, thus ruled the day as Canadian troops awaited the end of winter and the onset of a new fighting season. Rumours of a major Canadian battle circulated for weeks before Vimy, although some soldiers made no mention of it at all. David McLean devoted the last weeks of his life to describing the weather (almost uniformly awful) and itemizing the food parcels he received from home (slow in arriving but greatly appreciated when they finally appeared). Others were more forthcoming. While still training in the south of England, Will Mayse told Betty at the end of February that he expected to be in France very soon, because "it looks as though the big drive is commencing."[87] A month later Laurie Rogers mentioned, almost in passing, that his application for a commission would go forward only after this "next scrap comes off."[88] Few, however, were as daringly detailed as R.A.L. in a series of letters in which he wrote openly of where the Canadians would attack – the Germans, he opined, would have their hands full holding the Arras-Cambrai-St Quentin line – and spoke of General Julian Byng's careful plans in advance of the much-anticipated battle.[89] Making use of a green envelope, he wrote in early March 1917 more than he probably should have:

> I saw something this morning most interesting; a large number of our boys going through an attack as nearly similar to what they will have to contend with as possible. They used flares and worked in conjunction with aeroplanes circling a few feet above. The planes signaled, 'Morse code,' I think, with motor horns. It was most realistic. Signalling the lifting of the barrage was rather amusing. Two men with white flags advanced ahead, and were supposed to represent it. Hardly looked the real thing. Any thought of a home manoeuvre or sham battle, though, must be quickly dispelled, when you remember that in a very short while it will be done again through a hell of real fire.[90]

Days before the battle began – in another green-envelope letter that would arrive several weeks after Canadian newspapers had vividly described the heroics of Vimy – there was no apparent reason for reticence. R.A.L. sought to reassure his wife that the pending battle would be "very, very different from the Somme in many ways." Meticulous planning could not ensure that every man would survive, but it would make victory more likely: "All the way back here, the ground is marked out with tapes and flags, arranged according to our pictures exactly as Fritz has his trenches in front of the particular battalion which will take that section. So, if the officers get killed, the men know just what to do." Moreover, "Fritz must know what's coming. As far as I can see, we don't give a damn whether he knows or not."[91] Maheux asked only that Angeline remember him in her prayers: "we are in face of death every minute now ... dear wife write a long letter you will hear about us soon."[92]

The men who participated in and survived the assault on Vimy Ridge took pride in the Canadian success. When reassuring May that he had "just come through the last big push," Laurie Rogers admitted that he "sure [was] glad" he was there: "it certainly was grand."[93] R.A.L., who had only recently transferred into a combat unit, confessed that as he awaited his baptism by fire he was "plumb scared to death." Nonetheless, 9 April 1917 was, he averred, "the biggest day of [his] life."[94] Agar Adamson, a lieutenant-colonel in the Princess Patricia's Canadian Light Infantry and a much more seasoned campaigner, reported to his wife, Mabel, on the second day of the battle, that his brigade had taken "all [their] objectives yesterday pushing off at 5:30 a.m. in a rain storm." They had, of course, suffered casualties, including three officers killed and three hundred men (a number he alluded to indirectly as "equal double Beverley Street number"). Even though the rain had quickly turned to snow, he judged his brigade's performance "splendid" and had confidence that they would be able to secure their gains.[95] Similarly, Laurie Rogers was in equal measure impressed by the success of the operation, awed by its intensity, and saddened by the loss of life so evident in the aftermath of battle. "Surely it was awful the ground shook like an Earth-Quake when our artillery opened up and it seemed impossible to believe that anybody at the other end could live through the rain of metal that went over." As he advanced across terrain his company had just conquered, he observed that "the ground was just blown into great big holes and craters and the mud was something fearful every step we were over our knees in it." To compound the misery, "Fritzie was comming back at us with his artillery it was anything but pleasant that trip into we did not know what."[96]

Those who survived the Battle of Vimy Ridge quickly came to realize that this victory, however noteworthy and hard-won, had not ended the war. Vimy was to have been the opening salvo in a massive inter-allied campaign targeting a long-held German salient in northwest France. But when the Germans retreated in March to what became known as the Hindenburg Line, this strategic manoeuvre reconfigured the front lines east of Vimy and forced the French Army to reorient its plan of attack. A week after the assault on Vimy, French infantry – as sure of the imminence of victory as their Canadian allies – were thus compelled to attack in foul weather over the almost impregnable uphill terrain of the Chemin des Dames. Failure quickly followed, and widespread mutiny in the French ranks ensued. Canadian soldiers did not know any of this (or, at least, did not write about it). Nor, indeed, did the German high command, which would surely have moved to take advantage of the demoralized French army. Instead, the Germans continued to batter the Canadian sector with heavy shellfire, poison gas, flame throwers, and tactical assaults. In May and June, when civilians in Canada were basking in the reflected glory of recent victory, their husbands and sons experienced little respite from enemy fire and no rest. A month after Vimy, R.A.L. noted: "The boys are not happy or jolly this trip out ... Today is the ninth, just a month since the advance; and we've hardly been out of the line at all. There's a limit, and I think we've reached it. Five million men they say we have. Well, where in hell are they? Is it up to Canada to win this bloody war?"[97] As Adamson noted, a month later, if the German Army was demoralized by their defeat at Vimy, they showed little sign of it.[98]

⁕

Long before their husbands were sent into the water-logged wasteland that was the Battle of Passchendaele – a battle that would transform numerous Canadian war wives into war widows – many women in Canada had an unsettling understanding of war on the Western Front. Maheux was surely correct when he observed that Angeline did not know what it was to look out over a battlefield strewn with body parts, but he, Rogers, and others did what they could to close the existential gap that separated soldiers from civilians. While hometown newspapers offered a somewhat schizophrenic assessment of the realities of war – applauding the heroics of Canada's men in uniform, ascribing butchery and barbarism exclusively to the enemy, but also publishing letters filled with stark, unsettling accounts of combat – front-line troops told their wives a more nuanced story that downplayed their heroism and admitted their very human frailties.[99]

To concentrate exclusively on what these men conveyed in their letters home about the horrors of the war, however, would be to misconstrue the multifaceted, essentially conversational character of wartime correspondence. Interspersed with their descriptions of hell on earth were inquiries about mundane matters: Were the children healthy? Was the potato crop going to be adequate? And what about the weather-stripping, and the coal supply for the winter? Married soldiers never fully relinquished their civilian identities as husbands and fathers. Whatever their military rank or civilian occupation, they wrote home to ask about their children's health, inquire into the family budget, express concern about a wife's well-being. Husbands engaged from afar in their wives' disputes with overbearing in-laws or irresponsible tenants. The distant home front was as important to the men in uniform as the front lines were to those anxiously awaiting their safe return.

PART TWO

Staying Home

3

Coping

The Great War brought financial uncertainty, emotional turmoil, and daily challenges for many Canadian war wives, but for none more than a young mother of four children whose husband, having been unemployed for five months, enlisted in Winnipeg in early 1915. The economic downturn that fell upon the Prairies at the start of the war had plunged her family into destitution, leaving them to confront unpaid bills and a landlord who had not received his rent for months. Only the intervention of the Manitoba Patriotic Fund, which provided support to the families of enlisted men and, during the winter of 1914–15, to the most destitute of the unemployed saved them from eviction, hunger, and medical catastrophe.[1] In such desperate times, military service seemed a solution to the family's economic woes. Enlistment did not, however, liberate this family from all hardship. Having recently recovered from a difficult pregnancy, the young wife was anything but strong. She certainly could not go out to work, leaving her children (including newborn twins) to fend for themselves, and so she continued to depend upon the Patriotic Fund for emergency supplemental funds. In February 1915, she received a "special allowance of $10.00," for which she expressed her sincere gratitude: "I want to thank you for your kindness to me. I am sorry I had to ask for it but as I could not see anything else to do. With it I am getting a pair of shoes for myself and paying a couple of small bills. Thanking you again for your kindness." Life continued to treat her ill, however. In May 1915, she had to turn to the Patriotic Fund once again: she had received a bill for $33.50. From a funeral home. One of her babies had died. Six months later, the prospect of another Winnipeg winter alone with her children and her grief, far from family who could console her or help care for her children, was almost too much to contemplate. She asked the Patriotic Fund to help fund her passage to England where, she was sure, her "husband's people [would] look after her." The Patriotic Fund agreed and in December 1915 she and her three children returned to the Old Country.[2]

This young woman's experience of the First World War was worse than most. But the tragic narrative of her life – scarred as it was by economic privation, infant mortality, and unbearable loneliness – etches in especially vivid strokes the challenges that many Canadian war wives faced during the Great War. Mothers of young children, who represented the vast majority of Canada's war wives, often struggled to pay their bills, especially if their Separation Allowance was delayed, their Assigned Pay inadequate, or their budgets burdened by unexpected expenses. Women who depended upon the Patriotic Fund to supplement their Separation Allowance and Assigned Pay found by 1917, when the cost of living soared, when the winter was exceptionally cold and coal uncommonly expensive, that their budgets were stretched to a breaking point. In Canada as in Europe, 1917 was a year of crisis for many reasons; bitter weather, the resumption of submarine warfare, labour discontent prompted by wartime inflation, and the emergence of political and social strife placed severe stresses on all combatant nations and raised unsettling questions about their capacity to persevere. Some nations – most notably, Russia – broke under the pressure; others – Germany, Austria-Hungary, and Italy – came close. Striking women workers took to the streets of France, and British civilians worried about the effects of submarine warfare on the nation's ability to secure the food supply. In Canada, this fracturing ran along ethnic lines and, as Brock Millman has argued, "British Canadians" resented in equal measure "New Canadians," who appeared to be benefiting from full employment and high wages, and French Canadians, who vociferously objected to the possible imposition of compulsory military service.[3]

Canadian war wives, many of whom were recent British immigrants, would no doubt have been aware of the bitter political debates that divided the nation in 1917. They likely resented the immigrant miners of western Canada, whose strikes for higher wages made coal an increasingly expensive – but ever more essential – commodity; and they would have had little sympathy for those who took to the streets to protest conscription while their own husbands were fighting and dying in the trenches. In the weeks leading up to the national election of 1917, which enfranchised war wives, mothers, and sisters, May Timmins lent her moral authority as a soldier's wife to a political rally in defence of Robert Borden's Union government and its determination to conscript young, unmarried men. George Timmins worried that she was mingling with "those d— society people" but believed that she deserved her prominent place on the platform of the rally: "Mr Borden never knew the honour

that was his, at having a dear little woman like yourself at his meeting."
His further reflections are illuminating; public activism was, he believed,
the domain of "ladies who had too many interests to ever be able to stay
at home."[4] Most war wives, including his own dear May, were ordinarily
too busy for such public distractions. They had to devote their time to
a raft of domestic responsibilities, many of which were exacerbated by
their husbands' absence; contend with the rising cost of living; and
live with the anxiety that parents of young children knew all too well.

For the most impoverished among them, rent alone was often
beyond reach, requiring them to move frequently in search of ever
cheaper accommodation. And when children fell ill, a war wife had to
decide whether to confide in her husband and thus add to his worries,
or keep her concerns to herself, hoping that by the time a letter reached
the Western Front, the crisis would have passed. What, after all, could
a man thousands of miles from home do when his child developed a
rash that might signal scarlet fever, a cough that sounded ominously
like whooping cough, or a fever that perhaps suggested diphtheria?
These were worries that war wives struggled with. When the chores and
challenges of wartime life became too overwhelming – or life alone in
a community far from family too depressing – wives often wondered
whether they would be better off moving in with parents or in-laws.
Should they travel fifty kilometres to live with a widowed mother – as
Angeline Maheux contemplated – or five hundred to take advantage
of the comforts of city life – as Maggie Ormsby considered? Or should
they, like our poor Winnipeg wife, undertake a more daunting move
and relocate to Britain for the duration of the war? How a wife answered
such questions and adapted to these challenges depended to a significant
degree on where she lived, whether her income was sufficient to cover
her ordinary and exceptional expenses, and whether she had access to a
network of family who could provide comfort, consolation, and some
relief from the material and emotional strains of wartime.

⁂

When a soldier left for war, his wife acquired an indeterminate and
unfamiliar status: she was neither fully dependent on her husband nor
completely independent. By law and social convention, her husband,
now many thousand miles from home, remained the designated head
of his household. And insofar as his wife's income derived, with few
exceptions, directly from the benefits accruing to his military service,
his status as the family breadwinner remained intact. The fact that
a substantial proportion of married servicemen assigned more than

the requisite fifteen dollars a month suggests that they continued to take seriously their responsibilities; guaranteeing that his family was adequately supported remained a sacred charge. But although a war wife was both legally and financially dependent upon her husband, the practical reality of her everyday life required that she practise an independence she might previously not have countenanced. She would have to take on domestic tasks that would in peacetime have been her husband's responsibility: laying up fuel for the winter, weatherproofing a house, paying the monthly bills, and (perhaps) running the family business. As wartime letters filled with precise descriptions about such practical matters attest, she would often consult with her husband; but many decisions had to be made alone, and the burden of those choices rested on a war wife's shoulders.

Whether they lived in the country or the city, war wives had to take on back-breaking tasks essential to the upkeep of the family home. Unlike the hardy women of Alberta who won the accolades of neighbours and their champion Nellie McClung, May Rogers in the Eastern Townships did not plough the fields or drive a mower on the small acreage she and Laurie had purchased. She did, however, manage the poultry, tend to a cow, and care for a horse. Within months of Laurie's departure, she was facing the challenges of life as a "single" woman in a small farming community: the hired hand was obstreperous, a neighbour refused to pay his debts, the hen killed the ducklings, and the cats ate the chickens. By August 1915, Laurie reminded her it was time to think about preparing for winter: "I would suggest that you get in some dry hard wood. Get in a few cords at a time and even if you cannot put it all under cover have it filled out outside then you will not have any trouble in the winter and I believe you could get it cheaper than later on." The barn also required attention: "I would get the manure spread this fall if there is a very big pile or at least have it piled away from the barn as it will be much easier to clean out the stable if it dose not get way up to the window and it is better for the barn and the manure will be better for being in a good pile as it does not leech out so much. I am awfully glad you had the barn roof fixed up as it was in rather bad shape."[5] Laurie hoped she could hire a young man from his regiment, returned from England as medically unfit, to help with the farm: "He has been farming around that part ... for some years and knows just what to do and is not affraid of work altho he is not very strong but would be able and willing to do what little is to be done for you. It would save your poor old back and shoulders." If May set up a cot in the room over the kitchen, the young man could stay on the farm and look after the house should she and the children move away for the winter. This was not to be. Gossipy neighbours made the prospect of a young man living in the house with an unchaperoned woman too scandalous to consider: "I don't suppose you could take Turget in with that bunch but he is only a boy and rather innocent."[6]

Frank Maheux had no interest in Angeline taking in a hired man but he did worry about how his family would cope in his absence. He had hoped that his enlistment would give Angeline and their five children a life without care or want. Reality proved otherwise. For as long as he was away, Angeline had to care for the children – giving them an hour of schooling a day when the local teacher could not make her way to Baskatong Bridge – in addition to tackling an endless list of chores. As early as June 1915, Frank was offering advice on how to weatherproof their modest home: "Now don't forget to get the little chanty to take off the moss, and put lime even if you have to get boards for the roof, I want to see you well … I don't want you to get no hardship when I'll be away."[7] Sound advice, to be sure, but for as long as the weather held, Angeline had other tasks to occupy her days. She kept a vegetable garden where she grew radishes and onions; she tended the potato crop that she hoped would see her family through the winter; and she had to lay in a plentiful supply of wood. In 1915 she was able to hire a local man to help with the wood, setting Frank's mind at rest: "Poor Sam I am glad that he help you if he cuts your wood pay him well I am glad now so I wont be uneasy about it and the little chanty get it fixed well so you be able to pass a good winter, because my poor wife it is only the poor pleasure you have to be nice and warm."[8] The vegetables froze in the ground, however, and by September Angeline was looking to buy potatoes to supplement her crop, enough to last through the spring. She often sought Frank's advice: whether to relocate the family for the winter to be closer to her mother; whether to agree to a lease on a house when the landlord was asking $40 a month; and whether to buy a cow. Frank trusted her judgment – "do for the best" was his repeated mantra – even though he worried that the landlord was taking advantage of her situation. He agreed that buying a cow was a wise move: "for Salerre cow, do what you like I think it will be a good thing so you will have milk and cream this summer … if you get the cow, give him so much now and then the rest when he give you the cow in the spring, so you will be sure that he'll kept the cow in good order."[9]

Angeline proved more than worthy of Frank's confidence. By 1917 she had added pigs to her farm, the cow had a calf, her chickens were laying, and, at the end of the year, she signed a crop-sharing contract that gave her half the potatoes she grew on her landlord's farm.[10] As Frank observed with obvious admiration, she had become a "real farmer."[11] All this hard work came at a cost. Although only in her mid-thirties she was already suffering from rheumatism, which Frank found more than upsetting: "I am glad to see that you are all well only it is to bad for your Rhumatism you work to hard, that the reason I don't want you to work so hard as that."[12] As the winter of 1917–18 approached, the task of securing the season's wood supply returned. Angry that Angeline had had to chop her own wood in the spring of 1917, Frank suggested that she arrange a wood-chopping "bee": "Why don't you make a bee for your wood eaven if you pay them each, Dave should be able to get one for you, it is ashamed for men to leave a women alone cutting your wood, in a day they will cut enough for one stove for all winter, it is impossible for a women to cut wood ... I don't want you to cut it this fall."[13]

City life was less arduous – no cows to milk, pigs to slaughter, pota-toes to harvest, or fields to plough. But the maintenance of a house (and the almost universal tending of a vegetable plot) presented war wives with chores enough, as Jennie Hillyer discovered to her ongoing dismay. When she and Harry married in 1913, they bought a duplex in the Ville Emard neighbourhood of Montreal, hoping the rental income would help pay the mortgage. The plan was complicated, however, when Harry left for war, leaving Jennie to care for their infant son, deal with a tenant with an unseemly fondness for drink, and maintain the house. Like Laurie Rogers and Frank Maheux, Harry gave Jennie a detailed list of maintenance tasks, accompanied by sketched illustrations. In June 1916, long before winter set in, he reminded her: "Don't forget to paste the windows and doors upstairs before winter starts and put more ashes round the front side of the concrete step that leads upstairs and that will protect the step and the water pipes from frost; in fact you can build the ashes level to the top of the step if you have any spare."[14] He returned to this theme in subsequent letters, outlining how to fix the storm doors, protect the water pipes, and guard against drafts:

I think you can fix that with strips of carpet 3 or 4 inches wide. Tack the carpet all round the door the side where the hinges are you can tack out the frame as well. The sketch below will show you what I mean. Tack the carpet on the outside of the door and allow about 3 inches to overlap. The dotted lines represent the carpet, the side where the hinges are can be tacked on the frame work as well and don't forget to paste the windows upstairs before the winter starts and get the water turned off. If you have any money why not get in 3 tons of coal this summer while it is cheaper.[15]

He suspected that he was nagging and hoped that she would not "be offended" that he kept returning to these mundane topics, but he feared the consequences of neglect: "If you observe them and act upon them they will save you a lot of trouble and expense and perhaps next winter I shall be home myself and take all that responsibility off your hands."[16] When caterpillars ruined Jennie's vegetable garden, the drunken tenant proved a constant annoyance, and the prospect of frozen pipes and drafty windows made home ownership one burden too many, Harry and Jennie contemplated selling the house and having Jennie and the baby move in with her sisters.

Home maintenance also kept Betty Mayse fully occupied when she and her two children moved to Winnipeg from Pembina, Manitoba (where her husband, Will, had been the Baptist minister). She had no difficult tenants to worry about, but the neighbours were intermittently spiteful, the children susceptible to illness, and the house a constant work in progress. Like Angeline Maheux she wondered in the spring of 1917 how she was going to secure her wood supply for the following winter. Unlike Angeline, she had no interest in doing the job herself. She reported to Will that she was "delaying getting wood, till [she] got track of a 'splitter' – & also for another cheque to come." Fortunately, a kindly-disposed neighbour offered his help. One evening in late March, while she was busy "fixing the spout in case of rain ... Burchill came down the alley. He remarked that my supply of wood was getting low, & I said 'yes' that I was going to get some Tamarac one of these days – & he said: 'Well. I'll split it for you.' I said I'd be very glad to get it done if he'd let me pay him, & he said. 'Well, if you pay me I won't do it.' So that was very good of him."[17]

While Will was away, she also had to remove and store the storm windows and doors, a chore that taxed her strength and prompted her procrastination: "I have not the storm windows or doors off – only I took off the front bedroom one myself ... I'll get Mr. Burchill to take them off when he comes to do the wood. You-know-some folk that offer help make one tired – the man next door – Faulkner – always offering to do anything – but never doing a thing. Am sure he knows the windows are to come off – when he took his own off – but never asked if he could."[18] While waiting for help with the storm windows, she busied herself with a manic spree of spring cleaning: she repainted the kitchen, "gave all the wood work one coat put white oilcloth behind the sink & grouted the sink white – white oilcloth on the table & trunk, painted the 'little green' chair gray like the walls – & gave the woodbox a coat of that for the verandah floor." By the time she had given the trunk and pipes a coat of aluminum, everything looked "pretty fair now – clean anyway." And once she had attended to the curtains in the parlour and dining room, the "cleaning [would] be about done."[19]

These women had adequate, but by no means extravagant, sources of income. Angeline Maheux proved such an astute manager of the family budget that she was able to purchase a cow and a litter of piglets, thereby improving her children's diet. May Rogers was, by comparison, positively affluent: a well-invested stock portfolio produced an unexpected dividend of more than four hundred dollars, and Laurie suggested that if her total bank balance exceeded a thousand dollars, she should consult her father, a man of recognized business acumen, as to how to invest it: "There is no use letting too much accumulate [in the bank] and then it is only drawing 3 per cent ... while he can get you at least 6 per cent. He would not put it in anything he did not think sound and then he is in touch with the market. In any case it would not hurt to ask him about it."[20]

Even women of lesser means were reasonably well situated if they owned their family home. Provincial moratoria on mortgage payments that were offered early in the war to men in uniform eased their families' immediate financial obligations, as Harry Hillyer and Will Mayse were quick to remind their wives. Jennie Hillyer was not to worry if she could not "meet the payments on the house because they [could] not foreclose on the mortgage" while Harry was overseas.[21] If paying the mortgage proved no financial hardship, Betty Mayse, whose monthly income was eighty dollars, should continue payments, even though – as Will stressed more than once – they were "not bound to pay any of principle on mortgage ... they cannot even collect the interest on mortgage, as long as I am on service." In Will's judgment, there were advantages to paying down the principal – "we might as well invest our cash that way & make it earn 8%" – but in the final analysis it made more sense for Betty to skip some scheduled mortgage payments, put the money in the bank, and accumulate a small nest egg for emergencies.[22]

Many war wives, especially those who rented rather than owned their homes, would have thought themselves rich beyond measure if they had a thousand dollars in a bank account or an income of eighty dollars a month. Their ability to make ends meet eroded as the war progressed and the cost of living – especially high in the western provinces – ate into their modest incomes. Newspaper editors at the time often emphasized the inadequacy of war wives' (and widows') incomes, bringing to their readers' attention such instances of abject poverty as the soldier's wife with three children who in 1916 had to get by on less than forty dollars a month.[23] Such cases clearly did exist. Widows awaiting the approval of their pensions were, like Ellen Howe whose husband's death at Ypres in April 1915 remained unconfirmed for many months, stranded in the economic No Man's Land that separated a war wife from a war widow. The wives of men who enlisted in the British Army rather than the Canadian Expeditionary Force discovered to their chagrin that their husbands were not eligible for the Canadian-funded Separation Allowance; those whose husbands did not serve overseas were also forced to live on a more constrained budget.

These were the exceptions, however. Even though Patriotic Fund allowances varied from province to province, and from rural municipalities to large cities, allowances rarely fell below $15 a month (except for women with no children to support) and usually did not exceed $20.00. This meant that a war wife with children at home could ordinarily expect to receive a combined monthly income of between fifty and sixty dollars: $20 in Separation Allowance, $15 (or often $20) in Assigned Pay; and at least $15 from the Patriotic Fund. By no means an extravagant sum, but often equal to – and sometimes greater than – her household income on the eve of war. As Frank Maheux reminded Angeline, when justifying his decision to enlist, her monthly income of $60 – $20 in Separation Allowance, $15 in Assigned Pay, and $25 from the Patriotic Fund – far exceeded anything he had ever earned as a bushman. Surviving records from the Manitoba Patriotic Fund show that city wives in receipt of a similar income would also have been modestly well placed, at least at first. Many husbands, even among the ranks of the employed, had earned no more than $60 a month prior to their enlistment. One couple with a fourteen-month-old child had made do on the husband's income of $672 (or $56 per month); a father of seven children under the age of thirteen had worked for the railways before he enlisted in 1917, earning a paltry $50 a month. A woman whose husband had been a pastry chef before joining up – bringing home $60 a month – emphasized that he had "given up a good Position to enlist."[24]

By 1917, however, it became a challenge to live on a budget of $60 a month. By the end of 1916, as documented by the *Labour Gazette*, the cost of living had risen appreciably, as it would continue to do through the end of the war. The average cost of rent, food, fuel, and utilities for a family of five (including an adult man) in December 1914 had been $14.25 a week; two years later, it was $16.33; and by December 1917 was just shy of $20.00 a week.[25] Although rents had been manageable in the first year of the war – and, in fact, dropped significantly, at least in Toronto, at the beginning of the war[26] – affordable apartments soon became increasingly difficult to find, as one Hamilton woman (and her outraged husband), among others, discovered. From his artillery battery in northern France, Private Gordon Ross wrote directly to the Ministry of Justice in Ottawa: "My wife has been notified to vacate her residence by October 7 or the rent would be raised from $12.00 per month to $25.00." Although he did receive a reply, Ottawa could give him no satisfaction: "The Minister has no authority to control the landlord, and I can only suggest that your wife should endeavour, if the landlord will not be more reasonable, to find another house which can be had at a satisfactory rent."[27] Winnipeg women encountered similar difficulties and, like Katie Ross, had no choice but to seek out less expensive accommodations. In March 1916, at the height of the enlistment boom, a three-room "bachelor suite and bath" in the centre of Winnipeg rented for $30 a month, and even apartments near the railway yards – not the city's most elegant address – demanded as much.[28] Because Winnipeg experienced a surge in population between 1916 and 1917, when eight thousand new residents moved to the city, the demand for housing outpaced the supply and rents continued to rise. Some women defaulted on their rent: one woman who sought help from the Manitoba Patriotic Fund appears to have managed through the first year or more of her husband's mobilization but found herself in economic difficulty in January 1917 when she received a notice "for collection of rents from the premises you occupy." Her circumstances did not improve and by May 1917 she had to watch helplessly as the bailiff seized her property "to satisfy a claim of $30 and costs being rent now past due."[29] Other women simply moved from apartment to apartment in a relentless search for affordable rent. When Violet Cooper's husband, Ezra, enlisted in January 1916 and before he embarked for Europe in November 1916, he arranged for her and their two children to relocate from their rented home in the rural community of Boissevain to Winnipeg. Over the next thirteen months, she moved four times: in December 1916, March 1917, June 1917, and November 1917.[30]

The winter of 1916–17 proved especially punishing. The bitter cold that made life a misery for men in the trenches of northern France also afflicted North America, causing even the most hardened Canadians to remark on it. As Ruth Antliff in Montreal noted in a letter to her son, "we are having the coldest winter for years, and more snow has fallen than for 43 years."[31] Winnipeg fared no better; in mid-February the city suffered the "worst blizzard of the year," and forty-mile-an-hour winds and blowing snow idled the city's streetcars and stranded workers downtown.[32] For women on a constrained budget, soaring coal prices made the hardship even worse. In May 1915, when savvy customers were wise to buy their next winter's coal supply, it was possible to purchase coal for between $5.75 and $6.75 a ton; a year later the asking price was $7.50 a ton.[33] And then in the winter of 1916–17 a combination of forces pushed the price of coal up even further. Miners in western Canada went on strike, protesting inadequate wages; the anticipated entry of the United States into the war made heavier demands on American coal production; and – in the opinion of some at least – coal distributors were creating illegal combines to maintain inflationary prices.[34] By February 1917, coal was selling for $10 or more a ton and concerned citizens were convinced that Canada was facing a coal famine.[35]

Fear of a coal famine in Canada angered some soldiers and made others anxious. In southern Ontario, which depended upon coal imported from the United States, American shortages drastically reduced shipments of coal across the border.[36] As prices increased, families suffered the consequences. George Timmins was convinced that the local coal merchant in Oshawa was guilty of price-gouging: "Pretty rotten deal you are getting from the coal men eh? They should be shot as it surely isn't necessary to pile on the price like that. Just taking advantage of the times I guess."[37] Six months later, George Davidson, fearing that coal would be as scarce in the winter of 1917–18 as it had been expensive in 1916–17, wrote to his wife, Jeanie, in Macleod, Alberta: "I want you to make yourself as comfortable and cosy as you possibly can. Don't grudge a few dollars where warm clothing or fuel will help you to be more comfy … I hope you get in enough coal to put you through the winter alright. I dread looking forward to the coming winter it means such hardships for everyone."[38] For women like Ruth Antliff who had both the means and the foresight to do so, stockpiling coal in the spring of 1917 – a practice she would denounce a year later as hoarding – offered some protection against a second winter of coal shortages. From the relative comfort of her home in Montreal West, she purchased her entire winter supply in June 1917, believing that "next winter there will be a shortage and prices will probably go to $25.00 a ton … We got in our usual amount in May at $9.75, but Gr[andpa] thought we had better get the balance before we went away so got 4 tons more but had to pay $11.00 for it, and it is only sold for cash down, prices are going up every day."[39] Other women, less fortunate, had to resort to the generosity of the Patriotic Fund to keep them in wood and coal. By the end of the war, women who could not afford to buy their coal months in advance, and thus take advantage of lower prices, entered into contracts with the Patriotic Fund to pay for their coal and wood in monthly installments. A young Winnipeg mother who had paid $5 a month for rent when she arrived in the city in 1916 faced a fuel bill in 1918 of $86.40, for the purchase of "3 tons of

hard coal, 2 tons of soft coal and 1½ cords of wood." She agreed to have
the Patriotic Fund deduct $15 a month from her allowance until the bill
was settled in full.[40]

⟨꠸⟩

Cold homes, inadequate coal supplies, and the early onset of yet another
punishing winter contributed to what contemporary observers described
as the greatest public health crisis of the war years: the "Spanish flu"
pandemic, which proved especially lethal in the fall of 1918 and the
first months of 1919. Worldwide, as many as fifty million died; Canada
suffered 55,000 deaths, and families across the nation looked on in
dread as schools, churches, and movie theatres closed, hospitals were
overwhelmed with cases for which they had no known remedy, and
funerals became a daily ritual.[41] October was the cruellest month: in
Toronto as many as fifty flu victims died each day, thirteen hundred
during what was the worst month of the epidemic.[42] Montreal fared no
better. As Ruth Antliff, a particularly careful observer of everyday life in
her city, noted in mid-October:

> The streets have so many funeral processions all day long … All
> the schools are closed, all churches, movies, theaters, and every
> kind of meeting, even at funerals it is against the law to have more
> than 25 persons present. The shops all must close at 4 o'clock and
> do not open until 9 a.m. besides this they are nearly all disinfected
> every day, also every street car. The city seems stunned and one
> really can go nowhere because no one wants callers or visitors.[43]

If she had any inkling that the disease spread with marked speed in
Montreal because of military efforts to round up and then force into
close quarters conscripts who had refused to obey their call-up orders,
she did not say so.[44] She preferred to believe that "all the sickness and
Spanish flu we have with us is due to the fact that the houses are so
cold and damp with no fires and such terrible cold wet weather all
through Sept[ember]."[45] Whether the cold weather was really to blame
is debatable – the pandemic killed millions in India and equatorial
Africa, too – but the perception mattered. When the epidemic first
arrived in Winnipeg, some citizens blamed landlords who failed to heat
their apartments adequately: when "apartment dwellers were forced to
sit in confined quarters in the kitchen to stay warm [they] were at risk
of getting chilled."[46]

The Spanish flu was especially dangerous to young adults. Ruth Antliff believed, correctly, that "the worst cases are from 15 to 35" and, incorrectly, that "old people and children escape."[47] Although children were less susceptible than their elders, they suffered the flu's effects nonetheless. While some fell ill, others watched helplessly as their mothers became victims of the pandemic. One client of the Manitoba Patriotic Fund requested an advance of $5 on her monthly allowance in January 1919 because her "boy come home on Monday from King George Hospital had the flu and now I need to get him boots to start back school I did not expect him home so soon so I did not have boots ready for him."[48] This war wife, hard-pressed though she surely was, fared better than those whose children died during the worst months of the crisis. In Winnipeg alone "there were 225 reported deaths of children under age ten, nearly three-quarters of whom were under the age of three."[49] It is very probable that at least some of these were soldiers' children. Lilian Margaret Eardley, one of seven children born to Esther and Albert Eardley of Russell, Manitoba, died in Brandon in January 1919; Harold Harris, aged eight, in Winnipeg a month later. Without access to their death certificates it is impossible to know definitively that they succumbed to the flu. But their fathers' military service records indicate that in both cases their mothers were, by 1919, twice bereaved: Albert Eardley had enlisted in August 1915 and was killed at the Somme in October 1916; Abraham Harris had died of wounds in May 1917.[50] For these war wives – now widows – when sorrows came they came, in Shakespeare's words, "not single spies, but in battalions."

Long before the influenza epidemic cut its lethal swath across Canada, recurrent outbreaks of childhood diseases were a source of understandable frustration (and anxiety) to fathers too far from home to be able to offer care or consolation, and frequent concern to the mothers who were manning the home front. For married men who had enlisted because they hoped to keep their families safe from the depredations of war, their war experiences and their contact with the bedraggled civilian refugees of northern France reinforced their belief that their own sacrifices would be vindicated if women and children in Canada could be protected. Soon after George Ormsby arrived in France, he encountered a group of refugees whose village had been destroyed: "One particular group caught [my] eye – a man pushing a perambulator in which were two babies squalling and the mother walking alongside with two other children ... Well goodbye Sweetheart and God bless you and the children. Be of good cheer and thank God that your husband is fighting for the fatherless and the oppressed – everytime I think of that

poor refugee family it nerves my heart for the fight that is ahead."[51] Three
years later, in the spring of 1918, when the German Army had once again
advanced deep into northern France, George Timmins's awareness of
civilian suffering strengthened his much-battered morale: "I think we are
very lucky that the war is being fought in Europe on that account that
our babies can play around and grow fat without getting mixed up with
shells and things." He had watched as a group of children – including
a "poor little one that I had picked out for my especial notice, looking
as she did so much like my little girl did when I left home" – sought
refuge from incoming shells. When the danger had passed, the children
resumed their play "almost as happily as ever. I say almost, because the
look of trouble was still in that poor little ones eyes. God grant that
none of mine ever hear a shell coming. War's Hell all right."[52]

Any indication that families far from the fighting lines were in
danger would have disrupted soldiers' consoling conviction that they
were fighting to keep them safe from harm. Yet the greatest danger
confronting young children – and unsettling their parents – came
from a host of contagious diseases that had not yet been prevented by
vaccination or conquered by antibiotics: diphtheria, whooping cough,
polio, scarlet fever, and measles. Outbreaks of these diseases recurred
throughout the war years (as they had in the pre-war era, too), putting
children of all social classes, but especially the poor, at risk. If a child
fell ill and needed a doctor's attention, all parents would suffer anxiety
and apprehension; if a child died, the parents would grieve. But mothers
whose budgets could accommodate medical bills were better able to
withstand these threats than those who could not; and mothers who
could keep their household quarantined without compromising their
budgets were better placed than those who would have had to sacrifice
a teenager's income or a tenant's rent for as long as a quarantine was
in effect. Affluence and the access it provided to medical care made a
difference to war wives' ability to cope.

Even the children of well-to-do parents could not be fully protected
from the diseases of childhood, as May Rogers and Agnes Archibald could
certainly attest. But when their children fell ill or needed specialized
medical attention, both women were able to draw upon the informed
advice of friends and the professional attention of clinical experts. Shortly
after her husband left Montreal for overseas service, for instance, Agnes
Archibald faced two medical emergencies: one daughter, Joan, had to
have her adenoids removed (with the prospect of a further operation
to remove her tonsils); and a second daughter, Peggy, contracted scarlet
fever while the family was holidaying on the St Lawrence. Agnes was
understandably anxious about Joan's operation and waited until she

heard from her husband before proceeding. His opinion – contained in a letter from England in June 1915 – carried great weight in her mind: "I have no fear of the adenoid operation, and if Gordon advises it, as you say he does, you might as well go ahead. There's no dreadful hurry about it – I don't believe that, if she breathes quietly and easily thro' her nose when asleep, she is taking any harm from it … I should think it would be all right to have it done in September."[53] When Peggy fell ill with scarlet fever, an especially ominous and sometimes fatal childhood disease, Agnes once again sought her husband's considered judgment. He shared her apprehension: "Like you, I'm always afraid of scarlet. Make Gordon C. go over her carefully as soon as you get home, particularly her urine. I had quite got over my fear of her catching it from the Evans lot, as time passed. No doubt it came from them. Well, we have to be anxious about the kiddies now … Too bad, dear girl, that you should have such trouble always when I am away."[54]

A month later, Edward was relieved to learn that Peggy had fully recovered: "Your particular mention of the kidneys being all right was welcome … I had been worrying about the question of the kidneys, thinking that in the absence of a doctor they'd be more thought of; and that point is very important. I almost sent you a cable about it, but Jack advised against it, saying it was rarely serious in children."[55] As this and his previous letter suggest, Edward Archibald was more than a worried father. He was, in fact, a distinguished surgeon, a member of the McGill medical school faculty, and an emerging eminence in the Canadian Army Medical Corps. He and Agnes could draw upon the expertise of friends, the medical judgment of Canada's most prominent physicians – "Jack" was none other than John McCrae – and, just as important, a decent bank account. Assuring Agnes that she had done the right thing by hiring a private nurse to care for Peggy, he stressed: "Don't hesitate a moment about expenses. Get a doctor … if necessary; or anything. Expense doesn't cut the least bit of ice."[56]

Although May Rogers did not have immediate access to the expertise of the McGill medical faculty, she too had the means to consult specialists when her children's health required it. As was true of the Archibald children, Aileen and Howard Rogers both had health scares in the summer of 1915. Aileen had contracted polio before the war and her legs continued to give her difficulty; Howard developed problems – either with his tonsils or his adenoids – which would probably require surgery. From Laurie's vantage point at Shorncliffe Army Camp (where, had he known it, he could have consulted Edward Archibald), he could do little but offer May consolation: "[I am] awfully glad to hear that Aileen's leg is not so bad as I thought and hope Harvey will be able to get it into shape all right, was also glad Howard could wait as I did not like the idea of his having an operation during the hot weather wish I could be with him."[57] By the end of the year, however, it was evident that both children needed medical attention. Hopeful that surgery might improve Aileen's mobility, May arranged in November 1915 to take her to New York to consult a surgeon. Laurie followed their venture from afar, happy to hear that they had had a chance to visit the zoo, the shops, and the aquarium, and even happier to learn that "Charly decided not to operate as I don't like that kind of thing very much." Instead, Aileen was to wear a leg brace, a prescription she did not relish. Laurie could commiserate: "[I hope] it will console her a little if she knows that I wore one on each leg for some years when I was a little fellow but tell her not to do as I did and fall and break her arm."[58] Almost as soon as they returned home, May had to arrange surgery for Howard. Once again, Laurie was anxious for updates and unhappy not to be at home to provide moral support: "I was glad to hear that Howard had had that operation on his throat and I suppose by this time he has quite recovered. I wish I had been there as it would not have been so hard for the boy as I would have gone with him until he went to sleep. It must have been an anxious time for you and it was awfully good of Jean to go with you."[59]

More anxious times awaited May Rogers and other war wives, for there was scarcely a season when children, and infants most of all, were fully safe from diphtheria or whooping cough, polio, scarlet fever, or measles. The most lethal of all was diphtheria, which struck with cruel regularity: Ontario health records reveal its deadly grip during the winter of 1914–15, when 29 children died in December 1914 alone, throughout much of 1917 (a year in which 223 children lost their lives to the disease), and then again in March 1918 (when there were 347 cases and 23 deaths). So severe was the threat that the province spent in excess of two thousand dollars to purchase and distribute free of charge more than fourteen thousand units of anti-diphtheria toxin.[60] Although infants were most especially vulnerable to diphtheria, older children were by no means immune. When Daniel MacMillan, a farmer in New Brunswick, mentioned the diphtheria epidemic that ravaged the province in the fall of 1915 and closed schools in Fredericton and St Mary's, he noted the death of a local girl, fifteen years old.[61] Parents also had to contend with measles epidemics: the one that devastated Ontario from March through June 1916 tallied more than ten thousand cases and almost eighty deaths; a second epidemic, in early 1917, spread eastward from the Prairies to Ontario and Quebec, and then across the Atlantic to soldiers' encampments in the south of England.[62] In the wretched winter of 1916–17 – when war wives were adjusting to their husbands' departure, reading headlines about heavy casualties in northern France, and fretting about the much-anticipated Vimy campaign – polio, whooping cough, scarlet fever, measles, and diphtheria converged in a veritable concatenation of contagion.[63] For mothers beside themselves with worry, there was one source of consolation: the outbreak of smallpox, which had been so ominous in the summer of 1916, had been temporarily contained to Kent County, Ontario.[64] This most dreaded and disfiguring disease would reappear, however, in the last six months of 1917.[65]

Illness affected households differently, according to a family's means. When Toronto's William Coleman learned in October 1916 that his children had contracted whooping cough he was, understandably enough, "sorry to learn that [they] had been sick." He recognized how trying this must have been for his wife: "I can realize what a time you must have had with them at nights, and you all alone with no one so you could get a rest up in the day time."[66] At the very same time, polio was terrifying parents in Quebec and Ontario. Ruth Antliff noted that by mid-November 1916 "the infantile paralysis epidemic is supposed to be over and all the schools which have been closed open tomorrow ... but just the same there is a good deal of the disease in the city yet. There has been a law passed that no children under 16 are allowed to enter Ontario province from any place."[67] Because Aileen Rogers had already suffered its effects, Laurie and May knew full well how dangerous – or, at the very least, disabling – polio could be. Laurie tried not to be overly alarmist, however: "I am sorry to hear that there is so much Infant Paralysis about but I would not begin to worry too much, but I would go to Dr. Patrick and ask him if there is anything you can do for the kiddies as a kind of preventative as it is just as well not to leave anything to chance and if anything can be done he will do it for us."[68]

Della Coleman and May Rogers would have suffered the anxiety and uncertainty that parents everywhere experience when their children fall ill or are threatened by contagious disease. They would not, however, have had to worry unduly about paying for the medical care their children might then have required. As the wife of a captain, Della Coleman received a Separation Allowance of $40 a month (increased to $45 upon her husband's promotion to Major in December 1916), and $50 a month in Assigned Pay. And, as he reassured her, if she needed a little extra, he "still [had] a little money in the bank" in London.[69] Laurie Rogers, as we have seen, did not hesitate to suggest that May consult the family physician. Betty Mayse was perhaps more cautious. Her budget of approximately $80 a month was by no means miserly, but in her mind it allowed no margin for error or extravagance. She was, by her own admission, "always nervous when the cash [was] low for fear of sickness or anything." When Shirley Mayse contracted measles in the spring of 1917, she had such a mild case that Betty neither called a doctor nor kept her home from school. "Shirley got over her measles easily … We did not tell any one. She was outside all the time. They don't keep them in, only you are supposed to keep them home from school 8 days. It was just like prickly heat."[70] No doubt, if Shirley had been seriously ill, Betty would have called a doctor, but money was tight, Shirley was not so obviously sick as to be kept home from school, and Betty saw no need to seek professional help. Jennie Hillyer had a more difficult time when her baby fell ill with measles in the winter of 1916–17. She had to have both her duplex, now sublet, and her apartment fumigated, to reduce the danger of ongoing contagion; and she had to live with the worry of a sick baby and a husband in harm's way. Fortunately, the baby recovered quickly, easing Jennie's anxiety somewhat: "It worries me so when he's ill, knowing that you are in daily, hourly danger is enough without having him sick also. Still, now he is over them alright. I need not worry over measles."[71]

Betty Mayse was a meticulous manager of the family purse, always careful to put aside small sums to cover future expenses. When she learned in June 1917 that her Patriotic Fund allowance was soon to increase, the extra two dollars a month was welcome, for she complained: "[I don't] ever seem to get enough ahead to 'bury me.'"[72] The long-standing fear of the working classes – that they would die a pauper's death, without enough to pay for a respectable funeral – was probably just a figure of speech for the Mayse family. In other households of exceptionally modest means, it was an ever-present threat. Among the most impoverished beneficiaries of the Manitoba Patriotic Fund were women who faced repeated hardship when their children fell ill. In one instance, a mother of an infant born in the summer of 1914 was hounded by doctors' bills and dunning notices. Her son, not yet two, suffered recurrent illnesses in 1916: diphtheria in the spring and hospitalization six months later. When she sought the assistance of the Patriotic Fund to pay the hospital bill, she was firmly rebuffed: "the Directors of the Manitoba Patriotic Fund will not be responsible for these expenses." Nor would they help with the doctor's bill, which remained unpaid in the spring of 1917. She owed four dollars and the doctor was losing patience: "I think you are unreasonable," he wrote on the second notice, "in expecting me to allow this account to remain unpaid indefinitely. Would like to hear from you regarding same before April 30."[73]

It is not clear why in this very sorry case, the Patriotic Fund was so obdurate. Ordinarily, it did what it could to help women in comparable circumstances. Fund managers frequently authorized an advance on the next month's allowance, a stopgap solution to be sure, but at least a temporary fix. One woman – the mother of seven – relied so regularly on such advances that it is hard to know how the accountants kept track of what she had received and what she was still owed. Her needs, however, were indisputable. Shortly after her husband enlisted in February 1917, she registered with the Patriotic Fund and identified her ordinary expenses. She paid a mere $8 a month in rent, for a house so far from the centre of Winnipeg that it was not yet served by the streetcar lines; an additional $8 for heat and light; and $50 a month for food and incidental expenses. Her anticipated monthly income of $70 – $20 in Separation Allowance, $20 in Assigned Pay, and $30 from the Patriotic Fund – would cover her regular expenses, but left nothing to spare. When her youngest child contracted pneumonia in May 1917, she was desperately short of funds: her Separation Allowance and Assigned Pay had not yet arrived and she had a doctor's bill to pay. Her only recourse was to request an advance of "10 dollars and that will make half of my money I have the baby very ill with pneumonia Dr. [W.] of Transcona is attending at her and there is a lot little things to get extra for her and medicine to get as well." A year later, another child was hospitalized for two days, generating a bill for $3.50.[74]

When illness struck, even the most ordinary tasks became complicated and the most urgent needs went unmet. In September 1917, a Winnipeg woman who earlier in the war had had her furniture repossessed, found herself once again immersed in misery: her husband's Assigned Pay had not been forwarded from Ottawa, her grocery bill was in arrears, and she desperately needed an advance on her Patriotic Fund allowance. She would "have come down [to the Patriotic Fund offices] and explained things more clearer," she wrote, "but my children have both got whooping cough and I have no one to leave them in the care off."[75] These difficulties, real though they were, seemed almost trivial compared to the plight of a woman from rural Manitoba who was beset by debts, ill health, and her child's desperate need for medical attention. Because her husband had enlisted in the British Army, rather than the CEF, she was not initially eligible for either the Separation Allowance or the Assigned Pay given to the dependents of Canadian troops. For much of 1915, she had to support herself and her three children on the $25 a month she received from the Patriotic Fund. When the fund received confirmation that as of November 1915 she would receive both the Separation Allowance and Assigned Pay, her monthly stipend was reduced to $15. By the spring of 1916, she was barely getting by and begged the Patriotic Fund for an adjustment to her allowance: "I had a big bill to pay this winter for sickness and here I am with only one grinder in my mouth this was the months I was supposed to get my false teeth, but cannot for want of money to do it with … I am back in my monthly payment on the house when you half to pay for health it does not leave me very much to live and cloth was hopeing you will do something for me." And then, in July 1916, her life got even worse: "[My] little boy was run over by a wagon, which had 48 bushels of wheat on. The little fellow has never been right since. He does not walk right yet. The doctor advises me to take him to hospital in Winnipeg and have the Ex-Raye put on him. Now I cannot see my way clear to do this. Can you tell me if they will do this free of charge as I am a soldier's wife." In this instance at least, assistance was at hand. As the Patriotic Fund caseworker explained, "the medical profession in this city are giving their services gratis to soldiers dependents."[76]

Accidents and childhood illnesses were not, of course, unique to the war years. Nor, regrettably, was childhood mortality. As Cynthia Comacchio has shown, the most common epidemic diseases of child-hood were sufficiently dangerous as to make childhood mortality a dreaded fact of life: "Death from communicable diseases claimed at least 1 in 6 children under fourteen, and 1 in 10 children under five, in the early twentieth century."[77] A sample of Manitoba war wives shows that many had experienced the death of a child – often an infant – before the war, and just as many would be similarly afflicted while their husbands were in uniform. George Blanchett, for example, died at five months in September 1913; John Patrick Boult, the son of Frank and Mary Boult, died at two days in March 1912. Their mothers and others who had endured the death of a child had known inconsolable grief long before their husbands went to war. For others, the death of a child compounded incalculably the emotional distress attendant upon their husbands' absence overseas. When Thomas Harrison sailed for Europe in December 1915, he left behind his pregnant wife, Mary, and six children. Mary gave birth to a daughter – also named Mary – in May 1916, who died seven months later. William Donaghy had not rushed to the colours as quickly as Thomas Harrison; he was one of the many married men who waited until the early months of 1916, encouraged no doubt by the promises that his family – his wife, Emma, and their seven children – would be well cared for in his absence. Neither he nor Emma would surely have anticipated that their five-year-old daughter, Audrey, would die three months later in June 1916. George Gibson enlisted in July 1915 and then trained in Canada. When he sailed for Europe in May 1916, his wife, Ethel, was several months pregnant with their fourth child. Fanny Gibson, born a month after her father left Canada, died in Winnipeg at three months.[78] Like the distraught young woman whose sad tale of wartime separation and bereavement opened this chapter, Ethel Gibson opted to return to her parents' home in England three months after the death of her infant daughter. The war had not caused the deaths of these children, nor their parents' anguish, but the scourge of infant mortality intensified the emotional misery that was a war wife's constant companion.

☙⟡❧

A war wife's ability to cope depended on many things: her financial resources, her stamina in the face of hard work and relentless anxiety, and blind luck. Some children fell ill, others did not. But her resilience also depended on whether she could tap into a network of family who could help with the rent, provide companionship and childcare, and offer emotional support. This was as true for Canadian war wives as it was for their European counterparts. In Britain and France multi-generational households remained the norm in many rural and working-class communities and following the outbreak of war reasserted themselves in cities where nuclear families had become more prevalent. Peggy Bette has discovered that one-third of the war widows in the French city of Lyon moved during the war to live with parents, siblings, or in-laws. Although many of these women remained in their local Lyonnais neighbourhood, they occasionally moved further afield: the pregnant Mme Bonneaud, for example, travelled almost a thousand kilometres to go home and live with her family in Brest.[79] Loneliness and the high cost of living in Paris prompted another young woman, whose husband was mobilized in 1914, to relocate to her mother's rural village, where three generations – grandmother, mother, and young child – lived together for the duration of the war.[80] Economic calculations and emotional ties also moved Beatrice Oates, a mother of four living in a working-class neighbourhood in Leeds, to invite her parents to live with her following her husband's enlistment in the British Army. Together they could combine family budgets and take care of the children (one still a baby) as well as Beatrice's elderly father.[81]

For many working-class or recently arrived immigrant Canadian families, the multi-generational household was a fact of life too. A careful review of enlistment records and 1916 census data from Manitoba shows that some married couples were living with parents or in-laws prior to the husband's enlistment; in other instances, a young couple might make room in their home for a widowed parent. If it was not unusual for children, parents, and grandparents to live under one roof; nor was it unheard of for adult siblings to do so. The economic benefits of these multi-family households were clear. When Stafford Beaumont enlisted in 1916, for instance, he and his pregnant wife, Dorothy, were living with her parents. So, too, for Cora and William Lyle, who lived in Winnipeg with her widowed mother, four teenage brothers, and an eight-year-old sister, as well as their own four-year-old daughter. Following William's enlistment, Cora's presence in the family home would probably have made for a mutually beneficial – albeit rather crowded – arrangement. Not only would she and her mother have been able to share childcare duties, thus guaranteeing that the two little girls were well supervised, but her income as a war wife would have added substantially to a family budget based on the doubtless modest pay cheques of two teenage boys and her mother's earnings as a dressmaker.[82]

When the enlisted man and his wife were, for the purposes of the census, identified as the principal householders, and a widowed mother, mother-in-law (or, less frequently, father) lived with them, the financial benefits of a multi-generational household were less certain. One client of the Manitoba Patriotic Fund found herself in financial difficulties, even though her father lived in the household, because he was in frail health, could not undertake hard work, and had been recently laid off from his position as a dishwasher in a local restaurant.[83] Widowed mothers were also often in a poor position to contribute to the family purse. Thomas Hatcher enlisted in March 1917, at which point his infant daughter was not yet a year old. He no doubt hoped that his mother-in-law, who had lived with them since her arrival in Canada in 1915, would be able to help his wife with childcare and other household chores. A widowed, unemployed, sixty-year-old woman was likely not well placed to contribute much to the family budget, but the companionship she would have offered her daughter may well have been invaluable. Harriet Brown also needed company and help caring for her two young children, one of whom was a newborn in January 1916, more than she needed help balancing the family budget. Her husband, Ralph, enlisted in 1915, and as a Major in the CEF he was able to provide her with a monthly income of $95. By 1916, when the census was taken, she could afford a live-in maid to take on the heavy work of cleaning and laundry; her mother-in-law, no longer young, no doubt provided Harriet with the more intangible comfort of companionship – combined (perhaps) with some unsolicited advice about child-rearing.[84]

If war wives were not already living in a multi-generational household when the war began, their husbands' enlistment often prompted them to move closer to, or into the same home as parents, in-laws, or adult siblings. Sometimes this meant moving only a few blocks within the same city, as the paths of several Winnipeg women show. When

David Hilland enlisted in January 1916, he and his wife, Hilda, were young newlyweds living in the outer suburb of West Kildonan. Shortly after his departure for Camp Sewell, Hilda moved into the centre of the city, where, the 1916 census records, she lived with her two sisters. This arrangement would have benefited everyone: Hilda was several months pregnant; her sister, Elsie, was single and employed as a cashier at Eaton's; and her younger sister, Iris, was only nine. Together, the two women could pool their resources – Hilda received a monthly income of at least $45 and Elsie probably at most $10 a week – to guarantee a reasonable standard of living. As important, following the birth of her son in June 1916, Hilda would have been able to care for the two children while Elsie continued to work outside the home.[85] Arrangements such as this highlight the importance of family in the provision of childcare. Whereas it was customary for a war wife to remain at home with her children, as Hilda Hilland was able to do, she might occasionally opt to work for wages, if she could persuade her mother, mother-in-law, or sister to care for her children.

In February 1916 the *Toronto Daily Star* told the heart-rending story of the Harries family, where such an arrangement had unravelled for the most tragic reasons. John Harries, a Canadian-born resident of Toronto, had enlisted with the First Contingent, had arrived in Europe in the fall of 1914, and had died in the Second Battle of Ypres in April 1915. His death remained unconfirmed, however, until February 1916, leaving his wife, Mabel, and mother to worry incessantly over his fate. So acute was his mother's anxiety that, on the very day the family received confirmation of his death, she died of grief. Mabel Harries was then left in a most unenviable situation. Shortly after her husband had left Toronto, she had moved a few blocks to live next to her mother-in-law, who was able to care for her three children, enabling her to find work, first as a theatre usher and then as a department store clerk. Following the deaths of both her husband and her mother-in-law, Mabel was doubly bereaved, unable to maintain her job for want of childcare and, until her pension was approved, impoverished.[86]

While it was unusual for a married woman with a young child (or children) to work for wages, the formation of blended households also allowed childless war wives, like Jessie Beker, Elsie Bottomley, and Hazel Jackson, to retain their essentially domestic identity. Like Hilda Hilland, Jessie Beker moved from the distant edges of Winnipeg into the city centre to live with her parents and adult sister; Elsie Bottomley moved approximately a mile from the home she had shared with her husband to live with her widowed mother-in-law and two adult sisters-in-law. The 1916 census notes that the two unmarried sisters-in-law worked for the telephone company, where they probably earned about $35 a month, but Elsie did not work outside the home. Nor did Hazel Jackson, who shared an apartment near Winnipeg's City Hall with her sister-in-law, brother-in-law, and an unrelated boarder. Her sister-in-law was employed in a candy factory, where the wages were notoriously poor, and her brother-in-law was a caretaker. Hazel's income of $35 – from her Separation Allowance and Assigned Pay – would have allowed her to cover her share of the collective household budget without having to work for low wages and long hours outside the home.[87]

Financial calculations surely shaped in a significant way the choices these women made following their husbands' enlistment. But so, too, did the emotional advantages of a move close to family, as Jennie Hillyer's letters to her husband clearly demonstrate. In December 1916, having struggled to maintain the duplex she and Harry had purchased with such great hopes in 1913, and having endured one confrontation too many with her drunken tenant, Jennie decided to find herself an apartment closer to her mother-in-law and sisters. This decision helped dissipate the gloom that had become her constant companion since Harry left for war, so that when she wrote to him in late January 1917, she sounded almost happy. She had found two (suitably sober) tenants for the duplex and was beginning to feel settled in her new home (even though the landlord refused to turn on the electricity and she had to light the flat with gas lamps): "This little place begins to look quite comfortable and I feel heaps better than I did away out there. Mag was here all day yesterday and Mil called in the evening. I am expecting Jess this evening, so you see it is a lot better than when I was forever alone, except for company that was anything but congenial." Understandably, the stresses of daily life took their toll: "I do hope you will soon be home to attend to things yourself – so many little things to worry over all by myself. It doesn't seem to give me any chance to get strong, what with moving, looking after the other place, baby taking the measles … I've had some life lately however, it's over now."[88]

When Jennie Hillyer moved to the apartment on rue de Verdun, she travelled less than four kilometres. Other moves – within a province or across the country – were more complex but by no means beyond contemplation. Nine war wives from the Indigenous communities of James Bay, accompanied by their children, moved many hundreds of kilometres south, to Elk Lake, Ontario, in order to receive regular postal delivery and direct access to the offices of the Canadian Patriotic Fund. As Katharine McGowan has demonstrated, their stay in this predominantly white community exposed them to the systemic prejudices of their new and by no means welcoming neighbours.[89] Other women, recently settled in the west, opted to return to central or eastern Canada, where the cost of living was lower than on the Prairies and they could, as one military officer observed, "live more cheaply with relations."[90] Jeanie Davidson, of Macleod, Alberta, was of their number. When her husband, George, enlisted in August 1916, Jeanie and their three-year-old son persevered through the bitter winter of 1916–17, but by the summer of 1917 she was giving serious thought to pulling up stakes and relocating to Montreal. Like many married women living alone, she supplemented her income by renting out a room in her home. Her husband's reservations about the plan proved well founded, however, for Jeanie's "star boarder" proved anything but and had to be asked to leave. George could not help but say "I told you so." Even more disturbing were the actions of an overly nosy neighbour, who got hold of Jeanie's bank book, stole twelve dollars, and – George feared – was probably determined to come back for more: "The balance she saw there must certainly have opened her eyes and will encourage her to bum and sponge on you to no end. So if you can see your way clear to break with her I am sure you will be ahead in the long run." Unpleasant tenants and fast-fingered friends were bad enough; little "Binkie's" decision to head out into the streets of Macleod – where he was found "with a note in his hand crying" – was more than Jeanie could abide. George had family in Quebec and he was sure that they would welcome her and the baby into the family home: "You mention about moving and thought possibly about going to Quebec. Well, I know you would be welcome there and should you ever feel like doing so, why just go right ahead."[91]

May Rogers, Angeline Maheux, and Maggie Ormsby contemplated more manageable moves, from the Eastern Townships to Montreal, from the remote community of Baskatong Bridge to the somewhat less remote community of Maniwaki, and from the Okanagan Valley to Vancouver, respectively. May Rogers, who had grown up in Montreal and missed many of its amenities, found life in the small community of East Farnham, with its gossipy neighbours, physical labour, and relentless loneliness, increasingly wearisome. She was, however, reluctant to abandon the family home she and Laurie had made for themselves there, for this was the physical space in which their dreams of future familial happiness resided. She feared that to turn her back on their family home was to "abandon her post." Laurie was quick to dispel such reservations, for he recognized the benefits of returning to the city. As he tartly (but perceptively) observed: "[You would] have the advantage of being near relatives who may be grouchy and all that but they still have your every interest at heart. If you sell the place it will give you a little nest egg in the Bank with what you have and if you get your Father to invest the main portion of it for you it will bring in a little more and you could live very comfortably in Montreal." May remained undecided, however, and it was only in the fall of 1916 that she finally decided to close up the farm and return to Montreal, a decision Laurie quickly endorsed: "I certainly don't think you are deserting your post and am very glad that you have made up your mind to go to town for the winter and let the kiddies see something and get started on an education. Also you need a rest and with a heated house you ought to be able to get one." There would be difficulties to contend with in the big city – Laurie worried from afar about his children running in front of a streetcar – but life would be easier and somewhat less lonely. "I am awfully glad you decided to go to town for the winter and feel sure you will not regret it. First there will not be so much to worry about, only the cooking for yourselves, second you will be nearer the family if anything should go wrong. Thirdly you will be nearer your friends and will not get out of touch with civilization and last but not least the kiddies will have a chance of going to school and learning the ways of other people and be able to take their places with city people and not grow up like the clowns the E[ast] F[arnham] people are." By early 1917, he was even more pleased that she and the children were well established in Montreal: "It is a good thing that Howard and Aileen have the park to go to and the slide and rink to play on as it is even better than fooling around with the muts at E[ast] F[arnham]."[92]

Similar considerations prompted Maggie Ormsby to return, at least temporarily, to her parents' home in Vancouver. She and George had purchased a general store in Lumby, British Columbia, but shortly after his enlistment he advised her to sell off the merchandise and make do on her war wife's allowances.[93] Whether to raise additional cash, to make a move to Vancouver more manageable, or to protect her two young children from high-spirited horses, Maggie also decided to sell their two horses and cutter. But like May Rogers, she was initially reluctant to abandon her family home. She seems to have worried about the expense of moving to Vancouver. In George's mind this was a trifling consideration: "I note what you say with regard to your going home for the winter. Never mind the money part if you can get some one to look after the house, you will be much happier at home and your people will be glad to have you, Anna has already written me on the subject and she seems to think that it is I who am keeping you there. As I said before it is my desire that you have a good time during my absence, so please pack up and go home." By December 1915 it was clear that Maggie was not having "a good time" in Lumby: she had had a falling out with a neighbour and was more and more inclined to seek refuge in the friendly company of family. George agreed that there was no point in her staying in Lumby any longer: "guess it would be as well for you to pack up and go home." Thirteen months after George enlisted and almost a year after he arrived in Europe, Maggie and their two children relocated to Vancouver, where they lived with her parents through the winter months. Maggie clearly thought of this as a temporary respite rather than a permanent relocation, for she returned to Lumby in the spring. The same spiteful neighbour, nursing a grudge of unknown origin, continued to make life there a misery, ultimately prompting Maggie to rent out the family home and move into Vernon, where she and the children remained until George returned to Canada in 1918, following a lengthy convalescence.[94]

Angeline Maheux had no interest in city-living, but she recognized the benefits of being close to family. Baskatong Bridge was remote and lonely, the local school was open only when the teacher could make her way north, and – as we have seen – Angeline had her hands full caring for her children and attending to the many tasks that demanded her attention. If she were to move back to Maniwaki, at least for the winter months, her life would be somewhat easier. This, at least, was Frank's considered opinion. As early as July 1915, he was encouraging her to think about the advantages of moving south: "This fall if you believe you are going to have hard time to get your wood and the little chanty plastered stop the winter in Maniwaki, I sooner see you near your mother." By October, it seemed clear that she would spend at least some of the winter months in Maniwaki, and Frank was glad: "It won't be so lonesome for you this winter." Two years later, when Angeline was once again weighing the advantages of a winter in Maniwaki – a plan that would offer her mother consolation as she mourned the death of her eighteen-year-old son – Frank was quick to endorse the scheme: "Dear wife, you tell me you had a big notion to go down at Maniwaki do as you like I was thinking of that myself but I dint say any thing, because you know better than I how you are fixed for wood, and if you need something from the stores you wouldn be so far away, I tell you I was glad to get this letter, Baskatong is so far away, and worse when you have no horses." Maniwaki offered his wife companionship and his children a chance to be properly educated. Although he thought that Baskatong Bridge was "a good place," there were, he conceded "thousands of places better for schools."[95]

Angeline Maheux and Maggie Ormsby were formidable women, not easily daunted by the demands of everyday life or inclined to live under anyone's roof but their own. Maggie was, by all accounts, a woman of firm opinions and independent convictions. To live in her parents' home, where she would of necessity re-assume her role as a dependent daughter, was not, it seems, a solution that sat easily with her. However difficult life in Vernon might prove to be, it was the life she preferred. Other war wives – and perhaps especially those with very young children – preferred a life of semi-dependence to the prospect of unalleviated single parenthood or economic destitution. Eleanor Benny, the mother of a four-year-old son and a three-year-old daughter, relocated from Winnipeg, where her husband had been employed as a pharmacist, to live with her parents in Shoal Lake, Manitoba. Following her husband's death in a German prisoner-of-war camp, she and the children remained in her parents' household. Nellie Floyd followed a similar trajectory. In December 1916, when her husband departed for Europe, she was a thirty-year-old mother of three children, from the age of four down to four months. It certainly made sense for her to leave Winnipeg and return to her parents' home in the Interlake, while she awaited – and hoped for – her husband's homecoming. When she too was widowed, she and the children continued to live with her parents.[96]

Moving was a cumbersome and often costly task. As Frank Maheux observed, when thinking of Angeline's trek to Maniwaki in the last winter of the war: "You must had hell of a time to move all your stuff, pigs, cows in the winter poor wife it is to bad I believe us soldiers gets hard time and everything like that but still a women's get more and bother."[97] Very few war wives travelled with pigs and cows in tow, but those who owned a home had to make plans to close it up or rent it out; household goods had to be placed in storage or shipped. George Ormsby advised Maggie to secure the help of local men to help her prepare her family's possessions for shipment to Vancouver and reminded her that she could have them sent at the reduced rate assigned to "settler's effects." Complications sometimes arose, as Dorothy Yates discovered when she returned to California to live with her parents. In March 1917 her husband enlisted in Victoria, believing it "his duty to give up his position as a high school teacher" and join the CEF. Dorothy remained briefly at home with their seven-month-old son before sailing to the United States, where she and the baby reunited with her parents in Oakland, California. This was primarily an economic decision: she "live[d] with [her] parents in California now because it is impossible to live alone on a private's pay. Prices are terribly high and [she had] no private means." Before leaving Victoria, she arranged to rent the family home – for the very modest sum of $18 a month – having been reassured that she would not have to make any mortgage payments for as long as her husband was in uniform. The rent she received was, in her words, enough "to pay taxes, fire insurance, repairs, and my husband's life insurance for $3000."

It was not enough to cover the mortgage payments as well. It thus came as a most unwelcome surprise to learn that a change in provincial law, introduced after her husband's enlistment, made the owners of rental accommodations – including men serving overseas – responsible for keeping up their mortgage payments. This new obligation placed Dorothy in a very difficult financial situation. While living in California, she continued to receive her Separation Allowance and Assigned Pay, but Patriotic Fund allowances were paid only to residents of Canada, giving her a monthly income of $35 at most. Because her mother was in delicate health and not able to care for the baby, Dorothy could not, as she wrote, "seek employment until my baby son is old enough to be less care," and her father could "barely support himself and my mother."[98] Notwithstanding these difficulties – and what she took to be the patent injustice of the provincial law – Dorothy Yates remained in California until her husband joined them upon his demobilization in 1919.

⧆

When the daily challenges of single parenthood and the dreary prospects of life far from family became overwhelming, Canada's war wives had recourse to one remaining option that might mitigate the most emotionally debilitating effects of wartime separation: they could relocate to Britain. In this regard, the Canadian war wife's experience was importantly different from that of her French and British sisters in suffering, who only rarely undertook arduous and sometimes dangerous treks across a continent and an ocean such as would become familiar to many Canadian war wives.[99] To travel two thousand kilometres or more by train, as the recently bereaved Ethel Gibson and her three remaining children did in late 1916 when they left Winnipeg; then to endure an ocean voyage of eight to ten days in a third-class cabin – on a deck with too few toilets and no fresh air – this was not a venture for the faint of heart. Indeed, not every war wife who set out to return to the "Old Country" made it that far. One war wife, supported by the Manitoba Patriotic Fund, believed that she, too, would be better off close to her parents in England. A woman of fragile health, she had been hospitalized for several weeks in late 1916 and undergone surgery for an "intestinal obstruction." Unable to care for her eight-year-old son, she had placed him temporarily with foster parents, who were anxious to receive the $35 she owed for his room and board. A return trip to Britain, even in the depths of a brutal winter, was surely preferable to a life of illness, debt, and loneliness in Winnipeg. As was its practice, the Patriotic Fund authorized an advance to help defray her travelling costs, but by the time she and her son arrived in Toronto, German submarine warfare had resumed, trans-Atlantic travel was especially perilous, Britain was facing serious shortages of imported food, and Canada was curtailing most further emigration of war wives to Britain. In April 1917, she returned to Winnipeg.[100] The obstacles this young woman encountered were exceptional, however, and the timing inopportune. Before Canada acceded to Britain's request to stop issuing passports for all but the most urgent cases, at least twenty thousand Canadian war wives – and perhaps twice that number – had relocated to Britain.[101] Why they did so and how their experiences of war were shaped by this dramatic upheaval is the subject of the next chapter.

4

Returning to the Old Country

Alice Leighton had never seen London. Nor New York, which in 1916 rivalled London in size, if not yet in global influence. But in the spring of that year, she set out, alone, on a voyage of almost ten thousand kilometres, which took her from her comfortable home in Nanaimo, British Columbia, across Canada to Toronto; from there to New York and on to London. She undertook the journey for one simple reason: she was resolved to spend the duration of the war as close as possible to her husband, a newly commissioned lieutenant in the CEF. For several months leading up to and following his enlistment in September 1915, Alice and Arthur had discussed how she would cope with his absence. While his battalion was training in Vancouver, she would remain in Nanaimo, leading a simple life, tending the garden they both loved and volunteering her time to the many worthy war-related causes that occupied the lives of middle-class women everywhere. Although her hope that Arthur's company would be transferred, at least for a few weeks, to Nanaimo did not come to pass, she was able to cross over to the mainland often enough to ease her loneliness and temporarily tame her anxieties about the future. But both agreed that she would not stay in Canada while her husband was fighting in France. The prospect of indefinite separation was, for them both, unfathomable. Thus, when Arthur's battalion entrained in April 1916, destined for Halifax and from there to Europe, Alice finalized plans for her own trans-Atlantic trek.

Travelling in style and comfort, as befitted the wife of a successful small-town barrister, Alice arrived in New York in late May 1916, somewhat intimidated by the bustle of the big city but reassured that the staff at the stylish Breslin hotel would take care of a married woman of good reputation travelling alone. With a few days of leisure time on her hands – her ship's departure was unexpectedly postponed – she went window-shopping along Fifth Avenue, appropriately impressed by the famous stores, knowing that if her all-too-fallible sense of direction were to fail her, she could telephone the concierge and he would dispatch someone to escort her back to the hotel. If New York was daunting, London, the world's greatest metropolis and capital of its most expansive empire, was almost terrifying. For as long as Arthur's battalion was stationed in England, Alice took rooms in a hotel in either Folkestone or Hythe, near the staging grounds of the CEF and charmingly located along the Channel coast. But when he deployed to France in August 1916, she moved into London, a city of six million souls none of whom she knew.

In contrast to many Canadian war wives who relocated to Britain during the war, Alice had no immediate family in the "Old Country." Ontario-born and bred, she had married Arthur in 1908, and they had lived first in Minnedosa, Manitoba, before moving to the west coast in 1912.[1] Following Arthur's departure for France, Alice had neither sister nor mother to comfort her; nor could she count on the companionship of in-laws, for Arthur's own British-born parents were now well-settled in Victoria, where they battled elderly ailments and welcomed into their home Arthur's sister-in-law and young child while her husband also served in the CEF. In September 1916, Alice Leighton was well and truly alone. She found temporary refuge in one of the grandest hotels in Europe. Venturing out each day from the very posh Cecil Hotel, she explored the famous sites of central London: Westminster Abbey, St James's Park, St Paul's Cathedral, and the National Gallery (where she was amused to discover an empty picture frame, the Joshua Reynolds canvas having been spirited away for safekeeping). London was at war, but for the moment at least, Alice Leighton was a bedazzled tourist.

Alice's odyssey was far from unique. Perhaps as many as fifty thousand Canadian military wives and children temporarily relocated to Britain during the First World War. Only a few travelled in the style and comfort Alice enjoyed, for her adventure was very much that of an officer's wife. Other officers' wives also travelled across North America in the most comfortable train compartments, sailed first class across the Atlantic (occasionally accompanied by a nanny or nursemaid to care for their children), and settled either in the Canadian "colony" that grew up in the shadow of Shorncliffe Camp near Folkestone, or, if the family budget permitted, in London's toniest neighbourhoods. Like Alice, they relocated to Britain to be close to their husbands. The thousands of wives of rank-and-file soldiers who left Canada during the war, on the other hand, crossed the ocean in steerage class accommodation (paid for by the Patriotic Fund) and settled, sometimes quite uncomfortably, with parents or in-laws in towns and villages far from the parks and elegant environs of central London. They often struggled to make ends meet in a nation beset by wartime inflation, and when they returned to Canada frequently had barely enough money to buy a train ticket home. A meagre income – often no more than $35 a month – meant that these less fortunate Canadian war wives returned to Britain only if they could live with parents or in-laws and thereby pool their collective resources; and only if they could find comfort and child care in the company of family. Social status and military rank – which often went hand in hand – directly affected why Canadian war wives chose to relocate to Britain during the war, where they lived when they arrived, and how they then experienced the life and travails of a wartime wife.

A few women left Canada in the earliest months of the war: Hannah McDowell of Montreal departed in October 1914, accompanied by her four children, the youngest not yet two.[2] Like many immigrant families, the McDowells had arrived in Canada in stages: Hannah's husband came first and then she and the three oldest children joined him in August 1912. Settled in Canada a scant two years, Hannah and her children returned to her home in Ireland at the earliest opportunity. Many more Canadian wives bided their time: some were understandably reluctant to place themselves and their children in danger while submarines menaced maritime shipping in the early months of 1915; others had no reason to consider such a move until their husbands joined up at the high point of enlistment of 1916. The migration of Canadian war wives reached its peak in 1916 and abated soon thereafter. By February 1917 pressure from the British authorities prompted the Canadian government to stop issuing passports to Canadians hoping to relocate to Britain. Henceforth only civilians who could "satisfy the authorities that the reasons for the issue are weighty and urgent," and who could demonstrate financial self-sufficiency while in Britain were authorized to leave Canada. Hundreds of women met these criteria and the migration of Canadian wives to Britain continued through 1917, albeit at a much slower pace.[3] At the same time, many Canadian wives began returning to Canada. Some stayed in the "Old Country" only until their husbands were medically discharged from military service; others struggled to make ends meet, as wartime inflation ate into their meagre allowances; yet others responded to insistent government requests that all Canadian dependents leave Britain at their earliest convenience.

༺༻

Officers constituted a very small fraction of the Canadian Expeditionary Force: in an overseas army of almost 500,000 they numbered fewer than 19,000, only a third of whom were married.[4] The wives of officers were, however, more likely to relocate to Britain during the war than the wives of enlisted men. A survey of the military records of three hundred Manitoba men who were married when they enlisted shows that more than a third of all officers' wives in the sample moved to England during the war, in comparison to only one-sixth of the wives of enlisted men. It is doubtful that an officer's wife yearned with greater ardour than a private's wife to be close to her husband while he was overseas. It is almost certain, however, that she was better able to afford the venture and live comfortably once resettled. Men who earned their commissions before leaving Canada (as opposed to those who were promoted for valour on the battlefield) were drawn from the prosperous and professional ranks of Canadian society. Like Arthur Leighton, many (but by no means all) had accrued substantial savings in their civilian lives, certainly sufficient to cover the costs of their wives' trans-Atlantic travel and accommodation in England's more desirable districts. Alice Leighton gently berated herself for taking a room in the Cecil Hotel, for she knew it was a real extravagance. Nonetheless, she was pleased to report that her "finances [were] in a very happy condition" and she could pay her bill without doing serious damage to her bank account.[5]

At the time Alice Leighton sailed from New York in May 1916, trans-Atlantic travel was reasonably safe. Germany had suspended the first phase of its submarine campaign, fearing that another disaster comparable to the sinking of the *Lusitania* would bring the United States into the war on the side of the Entente powers. A year earlier, however, ocean travel had been fraught with danger, prompting some war wives to postpone plans to relocate to Britain. James Evans was a hardware and lumber merchant in a small Manitoba town when he enlisted in December 1914. He and his wife, Edith, had family in Wales who could offer her invaluable support when caring for her three young children while James was fighting in France. But could James and Edith in good conscience expose their children to the all-too-evident risks of trans-Atlantic travel and the increasing danger of Zeppelin raids that dominated headlines in early 1915? This is the question that, understandably enough, plagued Edith's deliberations and persuaded her to delay her departure until the seas were safe. In the meantime, she opted to move to Vancouver, perhaps to stay with a sister and brother-in-law. James supported her decision, even though he believed she was exaggerating the danger Zeppelins posed to English civilians: "Yes girlie I think your decision to go to visit Annie is a wise one, not so much the danger from Zeppelins which so far is a joke, but the danger in crossing the water, and as you say the children's lives are very precious to us both & not only the children's but yours is indescribably precious to me."[6]

Edith Evans continued to ponder the advantages and dangers of relocating to Britain, remaining undecided through the end of the year. James, however, grew ever more eager to be reunited with his wife and children, admitting to Edith in one letter that he often dreamt about her "and the little ones, and the dreams you can bet are very heavnly."[7] Although he was willing in September to let Edith make the final decision, confident that she would do what was best, by October he was becoming increasingly impatient. He knew that a move on the scale he proposed would be complex and expensive: Edith would have to close up their house, store the furniture, and perhaps arrange for a tenant whose rent would cover the mortgage fees. She would also have to come up with the funds for train fare to the east coast and sea passage for four to England. He offered to negotiate with his business partner in Manitoba an advance of $50, sufficient to cover the family's expenses until settled in England; he promised to write the local station agent to ask about discount fares for the children; and he suggested that she might be able to travel with a fellow officer's wife, who was also making plans to sail for England. He just desperately wanted his family to join him, and soon. If Edith started making arrangements immediately, he calculated that she and the children could be in England "long before Christmas."[8] When she still delayed, thinking it would be best to wait until after the New Year, he could not contain his impatience: "Well sweetheart I do hope you wont think I am hurrying you but great Scott, I certainly expect you can get here by Christmas."[9]

James Evans promised to find his family a small house in Hythe, Kent, a market town close to the Canadian base at Shorncliffe. They would, he was confident, find themselves in good company because by late 1915 "several of our officers have their wives & families living here."[10] In fact, Hythe and Folkestone became a veritable Canadian colony of officers' wives, not as elegant perhaps as London but ideally located for as long as their men were still supervising the training of troops in England. Maude Grant also gravitated to Hythe in the spring of 1916, several months after first arriving in England. Married to William Lawson Grant, a professor of Canadian history at Queen's University and future principal of Toronto's Upper Canada College – and daughter of the first administrator of the Rhodes Scholarship foundation – Maude Grant was a woman with her hands full when she embarked for England in late 1915: her oldest daughter was not yet four, the younger one only two – and she was five or six months pregnant. Unlike most war wives, who relocated to Britain only after their husbands had sailed from Canada, she opted to travel to England while William was still training his battalion in Gananoque. Recognizing that he would be otherwise occupied when she was recovering from childbirth, she travelled to England, where she could stay at her parents' home in a bucolic Oxford village until the baby was born and William's regiment had arrived in England. When their daughter, Alison, was born somewhat prematurely at the beginning of February 1916, Maude was able to rely upon her mother (and, one suspects, a servant or two) to help with the children until she regained her strength. Following William's arrival in England in mid-April 1916, she moved to Hythe.[11]

Stuart Tompkins also dreamed of having his wife settle in Kent, but unlike the Leightons and the Grants – who were so financially secure that they did not have to rely on the Assigned Pay most husbands routinely allocated for their family's upkeep – he and Edna Tompkins, only recently married and still making their way in the world, had to count their pennies. Nonetheless as soon as Stuart enlisted in 1915, they began to weigh the pros – and cons – of Edna's relocation to Britain. Stuart's position in the Alberta Department of Education was respectable but by no means as remunerative as Arthur Leighton's law practice. Without the accumulated savings that guaranteed Alice Leighton's material comfort, the Tompkins had to consider carefully the merits of Edna's relocation. Stuart, always prone to frame his arguments in an elevated, spiritual tone, recognized that "technically, it would be prudent for you to stay at home and get a job, but if it meant that the mighty epoch in which you were living would go by without the adding of one inch to your mental and spiritual stature, to stay home would be most lamentable. Prudent indeed but not wise." If, however, she were to accompany him to England she would be truly a partner in the great, redemptive adventure that he believed the war to be: "Oh my darling, how much more will we mean to one another, when we have lived through the stress and the strain of the present, when our souls shall have been lifted out of the common world on to the heights whence we will have caught the vision splendid of that new world which is to be."[12] All of which was well and good, but, upon his arrival at Shorncliffe, Stuart quickly realized that they would not have a minute to themselves: "Well, honey, I can see now, if you come over you are not going to see very much of me ... At present, there is no leave at all. What will be forth coming in a few weeks time I do not know." Ultimately, however, he wished with all his heart that she would make the journey, for it filled him "with a feeling of dismay to think of [her] being 6000 miles away."[13] To his great delight Edna arrived in England in July 1916 and for as long as Stuart's battalion remained at Shorncliffe, she lived nearby.

With its fresh sea air and boardwalk strolls, Hythe was certainly a charming place for a mother with young children. And as the Grants and Evans discovered, a house in Hythe allowed Canadian families to replicate the genteel customs of home. Although William Grant had to live in the officers' quarters at Shorncliffe, he took advantage of a weekend's leave to participate in his daughter's baptism, a respite from army life he greatly relished: it was, he declared, "delightful" to be with Maude and the children and "to live more or less quietly and not in a whirl of small duties."[14] He regretted that he could not get leave to spend their wedding anniversary together, but family life for the Grants had a tranquil familiarity for as long as he was stationed in England. So, too, for the Evans household, where every Sunday afternoon became an open house for the men in James Evans's company. Reflecting on the warm hospitality Edith had always shown to one and all, Private Alan Hodnett wrote her from France to express his gratitude: "Last Sunday we were on the move all day but every once in awhile either Coombes or I would make the suggestion that we go down to Evans' It seems strange to spend a Sunday any other place. I know we are going to miss the home terribly. After we have been out here for a few months we will begin to really appreciate what you folks did for us. We will never be able to repay all your kindnesses so just believe us when we say we are truly thankful."[15]

Many officers' wives made at least a temporary home in Hythe. Some, like Edith Evans, stopped first with family far from the Channel coast before settling briefly in Kent. When Edith's husband was transferred to the Canadian camp at Witley, she and the children left Hythe and rented a house in a country village within walking distance of Witley, where they would remain until he was sent to France in March 1918. Other wives, including Edna Tompkins and Alice Leighton, stayed in Kent only while their husbands were still in England, and then moved to London. The capital had much to offer: famous sites and fabulous shops, theatres and restaurants favoured by officers on leave, and charitable ventures ideally suited to the philanthropic impulses of their well-to-do wives. It was, however, also a target of aerial attacks which were frequent enough to set Londoners' nerves on edge. James Evans surely underestimated the danger to civilian life when he described the Zeppelin raids over England as a "joke." Starting in 1915, London and the Channel coast were targeted first by the slow-moving, lumbering Zeppelins, and in the last two years of the war by more lethal heavy bombers. One bombing raid, in June 1917, destroyed an elementary school in London's East End, killing 158 civilians including 18 children, another wrought havoc on an open-air market in Folkestone. On 31 May 1917 Georgina Lee, a perceptive English diarist whose wartime

experiences resembled in many regards those of Canadian officers'
wives, noted with dismay: "There has been a dreadful air-raid over
Folkestone. 16 German aeroplanes invaded the town on Saturday last,
when the people were at their busiest, between 5 and 6 o'clock doing
their shopping for the Whitsun week-end. Bombs were dropped ... in
the narrow part of the old town. About 80 people were killed, mostly
women but also 26 children."[16] British civilians and the Canadian
visitors who lived in their midst were therefore by no means fully
insulated from the dangers of war, and (as they would do during the
Second World War) Londoners who could afford it sent their children
deep into the countryside to protect them from nightly bombing raids.

If life in London was intermittently dangerous, it was always (and
increasingly) expensive, especially if one chose to live in Westminster,
Pimlico, or Kensington, as many Canadian officers' wives did. Annie
Collum, the young wife of a well-to-do Canadian officer and daughter
of a prominent Winnipeg politician, lived temporarily in Glasgow
before moving to London, where she set up residence in the Artillery
Mansions, Victoria Street; Ethel Hunter arrived in England with her
two young children in October 1916 and found a flat in Pimlico, a
neighbourhood where streets of elegant townhouses coexisted with
lodging houses of a more disreputable character.[17] And Helen Geddes,
whose husband enlisted in September 1914, moved first to Ireland and
then, following her husband's death at Ypres in April 1915, relocated to
London, settling in Kensington. Catherine Cameron, a newlywed in 1915,
moved to London six months after her husband first arrived in Britain,
and rented a flat on Northumberland Street, a short walk from the
National Gallery, Trafalgar Square, and Charing Cross Station.[18] These
central London addresses gave Canadian wives easy access to the London
branch of the Bank of Montreal, where (as Agar Adamson observed)
the manager became a font of Canadian war gossip.[19] Slightly further
west on Horseferry Road, the Quarter-Master General's office, which
included the Pay and Records Office for the CEF, became an equally
vibrant hub of Canadian activity, and for wives in search of clerical work
a source of employment.

Officers' wives could afford central London rents and the social
amenities of the city in part because their husbands often had professional incomes and accumulated savings; in part because officers'
salaries were sufficiently generous that the Assigned Pay they could
allocate to their wives guaranteed a comfortable living. Ethel Hunter,
for example, received $80 a month in Assigned Pay (when a private's wife
usually received no more than $20) and $50 per month in Separation
Allowance. The wife of a recently appointed university professor, she

probably had little in the way of private savings to fall back upon, but a monthly income of $130 (or approximately £30) would have given her an adequate income even in wartime London.[20] Alice Leighton, by contrast, received only $30 a month in Separation Allowance in 1916 and nothing in Assigned Pay. Her income from Arthur's law practice was sufficient, however, to allow her to live comfortably and contemplate investing in Canadian war bonds: "the government is about to issue Exchequer Bonds at 6% for three years and I think I'll invest. What do you think! While I think of it will you write me out a receipt, all properly worded, for Mr Ross when he sends money next time."[21] Mabel Adamson, the wife of a captain in the Princess Patricia's Canadian Light Infantry and the daughter of a wealthy Toronto family, was even more comfortably situated in her Kensington flat. Indeed, on more than one occasion, Agar had to ask *her* for an advance so that he could cover unexpected expenses.

Affluence made it possible for many officers' wives to pursue the activities deemed appropriate to their station. When she first arrived in London, Alice Leighton indulged an understandable desire to explore the city, happily reporting on daily excursions that took her to Westminster Abbey, the National Gallery, and Hyde Park. She dined with newly made Canadian acquaintances at elegant restaurants, and wondered, albeit briefly, if she was being too extravagant when she in turn invited them to dine with her at the hotel. She always knew, however, that she would not spend the rest of the war playing the tourist. As she explained to Arthur, she hadn't "seriously looked for anything to do yet" because she wanted "to find [her] way about first."[22] Once fully acclimated – and less fearful of losing her way in the winding streets of the West End – she would find some way to support the war effort. While still in Nanaimo she had volunteered with the Imperial Order Daughters of the Empire, which prepared parcels for men serving overseas.[23] Similar (and more interesting) opportunities abounded in London, where charities to support war refugees, prisoners of war, and front-line soldiers in need of clean socks proliferated. Uncertain how best to contribute, Alice first volunteered at a canteen for Canadian soldiers on leave, then wrote letters for wounded and convalescent soldiers in hospital, before ultimately deciding in 1918 to train as a Voluntary Aid Detachment nurse and take up a position at a convalescent hospital for blind soldiers.

Mabel Adamson, whose family wealth accustomed her to the finer things of life, was equally determined to do her bit for the war effort. From the moment she arrived in England in late 1914, she embraced the many obligations of an officer's well-heeled wife. While her young son was in boarding school, she paid courtesy calls to the wives of men in Agar's regiment; visited the wounded and convalescent in hospital; and invited her husband's close friends, temporarily on leave in London, to accompany her to the theatre. Even though these were the expected duties of a commanding officer's wife, Agar realized that such tasks, when combined with his repeated requests that she send him a panoply of articles, taxed her time. As he well knew, she had "so much to do."[24] For Mabel, like Alice Leighton and other comfortably situated officers' wives, devoted herself to an array of philanthropic ventures. Her first foray into wartime philanthropy was ill-fated: the Belgian Soldiers Fund, where she volunteered in 1915, soon fell under the gaze of suspicious police inspectors who doubted the probity of the plan's principal organizers.[25] Following the collapse of the Belgian Soldiers Fund, whose efforts had never been enthusiastically endorsed by the Belgian Army – and whose accounting methods were somewhat suspect – Mabel redirected her energies to a new project, the Belgian Canal Boat Fund, which would absorb most of her time and enthusiasm until serious illness forced her to retire from public life in 1917.

For those, like Edna Tompkins, who were less financially secure than either Alice Leighton or Mabel Adamson, London offered employment suitable for an educated woman of the genteel classes. Anticipating her husband's departure for France, Edna made plans to move into London, where she shared an apartment with the wife of a sergeant in Stuart's company and found work at the Canadian Army Pay office. It was not entirely clear that an officer's wife should be seeking paid employment, or so Stuart's comrades-in-arms seemed to suggest. "I told everyone quite frankly you have gone to work," he admitted. "No comment was made one way or the other."[26] And perhaps the seedier aspects of Horseferry Road, where Canadian and Anzac troops on leave were known to go in search of everything from a clean set of clothes to casual sex, gave a respectable woman (and her husband) pause.[27] Nonetheless, Edna Tompkins was not the only officer's wife hoping to secure a position at the Pay and Records Office, which by late 1916 employed a staff of almost three thousand.[28] Jessie Shouldice was also a newlywed not yet absorbed or encumbered by childcare duties. But her search for paid employment with the Pay Office came to naught and, Stuart reported, she decided to "stay here for a while and … then go … visiting."[29] However unconventional it might have been for a married woman of Edna Tompkins's social class to work outside the home, young wives without children could justify taking a paying job on the grounds that they were, as Stuart Tompkins put it, "doing something to release a man for the front."[30]

In her quest to do something useful for the war effort, Alice Leighton also worked for a short while in the Pensions branch of the Pay and Records Office. Inspectors, who "were quietly keeping track of how much work we did and the intelligence we displayed," thought she spent too much time chatting and not enough time attending to the piles of paperwork on her desk; she soon went in search of more rewarding work.[31] The Pay and Records Office would doubtless have been a hive of clerical industry. Pay records, suitably adjusted whenever a soldier or officer was promoted, had to be meticulously kept; and Separation Allowance records updated every time a war wife submitted a change of address. Such tedious work could also be heartbreaking, especially for a war wife worried about her own husband's well-being. Every soldier's death had to be noted in the payroll records; every Separation Allowance cancelled upon confirmation that a widow's pension had been granted. These constant reminders of the human cost of war would surely have depressed the wives working in the Pay and Records Office. Edna Tompkins felt that she could not afford to give up her job, but it was taking such a toll on her physical and mental health that she soon considered returning to Canada. Stuart, for his part, regretted that they were "so hard up" that she couldn't take a rest, and feared that he was to blame: "I know it has meant a lot of expense to have me over here. I am sorry that it has been so."[32] By January 1917, he was seriously worried about her health: "I know that you are not well and it worries me. I guess you should not have taken that job or held it so long. You are a dear brave girl and I certainly honour you for your grit."[33]

Edna Tompkins thought better of her plan to return to Canada. However demoralizing her work and however depressing her day-to-day life in the uncommonly cold, relentlessly grey, and always unlit London winter of 1916–17, she knew she would at least be able to see Stuart when he returned to England on leave. Indeed, she was so eager for their much-anticipated reunion in early 1917, that he felt it necessary to temper her enthusiasm with a dose of realism: "You seem very tired and dispirited. In a way I am sorry you are looking forward to my leave for it will seem all too short."[34] This was, of course, a common lament, but few soldiers would have foregone the opportunity to spend even a week far from the mud, grime, and soul-destroying misery of the front lines. And many wives in Canada surely envied those who had relocated to Britain, knowing that for one week at least they could enjoy something resembling real family life. As May Rogers, from her vantage point in Quebec, put it so poignantly in her last letter to Laurie, "if I only could see you, I think it would make a different woman of me loneliness is eating my heart out."[35]

Reunions with their husbands on leave, the most significant benefit of relocating to Britain during the war, was an advantage that officers' wives in London were well placed to enjoy. Whereas enlisted men, much to their annoyance, were given leave only once a year, officers enjoyed ten days of leave four times each year.[36] If they could afford it, they flocked to London, where elegant restaurants, amusing plays, and the pleasures of the flesh awaited. Not every leave went precisely as planned, of course, as Agar Adamson amusedly recounted to Mabel in July 1917:

> There is a pretty story of a certain lady of the Regiment who received the following telegram from Boulogne "Meet me Ryder Street 8 o'clock." She met her gallant, dined and went to the theatre and came back to supper alone and was surprised to meet her husband in the lift at 1 a.m. after supper. He also had sent a telegraph to her from Boulogne which she did not get. The gallant and the husband were old enemies, finding the lift too small for a proper ring encounter they fought it out in the passage landing. By 2 a.m. there were two vacant flats and two bills paid and Ryder Street will know them no more.[37]

Such misadventures notwithstanding, for most married couples leave was the only true respite they could count on during the war, and it was to be enjoyed to the full. Shortly after Alice Leighton arrived in London, she contemplated the advantages of volunteering at a Canadian soldiers' canteen in Westminster. Such work would give her something useful to do, but as important, it would allow her to adjust her schedule so that "if you came home or I wanted time off I could arrange for someone else to take my place. I didn't like the idea of being tied definitely as I would be if I took up nursing."[38] In this regard, the life of a prosperous Canadian officer's wife closely resembled that of her British counterparts. By the end of 1916, Mary Corfield, who found it hard to make ends meet on £300 per year, was seriously considering finding a job. Her husband was cautiously enthusiastic but insisted that whatever she chose to do she should be able to "give it up the moment I come home on leave or for other reasons." Nothing should interrupt the pleasures that only leave could offer.[39]

Life in Britain offered war wives two other, less expected benefits, one of which was certainly welcome, the other, perhaps less so. The mail moved quickly, sometimes arriving in two or three days, making it possible for those who were so inclined to write one another every day. Alice and Arthur Leighton did so, much to Alice's continuing delight and the amusement (or astonishment) of his English relations.

In March 1917, while visiting his extended family in Yorkshire, Alice reported: "Two more letters from you this morning dearie and it is so sweet of you. Aunt Edie is wonderfully impressed. She asked me how often you wrote and when I said 'every day' she had a 'that's all very well for a story' sort of look, but now when they do come every day or two every other day, she is lost in admiration."[40] Indeed, Alice became so accustomed to hearing from Arthur with every morning's post that even one day without mail could prove unsettling. Because all mail was systematically delayed in advance of or in the middle of major battles, it was not surprising that she went for two days without a letter in early October 1916, when the CEF was heavily engaged at the Somme: "Dearest old pal: There was no letter yesterday and of course none to-day [it was a Sunday] so I can hardly wait till to-morrow morning. It always happens like that, if I miss a letter one day, there is none the next either for the censor takes it into his head to have an investigation or something ... Then it is all made up by two coming at once. You have been splendid dearie, you don't know how I appreciate it but I just love every word of every letter."[41] Several months later, when reflecting on Arthur's admirable letter-writing habits, she confided, "if you never do anything else sweet in your life I shall always remember how you wrote to me every day when you were in France."[42]

Husbands also appreciated being able to hear from "home" more regularly than if their wives had remained in Canada. Even though delivery was still somewhat erratic – Agar Adamson noted, for example, that on 25 November 1916 he had received letters that Mabel had written on the 17th and 20th and that he expected "to get the 18th and 19th" the next day[43] – it was always much more efficient than anything sent from Canada. This was especially true of letters sent from London; because all mail, whatever its point of origin, was sorted first in London, letters sent directly from the capital often arrived in France before mail dispatched from the coastal towns of Folkestone, Hythe, and Hastings. Once in France, Stuart Tompkins was relieved to discover that as a rule Edna's letters reached him "within three days." Parcels, he noted, "have to be allowed a bit longer."[44] He might have added "but not nearly as long as those mailed from Canada."

Canadian wives in Britain were as committed as those remaining in Canada to providing their husbands with parcels that brightened life in the front lines. Some parcels were filled with gourmet delicacies and the accoutrements of middle-class life. From her flat in Kensington Mabel Adamson had convenient access to Harrods, where she became a regular client. Whenever Agar wrote from France, requesting everything from a fountain pen to a folding chair, from "trench gloves" to canned oysters, she made the rounds of London's prestigious shops – if Harrods could not fulfil her husband's many exacting orders, Selfridges, Fortnum & Mason, and bespoke tailors usually could – and then assembled parcels filled with a curious cornucopia of delicacies: "sardines, Bovril cubes, chicken and tongue, eye glasses, fountain pen, writing case, memo book, prawns, opium, saccharin, mints, chocolate, socks, films, acid drops, pushlight, Iodine, canteen, fountain pen."[45] Perhaps it was to be expected that some parcels would go astray, as Adamson lamented in May 1916: a box of liqueurs Mabel had ordered as a gift for one of his fellow officers had not arrived and he feared that "Harrods probably sent them to a prisoner-of-war."[46] Nonetheless, Mabel's parcels arrived at the front with exemplary regularity, satisfying her husband's special fondness for oysters and fountain pens. Stuart Tompkins, by contrast, craved intellectual and spiritual nourishment and cherished the Bible and other reading material Edna sent him. Everyone made use of shaving soap, tried out the latest version of louse powder (even if it didn't work), and relished chocolate and sweet biscuits.

Wartime residency in England also meant that Maude Grant, Alice Leighton, Edna Tompkins, and Mabel Adamson could attend to their husbands when they were convalescing from wounds, illness, or injury. William Grant's wartime service was short-lived and rather undistinguished: he was thrown from a horse in August 1916 only weeks after arriving in France and suffered fractured ribs and a head wound the attending physicians described as "dangerous." From a hospital bed in France he described (in a letter written by the resident chaplain) the accident somewhat vaguely: "I am not quite sure how my own accident occurred. I was galloping with a loose rein and I think the horse stepped into a shell hole. [I hope that] before I get through I shall be sent home to England and may have you to look after me but of this I am not sure."[47] A month after the accident and no longer in danger, he was invalided back to England and admitted to the IODE Hospital, Hyde Park, London. Discharged in October, he was granted three months leave with his family and at the beginning of 1917 was assigned to administrative duties at the Canadian base at Camp Bramshott. Arthur Leighton was also invalided back to England in March 1917, suffering from a swollen knee that saved him from seeing action at Vimy. Alice could not have been more delighted: "Your letter came from Etaples with the lovely news that you were on your way to Blinkin Blighty. Dearie, dearie, I am so glad. I could hardly breathe with the thought of it. And now you are in London – well I'll be there too pretty soon so you may be on the watch for me. I can hardly believe it!"[48]

Stuart Tompkins participated in the assault on Vimy Ridge but was hospitalized shortly afterward. He tried not to alarm Edna, reassuring her: "You don't need to do any worrying. It is just a little bronchial trouble. It wouldn't have bothered me at all, only I was about all in after the show." In fact, he was in much poorer health than he first admitted. Like many men who had endured the bitterly cold winter of 1916–17, military service in the insalubrious conditions that prevailed along the Western Front had undermined his physical and mental health. His "little bronchial trouble" persisted for months, and extensive bed rest in England did not restore him to full health. He lost weight, slept poorly, looked wan and run down, and, in the judgment of his examining doctors, was suffering from "the strain of service." He remained in England, on extended leave through most of 1917, and he and Edna returned to Canada in 1918.[49]

Officers' wives who relocated to Britain knew well, as did all war wives, the relentless psychological strain of wartime. That is one of the reasons they relished the week or ten days a husband was on leave: they knew that then, and only then, he was safe. But for as long as he was in France, there was no such assurance. In November 1918, when the war was finally won and Alice Leighton could rest easy in the knowledge that Arthur had survived, she confessed: "The last week dearie has been the hardest I have had for I was so afraid something might happen at the very last. I went down on my knees dearie when I knew for sure you were coming back to me."[50] In this regard, officers' wives were no different from the wives of enlisted men. Their relative affluence, however, protected them from the financial anxiety that hounded the daily lives of many less well-to-do Canadian wives who returned to Britain during the war. Whereas officers' wives could choose to live in Kent or London to be close to their husbands while training and on leave, the wives of enlisted men lived in towns and villages along the Channel coast only if their parents or in-laws were already settled there; those who lived in London stayed in humbler suburbs many miles from the chic West End; and many returned to the working-class neighbourhoods of their childhood in Yorkshire, Lancashire, or Scotland. Compelled to manage within budgets relentlessly eroded by inflation – food prices doubled in Britain between 1914 and 1916 – they often found life an unending struggle.

❧

In contrast to Alice Leighton, Edna Tompkins, Maude Grant, and other officers' wives who were Canadian-born, the wives of enlisted men who opted to relocate to Britain were, in the main, British-born immigrants recently settled in Canada. This, at least, is the pattern that emerges from the sample of married Manitoba soldiers and their wives. Of the forty-one wives of enlisted men and NCOs who relocated to Britain from Manitoba during the war, census data – when cross-referenced with birth, marriage, and immigration records – allow for the positive identification of all but three. Most of these thirty-eight women were young, and in several cases considerably younger than the men they married: three were not yet out of their teens when war broke out, and sixteen of them were under twenty-five. Only two of these women had been born in Canada; the rest were British-born and most had arrived in Canada during the great immigration wave of 1911–14. Some were already married when they initially embarked for Canada – Edith and William Crossland, for instance, sailed for Canada a month after their wedding in March 1912 – but many had come alone or with a sibling and had married only after settling in Manitoba. Margaret Moorey and her older sister left their family home in Yorkshire in 1912, destined for the small town of Melita, where they found work as domestic servants and, at least in Margaret's case, a husband. She married George Booker on Christmas Day, 1915, a month after he enlisted.[51] Grace Summerscales's path from Yorkshire to Manitoba was similar. In 1910, at the age of eighteen she and her brother Arthur arrived in Canada, intent on joining their brothers on a farm in Alberta. When the Alberta plan fell through, Grace moved to Winnipeg, where she met and married George Copsey.[52] In 1916, when she decided to return to Yorkshire she was, like the vast majority of the women in this sample, the mother of a young child.

Mabel Blyth, a British-born, recently married, mother of young children, matches this composite profile precisely. Born Mabel Shakesby in 1887 in Hull, Yorkshire, she had by 1901 moved with her parents across the river to Barton-on-Humber. In 1912, at the age of twenty-five, she sailed for Canada, destined for Winnipeg, where she married a few months later, perhaps having known her fiancé since childhood; Ernest Blyth, like his new wife, had also been born in Hull. By the time he enlisted in July 1915, he and Mabel were the parents of two young sons. Mabel and her boys, both not yet three, sailed from Saint John, New Brunswick, in January 1916 and, after a few brief stays in Hull – an important naval base which suffered civilian casualties when subjected to a Zeppelin raid in March 1916 – settled in Barton-on-Humber, near her parents and not far from her in-laws. She gave birth to her third child, a daughter, several months later.[53] Lacking the extended family networks in Canada that proved indispensable to women like May Rogers, Maggie Ormsby, or Jennie Hillyer, Mabel Blyth and many other young wives in comparable situations, hoped to find in England the comfort, solace, and support that would make wartime separation endurable.

Not every woman who opted to return to Britain during the war fit this profile as closely as Mabel Blyth. Some were considerably older;

others were new brides with no children to care for. Regrettably for our purposes, none documented their reasons for leaving Canada. In some cases, it is clear that they were abandoning a life of economic hardship or emotional misery. Edith Andrews was forty in 1915 when her husband, Ernest, embarked for Europe. Immigration and census records suggest that they had struggled financially since arriving in Canada in 1903. Ernest had travelled frequently to the States in search of work, sometimes alone and sometimes accompanied by his wife and son. When the war broke out in 1914, it was no doubt the prospect of steady employment that encouraged his prompt enlistment: by October 1914 he was in uniform and seven months later, in England. Physically separated once more from her husband and never fully settled in Winnipeg, Edith Andrews probably hoped to find a welcoming, familiar home for herself and her son when they arrived in Worcester in the spring of 1915.[54]

Poverty, loneliness, and ill health also encouraged a young wife attended by a Winnipeg physician to return home to the United Kingdom. As the doctor explained in his appeal to the Manitoba Patriotic Fund, this young woman was in a very bad way indeed. Her husband had struggled to find regular work, leaving his wife and infant child almost destitute. Following his enlistment in December 1915 and before she received her first Separation Allowance check, she had only ten dollars to see her through the month. To compound the misery, she was in extremely fragile health. Seriously injured in a car accident the previous year, she had "been an invalid ever since, being confined either to her bed or room most of the time." The doctor believed that if she were to return to "the Old Country," where she would live with her widowed mother-in-law, her health would improve: "The voyage home and the fact that she would again be among friends and relatives would in all probability completely restore her health." The Manitoba Patriotic Fund agreed to pay her passage home, and by August 1916 she was living once more in Belfast.[55]

These were perhaps the most unfortunate cases. But many other Canadian war wives, with very young children to care for and no family close by, would have found ample reason to relocate to Britain following their husbands' enlistment. Unlike Alice Leighton or Edna Tompkins, who initially looked upon Britain with a tourist's gaze, these women were going home: when they arrived in Britain, they almost always lived with, or near, their parents or in-laws. Having forfeited their claim to Patriotic Fund allowances, which were paid only to residents of Canada, these women had to get by on their Separation Allowance and Assigned Pay. Thirty-five dollars a month (or approximately £7) would have been a generous income by the standards of working-class life in pre-war Britain, when many households made do on one pound a week.[56] By

1916, however, when inflation had doubled the cost of basic necessities, £7 a month afforded few luxuries. For young women, like Anna Bella Galbraith, who returned to her mother's home in Scotland in December 1916 with her two-year-old daughter, the companionship of family and the financial benefits of shared accommodation were distinctly preferable to an apartment in Winnipeg where she had neither friends nor family.[57] Like Anna Galbraith, Mabel Bealey was also a very recent Canadian resident, having arrived in Canada in 1913. Two years later she and her infant daughter returned home to Exeter, where they spent the war. Older women also went home, to towns or villages they had not seen for a decade or more. Martha Atton, who had joined her husband in Canada in 1910, relocated to Bedford, living at first with her in-laws and subsequently with her parents.[58]

As best we can tell, many Canadian women who returned to Britain to live with parents or in-laws did find the support and emotional sustenance that they had lacked in Canada. They surely appreciated – as did their more affluent counterparts – access to a postal system that allowed soldiers to remain in close and regular contact with their families in the British Isles. Jack Ellis was not as assiduous in his correspondence as Arthur Leighton, but he wrote to his wife, Kitty, with admirable regularity following her return to her parents' home in Glasgow in October 1916. A devoted husband and the doting father of a baby daughter, Jack sent Kitty six letters in January 1917, while he was still training in England, and another six in March 1917, when in France. And like the British working-class wives who conscientiously included the cost of stationery and weekly packages in their wartime budgets, Kitty reciprocated, often writing several times a week.[59] When a letter mailed from Glasgow could arrive in the front lines in three or four days – Kitty's letters of February 8th and 9th were in Jack's hands by the 12th – regular correspondence acquired a conversational quality often lacking in letters from (or to) Canada. Nor did Kitty stint on the packages she and her mother prepared each week. Her homemade baking always elicited Jack's warm praise: he "sure [did] enjoy a little taste of wifeys goodies." A parcel of chocolates and dates, which arrived just as he was coming out of the front-lines, earned comparable (albeit less suggestive) praise: "many, many thanks for the lovely parcel I had left the trenches & walked about 8 miles arriving in rest camp about 4 am & nearly famished so that my chum & I between us devoured nearly all of it at once ... Oh those chocolates certainly hit the spot too, It is so long since I had some real good chocolate & the dates reminded me of those sweet old times darling that I pray will soon return." On other occasions, she (like Mabel Adamson) scoured the shops in search of obscure items indispensable to life at the front. The louse powder

Jack had requested was available only from a herbalist, so she sent a substitute instead. Perhaps it worked, but the battery she purchased certainly didn't. Unable to track down the "British battery no. 1678" Jack had specified, Kitty had been persuaded by a smooth-talking but not necessarily scrupulous salesman to purchase something "even better." As Jack observed, "that fellow who sold you the battery love didn't know what he was talking about my flash light is a little flat one that will fit in a vest pocket." Nonetheless, the cigarettes were fine and Kitty's mother's homemade dumpling much appreciated.[60]

Regardless of her husband's rank, then, a wife who relocated to Britain was able to correspond more frequently with her husband than she could have, had she stayed in Canada. The enlisted man's hope that he would be able to reunite temporarily with his wife and children while on leave or recuperating from wounds was less often realized. Leave was all too rare and convalescent hospitals only occasionally close to their family's British homes. Hannah McDowell was more fortunate than most in this respect. Although she moved frequently upon her arrival in Belfast in October 1914, she was able to reunite with her husband during his convalescence in the summer of 1915. Severely gassed and lightly wounded in the Second Battle of Ypres, James McDowell secured a transfer from his original hospital in the south of England to Belfast; and when granted convalescent leave in July 1915, he, Hannah, and their children lived briefly in Holywood, County Down. Like many a soldier reluctant to return to barracks, he overstayed his leave and reported late for duty to his new assignment at the Canadian military hospital at Bramshott. By June 1916, Hannah and her children had found a cottage in a small village nearby and family life resumed, free of the anxiety that always accompanied the life of women whose husbands were serving at the front.[61] Hannah McDowell's experience was exceptional, however. Kitty Ellis never saw her husband from the time she settled in her parents' home until his death from wounds in May 1917. And even if, as seems probable, Mabel Blyth was able to visit her husband while he was convalescing from wounds sustained in September 1916, she made no obvious plans to relocate to the south of England. With no guarantee that her husband would remain indefinitely at the Military Convalescent Hospital at Epsom, she would have uprooted her family only to find herself as alone in Epsom as she had been in Winnipeg. It was only when her husband was diagnosed with tuberculosis in the spring of 1917 that it became evident that he (and his family) would soon be returning to Canada.[62] Until then, it made good sense for Mabel and her children to remain in Yorkshire, near parents and extended family.

Women like Mabel Blyth, whose husbands were medically discharged and repatriated to Canada, clearly had no reason to stay in Britain. Circumstances such as hers had emerged as early as the fall of 1915, when Colonel W.R. Ward, the Director of Pay and Records in London, noted that "numerous cases" were coming to his attention "where the husband serving in the Canadian Contingent [had] been invalided and returned to Canada for discharge leaving his wife, and in some cases family, behind in England practically unprovided for and without means of returning to Canada."[63] Such women, eager to return home, discovered that the policy in place in 1915 offered them little in the way of financial assistance. When Canadian authorities in London inquired of Ottawa "whether widows of deceased Canadian soldiers and wives of discharged Canadian soldiers [were] to be returned to Canada at public expense,"[64] the response was an unambiguous "no." Circumstances and apparently compelling cases prompted a reconsideration. One such case caught the attention and elicited the sympathy of Colonel Ward: "Pte. W.F. Workman, 10th Battalion, was wounded on the 23rd April 1915 and returned to Canada on the 24th September. His wife was left in England with the matter of some £6 or £7 between her and utter destitution. She is urgently desirous of returning to her husband, who is now in Calgary, and I am endeavouring to arrange for an assisted passage for her to join him. As she is an expectant mother it is eminently desirable that she should rejoin her husband with as little delay as possible."[65] Fred Workman had enlisted at Valcartier in September 1914, had sought and secured permission from his commanding officer to marry in January 1915, and had been wounded at Ypres three months later. During the first year of the war, commanding officers granted permission to marry only to men who could attest that their engagement predated the war, for Canada had no interest in providing Separation Allowances to women whose affections were inspired by economic calculation. Yet it is doubtful that Fred and Louisa had indeed been engaged before he sailed from Quebec in October 1914: he had left Britain in 1901 at the age of ten (probably as a "Barnado Boy"), had worked as a farmhand first in Ontario and subsequently in Alberta, and had briefly sought his fortune in Australia before returning to Vancouver in 1912. When or how he could have met Louisa before he enlisted is a mystery. Nor is it entirely certain that she was pregnant in September 1915: their first surviving child was born in 1917.[66] So there is much about Louisa Workman's story that doesn't add up.

Nonetheless, the Workman case revealed a larger problem. Not only would Canadian wives resident in Britain understandably wish to accompany their medically discharged husbands on their return to Canada, but it would be financially disastrous to require that they remain in Britain. In the judgment of the Great War Veterans' Association, disabled returned men would, "find it almost, if not quite impossible to earn sufficient to keep themselves [in Canada], their wives in England, and at the same time save up sufficient to pay full fares to get their wives back to Canada."[67] Even an able-bodied discharged man would leave his wife in Britain in a precarious financial predicament: upon his discharge, she would no longer be eligible to receive either her Separation Allowance or her portion of her husband's Assigned Pay. Determined not to leave these women dependent upon the British public purse, Canadian authorities in London lobbied Ottawa to allow for "soldiers' wives and families [to go] back to Canada with their husbands whenever possible."[68] An Order in Council passed in April 1916 authorized the dispersal of $15,000 to assist destitute dependents arriving in Canada without the wherewithal to provide train and meal tickets home.[69] Officials in Halifax, Saint John, and Quebec were to purchase the necessary tickets and the Ministry of Militia would then collect from the demobilized soldiers the amounts advanced to their dependents. And as of August 1916, the wives of disabled or discharged Canadian soldiers could secure passage to Canada on military transports, paying only ten dollars for this rather uncomfortable privilege. To guarantee that no one abused the government's generosity, it was stressed that "It is not considered desirable that this authority should be made known or granted promiscuously, but is intended to help deserving cases."[70]

The need to repatriate the dependents of medically discharged soldiers – and the challenges this process created – grew ever more pressing as Canadian casualties sustained in 1916 and 1917 mounted appreciably. Port officials in Halifax conveyed their concern to Ottawa as early as December 1916 that many of "the wives and families of NCOS and men returning to Canada ha[d] landed at Halifax without the necessary money to pay their transportation from Halifax to their homes and, became, practically, a public charge until they arrived at their destinations."[71] The situation did not improve in 1917, when hundreds of women and children – some requiring immediate medical aid upon their arrival in Canada and many more without a penny to their name – left Britain. In April 1917, when the *Olympia* docked in Halifax, three hundred war wives sought financial assistance from the military paymaster. He supplied them with train tickets and meal tokens for their onward travels but strongly opposed authorizing any cash advances: "I hope the Department will not be unwise enough to ever authorize advances in instances of this nature. I consider that it would be illegal in the first instance and besides we will have thousands of these women returning during the summer and it would involve enormous outlay of money, and I doubt very much if it would ever be recovered." Ottawa agreed.[72] The most that returning wives could hope for was a third-class rail ticket to their ultimate destination and meal vouchers for the duration of their travels.

The financial duress evident in 1917 emerged from a convergence of circumstances. The ever-increasing cost of living in Britain made it difficult for war wives intent upon returning to Canada to save for anything beyond their ocean passage. And by 1917, with soldiers' dependents no longer allowed to return to Canada on military transport ships, their out-of-pocket expenses increased considerably, complicating their efforts to return to Canada at the same time as their husbands.[73] These new developments meant that, notwithstanding the obvious advantages of sending wives home at the same time (and to the same port of arrival) as their husbands, women and children usually travelled separately from the returning troops. The most fortunate families managed to schedule their return voyages so that everyone arrived in Canada at approximately the same time. When Ernest Blyth was repatriated to Canada in December 1917, Mabel and the children followed soon after. In the aftermath of the Halifax Harbour disaster, they had to travel by way of New York, but the entire family was back in Canada in time to mark the beginning of 1918. The Hale family was also able to coordinate their return to Canada with reasonable efficiency. Eleanor Hale had struggled to find stability in wartime England. She and her young son, Arthur, had moved at least four times following her arrival in Yorkshire in June 1915. Her husband, Percy, was seriously wounded in June 1916, hospitalized in London for several months and then assigned to a Canadian camp in the south of England before being repatriated to Canada in late March 1918.[74] Eleanor and Arthur Hale arrived in Canada – at least a week before Percy – destitute and dependent upon the good graces of the military authorities to purchase their train tickets to Victoria.[75]

However difficult their return voyage and however financially strained their family budgets, the Hales and the Blyths were among the fortunate. Other war wives, hard-pressed to scrape together the funds for even a third-class ticket to Canada, remained in Britain for months (or longer) after their husbands had been repatriated. By September 1917, Sapper A. Senier had been "back from soldiering over 12 months" but his wife and children were still in England. They had started the paperwork necessary to expedite their return several months earlier but to no avail; now Senier was eager to have them safely resettled in Toronto "before the weather sets in."[76] The desire for family reunion was widespread at the time. In 1917 and 1918 the Paymaster in London kept detailed records of repatriated Canadian soldiers with dependents still residing in Britain. A good number of these women were war brides; others were British-born parents or siblings now eager to settle in Canada; and a few were wives (and, often, their children) who had intended to emigrate to Canada before 1914 but had not yet done so when war broke out. But a significant number were wives who had travelled to Britain during the war and found themselves stranded there long after their husband had returned home.[77]

Upwards of 22,000 soldiers' dependents made the westbound voyage across the Atlantic in 1917 and 1918. Some were war widows, like Elizabeth Simons, who was living in Scotland when she sought the intervention of the Minister of Militia. Her husband had been killed in October 1916, and upon her doctor's advice she was eager to return to Canada: "As I have three little children I have been ordered by this country's doctors to get my children back to their own country."[78] Others were women who found life in wartime Britain unaffordable: as Florence Smith observed, it was all but impossible to support herself and six children on the $45 a month she received in Assigned Pay and Separation Allowance.[79] Yet others were women responding to the repeated requests of Canadian officials to return home voluntarily. Early in 1917, at the urging of the British government, Canadian authorities took steps first to stop the outmigration of Canadian dependents to Britain, and then to encourage in the strongest possible terms wives already relocated in Britain to return to Canada.

From the vantage point of British authorities, the repatriation of Canadian civilians was urgent. The winter of 1916–17 was exceptionally harsh in Britain as it was in Canada, but the deterioration of living conditions was more acute. Basic necessities – especially coal and food – were expensive and for those of limited means, scarce. Ethel Cove, an English housewife living in Harrow, worried in January 1917 about her parents' and in-laws' ability to cope with the bitter cold. Her parents were in a such a bad way – her father being forced to buy coal by the penny worth – that Ethel felt obliged to send them "2/6 [two shillings and sixpence] as it's dreadful to think of one of your own hungry and cold this weather."[80] Food shortages, evident from late 1916 onward and especially severe following the resumption of submarine warfare in February 1917, made life even more miserable. As scarcity bedevilled the lives of ordinary Britons, forcing David Lloyd George's government to consider (but ultimately postpone) the introduction of mandatory food rationing, every foreign civilian seemed a burden the British state could no longer accommodate. At the insistence of their British counterparts,

Canadian authorities in London thus urged every Canadian wife resident in Britain to return to Canada.

Rumours to this effect had circulated as early as January 1917. Stuart Tompkins told Edna that his commanding officer had requested "a return showing the names of officers and others whose wives were residing in England." He admitted that he did "not know the significance of the move" but hoped that Edna's employment would allow her to stay in England.[81] In March, Jack Ellis raised the issue with Kitty. She had read a notice in the Glasgow newspaper urging Canadian wives to return home and sought his advice. He was determined that she should stay put: "about that notice in the papers, don't you worry, if they want you to return to Canada they'll advise you & by jove if they do they should pay your fare back."[82] Canadian wives residing in Britain also received a notice enclosed with their Separation Allowance, urging that those "in the British Isles, who do not intend to permanently reside here, should, therefore consider the question of their immediate return to Canada, unless they are prepared to remain in England for at least one year after their husbands have been returned to Canada."[83] Many war wives ignored the notice, some because they feared returning to Canada at the height of the submarine campaign; others because they had successfully reintegrated into family life in Britain; yet others – Jack Ellis's insistence notwithstanding – because the government was not about to pay for dependents' return passage. It is clear, however, that significant numbers of Canadian war wives and their children did heed the government's warning and made plans to return to Canada. One sailing in May 1917 – at the height of the submarine war campaign – had only 30 men on board but 611 women, 188 children, and 69 infants; another ship sailed from Britain in September with 918 women and children on board.[84]

For many Canadian wives who found life in Britain costly and emotionally stressful, voluntary repatriation proved the better part of valour. Margaret Dickinson, Isabella Bunch, and Emma Piper almost immediately regretted their decisions to relocate to Britain. When Robert Dickinson sailed for England in April 1916, Margaret and her two young sons, then residing in Victoria, followed shortly thereafter. Several months pregnant in the spring of 1916, she made her way to Edinburgh, where life proved so difficult that by August 1916, she was longing to return to Canada, if only she could secure the necessary funds. Hoping to find the ear of a sympathetic civil servant, she wrote to explain her circumstances: "Just a line to ask if you could give me any help to get back to Victoria I left there on the second April for this country but have not been well since I came the doctor says I don't agree with this country and the quicker I get back the better I have three small children all boys the oldest is only 2 ½ years and the baby is six weeks." Having sold her home to buy her passage to Britain, she had little left in the way of private funds: "I have no way to raise it to get back unless you help me, it takes me all my time to pay my way in this country as every-thing is so dear." Moreover, she had found it impossible to settle in one place, moving from Edinburgh to Newcastle. As she so plaintively noted, "when I am not keeping well it makes it more difficult."[85] Margaret Dickinson secured an advance of $20 on her Separation Allowance "to assist passage to Canada" and returned to Victoria in November 1916.

Isabella Bunch arrived in London in the spring of 1916, finding temporary accommodation for herself and her three-year-old daughter with her sister-in-law in the predominantly working-class London suburb of Walthamstow. She soon found separate accommodations, no doubt to relieve the pressure her presence imposed on her sister-in-law's hospitality, but Isabella's stay in England was short, financially strained, and emotionally distraught. When her husband was killed in October 1916 and her budget was stretched to breaking point, she had little reason to remain in England. In January 1917 she opted to return to Canada, requesting (and receiving) a $40 advance on her Separation Allowance to cover her travel expenses back to Winnipeg.[86] Emma Piper also found life in Britain with three small children a constant struggle. She had returned to her family in Cheshire in October 1916, three months after her husband enlisted in Edmonton. And even though she gave her mother's address as her place of residence, she did not live there: "We have not had a minute's comfort since we came I have been in and out of lodgings nine times as no one will let me have rooms for long owing to the children's noise and I cannot make dummys of them and they have had cold ever since we came and nothing seems to cure them." Unlike Isabella Bunch and Margaret Dickinson, Emma Piper failed to secure the advance she needed to cover her travel costs. Her timing was not opportune, for she submitted her request only days before the German navy resumed its campaign of unrestricted submarine warfare and at a time when Canadian authorities in London were no longer authorized to approve advances on Separation Allowances. Emma and her three unhappy children remained in Britain until July 1917.[87]

Emma Piper's return home was probably as miserable as her months in the cramped rooming houses of Cheshire. This, at least, is the strong impression conveyed by another Canadian wife who sailed from London in September 1918. Florence MacKenzie left England against her better judgment and at considerable personal expense. The Canadian authorities in London had, she contended, "frightened a lot

of us into returning at once at the risk of our lives and children." The
ocean crossing, which depleted her savings, was marred by bad food and
worse weather: even though she had paid more than £7 for a third-class
ticket (and half-fare for her child), she was convinced that the two of
them "did not eat 10/- worth of food. It was the worst food I ever had
in my life, the whole voyage we had to buy biscuits and ginger ale, that
is what we lived on. All the other passengers can tell the same story."[88]
Emily Smallman encountered similar difficulties when she also heeded
the government's request to return to Canada before the end of the
war. She had relocated to Wales, where her elderly mother was in poor
health and she could offer her mother much-needed help, hoping to
be closer to her husband and two sons, all three of whom served in
the CEF. Following the deaths of her sons, she would have preferred to
remain in Wales while her husband was still stationed in England, but
when the government implored Canadian women to return home, she
obeyed: "to help the government in their work I was quite willing to
return, expecting my husband to return with me." Emily Smallman's
sense of patriotic duty cost her dearly: travelling at short notice from
Wales to London, sailing from there to Quebec, and then travelling by
train to Winnipeg (where she was temporarily laid up due to the flu)
and then onwards to Souris, she found herself $115.35 out of pocket. Yet
she was ineligible for reimbursement for any expenses beyond her rail
fare: only dependents who returned to Canada after the Armistice were
to be compensated for their full expenses. As Emily Smallman later so
justly wrote to the Ministry of Militia and Defence: "Those who have
done all they could for their country and came back when the danger
was so great on the seas, to try to help the government should have the
same benefits as those who stayed in England, till the danger was over."[89]

Emily Smallman's complaint was well founded and much repeated.
She and others who at their own expense had returned to Canada prior
to the Armistice were outraged when women who remained in Britain
until the end of the war received free return passage. Emily Smallman's
plea for retroactive reimbursement was polite; Mary McLuskie's was
more indignant. A resident of Vancouver, she had returned to Scotland
during the war and had then left Britain in September 1918. Her husband,
loath to contemplate an even longer separation than they had already
endured, urged her to act on the government's advice that she return
at once, for "if he got back to Canada he would not like it if [she] had
to stay in the old country for a year or two after he got back." Having
done what the government (and her husband) had urged her to do, she
now wanted "to understand why you were pressing me to get back to
Canada, and then when a lot of us came back you bring the rest back

free, we all had to come in a transport just the same as the dependents are coming now, why were we not brought free, please explain it to me."[90] Many women who returned prior to November 1918 had had to scrimp and save to pay the costs of their return travel. Steerage-class accommodation had more than doubled in price, from the "charity rate" of £3 to £7/10 for adults and half fare for children. The cabin rate, which afforded noticeably better accommodation, was £13.[91] Many a returning wife discovered this only when it was too late to change her plans. A Mrs Christie of Toronto, attentive to the repeated injunctions to return to Canada, arrived in Liverpool with her three children believing that her fare would be only £3. When informed that it was in fact now £7/10, she had no choice but to pay the higher fares for transportation that was decidedly inferior: she was assigned a "Cabin ... with not a seat to set on or a looking glass or a glass of water in the Cabin for the Children." As her irate sister-in-law exclaimed in her letter to the ministry: "Is that the way that a Woman is Serve when her Husband is in France and Cannot protect He interest?"[92]

Wives who had borne these additional costs would perhaps have been less indignant if the women who had ignored the government's repeated messages had in fact been forced to stay in Britain long after their husbands had been demobilized, but the government never acted on that threat and began the repatriation of Canadian civilians within weeks of the armistice. From November 1918 through the summer of 1919, upwards of fifty thousand women and children set sail for Canada.[93] Some – and perhaps the majority – of these dependents were war brides, but a significant number were wives and children who had relocated to Britain for the duration of the war. Women of independent means returned to Canada in the comfort to which they were accustomed. Dorothy Morris, of Westmount, Montreal, expected reimbursement for travel expenses she incurred upon her return voyage from London to Montreal. In addition to the £13 she paid for her own passage on the SS *Northland* and £6/10 for her child, she sought "£1.10.00 in tips while on the steamer" and $9.30 for rail transportation and meals from Halifax to Montreal.[94] Other returning wives had to make do with steerage accommodation in ships ill-equipped for the transport of pregnant wives and seasick children. Indeed, as the scandal that emerged in late December 1918 following the arrival in port of the *Scandinavian* made clear, conditions on board were abysmal, sanitary arrangements grossly inadequate, and the food deplorable. A report filed in January 1919 admitted as much: "The quarters are cramped, congested, stuffy and being located in the forward and aft sections of the ship, the motion is extreme during rough weather. The propeller, when out of water, creates a sickening vibration, which puts the strongest organism to a severe test. I have known strong men to complain bitterly of the shaking up they experience followed by an acute head ache when forced to remain in these quarters during rough weather." Nor was the staff assigned to steerage class passengers uniformly capable or compassionate: "The class of Stewards and Stewardesses in the steerage is most indifferent. Few of them are trained and altogether they are not the sort to bring comfort to nervous, ailing women and sea-sick children."[95]

Canadian authorities took steps to improve conditions: representatives of the YWCA, who were assigned to each crossing, conducted daily inspections to guarantee that sanitary conditions were at least minimally acceptable; on-board entertainment helped pass the time (although at least one observer noted wryly that recently reunited husbands and wives had little interest in such distractions); and passenger surveys revealed general satisfaction. Or so the YWCA inspectors contended: "in 3rd class, rooms, alleyways, lavatories, etc., were cleaned and disinfected each morning." Families did complain that children who had to be vaccinated for smallpox before being allowed to enter Canada suffered the ill effects of vaccination while on board, but in other regards reported that the crossings were uneventful.[96] Other reports were less sanguine. As late as April 1919, months after the *Scandinavian* had exposed the horrors of steerage-class accommodations, the Superintendent of Immigration remained concerned about sanitary conditions on board the ships routinely used to return troops and their families to Canada.

Some of these problems were the inevitable consequences of an enormous task undertaken in the dead of winter. Each of the three phases of repatriation was complicated by bad weather, compromised by the amenities available to steerage-class passengers, and confounded by the logistics of disembarkation. When the *Melita* was scheduled to sail from Liverpool in March 1919, the weather was so foul – "snowing and blowing a gale, a regular old-time 'Western' blizzard" – that the ship could not approach the embarkation station. All passengers "had to be moved by wagonettes approximately 3 miles to the dock where they were able to board the ship."[97] Once on board, even on the better class of ships, passengers in the lower decks found that lavatory facilities were grossly inadequate. The *Megantic*, for example, had no lavatories below the middle deck, and yet it was considered "somewhat better than several of the ships" commissioned to return Canadians home.[98] Steerage-class passengers seeking fresh air were restricted to decks that lacked deck chairs or shelter from the rain. When they received permission to use the deck chairs reserved for cabin passengers, those who had paid for cabin-class accommodation objected and even this minor concession to comfort was abandoned. Not surprisingly, soldiers complained that their wartime sacrifices appeared to matter little to those who treated the wives and children of rank-and-file returning men with such contempt.[99] Similar distinctions between families able to afford cabin accommodation (almost invariably the wives and children of officers) and those confined to steerage class resurfaced at the time of debarkation. When the *Melita* docked at Saint John at 3 p.m. on 5 April 1919, cabin passengers' arrival documents were quickly processed and their disembarkation complete by 4:45 p.m. Only then could women and children in steerage class move slowly through the disembarkation sheds, hoping to secure their luggage and reunite with their husbands in time to catch the last train leaving Saint John after midnight.

As of May 1919, trans-Atlantic ships docked in Quebec City rather than the Maritimes. The first to arrive, the *Metagama*, carried 1,136 third-class passengers, including 220 children and 48 infants. A report submitted by the YWCA representative who accompanied the ship acknowledged that the voyage had been a "strenuous one." She was of the opinion, however, that "the people on the whole were content and were given as little opportunity as could be for dwelling on grievances, passing or real." She highlighted the musical entertainment offered on board, the creation of a lending library, story hour for children travelling third class, and one man's generous donation of five pounds to tide over the families whose Separation Allowances for April had not been delivered prior to departure. She insisted that many passengers expressed their sincere appreciation for all she had done for them.[100] A very different story emerged from disgruntled returning men who did not hesitate to voice their complaints to anyone who would listen, including local and national representatives of the Canadian Patriotic Fund. The men resented that their wives and children had been assigned to berths on the lowest deck, where ventilation was poor, the movement of the ship most noticeable, sanitary facilities deplorable, the food poor, and the ship's stewards corrupt.[101] Knowing that the meals available in third class were far from filling, the stewards had taken advantage of their passengers by selling supplemental rations – meat pies and French fries – at exorbitant prices.

To add insult to injury, the special train carriages laid on for soldiers and their families were grossly inadequate. They were often dirty and the seats were slatted boards with no upholstery. Because there were no privacy curtains around the berths, women had either to sleep in their clothes or undress in public. The absence of lights in the lavatories made it difficult for women to care for babies and young children.[102] Recognizing that passengers assigned to colonist cars could not travel a thousand miles or more without blankets and pillows to soften the slatted seats, the department of Immigration and Colonization contracted with the CPR to provide the families of returning men with these basic supplies. In some cases, however, civilian passengers appropriated both the bedding and the berths assigned to returning women and children, forcing the soldiers' dependents to take seats in day coaches; in other instances, blankets were available but had not been cleaned; and at least one shipment of blankets and pillows, heading east from the Prairies to be cleaned in Montreal, was delayed by the Winnipeg General Strike.[103]

The repatriation of returning men, new brides, and the wives and children who had temporarily relocated to Britain was a logistical task of unprecedented scale, and for passengers confined to third-class accommodation, far from comfortable. When women and children, having endured an ocean voyage of ten or eleven days, had to wait hours (and sometimes overnight) before they were given permission to disembark; when the trains that carried them home were uncomfortable and poorly outfitted; when, as occasionally happened, they arrived late at night into a railway station with no one on hand to greet them, homecoming was a gruelling and often bitter experience. Yet repatriation succeeded in bringing home thousands of men who had fought overseas and the wives and children who had found a temporary home in "the Old Country."

Most surely hoped that the future would be easier than the immediate past; that the misery they had suffered and the separation they had endured were well and truly behind them. They fervently believed postwar Canada would be a place of peace and plenty. For some this was indeed the case. But not for all. As crowds thronged railway stations across Canada in the spring and summer of 1919, welcoming returning soldiers and acclaiming the victory they had helped secure, lost in the shadows of national celebration were women recently widowed and wives accompanying wounded husbands whose compromised health would condemn them to premature death. There were men who feared that the war had irrevocably ruined their marriages, and others who opted not to return home at all. Widowed, deserted, and divorced women: these were the domestic casualties of wartime separation.

PART THREE

Après la guerre

Après la guerre

The Postwar Lives of Canadian War Wives

In 1919 May Timmins would have considered herself more fortunate than many, for both her husband – and her marriage – had survived the war. George Timmins returned to Oshawa in February 1919 and, it would seem, adjusted well to civilian life, their concerns about the prospects for returned men notwithstanding. During the war he and May had both worried that the men who remained in Canada would benefit from the riches generated by a wartime economy, while those who had enlisted would have a hard time re-establishing themselves upon demobilization. George refused to give in to despair: "Say hon. don't you let the fact that so and so is doing so well worry you that don't amount to a row of pins. You bet we'll be all right. If good jobs are scarce I guess I'll be able to hunt one."[1] His optimism was not misplaced. Census records of 1921 show the Timmins family residing in the house on Golf Street in Oshawa where they would remain for the rest of their lives. George had secured a full-time job, supplemented by a part-time position as the census taker for their district; May was a housewife; and the three children were in school. In an age when children often went out to work at fourteen, Winnie, having turned fifteen, was training to become a stenographer.[2] Although May had briefly contemplated taking a paying job in 1917 – a prospect George dreaded and urged against – the domestic routine of a male breadwinner, well-established before the war, re-asserted itself upon his return.

There had probably been some difficult moments of readjustment. Throughout the war, George had consoled himself with thoughts of home, of domestic happiness, and – perhaps more than anything else – of Mollie, their youngest child, who was not yet two when he sailed for Europe. In December 1916, shortly after arriving in France and in gloomy anticipation of a cheerless Christmas, he dreamed: "[I was] home and you were so pleased to see me Mollie was in bed you said so

I went upstairs and woke her and she jumped up with both arms out and shouts 'Daddy'. Say I did'nt want to wake up I tell you. You'd laugh, if you were here sometimes."[3] It is unlikely, however, that Mollie greeted him with such exuberance when he returned home three years later. Like most children whose fathers went to war, she had "written" him notes and, at her mother's urging, had sent him her love. If she remembered her father at all, she surely would not have recognized him as the now greying man who stepped across their threshold in February 1919.

Soldiers in all combatant nations worried that upon their return home – *après la guerre* – their children would not know them and, their best efforts notwithstanding, this was often the sad truth. Elderly French citizens, interviewed many years after the war, still recalled the emotional dislocation attendant upon their fathers' return from war: who was this stranger in their midst, and why did his often brusque and intimidating orders so quickly supplant their mother's gentler tones? One young girl, an infant when her father left for war and only five when he returned, could not curb her tongue: "I prayed to the good Lord that you would return home from the war, and now I'm going to pray that you go back there."[4] Let us hope that Mollie Timmins was somewhat more tactful, even if she may have had similar feelings. She would, no doubt, have gradually accustomed herself to the new routines of family life, as would May and the older children. But as Manon Pignon reminds us, we should resist the urge to romanticize the return to domestic life of men who had been away at war, connected to wife and children primarily by the lifeline of regular correspondence. Homecomings were not always the imagined blissful reunions that had sustained the spirits of men consigned to perpetually damp, mud-filled, rat-infested trenches. And if this was the case for European soldiers, who had at least enjoyed the intermittent luxury of returning home on leave, how much more wrenching might the homecoming be for Canadian families who had been separated for two years or more?

Whatever challenges the Timmins family encountered in the immediate postwar years, many war wives would have envied them their relative economic comfort, and countless war widows would have looked wistfully upon George and May's marital reunion. Even though some (and perhaps most) returning veterans stepped successfully into their civilian lives, others faced a future of economic uncertainty, aggravated in the early twenties by a worldwide recession whose scope and severity felt very real to those who lost their jobs, fell into debt, or scrambled to make ends meet. Only the even more acute crisis of the Great Depression would efface from popular memory the misery of those hard times.

Desperate to keep families together and the rent collector at bay, the most economically afflicted couples continued to struggle through the early years of the postwar era. Others grappled – not always success-fully – with the lingering and often pernicious psychological effects of wartime service. Some men drank too much; others suffered shell shock so severe as to require their hospitalization; yet others had contracted venereal diseases which, if not fully cured, would have endangered the health of their wives and the lives of unborn children. This surely was not the fate that wartime wives, who had sustained themselves and their children with the promise of better times after the war, had imagined. For war widows the future was even more uncertain, the prospects for happiness even more precarious.

☙❧

It is probably not true – Tolstoy's aphorism notwithstanding – that "all happy families are alike." Some find happiness in the joy of children, others in marital companionship and mutual respect; some couples find meaning and satisfaction in the daily routines of a familiar community, yet others explore a world far afield. All, no doubt, experience occasional (or frequent) hardship and intermittent heartache; children fall ill, jobs disappear, partners succumb to sickness. Yet their marriages endure. This is the story of resilience that emerges from the postwar experiences of some of the more fortunate couples we have encountered here. Stuart and Edna Tompkins returned to Edmonton in 1917 and a year later, as the Entente powers prepared to dispatch an expeditionary force to Russia, Stuart volunteered for military service again. His brief encounter with Russia – a nation in the throes of civil war amid the Bolshevik consoli-dation of power – forever transformed his postwar life. Having spent the 1920s as a teacher in Lethbridge and, subsequently as the superintendent of schools in the Yukon, he embarked in 1928 on a graduate career in History at the University of Chicago. Upon completing his degree, he and Edna moved to Norman, Oklahoma, where Stuart earned a reputation as an expert in Russian history and served on the university faculty for the next twenty-five years.[5] Arthur and Alice Leighton were less intrepid: upon demobilization, they re-established themselves in Nanaimo, where Arthur resumed his law practice and Alice, as was fitting for a woman of her social standing, devoted herself to many important public and philanthropic causes.[6] Perhaps they crossed paths on occasion with the Mayse family, who also found themselves in Nanaimo in the early 1920s, when Will took up a living as a Baptist minister. But his young son's recollections of a rather rough and tumble life in the gritty coal-mining town suggest that the Mayses and the Leightons probably moved in rather different circles after all.[7]

Money was certainly scarce in the preacher's home, as it was (and always had been) for Frank Maheux's family until he secured a permanent position with the Ottawa post office in the late 1920s.[8] During the war he had read of a government plan to provide returning soldiers with free land and the means to economic self-sufficiency. He was sure this would be their ticket to a postwar life of ease: "I see in the papers the Canadian Government will give us land … I might go farming."[9] Perhaps it was for the best that he abandoned this dream following his return to Canada in 1919, for the rumour of free land was – like many rumours – only partially true. The Soldiers' Settlement Acts of 1917 and 1919 did disburse some land at no cost as homesteads to returning soldiers, but much of the most desirable arable land was available only for purchase. Whether a soldier had to buy his quarter section or acquired it as a homestead, the Soldiers' Settlement Board provided him with a loan of up to $3,000 to cover the cost of equipment, seed, and livestock. A well-intentioned plan, the Soldiers' Settlement scheme soon turned sour. Many of the veterans who tried their hand at farming acquired poor land at high prices, assumed unwieldy debts, and ran straight into the depression of the early 1920s.[10] George and Maggie Ormsby learned first-hand the limits and liabilities of the Soldiers' Settlement Act. When George returned to Canada, having been seriously wounded in 1916, he and Maggie settled once again in the Okanagan Valley, hoping to make a life for themselves and a future for their children. Like many veterans who acquired land through the Soldiers' Settlement Board, they laboured to make their allotment productive. Although more fortunate than many in comparable circumstances, they persevered in the face of economic adversity and George's lingering ill-health. Life was not easy in the Okanagan, but the Ormsbys made a go of it, ensuring that their children would thrive in careers well suited to their intellectual talents.[11]

Whether they hoped to make a living on the land or opted for life in the big city, many veterans and their families encountered a postwar life of modest prospects at best, and dire poverty at worst. In Toronto, where jobs were scarce and affordable housing even scarcer, real misery plagued many veterans' households.[12] In November 1921, the chaplain of the Toronto branch of the Soldiers' Civil Re-establishment Department reported on several "typical" cases he and his colleagues had encountered in the previous months. Returned men and their wives and children were living in shacks, almost entirely unfurnished and offering scant protection from the elements. One man, thirty-seven years old, unemployed and of miserable appearance, had had to relinquish his two young children to the care of the Soldiers' Aid Commission. For want of proper furniture, he and his wife slept on the floor. Another equally lamentable case found a forty-two-year-old returned man, his wife, and six children living in "a shack which he [was] trying to improve." But his pension of $25.50 a month made any real improvements beyond their means: the interior rooms were separated by partitions constructed of "cardboard from shredded wheat boxes." And there was the case of a thirty-one-year-old man – so worn down by the hardships of war that he could have passed for fifty – living with his wife and five children, all under fifteen, in a three-room shack on Yonge Street. Lacking proper bedding, the children had to "sleep on old clothes" and the husband, whose war debilities made it difficult for him to work, had to "pawn [his] wife's wedding ring to get car fare." These men, the chaplain attested, were all hard-workers and of good character, but they had fallen on very hard times and each case was "worthy of every consideration."[13]

The physical and psychological effects of wartime service made readjustment to civilian life especially challenging for some returning veterans and, by extension, their wives and children. A particularly poignant case came to the attention of the Toronto clergy in January 1921. A returned man had enlisted in late 1914 against his wife's better judgment; upon his demobilization in 1919 he had been ineligible for any pension beyond the wartime demobilization gratuity. He soon discovered that "the long years of service, trial, hardship and frequent exhaustions of body and mind in the mud and slime and rain in France had sapped his energy and burned out his reserves." An experienced stonemason, he had "found that he was incapable of carrying on as before or competing in his trade with those whose strength was greater than his." Unable to hold a job, despite his best efforts, he and then his wife, who had gone "to work in a factory to support the family," became casualties of the great recession of 1920. In the weeks before Christmas, when the family fell behind on the rent and their only income was "what was earned by the ten-year-old selling papers after dark upon the streets and before daylight," the bailiff came to call, twice. He first compelled the sale of most of the family furniture – leaving only "one bed for the family of five, a table, a stove, and a few chairs of very inferior quality"; and then, on a second occasion, threatened eviction if an outstanding debt of $18 was not immediately paid. Only the generosity of a kind-hearted bureaucrat from the Department of the Militia, who paid the rent and passed the hat among his colleagues at the Masonic Lodge, saved the family from eviction in the dead of winter.[14]

Physical ailments sustained in active service could sap the energy and make regular employment a challenge. A dependence on alcohol, often developed during the war and persisting upon demobilization, afflicted many returning veterans – although it is impossible to know how many – and made the postwar lives of husbands, wives, and children miserable. Albert Jesson, for one, died of acute alcohol poisoning while on furlough in Winnipeg, after drinking rubbing alcohol obtained from a Turkish bath in one of the city's rougher neighbourhoods. Whether his alcohol consumption was an attempt to deal with the psychological effects of war service – he had enlisted in 1914, been gassed at the Second Battle of Ypres, and wounded at Festubert – or was, as one doctor opined, simply the habit of a "typical alcoholic" mattered little to the pension board, which denied his wife's application for a pension.[15] Bert Mason also struggled to control his appetite for alcohol and saw his marriage founder as a result. As Jonathan Vance notes, when Mason returned to small-town Ontario in 1919, he "drifted from farm to farm, turning to alcohol to soothe his restlessness … His war bride hated Canada and soon took their daughter back to England," apparently severing all further contact with her husband.[16] In another case, cited by Veronica Strong-Boag, a family member reflected on the tragic after-effects of one man's military service: "We thought the war would have done great things for B … but indeed the effect seems to have been quite the reverse. Since his return he has been drinking heavily, and has been horrible to M … in every way. She could get a divorce if she wished but she has not the money, in the first place, and she dreads the publicity for the children's sake."[17] Isabella Petrie found herself in a similar predicament. By the time of her husband's discharge in 1919 he was suffering from acute alcoholism, unable (or not inclined) to work, and ill-disposed to married life. He drank too much, accumulated debts, and abandoned the family's Alberta farm. A brief reconciliation was for naught; by December 1923 he was gone again, refusing to provide any support for his ailing wife or young son.[18]

Alex Petrie suffered from more than one wartime affliction. Seriously wounded in 1917, he had been reassigned to base duties in England for the remainder of the war. In November 1918, he was hospitalized with syphilis, contracted (according to his police testimony) from a liaison with a married woman in Folkestone.[19] He was just one of a dismaying number of married man far from home to contract a venereal infection while on active service. Indeed, Canadian military and medical officials had been concerned since the earliest months of the war that the CEF's fighting strength was being profoundly compromised by what amounted to an epidemic of venereal disease. The problem arose almost as soon as the First Contingent arrived in England, having sailed from Quebec in October 1914. Well-paid and by no means immune to the charms of local women, Canadian soldiers found plenty of opportunities to be led astray. By the end of 1914, four hundred venereal cases were being treated each month and in the next year fully 28.7 percent of men serving in the CEF were diagnosed with a venereal infection. By the end of the war, official statistics calculated that the CEF had suffered 66,083 cases. As Jay Cassel has pointed out, that number needs to be interpreted with care: some soldiers were treated more than once, while others somehow escaped detection altogether.[20] But if an infection rate of 15.8 percent is more an indication of a widespread problem than an entirely accurate count, it is significant nonetheless. Like their Australian and New Zealand allies, Canadian soldiers serving overseas were (perhaps not surprisingly) much more likely to contract a venereal infection than their British and French comrades-in-arms, who had the chance to spend their leave with their families.[21]

Because venereal disease placed otherwise healthy men out of front-line service for up to two months, it was a bane to armies. It was also a curse to married couples, whose unborn children might suffer its baleful effects; and a subject of anguished professional and public debate in all combatant nations during the war years.[22] In France, where the birthrate at the beginning of the twentieth century was uncommonly low and the mortality rate inflicted by the war uncommonly high, the prospect of stillbirths, miscarriages, and children born blind – all possible consequences of venereal infection – was especially alarming. In nations with more robust birthrates, including Canada, eugenicists feared that an epidemic of venereal disease would lead to "race suicide." If Anglo-Canadian soldiers infected their wives or fiancées with a venereal disease upon their return home, an entire generation of children might be born with lifelong debilities.[23] To mitigate the effects of this threat to public health, Canadian military authorities took steps to educate men in uniform about the dangers of untreated venereal infections and to subject all returning troops to medical examination before approving their passage home. Federal and provincial governments funded clinics to treat venereal infections, compelled the treatment of those known to be infected, and punished with substantial fines anyone who knowingly infected a partner with a sexually transmitted disease.[24]

To protect the women of Canada from the unfortunate consequences of their husbands' (or fiancés') transgressions, Canadian military authorities in London became convinced that modern technology – so effective in encouraging enlistment in the first place – could also be used to remind men in uniform of their obligations to hearth and home. Whereas the French army required its troops to watch slide shows sparing no details about the symptoms and consequences of venereal infection, the British and Canadian forces offered the same lesson in narrative form.[25] Brent Brenyo demonstrates how *Whatsoever a Man Soweth*, a silent film produced and distributed in 1917, impressed upon soldiers their moral responsibility to remain monogamous. The film traced the paths of three Canadian soldiers – two single, one married – on leave in London. Although "Dick" successfully resisted repeated propositions from importunate prostitutes, his two comrades, "Harry" and "Tom," were less stalwart in the face of temptation. For Tom the consequences were especially tragic: having refused to seek professional treatment for the symptoms of syphilis that appeared following one assignation, he returned home to Canada where his wife, unaware that he had also infected her, gave birth to a sickly, blind infant. Brent Brenyo observes that "the film exhorts soldiers not to take a chance with illicit sex and instead promotes a 'culturally appropriate' form of sex – monogamous marriage with an emphasis on childbearing."[26]

Were the intemperate married Toms, whether of the CEF or other armies, more likely than the resolute single Dicks to fall for the seductive promise of casual sex? Historians differ widely in their judgment. Some argue that it was the young, single, and perhaps still innocent men who patronized the prostitutes of French brothels and London street corners: after all, it would be a terrible thing to die a virgin![27] Others suggest that married men were more inclined than their single comrades to seek out casual liaisons, accustomed as they were to regular sexual relations.[28] A dramatic increase in venereal infections among the wives of French soldiers suggests that married men were by no means always abstinent when away from home.[29] Canadian military officials feared that their married troops were also susceptible to temptation. It is possible, however, that the married men of the CEF were not as promiscuous as *Whatever a Man Soweth* implied. A sample of 187 men, drawn from the database of married men who enlisted in Manitoba, suggests that married men on active service were less likely than their single comrades to be diagnosed with and treated for a venereal infection. In a fighting force contending with a 15.8 percent rate of venereal infection, only six of these 187 married men received treatment for either gonorrhea or syphilis; of those six, two had contracted the diseases prior to the war. Perhaps this sample under-represents the reality, but it certainly suggests that long before 1917, when Canadian troops were reminded of the dire consequences of sexual license, the married men in their ranks were more attentive to their marriage vows than the unfortunate Alex Petrie (or, indeed, Frank Maheux).

The war weighed on some men – and, inevitably, their families – in other ways, too. Soldiers suffering from shell shock found readjustment to civilian life difficult or even impossible. The *Toronto Daily Star* calculated in December 1918 that there were perhaps five thousand Canadian soldiers suffering from shell shock; recent scholarship has shown that probably three times that number, constituting 2.5 percent of all enlistments, returned from war with nerves strained to the breaking point.[30] Desmond Morton and Glenn Wright cite the case of Arthur Tooke, who had been buried alive during a German barrage and had suffered "a fair case of 'shell-shock'" as a consequence. When he returned to Canada, having been medically discharged in England, he struggled to support his family on the miserly military pension of $2.66 a week. "Only a good-hearted employer in an Ingersoll foundry kept the Tookes from starvation."[31] In even more extreme cases, returned men required permanent institutionalization. In May 1917, for instance, a soldier whose family received support from the Manitoba Patriotic Fund returned to Canada suffering the severe effects of shell shock; his wife and child, who had spent the previous year or more with family in Ireland, joined him in Winnipeg two months later. They did their best to support themselves and re-establish the domestic routine that had characterized their pre-war lives: they rented an apartment, he found menial work at the CPR yards, and she gave birth to their second child in the summer of 1918. Their caseworker noted, however, that his "nerves [were] badly shattered and [he was] not accountable for his actions at times." He could not work regularly and by late 1919 it was evident that he needed permanent, in-patient medical care. In January 1920, his Patriotic Fund caseworker concluded: "This is one of the most distressing cases on our books. The man has been transferred to Selkirk and the wife states that the Dr. there has told her that her husband is in the worst condition of any patient there."[32] He might well have been the most adversely afflicted victim of shell shock treated at the Selkirk Asylum, but many others were similarly tormented. Mark Humphries has determined that by 1921 seventeen hundred veterans were "under care for 'nervous' or 'mental' conditions at government hospitals."[33] If married men were no more – and no less – susceptible to shell shock than their unmarried brothers-in-arms, then it is reasonable to conclude that more than three hundred married couples experienced the debilitating and disruptive effects of psychological trauma brought on by wartime service.

Clinical psychologists who study post-traumatic stress disorder (the contemporary iteration of shell shock) recognize that a veteran's family – his wife and children – are often its secondary victims. Wives who have to manage a family home, ever alert to their husbands' irascible outbursts, experience high levels of "secondary traumatization"; in the most extreme cases they and their children are more likely to be victims of domestic violence than the wives of veterans unaffected by PTSD.[34] Could this explain the tragic case of John Buchanan Pirie who in 1924 murdered his wife and two children? Pirie had served during the war in the Royal Flying Corps and relocated to Canada in 1921, settling in Ottawa with his wife and young daughters. Physically disabled as a result of war injuries and allocated a British pension of only £84 per year (less than $400), Pirie tried his hand at various ventures, and failed at all of them. He was not fit enough to be a travelling salesman, his clerical position with the Ottawa electric company paid – in his words – "starvation wages," and lacking prior experience, he found no business willing to train him on the job. Unemployed, disabled, and deeply in debt, he concluded that his condition was hopeless, his prospects non-existent, and his family destined for a life of destitution. Convinced that it was "too expensive to live, and too risky for [his] wife and family" to live without him – unprotected women would, he feared, be preyed upon by rapacious men – he decided that he, his wife, and the little girls would be better off dead. As he explained in what he intended to be a suicide note: "Rather than seeing my wife and children starving, and absolutely lacking for the necessities of life, and allowing my children to grow up handicapped by my inability to clothe and feed them I have decided to cut the slow torture of living short." He suffocated his daughters, bashed in his wife's skull and then strangled her. When it came time to take his own life, his nerve failed him. Aghast at what he had done, he turned himself in to the local constabulary and at the end of 1924 stood trial for murder. The Great War Veterans' Association, a contingent of war widows, a local spiritualist, and a psychiatrist convinced that Pirie suffered from manic depression all came to his defence, for although his crime was abominable his plight as a veteran unable to secure a respectable living was surely a tragic indictment of postwar society. Condemned to death in March 1925, Pirie had his execution stayed at the last moment.[35] The Pirie case was certainly exceptional: very few veterans suffered such debilitating depression; and no other family suffered such dire consequences. Yet the Pirie case, when placed at the far end of a spectrum of postwar readjustment, reveals how fortunate George and May Timmins – and many other reunited couples – truly were. Domestic re-establishment was certainly possible, but it was by no means guaranteed.

☙❧

For the more than thirteen thousand Canadian war wives who were widowed during or shortly after the war, a return to the domestic life they had long imagined was all but impossible. War widows and their children were living reminders of and memorials to the men who had died. As such, they earned the support of Canada's veterans' associations, the public advocacy of journalists ever attentive to a widow's miserable lot, and the esteem of the nation: theirs was a privileged position, second only to that of bereaved mothers, in the cultural landscape of postwar Canadian commemoration.[36] This respect did not, however, secure a postwar life of material comfort or psychological ease. Welcome though the federally funded widows' pensions were, they were usually too small to ensure Canada's war widows an independent, self-sufficient existence. As they had done during the war, these women depended upon the emotional and economic support of family, relying on networks of kinship and community to sustain them through the trauma of bereavement and the trials of single parenthood. Some found support close at hand; others returned to Britain; and thousands remarried.

Bereavement could come at any time, as Jennie Hillyer learned in March 1917, when her husband, Henry, was killed ten days before Canada's big offensive at Vimy. All of Jennie's hopes that he would be home in time to help her prepare for the next winter were for naught. Ezra Cooper also survived the "big shows" of 1917 only to be killed in action on a relatively unremarkable day in mid-November. There was clearly no guarantee that a quiet day on the Western Front would protect the men who served there or the women who waited for them at home. But not surprisingly casualty rates spiked when the Canadian Corps was directly engaged in pitched battle: in the last months of 1916 at the Somme; in the three campaigns of 1917 – Vimy in April, Hill 70 in August, and Passchendaele; and in the famous (and subsequently much disputed) Hundred Days campaign that ended the war. Because married men had responded in especially large numbers to the recruitment campaigns of early 1916, many had arrived in Europe in time to participate in, and become casualties of, these major Canadian campaigns. Laurie Rogers, who was killed on 30 October 1917, was one of at least 2,500 married Canadian men who died in 1917; another thousand or more fell in the last two months of the war. The year 1917 proved the mettle of the CEF; but it also brought anxiety and grief to parents, wives, and children across Canada.

Many a war widow would discover that the way her husband died – as opposed to simply *that* he had died – had significant (and sometimes disastrous) consequences for her economic well-being. She would qualify for a widow's pension only if her husband's death could be directly attributed to his military service. If there was no doubt or ambiguity as to the cause and circumstances of a soldier's death – as was the case for Bert Ewen or Laurie Rogers, both of whom were killed by direct shell fire – then his widow's pension would be quickly granted. But military medical records remind us that soldiers also succumbed to pneumonia, nephritis, influenza and a host of other diseases aggravated by the miserable conditions of life in the front lines. Indeed, some men died without ever seeing combat: a weak heart, untreated epilepsy, or accidents (sometimes caused by an excess of alcohol) claimed their lives far from the fighting lines. Whether a soldier died in the maelstrom of battle, in a casualty clearing station behind the lines, or in camp at Shorncliffe, the emotional effects of his death would – in most cases, at least – have been the same. But would Isobel Kell, Elizabeth Jones, and Lilian Atha also qualify for a widow's pension, given the circumstances of their husbands' deaths? John Kell suffered a fatal head injury when he climbed on a gun limber while drunk, fell off, and was crushed under its wheels. Arthur Jones died of a heart attack while still in training at Shorncliffe: the inquest reported that he had been sitting on the edge of his cot, stood up, grabbed the tent pole, and fell over on his side. He was thirty-eight years old. A weak heart also killed Walter Atha, who died in the Winnipeg General Hospital in May 1918. Although he had been declared fit for overseas service when he enlisted in March 1916, chronic health problems became evident following his arrival in England: he was hospitalized, diagnosed with myocarditis, and repatriated to Canada, never having served in France. In all three cases, the pension board granted widows' pensions.[37]

The pension board was often criticized for its less generous judgments. Because shell shock was not always attributed to the stresses of war, the widow of the Manitoba soldier who was institutionalized in the Selkirk asylum was denied a pension on the grounds that his disability could be "traced to causes other than [the] war."[38] So, too, for Marjorie Jesson, whose husband died of acute alcohol poisoning while on furlough in Winnipeg. Neither of these cases generated the public outrage and newspaper coverage caused by the piteous case of Mrs Lily Tarrington, a widow with nine children, whose application for a pension following her husband's death in April 1918 failed to persuade the pension commissioners. The *Toronto Daily Star*, always vigilant in its defence of impoverished widows, first brought the case to the attention of its readers a week after James Tarrington died in a Toronto hospital. The case for a pension was by no means clearcut; Ottawa contended that Tarrington's war-related injuries were not so severe as to impede his ability to work and support his family following his discharge from the army in October 1916. Mrs Tarrington begged to differ. Her husband had been gassed while serving in France, directly contributing, in her judgment, to his lingering ill health and, ultimately, to his death from pneumonia. Left to raise nine children, only one of whom was old enough to work, Lily Tarrington easily won the support of the West Toronto branch of the Great War Veterans' Association and the attention of sympathetically inclined journalists, who for the next eighteen months converted her private plight into a campaign for compassionate pension reform.

Through the summer of 1918 the GWVA sponsored fundraisers to support the family while simultaneously lobbying the Pension Board to reconsider the Tarrington case. The family's circumstances remained desperate, however, and by December 1918, Lily Tarrington was taking steps to break up her family. Following their move to Toronto in late 1917, she had found employment working an afternoon shift in a munitions factory, a schedule that allowed her to be home with her children in the morning and then again at bedtime. When the munitions factory closed at the end of the war, she took a job in a flour mill; working from 7:30 a.m. to 5:30 p.m. for the princely sum of $12 a week, she had to leave her youngest children alone at home, supervised only by their nine-year-old sister. Quite properly, she feared that this was not a safe or appropriate arrangement. Unable to give up her job, for she had no other source of income, she took steps to place the youngest children in the care of others: two daughters went to a family in the country, a third was about to leave to be cared for by a "well-to-do family who ... promised to give her the best attention," and the nine-year-old was to be taken in by relatives in Winnipeg, who would provide her with a comfortable home, a respectable education, and a promising future. The baby of the family was to be placed in foster care. Only the boys were to stay at home: the oldest, now fourteen, was employed at the flour mill with his mother and the two younger boys were enrolled in school, fulfilling her husband's explicit wish that "the boys should get a good schooling."[39]

Reported so assiduously by the *Daily Star* (and intermittently by the *Globe*); embraced so fervently by the local branch of the GWVA, the "Tarrington case" soon became synonymous with the suffering of widows and orphans whose financial well-being was endangered by bureaucratic indifference and government parsimony. When a soldier's widow in London, Ontario, was also denied a pension on the grounds that her husband's death could not be attributed to his war service, the *Star* pronounced that "'the Tarrington case' of Toronto has been repeated here."[40] Whether it was the persistent attention of the Toronto press or the determined lobbying of the GWVA, the Tarrington case helped bring about a significant change in government policy. An Order in Council signed in January 1919 authorized the Pension Board commissioners to accommodate "special cases of hardship which are not covered by the pensions regulations."[41] Among the potential beneficiaries of this new regulation were the Tarrington children (although not, apparently, Mrs Tarrington herself), who would collectively be eligible for an orphans' pension of $130 a month; a Canadian widow whose French-born husband, having returned to France to fulfil his military service obligations, remained missing at the end of the war and was presumed dead; and a "woman of culture" who had invested all of her savings in the private school education of her only son, and faced a future of penury following his death in France.[42]

The Tarrington case did not end happily. In September 1919, Lily Tarrington died of typhoid fever, leaving her children completely orphaned and – presumably – dependent upon the kindness of strangers and the $16 a month each dependent child would have received from the Pension Board.[43] The case did, however, reveal the determination of Canadian veterans and their allies to defend the interests of war widows and their children. When the government issued a war service gratuity to returning soldiers and their dependents, but not to the widows and orphans of men who had died in uniform, various veterans' groups demanded justice on their behalf. The Veterans of France and Comrades of Hamilton, for example, petitioned Ottawa to "suspend all further negotiations regarding proposed increases to pensions, gratuities or other monies for services rendered ... until next of kin, or dependents of all soldiers who dies [*sic*] in the service, or were killed in action, be granted their legitimate and justifiable portion of the war services gratuity as paid to the dependents of those who were more fortunate to return to their families, home and country."[44] The Vancouver branch of the Widows, Wives and Mothers of Great Britain's Heroes' Association made a similar plea: How was it just that "widows with children, orphans, and fatherless children have never received one cent of the Gratuity which 'dad' would have received if he had come back alive?" How was it fair that widows with children, orphans, and fatherless children were excluded from any of the "scheme[s] of re-establishment, vocational training, special high-school or college training, agricultural training, hospital accommodation, sanatorium accommodation, or land settlement" offered to returned men?[45] Surely justice required that the bereaved dependents of men who had died for Canada and the Empire be granted the same opportunities offered to men who had served and survived.

The plight of widows – and the economic challenges they faced during and after the war – thus became a subject of social and political discourse: was Canada doing enough for the widows and orphans of men who gave their lives for the "sacred cause"? Were the economic hardships of widows a fitting fate for women who had lost a husband – and, not incidentally, a breadwinner – because of the war? Attentive to these concerns and to the persistent efforts of veterans' groups that championed the widows' cause, the federal government increased the war widow's pension, effective September 1919, from $480 to $570; she would also receive $180 per year (an annual increase of $36) for her oldest child and pro-rated supplements for each additional child.[46] In 1920 the federal government also acceded to the demand that widows receive the same war-service gratuity already afforded the wives of returned men. Some widows fared reasonably well. The 1921 census reveals that May Rogers was residing in the elegant neighbourhood of Outremont with her seventeen-year-old son. Employed in an office, she reported an annual income for the previous year of $1,260 and Howard had earned $660.[47] When added to her pension this would not have represented extravagant wealth, by any means, but would more than adequately have covered their monthly rent of $45 and left enough for the necessities of life.

Widows of less affluent background struggled. A pension of $48 a month would provide a widow with no children an income equivalent to the minimum wage established after the war for working-class women in central and western Canada. When the Ontario Minimum Wage Board set out to determine a saleswoman's annual budget, it calculated that she would need at least $653 a year to cover room, board, clothing and necessary incidentals. And this presupposed that she would pay only $7 a week to rent a single room.[48] To cover her most basic costs, a childless widow receiving an annual pension of $570 would have had to find work outside the home or, if she wished to conform to the prevailing norms of social respectability, live with parents or siblings. Women with small children often found that even the supplement provided to cover the care of dependent children was inadequate. They battled landlords intent on raising their rent and coal merchants with little tolerance for unpaid bills. In September 1920, when the recession was at its worst, one war widow in Toronto complained that the rent she paid for one room (which she occupied with her three children) had "jumped from $6 to $11 a week."[49] Nor was this an isolated case. A close analysis of census records from 1921 shows that Manitoba war widows with no extended family to turn to rented rooms in the homes of strangers. Both Mabel Huggins and Alice Gorringe had lived in

Winnipeg when their husbands enlisted; both had relocated to Britain during the war and then returned to Canada after the Armistice. In 1921 both were tenants in boarding houses in central Winnipeg. Alice Gorringe was childless; Mabel Huggins had a two-year-old daughter to support. When she had returned to Winnipeg at the end of the war, she no doubt hoped she would soon resume her married life. This was not to be. Her husband, who had suffered a range of illnesses during his military service, was hospitalized immediately upon his arrival in Winnipeg and died in January 1919, leaving Mabel and their daughter in straitened circumstances. They moved frequently in the early 1920s, living at several different addresses before the census taker located them in 1921, renting a room in a house occupied by four other adults and three children.[50]

Widows with more robust family networks fared better. Mothers with young children continued a practice that had proved invaluable during the war: they husbanded their meager resources and found companionship and childcare by living with their parents. This was true of Elizabeth Beckett, Eleanor Benny, and Ellen Ewen, all of whom were sharing a home with their parents at the time of the 1921 census.[51] In an age long before daycare, such arrangements provided valuable (and, presumably, affectionate) assistance with child care. Indeed, Elizabeth Beckett probably depended upon her parents to mind her children while she worked as a stenographer. Women with teenage children old enough to work could count on at least one pay cheque, however modest, to supplement the widow's pension, thus providing a degree of economic security and household stability. This was true for Alice Adderly and Charlotte Adams, both of whom had stayed in Winnipeg throughout the war; in 1921 they were living at the same address as at the time of their husbands' enlistment, and both had at least one employed teenage child living at home. Older women – like Janet Gardiner, who had been born in 1871 – lived with their adult children, either as the head of a multi-generational household or as the mother (or mother-in-law) of the "man of the house."[52] For these women, postwar life in a multi-generational household alleviated the economic strain of single parenthood and the emotional stress of widowhood.

Even childless widows could benefit from the companionship and respectability that a blended household could offer. Annie Collum had relocated to Britain during the war, where like many officers' wives she had settled in one of London's elegant neighbourhoods. When her husband, a financier who had secured a commission upon enlistment, died of wounds in the summer of 1917, she remained in Britain, apparently indifferent to the government's pleas that Canadian wives return home immediately. It was only in 1920 that she sailed for Canada to live with her widowed father, a prominent Winnipeg citizen, in his grand home in Armstrong's Point.[53] Flora Lindsay found herself in similar circumstances. After her husband enlisted, she lived temporarily with her sister and brother-in-law (both of whom were physicians), before relocating to Britain in 1916, where she lived in London. When she returned to Canada in 1920, she once again shared her sister and brother-in-law's Winnipeg home until she remarried in 1924.[54] Financial calculations were probably not uppermost in her mind; unlike many war widows who had few employable skills, Flora Lindsay was, like her sister, a professional woman, employed as a pharmacist and earning a respectable income. The family affection, intelligent conversation, and companionship she would have found in the company of her sister and brother-in-law were no doubt invaluable to a childless widow coping with grief.

Annie Collum and Flora Lindsay were but two of many wives who relocated to Britain during the war and then returned to Canada following the death of their husbands. For those with close or long-standing familial ties in Canada, this made good sense. Like Annie Collum, Muriel Birkett was a Canadian-born war wife who had lived in Britain during the war and had remained there for two years following her husband's death in September 1916. When she learned that the Canadian government intended to reimburse the travel expenses of wives who returned home after the Armistice, she sought compensation for the expenses she had incurred in October 1918. She had found it difficult to fund her return trip, even though as a childless woman she had been able to support herself as a mechanic (presumably in the war industries) while living in England. Nonetheless, she made her case: "As I am absolutely dependent on my pension this made it very hard for me and I wondered as others are having their passages paid, if you could possibly help me to get the whole or even part of what I had to pay refunded." Such pleas usually fell on deaf bureaucratic ears, and there is no evidence that Muriel Birkett's request was an exception to that rule. Out of pocket, alone and childless, she moved west and lived with her widowed father in Vancouver.[55]

Just as close family connections prompted some widows to return to or remain in Canada, the same consideration encouraged others to remain in or relocate to Britain after the war. Three examples make this clear. Edith Andrews's husband had enlisted in October 1914, and she had followed him to Britain in March 1915, settling first in Worcester, where her husband was born. Three months after his death in April 1916, she moved to a suburb of London where she would remain through at least the early 1920s.[56] By contrast, Nellie Pell had stayed in Canada for the duration of the war but in February 1919 she asked if the Canadian government could help pay the steamship fares for herself and her two children to return to Britain: "Having lost my husband in France seventeen months ago and not having any relatives in Canada I am wanting to go to England with my two children to live with my widowed Mother. And as the soldier's wives are being brought back from England I wondered if any reduction was made for those wishing to go to England to live with their own people."[57] Denied support, she had no choice but to cover her own expenses: she and her two children sailed from New York to Liverpool in April 1919. Mabel Blyth and her three children had returned to Canada in December 1917, following her husband's medical demobilization. Her husband's health remained precarious, however, and he died in March 1919. Six months later, Mabel and her four children – the oldest of whom was six and the youngest ten months – left Canada, destined once again for Yorkshire where they would live with her mother.[58] The migratory upheaval that had characterized the lives of so many Canadian war wives between 1914 and 1918 thus continued for widows after the Armistice; some relocated within Canada, others returned to Canada from Britain, and yet others made the return voyage home to Britain, ending the experiment in Canadian living they had embarked upon, often as young wives, before the war.

Although war widows often won the sympathy of veterans' groups and the attention of indignant journalists, they did not enjoy the unparalleled social esteem granted to mothers who had given their sons for the cause of liberty and the defence of the British Empire. The bereaved mother and her fallen son represented both the tragic cost of war and the filial relationship of Canada to Britain. As Jonathan Vance has so perceptively argued, the "soldier-mother bond symbolized the relationships between the individual Canadian and his country, and Canada and Britain."[59] Unlike mothers, whose fidelity to the memory of their fallen sons was unimpeachable, a widow's faithfulness was more contingent. She could properly honour her husband's memory only if she did not remarry. Yet the reality for many war widows in all combatant nations – Canada among them – was that only remarriage allowed them to struggle through. Whether burdened by the demands of single parenthood, the inadequacy of a widow's pension, or the emotional strain of bereavement, a significant minority of war widows remarried: by 1924, 40 percent of war widows in France, Germany, and Britain had remarried.[60] In Canada, remarriage was less prevalent than in Europe but it became a subject of moralistic hand-wringing nonetheless. In October 1922 the *Toronto Daily Star* summarized a government report on the status of war widows and stressed that of the 13,000 women who had been widowed by the war and thus were initially eligible for a Canadian pension, 3,251 (25%) had remarried by 1922. Although remarriage was evident from 1916 onward (when 80 Canadian war widows had remarried), most remarriages occurred, not surprisingly, after the war: 897 in 1920, and 772 in 1921.[61]

For the journalists of the *Daily Star*, the remarriage of war widows was regrettable. They feared that men who might otherwise have married young single women chose a widow instead because she would bring to the marriage the federal "dowry" of $720 bestowed on widows who upon remarriage forfeited their pensions. As was the case in England, where the dowry system also obtained and similar fears captured the public imagination, these venal calculations supposedly doomed a generation of young girls to life as spinsters. This belief that war widows were "stealing" eligible men and thereby depriving single girls of the chance of marital happiness also made its way into popular culture, albeit in a more humorous vein. The 1919 film *A Widow by Proxy*, which screened in Toronto in February 1920, was the "story of how a bachelor girl won a husband while posing as a war widow."[62] But if a sense of fair play was not enough to keep war widows from remarriage, perhaps common sense would suffice. According to several stories in the *Daily Star*, war widows frequently regretted their decision to remarry. In one instance, an unsuspecting Toronto woman remarried only to discover too late that her new husband was a bigamist; in another, a wife took her feckless husband to court for non-support: in the judge's opinion, "How any woman can give up a pension of $75 a month to marry an idle, worthless vagabond is entirely beyond my comprehension."[63]

These cautionary tales notwithstanding, more than a few Canadian war widows did remarry. A sample of wives who were living in Manitoba at the time of their husbands' enlistment, all of whom became war widows, reveals that at least 70 remarried (25%).[64] Census data from 1916 and 1921, read in conjunction with available vital statistics records, allow for a closer reconstruction of the path from first marriage through widowhood to remarriage of 62 of these 70 widows. As might be expected, most of these women were young and had been married for only a few years when they were widowed: 44 of the 62 had been married eight years or less, and the average length of first marriage for all 62 women in the sample was 6.9 years. There were, of course, outliers at either end. Two, including the very young Gladys Little (née Cousins), became widows before marking their first anniversary. Gladys Cousins was eighteen when she married Thomas Little in November 1917. Only they would have known whether this was a genuine love match or a marriage of expedience to protect Thomas, who was twelve years her senior, from conscription, but he was conscripted nonetheless, deployed to Europe in time to participate in the Hundred Days campaign, and was killed in September 1918. Gladys remained in the rural municipality of Whitemouth, where she had grown up, and in 1922 married again.[65]

That a twenty-two-year-old young woman living in a rural community where young men went in search of work would remarry is surely not surprising. But a substantial number of the war widows in this sample were much older than Gladys Little. Of the fifteen women who had been married for a decade or more when they became widows, Lilian Atha was thirty-nine when her husband enlisted, and Elizabeth Jones was forty-one. Both women had first married in 1899; both husbands were in their late thirties when they signed up and suffered from poor health which prevented them from seeing military action. Walter Atha, as we have seen, was hospitalized shortly after arriving in England, was repatriated to Canada, and died in the Winnipeg General Hospital in March 1918. He left a wife and four children, the oldest nineteen and the youngest five. His widow married Thomas Potts, a widower, in April 1920.[66] Elizabeth Jones had no dependent children when she married Frank Honeybell in London in 1916: she had returned to England in July 1915 and was widowed only weeks later, when her husband, Arthur, died of a heart attack at the Shorncliffe staging camp. Elizabeth and Frank Honeybell sailed from England to Canada in June 1919, destined for Winnipeg.[67]

A very small number of these war widows remarried in what would have been deemed unseemly haste. When protocol dictated that a widow should wear mourning for at least a year and should withdraw from all forms of social life for six months following her husband's death, to remarry within three months, as Millie Cockriell, did following the death of her first husband in April 1917 – or within a mere three weeks, as Athalie Clemis did – was to flaunt convention and decorum.[68] Most, however, waited until after the war to remarry, and the average length between the death of a first husband and remarriage was 3.3 years. If it is possible, therefore, to describe the "average" war widow and the path she took to remarriage, she would have been married for six or seven years before her husband's death, would have stayed in Canada throughout the war, and would have remarried in the early 1920s. In fact, she would have closely resembled Violet Kaslake, who had emigrated from England in 1907 and had married her Canadian-born husband, George, in Winnipeg two years later. By the time he enlisted in March 1915, they had been married for six years and had three children, the oldest not yet five and the youngest, a baby born in September 1914. Violet and her children moved often during the war, living at six separate addresses in Winnipeg between March 1915 and October 1916, when George Kaslake was killed at the Somme. Three years later, in November 1919, Violet married James Andrews in Winnipeg, and the family, which by 1921 included Violet's three children from her first marriage and an infant, continued to be buffeted by the winds of economic hardship. James Andrews had been unemployed for thirty of the previous fifty-two weeks, and the family's annual income for the previous year had been a scant $500.[69]

Isabella Bunch, whom we last encountered living with her sister-in-law in London, was widowed in October 1916. Having secured an advance on her separation allowance, she and her three-year old daughter, Mildred, returned to Canada in early 1917. How or when she made her way to the west coast is unknown, but this was a path taken by many Manitoba widows after the war. For Isabella Bunch it led to remarriage: in the spring of 1919 she married Edward Alfred Dawn, an English-born widower with two children, thirteen years her senior, in Vancouver. By May 1920, they were on their way to the States, sailing from Victoria to San Francisco in May 1920 and settling shortly thereafter in the Highland Park neighbourhood of Los Angeles. Isabella gave birth to two children, in 1920 and 1921, and applied for American citizenship in 1941.[70] Isabel Harris followed a strikingly similar path from widowhood to remarriage, and from Winnipeg's endless winters to southern California's eternal summer. Born in 1890, she was, like Isabella Bunch, twenty-four years old when the war broke out. Her husband enlisted immediately and was declared missing in April 1915; it would not be until August 1916 that he would be officially declared dead, leaving his young widow to mourn him and care for their two children. Isabel no doubt depended for emotional and financial support on her mother and four siblings, with whom she lived in central Winnipeg. In October 1919, however, Isabel and her children sailed from Canada to Liverpool, and a year later she married Alexander Munro in Edinburgh. They, too, moved to Los Angeles in 1921; she had two more children and, like Isabella Bunch, applied for American citizenship in 1941.[71]

Relocating to the United States following a second marriage was not an unusual path for Manitoba's war widows – Lucy Chatfield and her second husband were living in Detroit by 1930, and Athalie Clemis ultimately settled with her fourth husband in Michigan – but many more stayed in Canada. Those who left Manitoba frequently moved westward to the more temperate climate of British Columbia. Both Kate Greenwood and Fanny Diplock had married their first husbands in England (in 1902 and 1905, respectively), before emigrating and settling in Winnipeg. Neither was, by the standards of the day, a young

woman when their husbands enlisted: Kate was forty-one and Fanny
thirty-three. They were the mothers of young children and both stayed
in Winnipeg for the duration of the war. By the early 1920s, however,
they had relocated to the west coast, where they remarried. In 1921, Kate
Greenwood was living with her two young sons in New Westminster,
where a year later she married William Hugh Rogers. In 1920, Fanny
Diplock married Frederick Gent in Victoria, and by the time of the 1921
census she, her new husband, and her three children were living with
her new father-in-law in Nanaimo.[72]

Remarriage did not necessarily signify betrayal of or a lack of affection for a widow's fallen husband. Psychological studies of bereavement
show that "resilience" in the face of loss – which might be made manifest
by the ability to form new emotional attachments – is neither a rare
nor a pathological response indicating a cold, affect-less, or unloving
attachment to the lost partner. Rather, resilience occurs quite frequently
in individuals who are clearly emotionally well grounded.[73] This
recognition might help us understand the relatively high incidence
of remarriage among war widows. They did not necessarily forget
their first husbands, and, indeed, in their acts of commemoration they
publicly avowed their affection. When Alice Beasant chose the words to
be inscribed on her first husband's grave, she praised him as "A Faithful
Husband, a Faithful Friend, a Faithful Soldier to the End." Effie Dorman,
who remarried in 1921 four years after the death of her first husband,
opted for the simple but significant pledge: "Gone but not Forgotten,
His Wife." And Marion East, whom the Canadian army categorized as an
"unmarried wife" refused such second-class status when memorializing
her first husband: "Though Divided in Death Memory Still Clings From
His Loving Wife and Son."[74]

Domesticity defined the lives of postwar wives and widows. As Veronica
Strong-Boag has clearly demonstrated, there was, no "New Age" for this
generation of newly enfranchised but not yet liberated women.[75] That
this would have been true for women whose husbands survived the war
is not surprising; married men had enlisted to defend their families from
the "barbaric Hun" and, as important, to defend the familial ideal of a
male breadwinner and a dependent wife and children. It is perhaps more
surprising that widows too would have found refuge in the domestic
routines and resources that had defined their prewar lives and had
sustained them during the years of wartime separation. The available
(and far from comprehensive) evidence suggests that these "single"

women only rarely embraced – or were interested in assuming – an identity as an "Independent Woman." Only one example, drawn from our data base of Manitoba war widows, emerges from the 1921 census. In 1920 Harriet Brown, widow of Major Ralph Brown of Winnipeg, resumed the position she had resigned in 1913 when she married: Art Supervisor in the Winnipeg Public Schools. She probably could not have done so, however, if her mother-in-law had not been available to help care for her two young children.[76] Like the war widows who still had children to raise, even the childless war widow existed in a world defined by domesticity: she lived with extended family (siblings, parents, or in-laws); she remarried; and if she had to support herself, because her pension offered an inadequate source of financial support, she did what widows had long done: she took in boarders, she bought a sewing machine on time; she worked at low-skill jobs. Some widows with young children took up positions as housekeepers for widowed or single farmers.[77] Whether childless or the mothers of young children, these war widows resemble – in the choices they made (or were made for them); in their reliance on family; and in their continued identification with domesticity – the widows of earlier generations. Like the widows of nineteenth-century Canada whom Bettina Bradbury has studied, Canada's war widows relied upon the resources of family and the respectability of domestic life.[78] War wives and war widows did not, therefore, represent a threat to Canada's core social values of domesticity and conjugality. Much more disruptive of this social order – at least in principle – were the war wives whose marriages succumbed to divorce or desertion, for their unhappy circumstances gave credence to the belief that the war had brought in its wake a "crisis of marriage" caused, it was alleged, by the infidelity of Canada's war wives.

Till Divorce (or Desertion)
Do Us Part

Captain Ralph Holmes enlisted in March 1916, one of many men who responded to the increasingly urgent pleas of local recruiters. He and his wife, May, had married in 1911 when both were young; she was only eighteen, and he twenty-two. By the time he enlisted, they were the parents of a son and two daughters, and May was pregnant with their fourth child. Although it is impossible to know whether the marriage was happy and whether Captain Holmes corresponded regularly with his wife and children while he was overseas, by the time he returned to New Brunswick in 1919 it was abundantly clear that his marriage had collapsed. For the past year (or more) his wife had been having an affair with the local Baptist minister, Reverend W.N. Stackhouse, and had borne him a child in January 1919. The disgraced minister, having resigned his curacy before his supervisors learned of his indiscretions, had departed for New York. Neighbours believed that May was working as a nurse in Boston. Faced with this incontrovertible evidence of betrayal, Holmes filed for and was awarded a divorce. Neither his wife nor the delinquent Reverend Stackhouse appeared in court to contest the charges or defend their besmirched reputations, but in an affidavit submitted to the court May admitted that the minister was indeed the father of her child. A young woman who had taken rooms in the family home while Captain Holmes was overseas testified to the "frequent visits Mr. Stackhouse paid, and gave direct evidence of infidelity on the part of the wife in April 1918."[1]

The saga of Captain Holmes's marital woes captured the attention of Canada's national press, for it seemed a paradigmatic example of the disruptive effects of the war on marriage and respectable family life. Certainly, the involvement of a Baptist minister added a *frisson* of scandal to a story that journalists would be loath to ignore, as did May Holmes's abandonment of her young children. Most compelling of all, however, was Captain Holmes's military status; a returning soldier who had risked his life to defend his family, his home, and his nation from Teutonic barbarism, he was the innocent victim of wifely infidelity. His petition for divorce made palpable a deep and demoralizing cultural anxiety: that the Great War had exacerbated a crisis of marriage that had unsettled Canadians – and especially those who were determined to protect the nation's Anglo-Celtic identity – since the late nineteenth century. Canadians feared that the institution of marriage, the bedrock of national strength and moral order, had been eroded by the forces of modernity and, perhaps especially, by close proximity to the "pernicious, corrupt and immoral influence of the United States, where it was understood that the marriage tie was loose and lax."[2] The war and the long separations it imposed on couples did nothing to allay this fear. And as the Holmes case made abundantly clear, blame now came to rest not with immoral Americans but with apparently respectable but demonstrably unfaithful Anglo-Canadian wives.

At the same time, attention to the misdeeds of Canada's war wives obscured the ways in which they were victims in the national drama of war-induced infidelity; and discussions of divorce obscured the equally unsettling evidence of desertion as a marker of marital disintegration. Long-term absence certainly created opportunities for Canadian wives to abandon their marriage vows; but it also allowed Canadian soldiers who were so inclined to engage in extra-marital relationships while serving in Europe. Evidence of these affairs and their disruptive effects on the lives and marriages of Canadian war wives appears in various sources: in divorce petitions brought by aggrieved English husbands; in criminal trials for bigamy reported by both the British and Canadian press; and most poignantly in stories of the sorry plight of Canadian women like Mary Palmer whose husbands deserted them at the end of the war. Douglas Palmer, a corporal in the CEF, bade Mary farewell in 1916, wed another woman in Scotland and, rumour had it, a third in England. Mary knew nothing of these marital adventures until her husband returned to Canada in 1919, accompanied by his Scottish wife. Charged and convicted for bigamy, he served a four-month sentence, but rebuffed Mary's offer of reconciliation and refused to provide her and their child with any financial support.[3] For deserted wives like Mary Palmer the economic and emotional hardships of the war years persisted well into the next decade. They struggled to maintain their family home, to care for their children, and to sustain themselves through episodes of ill health. If they were fortunate enough to live in a province that provided support to deserted wives, they had access to modest monthly allowances and, as needed, emergency funds to address the intermittent crises of domestic life. If not, they did what Mary Palmer had to do: they took jobs at low pay and turned to their families for support. Unlike the bereaved widow, the deserted wife had little (or no) claim on the nation's purse and less still on its compassion.

৵৵

Cultural apprehension about the disruptive effects of the war on married life was by no means unique to Canada. Divorce rates increased appreciably across postwar Europe. In Belgium, a nation of fewer than eight million, and in Germany, with a population approaching seventy million, the number of couples filing for divorce almost doubled between 1913 and 1920.[4] In France, the increase was not as dramatic but nonetheless noteworthy: 13,500 French couples divorced in 1913; 19,465, in 1919, when for the first time husbands were more likely than wives to file for divorce. Whereas men represented only 40 percent of divorce petitioners in 1913, by 1919 they represented almost two-thirds of those seeking a legal end to their marriage. And, whereas only 10 percent of all divorce petitions filed in 1914 had cited female infidelity as the principal cause, 18 percent of petitions filed in 1919 did so.[5] In England and Wales the divorce rate in 1912 (calculated as the number of divorce petitions filed per 10,000 married women aged between fifteen and forty-nine) was 1.89; in 1919 it reached what then seemed to be the outrageous heights of 9.46. As in France, more and more petitions were being brought by aggrieved husbands: in 1912, 45.1 percent of petitions were filed by women (even though the English divorce laws made it considerably more cumbersome for women to divorce their husbands than vice versa); in 1919, only 20.3 percent of all divorce petitions were initiated by women.[6]

Many factors contributed to this dramatic increase in divorce. Wartime separation had temporarily alleviated the marital stress that might otherwise have resulted in divorce petitions between 1914 and 1918. Patriotic sentiment discouraged divorce petitions against men in uniform. Couples who married hastily during the war might have discovered their essential incompatibility upon reunion in 1919. And in Britain, changes to the law introduced on the eve of war in 1914 exempted the poor from the prohibitive costs that traditionally accompanied divorce petitions. Any one or all of these factors might have stemmed the flow of divorce petitions during the war only to open the floodgates immediately thereafter. But in the minds of contemporary observers, it was the infidelity of war wives that was uniquely responsible for a purported "crisis of marriage." Women indifferent to their marriage vows became the anti-heroines of literature and the principal focus of national debates about the unsettling prevalence of divorce in postwar society. In France, Roland Dorgelès's 1919 novel *Wooden Crosses* gave voice to the anger of a soldier returning home to find that his wife had run off with another man. Nor were such tales restricted to the realm of fiction. In January 1919 *The Times* alerted its British readers to similar incidents in an article with the unambiguous title, "Faithless Wives"; as in the Holmes case, two English servicemen returned home only to discover that their wives had been unfaithful and had given birth to children out of wedlock.[7] Dishonest, duplicitous, and unworthy women came to represent a personal betrayal, a symbol of home-front immorality, and indisputable evidence that marriage as an institution indispensable to the survival of respectable society was under threat.

In Canada the much-lamented epidemic of divorce, which so unsettled postwar Europe, caused comparable anguish in the ranks of the nation's moral arbiters. Before 1914, divorce had been so rare as to be almost unheard of: in 1900 only eleven Canadian couples secured a divorce and, although the numbers increased slowly thereafter, divorce remained both exceptional and morally offensive. In most provinces, the procedure for legally dissolving a marriage was intentionally cumbersome, time-consuming, and expensive. As determined by legal provisions in place when their provinces entered Confederation, residents of the Maritimes and British Columbia could apply for a divorce by taking their case to a duly designated provincial divorce court. All other Canadians seeking the legal dissolution of their marriage had to file a petition with the Senate in Ottawa, which (like the House of Lords in Britain prior to the passage in 1857 of the Marital Causes Act) had the authority to grant a divorce through a private act of Parliament.[8] Parliamentary divorces were expensive: petitioners had to tender a filing fee of $200 and arrange for witnesses to travel to Ottawa to testify in person. Because few unhappy husbands or miserable wives could afford to file for divorce under these conditions, the Senate had a light caseload: of the seventy divorces finalized in Canada in 1914, the Senate adjudicated only thirty-three.

By 1920, however, when all returned men had re-established themselves in Canada and the misery of mismatched marriages had reasserted itself, the Senate saw a significant increase in the number of divorce petitions filed. In 1919, it approved fifty-five; a year later, ninety-eight.[9] Moreover, these Parliamentary divorces represented but a fraction of all divorce cases generated in the aftermath of the war. In 1919 the three Prairie provinces finally won the right to adjudicate divorce petitions in provincial courts, thus substantially reducing the cost of divorce for residents of these provinces and, concomitantly, the Senate's caseload. This single reform created an apparent tidal wave of divorce petitions. In March 1919 the Office of the Manitoba Attorney General anticipated that "several hundred" petitions would be filed as soon as the Imperial Privy Council in London confirmed the province's right of adjudication. By August more than eleven hundred petitions for divorce had been filed in Manitoba, the majority from "soldiers who have returned to find their wives have been unfaithful."[10]

This notable rise in divorce caused considerable alarm, for many Canadians found the very idea of divorce abhorrent. When the Hollywood movie *The Blindness of Divorce* played in Toronto theatres in the summer of 1918, illustrating the unintended and regrettable consequences of easily won divorce, the *Globe* was quick to speak of divorce as "a curse to society and a menace to the home."[11] The *Edmonton Journal* was of much the same opinion. In 1919, when the Alberta Supreme Court secured the right to adjudicate divorce cases, the *Journal* spewed indignation: "It is axiomatic that the marital relationship lies at the basis of all civilized institutions, and it must be clear that the constitution of a Democratic state could not survive a general dissolution of this most fundamental of human relationships."[12] The most conservative jurists of the Canadian Bar Association opposed any reform "that would facilitate the granting of divorce." And their more moderate colleagues, open to the possibility of some reform, nonetheless insisted that "there should be no cheapening or weakening of the divorce laws, for it should only be granted on the highest grounds."[13] In the past, Canadians had often disparaged "easy divorce" as an American abomination, yet by 1919 an even more damning association had come to light: the greatest proponents of easy access to divorce were – it was claimed with some justification – the Bolsheviks.[14]

Anxieties about the corrosive effects of divorce on the foundations of the family and the nation itself coexisted, however, with a new reality. When returning men confronted evidence that their wives had taken lovers, and, in some instances, abandoned the family home, they called upon Canada's veterans' organizations to press for divorce reform. As early as October 1917, the Great War Veterans' Association remarked: "Some very painful cases are coming to our attention of returned soldiers coming home to find that their wives have been unfaithful to the marriage vows during their absence, and some disagreeable and ugly situations have arisen."[15] Letters submitted by aggrieved husbands to the minister of justice in Ottawa made this painfully apparent. When Private Stratfull returned home to Brandon he discovered that, only two days after he had enlisted, his wife had begun "living as man and wife with another man, her having one child by him." Unable to care for his own five children, he had had to place them temporarily in the children's home in Winnipeg where, he was relieved to note, they were being well cared for.[16] John Coyne and René Meysonnier found themselves in similar predicaments. Shortly after his return to Saskatchewan, Coyne learned that his "wife had been living a part of the time while [he] was away with one Thompson a farmer whose wife is in an asylum and some few months [later] she left her home and has been living ever since with Thompson on his farm some few miles from here."[17] And in an especially impassioned (and quite lengthy) letter, Meysonnier, a reservist in the French Army, laid bare the misery of his now-defunct marriage. He asserted that "many war wives had taken advantage of their husbands' prolonged absence to give themselves over to the most ignoble debauchery." He was himself a "victim like so many others of the wickedness of such women." When he returned to Saskatchewan, wounded and, he insisted, in great need of a woman's gentle, healing touch, he discovered that his wife, upon learning of his imminent return, had "fled to the United States with her lover, a miserable no-good, a ravager of women the likes of which you find in the lowest ranks of society." And if that was not bad enough, the womanizing miscreant was a Swede![18]

The case of Grace Henderson in Toronto is also illustrative. Evidence of her infidelity, and the steps she took to hide it from her husband, came to light in the summer of 1919 when she was arrested in Toronto and charged with murdering her newborn son on 7 June 1919. She was a young woman, at twenty-two already the mother of a two-year-old daughter, and a recent transplant to Toronto, where she met and had a brief but tragically consequential affair with one Corporal Harman. According to the testimony of a neighbour, who had remarked upon a pungent odour in Mrs Henderson's apartment, Grace had then taken a suitcase from a closet, opened it, and unwrapped the remains of her recently born child. She confessed that she had "had to get rid of it before her husband arrived back from overseas." Because the medical evidence was ambiguous – it was not clear that she had intentionally killed the child, even though she admitted as much to her neighbour – she was acquitted of the more serious charge of murder but was found guilty of concealing the child's birth. Citing "circumstances surrounding the case" which led the judge to "take a lenient view of the matter," Grace Henderson received a suspended sentence.[19]

Whether her husband was as forgiving as the judge remains unknown. Other men in less tragic situations certainly were not. Corporal John Weaver, a returned man serving with the Military Police in London,

Ontario, was determined to secure a divorce from his wife, who was "living with another man age 24 years as Man and Wife, and she is 44 years." Weaver's marriage would appear to have been of very short duration. When he had first enlisted in August 1915, he identified himself as a widower and named his daughter his next of kin. At some point thereafter he married, only to discover upon his return from overseas in 1918 that his wife had abandoned the family home. For Weaver, a man who had enlisted twice (once in 1915 and then again in 1917), it was particularly galling that his wife was now living with a man twenty years her junior: was it possible that the younger man had rushed to marry in order to avoid conscription?[20] Albert Adams, much younger than Weaver, was also newly married when he went overseas. He had enlisted in June 1916, had married his nineteen-year-old bride in August, and sailed for Europe in November. He, too, discovered upon his return to Canada that his wife "had been and [was] still continuing to be unfaithful." Lest the minister of justice doubt his claim, he added: "For which I have ample proof."[21]

Incensed by such evidence of wifely infidelity, veterans and their organizations demanded divorce reform as a matter of justice. At the very least, they argued, the federal government should take steps to reduce the cost of divorce. When a divorce petition submitted to the Senate might cost as much as $900 – a sum far beyond the means of most rank-and-file soldiers – some financial assistance was imperative.[22] It is not surprising, therefore, that soldiers eagerly believed a rumour, derived from an article first published in the *Ottawa Citizen* that "returned soldiers whose wives have proved faithless in their absence are to be facilitated in seeking that relief which the law allows by way of divorce."[23] It was believed that Parliament was about to introduce a "soldiers' divorce" that would eliminate the Senate's $200 filing fee. The rumour spread quickly and widely in early 1918, eliciting inquiries to the Ministry of Justice from across the nation. There was, however, no truth to the rumour of low-cost divorce, as the Ministry of Justice had to stress repeatedly: "The report in the public press that special provision has been made for the remission of parliamentary fees in the case of returned soldiers who petition for bills of divorce, is incorrect." The most that could be hoped for was the beneficence of the Senate: "It has been the custom of the Senate to remit payment of the fee of $200 required by rule 140, whenever the Committee on Divorce is satisfied that the applicant is in good faith, and is not able to afford payment."[24]

Some form of financial assistance for soldiers seeking a divorce thus remained an urgent demand of returned soldiers and veterans' associations, and a recurring topic of political debate. At the very same time that Manitoba (and shortly thereafter Alberta) was calling for the creation of provincial divorce courts, veterans assembled for the annual meeting of the Ontario Great War Veterans' Association (GWVA) endorsed the principle that local courts be given jurisdiction over divorce. If that proved untenable, then the existing procedure should at the very least be made less expensive.[25] When a group of returned soldiers from Windsor, Ontario, met with their local MP in October 1918, they impressed upon him their demand that "the Government assist returned men to procure divorces from their wives who had left them while they were overseas."[26] Six months later, when most of the men serving overseas had been repatriated, the issue of divorce reform became even more pressing. Ontario veterans convening in Windsor for the annual meeting of the GWVA reiterated a complaint frequently heard: the system by which divorces were granted only by a private act of Parliament favoured the rich and discriminated against the poor. On rare occasions a returned man without personal resources might secure the pro bono services of a benevolent law firm, as William Canahan learned in February 1918 when the law offices of Sydney Mewburn, the minister of the militia and a fellow resident of Hamilton, covered the fees associated with his petition "on account of the fact that the petitioner is a returned soldier."[27] Few other men were so well placed, however, and Albert Adams spoke for many when he confided that he was not "in a possation to pay any large sum for a divorce."[28] In advocating for Canada's returned men, the GWVA did not demand that the recognized grounds for divorce be expanded – and there was certainly no call for divorce on the grounds of incompatibility alone – but only that it should be "equally easy for rich or poor to secure."[29]

The creation of provincial divorce courts did make divorce easier to obtain for men (and women) in the Prairies. In Alberta, for example, only thirty-six couples secured a divorce in 1919; a year later, 112 did.[30] Financial obstacles remained a serious impediment, however, for unhappy couples in Ontario and Quebec. Whereas divorce remained rare in Catholic Quebec, in Ontario men (or women) hoping to extricate themselves from a ruined marriage had two choices: if they could afford it, they could file a petition for Parliamentary divorce; or they could head across the border and obtain a divorce in the United States. As Canadians knew at the time, and historians have subsequently stressed, many Canadians, of many different social classes, travelled south to the States where, upon establishing residency after only a few months, they could secure an American divorce and thus avoid entirely the process of petitioning Parliament for a divorce. Upon their return home, they hoped (in vain) that Canada would recognize both their divorce and

their remarriage as legal. Some Canadians condemned such practices
as immorality of the highest order. In August 1919, a woman, who
represented herself as a "London West Mother," wrote to the Ministry
of Justice in Ottawa to express her outrage at how easy it was "to get
rid of a wife" simply by moving south of the border. In point of fact, the
story she recounted revealed how easy it was to get rid of an unwanted
husband, but her larger point – about the ease with which Canadians
who lived close to the border could secure an American divorce – was
well taken. She told of a soldier's wife who became enamoured of a
sergeant assigned to the London armoury. To free herself of her first
husband, the woman moved temporarily to Toledo, where she received
frequent visits from her new admirer. After six months of residency in
Ohio, she filed for and won a divorce from her first husband. The new
couple quickly married and returned to London, Ontario, where they
lived as man and wife.[31] The available evidence, limited to data from
1922 collected by the US Census Bureau, suggests that in that year at
least twice as many Canadians sought a "migratory divorce" as pursued
one through the Canadian courts. How many of these petitioners were
returning soldiers is unknown – and perhaps unknowable. Insofar as
women were more likely than men to resort to a "migratory divorce"
of this type, it is likely that Canadian veterans constituted only a small
fraction of those who secured an American divorce.[32]

A "migratory divorce" offered one alternative to the Canadian court
system. Informal petitions, submitted either to provincial or federal
authorities, gave voice to the widespread belief that a kindly bureaucrat
or a well-disposed politician could grant a divorce by simple fiat: all
that was needed was demonstrable cause and the petitioner's unhappy
marriage would be legally dissolved.[33] For men (and women) of modest
means and imprecise knowledge of the legal system, the informal
petition thus seemed an invaluable avenue to securing a divorce. As
the many plaintive letters submitted to the Ministry of Justice make
clear, these informal petitioners often requested the right to end their
marriage because their spouses had deserted the conjugal home. In May
1916, Frederick Ledger, a recently returned Canadian soldier, conveyed to
the Attorney General in Ottawa the sorry tale of his unhappy marriage:
he had, he confided, been married for nine years and six months. "I was
married two months," he continued, "when my wife ran away with
another man I tried in vane to find her for nine years and could not
till six months ago I found her in Rochester NY with a nother man I
brought her back to Canada and after three days she ran a way from
me againe and went to the States so I did not bother going after her
againe … now what I want is to ask you if you will grant me permit to

get married over a gaine for my life is spoilte now and I beg of you to do this for me I am 30 years old now ... She also has a daughter but not mine."[34] However unfortunate the circumstances of his marriage, it is clear that it was ill-fated from the start and not an uncounted casualty of the Great War.

⇛❦⇝

Although much of the rhetoric animating discussions of marital breakdown in the aftermath of the war concentrated on the unfaithfulness of soldiers' wives, the reality was more complex. Some women were not guilty as charged, for rumours and allegations of infidelity were not always true. When the Manitoba Patriotic Fund investigated a charge of infidelity brought by a soldier who was eager to distance himself from his wife, the caseworker who reviewed his charge found no evidence to corroborate his allegation.[35] As in Britain, where caseworkers launched 40,000 investigations of infidelity but found substantiating evidence in only 13,000 cases, rumours (or self-serving allegations) of wifely misconduct often seriously misrepresented the reality.[36] Perhaps this explains why only a small fraction of the eleven hundred divorce petitions filed in Manitoba in 1919 proved successful: only eighty-eight divorces were finalized in Manitoba in 1919 and forty-two in 1920.[37] If some women were unjustly accused of adultery, others discovered that their husbands were the ones primarily responsible for a breakdown in marital comity.

Evidence of soldiers' infidelity and its effects on wartime marriage emerges from four quite distinct sets of sources. Parliamentary records reveal that soldiers' wives sometimes filed for divorce, citing their husband's adultery as the principal cause. The British press denounced Dominion troops who were named as co-respondents in divorce cases or as the bigamous seducers of young, respectable women. The Canadian press, unusually reticent when reporting on divorce cases brought by a war wife against her wayward husband, did pay attention to criminal charges of bigamy brought in Canada against returning soldiers. And because deserted wives living in Manitoba were able to seek assistance from the Soldiers' Deserted Wives Fund (SDWF), the fund's extant files offer rich and detailed accounts of how the war precipitated marriage breakdown, soldiers' desertion of the family home, and the challenges that deserted wives then contended with in the postwar decade.

War wives whose husbands had been unfaithful while overseas hoped that divorce reform would serve them well. When the rumour circulated that the federal government would provide free (or inexpensive) divorces for returned soldiers, war wives and their advocates believed they too should be eligible for such consideration. In February 1918, only weeks after the story of "soldiers' divorces" had first appeared in local newspapers, the secretary of the Saskatoon branch of the Canadian Patriotic Fund inquired of the Ministry of Justice whether the "same regulations will be applicable to soldiers' wives ... seeking divorce from their husbands." He had, he wrote, to his considerable regret, been "dealing with one or two cases here."[38] There were certainly more than one or two cases of wronged wives in postwar Canada. As in England, Canadian law prior to 1925 allowed men to file for divorce on the basis of adultery alone, but required women to demonstrate that their husbands were guilty also of a second offence: desertion for at least two years, physical or mental cruelty, or rape.[39] These restrictions notwithstanding, some Canadian war wives did successfully obtain divorces in the years immediately following the war. In Alberta, where the first divorce granted by the provincial court was to a returned veteran, there were by September 1919 twenty-four pending petitions before the provincial Supreme Court: fifteen brought by husbands, nine by wives.[40] In Ontario, of the twenty-seven women who successfully petitioned Parliament for a divorce in 1920, fourteen were war wives. Hardly evidence of an epidemic of wartime infidelity, but significant nonetheless: even though military wives represented a very small proportion of all married women in Ontario, they accounted for slightly more than half of all Parliamentary divorces granted on the grounds of a husband's infidelity.[41]

More revealing than the fragmentary evidence preserved in the Parliamentary record is British evidence of, and anxiety about, the extramarital conduct of Canadian soldiers abroad. The Canadian press paid only occasional attention to cases of soldiers' infidelity. In July 1918, for example, the *Globe* reported that Major Andrew Cory had been court-martialled for refusing to return to Canada as scheduled. In his defence, he claimed that he needed to stay in London, where he had been named as a co-respondent in a divorce case. He indicated that he hoped his English lover, who was being divorced by her husband, would then return to Canada with him. He acknowledged, however, that he had a wife already in Canada.[42] The British press was less reluctant to expose the marital misadventures of Canadian soldiers, for defenders of British morality became increasingly incensed over the course of the war by what they took to be the promiscuous ways of Dominion troops temporarily stationed in England.

Between 1914 and 1918 more than a million men from Britain's "white Dominions" enlisted for (or, in some instances late in the war, were conscripted into) military service. Many of the men from Canada, Australia, and New Zealand who returned to Europe to defend the Empire had close – and sometimes very entangled – family ties in "the Old Country." When William Harvey married Mary Sutherland in Winnipeg shortly before the war he presumably did not tell her that his Scottish wife, Elsie, was still alive. Nor, presumably, did he alert her to the fact that, while serving in Europe, he and Elsie had resumed their married life. But upon his death, when the pensions office in its Solomonic wisdom had to decide which "wife" was to be deemed his legal "widow," both Mary and Elsie had to make do on a partial pension.[43] Other men had no reluctance to forge new ties even though they had a wife and children at home. Evidence of this was to be found in the sad stories of young English girls seduced by married men from the Dominions; and in divorce proceedings heard before the Admiralty, Divorce and Probate Court and reported in the pages of Britain's popular and prestige press.

Both the *Daily Mirror* and *The Times* followed closely the case of Major Francis Saunders, heard in April 1920, who contended that his wife had committed adultery with a Canadian officer, Major William Inglis. Inglis, a married stockbroker from Edmonton who had enlisted in October 1915, made the acquaintance of Major Saunders's wife in the spring of 1917, while Saunders was still serving in France. Several servants testified that they frequently found Inglis in Mrs Saunders's London apartment, and on at least one occasion in her bed. She denied this vigorously, insisting that her servants were liars. To support her claims of innocence and to defend her honour, she needed Inglis, who had returned to Canada in 1919, to provide exculpatory testimony. She thus took it upon herself to write to his father-in-law, stressing how important it was that Inglis deny the charges of adultery. If he did not do so, she wrote, he would leave her to "bear the brunt" and would be, in her judgment, a "rotten man." The judge put little stock in Inglis's denial of misconduct, finding the testimony of the three charwomen more compelling, even though they were, as he observed, "persons in a humble position in life." He granted Major Saunders a decree nisi.[44]

In another case involving a Canadian man cited in a postwar English divorce case, Rupert Inkster was in January 1920 named as the co-respondent in an uncontested petition for divorce brought by Sergeant Richard Smith. Inkster, a married man with a wife and six children living in Winnipeg, arrived in England in September 1917. Assigned to the London offices of the Canadian Forestry Corps, Inkster met Smith's wife when she went to work there. Passionate exchanges ensued, and incriminating letters discovered by the wronged husband proved decisive in the judge's deliberations. Whether Inkster, who had returned to Canada in October 1919, ever paid the substantial sum of £400 awarded in damages to the man he had wronged remains unknown.[45]

Perhaps even more alarming than the evidence heard in divorce proceedings were the stories of bigamous marriages recounted in England's criminal courts. Bigamy, the British feared, was very much on the rise in wartime England and in many cases blame rested firmly on the shoulders of Dominion soldiers like Edward McGonigle, who stood trial in Dorchester in January 1918. Originally from Scotland, he had emigrated to Australia before the war, leaving his wife and children in Glasgow. Enlisting under a false name, he had served with distinction at Gallipoli and on the Western Front and was subsequently discharged. Rather than return to his wife and children in Glasgow, however, he married a young English girl with whom he had a child. Although his commanding officer spoke well of McGonigle's military service, the assizes judge was unsympathetic: bigamy, he charged, was "getting too common, especially among soldiers," and McGonigle was sentenced to four months in prison.[46] While McGonigle awaited sentencing, *The Times* published two letters, both protesting the duplicitous ways of still more "bounders" temporarily residing in Britain. In the words of one outraged father, his respectable daughter had "narrowly escaped falling a victim to the bigamous instincts of an overseas warrior." Because it was almost impossible to ascertain from afar the true marital status of such men, he urged parents to be especially vigilant if their daughters were being courted by Dominion soldiers purporting to be single.[47] The view that married Dominion soldiers represented a unique threat to the reputations of young English women also unsettled some Members of Parliament. In April 1918 the Liberal MP for the riding of Thornbury rose in the House to protest what he believed were the unscrupulous ways of married men far from home, alleging "that many thousands of marriages between overseas soldiers and British women had taken place, and that there was evidence that some hundreds of these were bigamous." The Under-Secretary for War hoped that the Right Honourable Member was mistaken in his understanding of the severity of the problem but insisted that the War Office could neither introduce legislation on the topic nor "facilitate the obtaining of legal evidence from the Dominions."[48]

Young women and their parents were wise to be wary. Ella Caddey had the good sense to contact authorities in Ottawa, seeking reassurance that her fiancé was, as he insisted, well and truly divorced. According to her Canadian suitor, who admitted that he had been married and had two children in Toronto, he and his wife had received a divorce "between the years 1913 and 1917." Ottawa could offer Ella no such assurance, however, for a "search of the statutes fail[ed] to disclose any Act granting a divorce between Harry Altman Lee and Emily Jane Lee, formerly Emily Jane Turner, of Toronto."[49] Other would-be brides were more gullible, beguiled perhaps by the promise of life in a far-away land. Australians (like Frank Cox) and New Zealanders (like Vincent Roberts) also found themselves in court, facing charges of bigamy. Cox, a 2nd Lieutenant in the Royal Warwickshire Regiment, had a wife in Australia when he married Dorothy Dyer in London in May 1916.[50] When Roberts appeared before the justices of the Old Bailey in January 1918 his tale of marital misadventure was enough to raise the eyebrows of even the most jaded court recorder: "One day, while standing in Regent Street, Westminster, he accidentally knocked a bag out of the hand of a woman clerk named Bennett. He introduced himself, said he had been wounded in Gallipoli, and suggested that they should become engaged and be married almost immediately. The young woman replied, 'This is sudden, is it not?' but she accepted the proposal of marriage and a few days later they were married at a church in Brixton. It was subsequently discovered that the prisoner was already married." Not surprisingly, the recorder at the Old Bailey shook his head in dismay. Having noted his disgust at the number of bigamy cases before the court, he opined that there had been "considerable carelessness" on the part of many of the young women who had failed to make the appropriate inquiries of the men's regiments.[51] A year later, he had no reason to be more sanguine: the number of bigamy cases brought before the court was, in his judgment, "most appalling," and "this referred not only to our own men, but also to Australians, Canadians, and New Zealanders."[52]

From the vantage point of British jurists and journalists, there was little to distinguish one devious Dominion soldier from another: Canadians, Australians, and New Zealanders were all of a piece. From the vantage point of Canadian war wives, jurists, and journalists, however, only the misdeeds of Canadian men mattered. As in England, cases of bigamous marriage entered into while a soldier was in uniform or following his demobilization gained the attention of Canadian newspapers and the opprobrium of Canadian judges. However valiant their overseas service, high-ranking officers who abandoned their wives and deceived unsuspecting women were especially blameworthy. In 1915 Major William Stewart (who also went by Stitt) left his Toronto wife of many years to take charge of a recruiting campaign in Calgary, where he met and married a Miss Lillian Tipping. Even though his commanding officer spoke highly of his subsequent service in France, this commendation counted for little when Stewart appeared before an

Edmonton judge on a charge of bigamy. Stewart received the unusually harsh sentence of four years in the Edmonton penitentiary. Rank-and-file soldiers who offered the much-used excuse that because they suffered from shell shock they had no memory of ever having been married, fared somewhat better. One soldier, who had left his first wife destitute and dependent upon the good will of public charity and had then "deceived" a seventeen-year-old girl, pleaded temporary insanity. The judge found the "shell-shock" defence unpersuasive and sentenced him to two years in the Kingston Penitentiary. The shell-shock defence did not disappear, however: in 1922, James Wright, a former soldier, appeared in Police Court in Toronto on a charge of bigamy. He claimed that he had suffered "a lapse of memory due to war service" and had "no recollection of his first wife at the time he married the second."[53]

When divorce was expensive and a marriage no longer sustainable, bigamy was – at least in the judgment of one returning soldier – a man's only recourse.[54] His judge thought differently and sentenced him to jail. For those not willing to court a jail sentence, desertion was less expensive than divorce and harder to prosecute.[55] Desertion had so long been a common enough solution to a miserable marriage, in Britain as in Canada, as to be called "the poor man's divorce," but it was only in the years immediately preceding the war that social commentators in Canada and members of the judiciary grew especially worried about its proliferation.[56] As the western provinces opened up for settlement, it was all too easy for a husband to desert his home and abandon his familial obligations. This, at least, was the considered opinion of one Crown Attorney in Ontario who in 1914 observed that desertion had "become much too common, encouraged doubtless by the immunity from pursuit where refuge is taken in the far West."[57] The war did nothing to calm such concerns. By the early twenties, social workers were increasingly alarmed by what they took to be an upsurge in family desertion and the economic misery to which it condemned deserted women and children. As the *Globe* so pithily stated in 1923: "Runaway Husbands Create Big Problems for Social Forces."[58]

Desertion was not an exclusively male offence. Runaway wives caused their wronged husbands considerable heartache, too, as many plaintive letters submitted to Ottawa made clear and as Wilfred Whitely, a victim of his own impetuous passion, learned to his dismay. Only days before he sailed for France in 1915, Whitely met and proposed marriage to Daisy Louise French in Windsor. Following his return from the war, he persuaded her to relocate with him to Detroit, where she found work as a nurse and a new love: a convalescent American soldier. Daisy and her American lover soon decamped to Winnipeg, leaving Wilfred to care for his infant son.[59] But if the emotional toll of desertion fell on abandoned husbands as much as on deserted wives, wives suffered more acutely its economic effects.[60] Unlike war widows, who were almost always eligible for a pension, deserted wives were not. They were eligible for temporary relief under the terms of the Canadian Patriotic Fund Post Discharge Relief Act, which authorized the CPF to distribute all funds remaining in its account to the widows and orphans of men who had died prior to January 1921 "from causes not directly attributable to his war service"; to "deserted wives and deserted children where the soldier has been discharged and has disappeared"; and to "the unmarried wife with children, recognized during the war by the Government or Patriotic Fund, but abandoned by the soldier within three months after discharge."[61] In each instance, the maximum grant was to be $100 a month, and allowances would continue only until the funds were exhausted. Deserted wives received no further promise of ongoing support. Nor were they ordinarily eligible for the "Mothers' Allowances" first introduced in Manitoba in 1916 and, by 1920, in all provinces west of Quebec.

Manitoba granted Mothers' Allowances only to widowed mothers or "if [the] husband is in prison or asylum or physically disabled." Ontario also excluded deserted wives when it introduced a comparable program in 1920. On the grounds that it was a husband's moral and legal responsibility to provide support for his wife and children, Ontario legislators feared that if his dependents were to receive a state-funded allowance, he would too easily abandon his responsibilities. An amendment to the Ontario law passed in 1921 allowed deserted wives to receive a Mother's Allowance if their husbands had abandoned the family home at least seven years earlier; a subsequent amendment, passed in 1925, reduced the period of desertion to five years. It was therefore only in 1925 that Ontario war wives who had been deserted in the immediate aftermath of the war became eligible for these very modest allowances. Even then, women whose husbands had deserted the family home – whether prior to or after the war – constituted only a small percentage of all recipients.[62] The British Columbia mothers' allowance program, also introduced in 1920, was more generous in its funding and more expansive in scope. Deserted mothers were eligible for support from the outset and could receive a monthly allowance of up to $42.50 a month (for a deserted wife with one child at home) and an additional $7.50 for each additional child. When Nova Scotia debated the merits of mothers' allowances in 1921, legislators recognized that "there were strong arguments to support the granting of pensions or allowances to all worthy women, bearing alone the responsibility of providing for their young children." But insofar as the Nova Scotia treasury could not countenance a program as expensive and expansive as that in place in British Columbia, only widowed mothers with young children at home were eligible for support.[63] Throughout most of Canada, therefore, deserted wives had to fend for themselves, finding work when they could, relying on municipal relief and private charity, and struggling – often unsuccessfully – to keep their children out of institutional care.

War wives were not the only women to suffer the effects of marital desertion. One social worker estimated that in Toronto alone there were as many deserted wives as there were widows receiving a mother's allowance.[64] Although it is impossible to know how many of these women were war wives, fragmentary evidence strongly suggests that many of them surely were. In September 1923, when the annual meeting of the Ontario Great War Veterans' Association convened in Welland, the delegates called for an amendment to the province's Mothers' Allowance law to include women who had been deserted for three years or more.[65] Why would Canadian veterans insert themselves into political debates about the fate of deserted wives – insisting that women abandoned as recently as 1920 receive much needed financial assistance – if they were not concerned about the plight of war wives and children left to look after themselves in the aftermath of the war? The case of one Mrs Lambert, which made headlines in early 1923, revealed how necessary such support could be. A war bride, Mrs Lambert had met her Canadian husband while he was serving in the CEF. They had two children before they returned to Canada and another two in Canada. When Lambert decamped for the United States, he left his family in desperate straits, living in a "hovel in the township of Thorold with very little clothing, no food, and in a deplorable condition." His wife feared that, if she remained in Canada, her children would ultimately have to be placed in care: "she does not want to remain if her children are taken from her as they will have to be if she does remain."[66] She was understandably anxious to return home, where her parents could provide the care and attention she and her children so desperately needed.

Deserted wives ineligible for provincial support managed as best they could. Like Mary Palmer, they sought work where and when they could; and relied on the support of family, if possible. Whereas families had been a reliable (and probably willing) source of support during the war – when wives could contribute their Separation Allowances to the household budget – deserted wives were not always welcome additions to families with other obligations. As Annalee Lepp has demonstrated, the fathers and brothers of deserted wives often believed – with some justice – that the husband was responsible for his wife's upkeep. For a family to provide room and board to a deserted wife and her children was, in effect, to let her husband off the hook. Sorry though their circumstances surely were, "deserted and neglected wives were frequently constructed as economic liabilities by family members, close neighbors, and local officials"[67] Deserted wives were therefore under greater pressure to support themselves than was customary for married women. Mary Palmer's experience in this regard is revealing. Like many war wives, she and her daughter had lived with her parents while her husband was overseas. When it became clear that her much-married husband had no intention of returning to his first wife and child, she found work, first at a printing shop in Toronto. When it closed at the end of 1920, she accepted a position in Thessalon on the *Algoma Advocate* staff, where, she complained, "I had to work both day and very often half the night until my nerves were a perfect wreck so I came home here to take a rest." While working in Thessalon she presented herself as Miss M.E. Palmer: "it is hard for a married woman to get a job in the printing and so I went by Miss as I could not afford to be without work."[68] Although she made no mention of it, she probably left her daughter in Toronto to be cared for by her parents. Daycare facilities were rare, and probably non-existent in small towns in northern Ontario. The few that did exist in Toronto catered exclusively to women – categorized as "unfortunates" – who had no choice but to seek paid work: the wives of unemployed men, separated or single mothers, and deserted wives.[69]

Marriages hastily undertaken on the eve of mobilization were perhaps especially prone to desertion. Hilda McQueen's story of a hasty marriage followed quickly by the birth of a baby traces a trajectory from wartime marriage to postwar abandonment. She and her husband had married in December 1914 a few weeks before he left to train at Camp Hughes in Manitoba and four months before their daughter was born. While overseas, she wrote the minister of justice, he had written "regular until Sept. 6 1916 then there was ten months or until June 6 1917 I never had one letter from him then he wrote saying our marriage was all a mistake ... He came home on March 1st 1919 from overseas but he never came back to me nor have I had a word or a cent of support from him since March 1 1919. Now what I want to know is this is it possible for me to get this marriage annulled so I could marry again."[70]

Some longstanding marriages with many children also collapsed in the aftermath of war. In August 1919, Thomas Keeler was arraigned in magistrate's court in Cobourg, Ontario, charged with deserting his wife and five children and (not incidentally) having entered into a bigamous marriage following his release from the Kingston Military Hospital.[71] Wilfred Eadie, born in 1873 in Ontario, married his wife, Annie, in 1898 and by the beginning of the war had settled, with their four children, in Winnipeg. He enlisted in April 1916 and upon demobilization chose not to return to Winnipeg, opting instead to take a farm in Ontario under the government's veteran's settlement plan. He married for a second time in 1919, claiming that "his reason for not wanting to go back to Winnipeg was that he didn't want to live in the same house with his mother-in-law." He received a sentence of three months of hard labour in the Ontario Reformatory.[72] A hasty, ill-advised marriage, the traumatic effects of wartime service, a newfound love far from home – any (or all) of these factors might precipitate marital desertion.

The records of Manitoba's Soldiers' Deserted Wives Fund (SDWF) shed further light on the manifold causes of marital desertion, the material challenges deserted wives contended with in the decade after the war, and the strategies they embraced to keep their households intact. The brainchild of Edith Rogers, the first woman elected to the Manitoba legislature, the SDWF was intermittently subject to budget cuts and faced opposition from politicians who, like their counterparts in other provinces, had little interest in supporting the dependents of men who refused to fulfil their familial responsibilities. These obstacles notwithstanding, the fund lasted into the late 1920s, providing modest – but invaluable – assistance to war wives who discovered in 1919 (or shortly thereafter) that their husbands had no intention of returning to the family home. A demobilized soldier reluctant to resume married life, whether because wartime separation had exposed the fault lines of an already unhappy marriage or because the strains of war had made marital reunion well-nigh impossible, might decide to remain in Europe at the end of the war; might disappear into the crowds of demobilized men disembarking in Halifax or Montreal; or might linger at home for a while before leaving for good. One Manitoba woman who had relocated to Britain during the war expected her husband to follow shortly after she and her three children embarked at Liverpool. He had accompanied the family to the ship when they set sail for Canada in the spring of 1919 and had "stated that he was quite pleased to see the three children, ages 14, 7 and 4, and myself leaving for Canada and that he would join us in Canada before Christmas 1919." Within a month, however, he had indicated to his military superiors that he had no intention of returning to Canada nor, it would seem, any plans to support his family. Since her return, she reported: "[I have] received not one cent of support for myself or children from my husband ...

the only sum I have received since arriving in Canada is a Cheque for ninety dollars representing War Service Gratuity." Subsequent inquiries revealed that her husband was living in England with a Belgian woman whom he identified (misleadingly) as his wife. A year later they were living in Belgium and thereafter in Chicago.[73]

More common than the husband who remained in Europe at the end of the war, usually in something that resembled a bigamous marriage, was the man who disappeared as soon as or shortly after returning to Canada. A Manitoba wife, the mother of nine children (including three sons old enough to enlist in the CEF and a toddler born in 1916), struggled to support her children when it became evident that her husband had abandoned the family. Upon his return to Canada in December 1918 he had remained in Halifax while his fellow Manitobans made their way home. By June she discovered that her husband had returned to England where, according to a neighbour, he was "living with a woman who knows he is married and [is] worse than him."[74] In another case also supported by the Manitoba SDWF, the husband returned to Winnipeg in April 1919 and lived with his wife "intermittently" over the next few months, before abandoning her and his two children for good in September. Rumour had it that he had headed west to Vancouver, having contributed nothing to the household "for some time prior to that."[75]

Provincial and federal law required a husband to support his wife and children. Enforcing those laws in a vast nation with a relatively porous international border proved next to impossible. Errant husbands were hard to locate and, even if found, difficult to prosecute. Alberta's deputy attorney general wrote in June 1923, when consulted on the Alexander Petrie case, that "a husband is under obligation to provide for his wife, but whether or not he can be compelled to do so depends upon his financial circumstances. If Petrie has no money and is without a job nothing is to be gained by bringing him back to this Province for trial."[76] Court orders were equally hard to enforce if a husband left the country. However difficult the process, wives, their parents, and, in Manitoba at least, the provincial authorities had a strong interest in pursuing such cases. Under pressure to pare its expenses as best it could, without leaving women and children in desperate circumstances, the staff of the SDWF made repeated and often lengthy efforts to locate deadbeat husbands. When they tracked the Winnipeg soldier who had "married" a Belgian woman to Chicago, they sought the assistance of the Chicago police chief: could he "send one of [his] men to interview him and see if it was not possible to get him to make some regular allowance towards the support of his wife and family"? These inquiries proved fruitless, and the family remained dependent upon the resources of the deserted wives' fund.[77] In yet another case, the SDWF paid a Winnipeg woman's train fare to Los Angeles, where she went in search of her husband. If she could find him and "make him assume his responsibilities," so much the better; if not, then at least she would no longer be a charge on the Manitoba fund.[78]

An especially diligent yet ultimately fruitless campaign to compel support focused on a husband who deserted his wife and two children shortly after returning to Canada in the spring of 1919. Home barely a month before he set sail again for England, he refused categorically to live with his family in Winnipeg, where, he claimed, he had been obliged against his will to support his wife's extended family. Whether he had ever done so was, according to the Manitoba investigators, open to doubt. It was certainly no excuse for failing to provide for his wife and two children. Starting in the spring of 1920 and continuing for the next five years, the SDWF engaged in an extensive correspondence with the Canadian Investigation Office for Overseas Military Forces in London, the Canadian High Commissioner's office, and the English Police Commission, with the objective of securing regular support payments for the Winnipeg family. All that materialized were excuses, lies, stories of failed business ventures, and various small remittances. When first interviewed in 1920, the husband claimed that he had arranged for his immediate family to receive $75 a month from his Winnipeg partnership, but the business was not doing well and the most he could promise to provide was £10 a month, to be sent from London forthwith. More than a year later, that was the first – and only – payment his wife had received. Once again, the Manitoba offices intervened with the London authorities: "you say that he is sending his wife the sum of £10 … from that date to this he has not sent another penny." Threats to have him deported were in vain – he was a British citizen and could not be forced to leave his homeland – as were renewed efforts to secure regular support payments. In 1923 the Office of the Canadian High Commissioner reported: "Since his business closed up he has been out of work, and in great difficulties. He has at last succeeded in finding a situation and … he has promised to send at least £5 within the next three weeks, and will increase this as he may be able." That promise, too, went unfulfilled. In 1925, the SDWF caseworker calculated that, for all their efforts, "since his discharge [he] has sent various amounts to his wife and children amounting to approximately £40, the last amount sent was £2 Xmas time 1923."[79]

Even when they were eligible for provincial support – as they were in Manitoba and British Columbia – deserted wives often had to struggle to make ends meet. The Mothers' Allowances, which constituted the

basis upon which the Soldiers' Deserted Wives Allowances were calculated, were ordinarily less generous than war widows' pensions, and
budget cuts imposed on several occasions through the 1920s reduced the
number of women supported by the fund and the amount they received
each month. Recipients were expected to supplement their allowances
by working outside the home, by taking in lodgers, or by sending their
teenage children out to work. Paid employment for women of few skills
and little education was rarely very remunerative, largely because, when
minimum wages for women's work were established shortly after the
war, they were based on calculations of what was necessary to support a
young, unmarried woman still living at home.[80] Twelve dollars a week,
the established wage for retail clerks in Manitoba, might have sufficed
for women with no dependents, but a deserted wife with two young
children at home who earned $14 a week in 1920 as a sales clerk in a
Winnipeg department store found it difficult to work, pay for childcare,
and cover her other expenses. At the end of the decade, one woman
who earned $9 a week working half-days as a waitress, and another, who
earned $55 a month as a cleaning lady would have been living on the edge
of economic disaster.[81] Waged labour of this sort, however modestly paid,
was possible only if child care was available, and women without family
to call upon could only adapt as best they could. A woman employed as
a sales clerk requested $25.00 a month from the SDWF so that she could
keep her job and "pay a woman to look after the children in the day
time." Another woman, who worked as a caretaker in her apartment
building, supplemented her meagre income by "going out to wash to
earn money for the maintenance of herself and 3 children."[82] And a
deserted wife who gave birth shortly after her husband permanently
abandoned the home opted to share a house with another woman in
similar circumstances. While the more robust woman went out to work,
the new mother looked after both families and took care of the house.
The SDWF gave her an allowance of $40 per month.[83]

Even though Manitoba expressly prohibited women in receipt of
Mothers' Allowances from taking in male boarders – a practice deemed
injurious to the moral well-being of women and children alike – deserted
war wives who could afford the upkeep on a house did rent out rooms,
hoping to find reliable tenants and a regular source of income. In some
cases, they succeeded. One woman of a most enterprising spirit first
found work in a doctor's office, "where she earned $12.00 per week when
she puts in full time." This was far from a perfect arrangement: after her
husband deserted the home, she was in poor health – "on the verge of
a nervous breakdown," in the opinion of her caseworker – and rarely
able to work full time; and when she could work she had to keep her

ten-year-old daughter home from school to mind the three-year-old. Renting a large house and then taking in lodgers proved a more reliable road to self-sufficiency. By 1925 she was paying $72 a month in rent but was able to recoup $120 each month from her lodgers. In the admiring words of her caseworker: "the appearance of [the wife] and her home does credit to her as a careful manager." A large house was expensive to heat, requiring even the most careful manager to seek support from the sdwf. Once her winter coal bill was paid off, the caseworker was confident that "she will be able to manage without further assistance, and we will consider the account closed."[84] Other women fared less well. In April 1920 a woman whose husband had deserted her six months earlier was trying to meet the mortgage payments on her home by renting out a room. But her tenant, who had contracted measles and was unable to work, fell behind on his rent and owed her $40. Problems continued to mount to the point that by October 1924 the mortgage was "more in arrears than ever."[85]

When a father deserted the family home, his teenage children were expected to work. This was easier for families in towns and cities than for those in the countryside, where jobs were often far away and poorly paid. Although teenage wages everywhere were paltry, they were important components of a family budget. The Winnipeg family whose husband and father had abandoned them on the dock at Liverpool was by August 1919 on the very brink of destitution. The mother was facing an imminent confinement; her sister-in-law would care for the children while she was in hospital, but she was already in debt to the grocery store, facing a rent bill of $10.00 at the end of the month, and medical bills amounting to $37.25. By November 1919 her fourteen-year-old daughter had secured a job in the mail order department at Eaton's but, as the city's Social Welfare department reported: "[she is] very weakly and lacks clothing. In this severe slushy weather she has nothing for her feet but a pair of low shoes, with a gaping hole in the side. The younger members of the family who should be at school have been kept home owing to lack of clothing." The sdwf calculated that "the necessary expenses of the family at present amount to a minimum of $84.00 per month." The daughter earned $36 a month; a lodger might bring in another $20, leaving the family almost $30 a month shy of the basic income needed to survive. Recognizing that the family also had to pay medical bills, make installment payments on the household furniture, and purchase adequate winter clothing for the children, the fund authorized a monthly grant of $65.[86]

If an extra year or two of schooling or vocational training beyond the official school-leaving age of fourteen could help a teenager secure a higher wage or a more reliable job, then the sdwf was willing to continue its family support. Secretarial courses were a favourite choice of young girls, even though work was not guaranteed. One family received support through April 1925, but was expected to support themselves as soon as the eldest daughter, having just turned sixteen, had finished her "business course and [was] ready to work."[87] The SDWF also looked kindly on a request from a woman who had moved her family out of Winnipeg to a town in the Interlake region, where the cost of living was more manageable and she could grow vegetables and raise chickens. By 1927, when both of her children were in their mid-teens, the Winnipeg office indicated that she should now be able to fend for herself. She made a convincing case for continued support: "My children are both going to school and are in the 7th grade the boy lost a lot of schooling when he was little through sickness but is doing fine now I had hoped to keep him in school until he passed the 8th grade the girl longer as the grades go to eleven in our school and then they would be in a better position to earn a respectable living."[88]

Farmhands and domestic servants – the jobs available to teenagers in much of rural Manitoba – were hard-pressed to support their mothers and younger siblings. The woman whose husband deserted her in 1919, leaving her to support six children under sixteen, remained dependent upon the SDWF through the end of the 1920s, even though several of her children were by that point earning wages. In August 1923, when provincial funds for the year had been exhausted, the administrators of the SDWF were forced to reduce its caseload, removing from its books beneficiaries whose children were old enough to work. Faced with the reduction of her allowance from forty dollars to twenty, this deserted wife set forth the circumstances of her difficult existence:

> I have two sons working on the same farm together out west hired for 6 months one is getting $35 and the other $40 … These two young men want to try and rent a farm next spring as they cannot get along on such small wages and cannot possibly support me and my home and children they have to raise themselves first, they always do their best to give me what they can when they get their wages in the fall which is not very much. I have a daughter just 17 in Minnedosa earning $12 a month and she is only able to send me $2 each month as she has to buy all her own clothing. I have another boy only 14 years of age who should be at school but through my allowances coming down so low was compelled to send him on a farm, the farmer had to teach him first so was only able to give him $10 to start for the first three months and $15 for the other three, he will only get his board in the winter, he has to find himself in clothing out of his summer wages.

When her adult children could offer only the most minimal assistance, and she still had three children of school age, she could not imagine how she would survive on $20 a month: "Our house is fearfully cold in the winter and freezes things solid when a cold wind is on it with two stoves going I cannot think what it would be like with no fire at all. I hope I am not taking too much of your valuable time Sir in writing such a long letter but I have explained as briefly as it was possible."[89] This careful accounting – and a strong letter of support from a municipal councillor – failed to overturn the SDWF's original judgment: from September 1923 through the end of the decade, she would receive an allowance of $20 a month.

Cobbled together in this way, a deserted war wife's monthly income was rarely robust enough to cover emergencies or unanticipated expenses. Illness was a constant worry, as it had been during the war. In September 1922 one woman was hospitalized for six weeks, amassing a doctor's bill of $177. She was subsequently diagnosed with tuberculosis and was admitted to the provincial sanitarium in Ninette.[90] In another case, a woman was hospitalized on three separate occasions between 1922 and 1924, making it impossible for her to care for her two children. They were taken into foster care and their upkeep – totalling $37 per month – was covered by the SDWF. But the mother's health remained precarious and by 1926 she owed more than $70 in unpaid hospital bills. The Fund intervened once again and explained to the collection agency that "any worry is liable to put her back in Hospital again. Her little shack is paid for, thanks to eldest son who is now married leaving the mother one boy ten years of age." She had a monthly allowance of only $35, out of which she had to "keep and clothe herself and her boy ten years of age, buy fuel and pay Taxes and incidental expenses she has very little left to pay Hospital bills."[91] Poor health also troubled a young wife whose husband disappeared to the States in 1919. She was too ill to take, and keep, a job and, as her caseworker astutely recognized, with three children at home, the youngest only eight, it would have been difficult for her to care for her family while also working outside the home. From 1920 to 1925 she did what she could to improve her circumstances. She completed a stenography course but could not find a position, and in the spring of 1925 an operation left her unable to take on any heavy work.[92]

As had been the case so often during the war, children's ill-health only added to the emotional and economic burden of mothers attempting to manage on their own. One deserted wife, the mother of four children, found it difficult to work outside the home when her children fell ill. In January 1921 she wrote asking if she could have her cheque a little earlier that month, "as with the expense of moving and my little girl has been sick that I have not been able to work and … you know work of any kind is hard to get just now and we are nearly out of fuel I hope you wont think me bothering too much." By October she was once again in difficult straits: "One of the children are ill in Hospital and have been for the past 5 weeks with diphtheria I expect him home this week of course that prevented me from working nearly two weeks as we were not allowed out. I understand the City is going to pay the Hospital."[93]

⁕⁓⁕

Because the Soldiers' Deserted Wives Fund was usually willing to provide the supplemental funds needed to cover hospital expenses, heating bills, and children's boots, it remained through the 1920s an invaluable source of much-needed assistance to Manitoba's most desperate war wives. Although grants were often modest, and became more so by the mid-twenties, the women who received them recognized how much they depended upon this support. In 1927 the mother of four who had struggled to get by when her children were ill, expressed her genuine gratitude: "I must thank you for all your trouble and kindness to us which enabled me to keep my children with me and keep and clothe them properly I can assure you we do appreciate your kindness very much."[94] Deserted war wives who lived in provinces that did not provide such support faced even more difficult circumstances. Dependent upon the slight support offered by municipal relief and private charities, they had no choice but to work outside the home, often for wages insufficient to cover their expenses; their children had to fend for themselves, with older children staying home from school to mind their younger siblings; and when all else failed, deserted wives had little choice but to surrender their children to institutional care. Social workers recognized that this was far from ideal. The Toronto director of the Division of Social Welfare regretted that, notwithstanding improvements to the Mothers' Allowances program, which by the end of the decade allowed deserted wives to qualify for support after three years, they often struggled in the early years to keep their families together: "We find that even with the three years, there is a very strong tendency to place children in Homes rather than give adequate relief to the family."[95] Suzanne Morton's study of "single women" in working-class Halifax reinforces this observation: deserted wives were more likely than widows to surrender their children to foster care or adoption; and, at least in Halifax, municipal authorities hesitated to rent to them.[96]

Two accounts from outside Manitoba of deserted war wives struggling to manage confirm this impression of a life of oppressive hardship in the aftermath of the war. Hilda McQueen and Grace Pelton had very little in common: Hilda was twenty-one and a pregnant newlywed when her husband left for war; Grace was in her late thirties and had been married since 1901. But after the war, both were deserted wives with almost no means of support. Even though Hilda had taken a position as a housekeeper for a young farmer in Saskatchewan, she had no income to speak of: "I have no home nor no money and times are very hard all over and I cannot get things for myself and Baby without help … Why I have only had 50 ¢ to spend in the last month."[97] Grace had no child to support but was burdened with debts, plagued by ill-health, and dependent upon the kindness of friends. While her husband, his new "wife" and three children lived on a small farm in Nova Scotia, Grace found work in Saint John with the Salvation Army. For as long as she was employed, she had been allowed to run a tab at the local store "and pay each week, and then when I got settled up I could do likewise again." Illness kept her home from work, adding to her debts and leaving her all but homeless: "I also owe board and had to settle my board bill on the Salvation Army Officers before I could claim what few clothes I possessed. Now I am at friends of mine until I see what can be done here. They have all they can do themselves. I cannot remain here because they cannot keep me without paying my board. I will have to have clothes and money to live on, and will ask your advice what I can do or what can be done. I am not able to work because that is why I was discharged is because I lost so much time with sickness."[98] The authorities in Ottawa to whom both Hilda and Grace addressed their pleas could neither grant the divorce that would allow Hilda to marry her young farmer nor compel Grace's husband to support her. Lives of quiet destitution were the lot of many a deserted war wife.

Conclusion

The Invisible Wounds of War

By April 1917 Betty Mayse appeared on the edge of a nervous breakdown. Her husband, Will, having enlisted in January 1916, had spent the best part of that year in training camp in Brandon, Manitoba, a deployment that allowed him to spend the occasional weekend with Betty and their two children in Winnipeg. His regiment sailed for England in November and by the spring of 1917, he – like so many other Canadian men – was preparing for the "big show" at Vimy. Indeed, when Betty went for weeks without word from him, she was sure he must be in the thick of battle and feared the worst. By the end of April, she was close to utter despair. To occupy her mind, while newspapers reported on Canadian heroics and Canadian casualties, she gave herself over to a cleaning frenzy, the likes of which would put most of us to shame:

> I have got nearly to the end of cleaning – the hardest part anyway. I spent all the spare time this week in the kitchen. Gave the ceiling 2 coats of white Kalsomine – & oh laud – the back and neck ache I've had – but it was worth it. The walls just needed a coat – real deep pinky cream – & its real nice. I stuffed all the cracks and holes with plaster paris & there is hardly a crack showing. I did the pipes & the board they are painted cream too … This evening I gave all the woodwork one coat of silver grey paint, and gave the stoves & pipes range a proper cleaning. That is where I am now, but today I gave the whole place a sweep – scrub and clean up for Sunday. I am feeling rather tired, but now that the dirt is cleaned out, & the place clean, I can take my time.

Hard work kept the most disturbing fears at bay, but when a letter arrived on April 27 with word that Will had missed the battle, quarantined as he was in England, Betty broke down in floods of tears. "Imagine my surprise," she wrote, "to find you are still in England. I don't think I knew how much I had been pushing it, till your letter came. I nearly had a fit between the letter and the kids. I was crying & Shirley ran to get a big handkerchief & got one arm around my neck & started mopping it off. She says, 'Billy, run & get a dish to catch them', & Billy hiked to the pantry and got a bread pan. By this time, I was able to tell him I'd manage now." Two days later she reflected: "I do not know how we will stand it when you do get over to France – it was hard, for the week & a half we thought of you there – but this 'reaction' had helped: only then – there will be no 'reaction' – only to hope, trust & pray – I'll stop now: Your letters come oftener now."[1]

Betty Mayse's experience reveals how the war and the enforced separation it imposed on married couples made psychological malaise an invisible but insidious companion in the lives of Canadian war wives. Dependent as they were on a mail service that was often maddingly unreliable, the wives who remained in Canada had only imprecise and much-delayed knowledge of their husbands' whereabouts and well-being. And, although hard work could temporarily tamp down their most unsettling fears, the life of a single parent, burdened as it was by the chores of home maintenance, the anxiety that accompanied children's illness, and the relentless penny-pinching that became more necessary in the last years of the war, eroded the resilience of many war wives, setting their nerves permanently on edge. Those who struggled with financial insecurity worried when a long-awaited and inexplicably delayed Separation Allowance cheque failed to arrive in time to pay the rent; their only recourse was to swallow their pride and ask the Patriotic Fund for an advance on their next month's allowance. As "single parents" solely responsible for the health and behaviour of their children, they fretted over fevers and dreaded any outbreak of epidemic disease. These domestic responsibilities alone would have made life difficult but, unlike other single mothers, a war wife also had to live with the corrosive knowledge and consuming fear bred of the realization that her husband's life was all too often in danger. Women coped as best they could, finding refuge (if possible) in the companionship of family, seeking solace (if they were so inclined) in prayer, and finding temporary release (if handicrafts appealed to them) in such unexceptional tasks as knitting. When these coping mechanisms proved ineffective – when the mail did not arrive or brought with it distressing news; when single-parenthood afforded no relief from the quotidian worries of ordinary life; when anxiety was constant – nervous strain was inevitable. In the most desperate cases, illness, hospitalization, and psychological collapse ensued.

For Canada's war wives, like their European counterparts, regular letter writing was the thread that kept their marriages intact. But Canadian wives discovered, to their great anguish, that their sheer distance from the fighting lines made it a sometimes-fragile thread. Letters moved more slowly than they did in Europe, delivery was more susceptible to interruption, and the conversational quality often apparent in European wartime correspondence – a quality dependent upon the daily exchange of letters – was more muted. It was not unusual for European couples to write one another every day, knowing their letters would be delivered within the week. When delivery was likely to be delayed, as it was in advance of major battles, husbands realized that the inevitable silence thus created would cause their families exceptional anxiety. When Robert Pöhland was serving on the Western Front in 1916, he took care to alert his wife whenever mail destined for the German home front was to be embargoed: "What will you be thinking?" he wrote. "You won't be able to shake off the fear. Because I've heard that this time the postal ban is going to last ten days. That means ten long anxious days and nights."[2] Delays of ten days or more, while exceptional and unnerving for European couples, were the ordinary lot of Canadian husbands and wives. And because mail was not shipped across the Atlantic every day, many Canadian soldiers became used to writing only once or twice a week. When they did write, censorship often constrained them in ways not seen in the wartime correspondence of French and German soldiers. Many letters were formulaic in their descriptions of front-line life and modest in their affirmations of affection; yet honest – often brutal – appraisals of battle did make their way home, the writers' reticence notwithstanding. Writing about their experiences probably offered soldiers a measure of psychological release that their wives could not share on reading about them. Even though wives often insisted that their husbands be as candid as they could, knowing about the horrors and unpredictable outcomes of combat was in no way reassuring. War wives worried about what they did know of combat and about what they didn't.

Unexplained and worrying gaps in mail delivery could not be offset in Canada, as they were in Europe, by more immediate and irrefutable evidence that a husband was, for the moment at least, alive and well. Distance from the fighting lines made home leave for Canadian soldiers almost impossible, depriving husbands and wives of the emotional respite that temporary reunions almost always granted to European couples. Recently married French couples like Paul and Marie Pireaud could dream about the pleasures that awaited them when Paul returned home on leave; somewhat older but still amorous couples like Frederick and Mary Corfield could plan decadent weekends in luxurious London hotels.[3] This was not an indulgence available to husbands and wives separated by the Atlantic. When Canadian men enlisted – pledging to serve "for the duration of the war plus six months" – their wives signed on to a similar term of enforced and uninterrupted separation.

The Canadian women who relocated to Britain could of course enjoy the benefits of their husbands' leave, officers' wives more often than the wives of enlisted men. And like other European war wives, Canadian women living in Britain could also learn indirectly of their husbands' well-being. It was customary in France, for example, for local men headed home on leave to carry with them letters written by their front-line comrades and intended for their wives or mothers. These letters and the informal visits that usually accompanied their delivery gave war wives the welcome assurance that twenty-four hours ago at least their husband was still alive.[4] Such assurances were never entirely satisfactory and certainly not as welcome as leave itself, but they were better than the weeks-long silences that Canadian war wives like Betty Mayse often had to endure. Not only did distance from the fighting front deny Canadian women the occasional conjugal companionship enjoyed by European couples but it also deprived them of the less intimate reassurances that a regular leave rotation could (and did) offer European war wives.

Distance from the fighting front did, of course, protect Canadian wives from the worst effects of war on the home front. The lot of Canadian war wives was not burdened by the abject material misery that tormented women and children in Germany, Austria-Hungary, and the Ottoman Empire; and the need for them to find work outside the home was less pressing than in Britain or France. The food crisis in each of the Central Powers was acute, at best, and disastrous, at worst. In Germany and Austria, where by the last years of the war all but the most privileged workers had to get by on about 800 calories a day, children were especially prone to malnutrition and the diseases that preyed on the underfed.[5] In the Ottoman Empire – affected as its allies were by the naval blockade, the conscription of men, and the forced requisitioning of farm animals – famine devastated much of civilian society from 1915 onward.[6]

In Britain and France life was much less harsh. Separation allowances, which Britain granted automatically to the dependents of enlisted men, were, through to the end of 1916, adequate to guarantee working-class women a degree of economic security and self-sufficiency many had never known before. A survey of the weekly budgets of British soldiers' wives reveals that when a husband's irregular peacetime wages were replaced by regular monthly stipends, his wife was

.able to budget more efficiently, live more comfortably than before the war, and factor into her budget two items now considered household necessities: stationery and the weekly care packages sent to her husband at the front.[7] Inflation and disruptions to the food supply caused by the resumption of unrestricted submarine warfare in February 1917 significantly eroded this modest affluence. In France, by contrast, war wives did not receive a separation allowance as a matter of course. Rather, they had to demonstrate need: they would qualify for a separation allowance only if ill-health prevented them from contributing to the family economy or if their household income, in the absence of the male breadwinner, was inadequate to meet their family's needs.[8] Whereas French war wives were expected to work, Canadian war wives, everyone agreed, should not have to do so. As recipients of Separation Allowances, Assigned Pay, and Patriotic Fund stipends, they were expected to remain at home, caring for their young children and reassuring their husbands that the war had not undermined the cultural presumption that males were the breadwinners. The economic challenges of wartime Canadian life were real enough, as the Manitoba Patriotic Fund records make evident. Food was costly and living conditions often uncomfortable, especially in the dead of winter when coal was scarce, rent was high, and apartments poorly heated. But outright famine was never a threat and abject economic misery was more exceptional than ordinary.

Distance also put most Canadian war wives and their children beyond the reach of aerial bombardment, enemy occupation, and forcible deportation. With the singular and significant exception of the women of Halifax, war wives in Canada did not have to fear for their lives. Nor did they have to contend with forced relocation from their family homes, with sexual assault, or – in the most severe instances – with the annihilationist policies of ethnic cleansing that women living in war zones across Europe and the Middle East often did.[9] In the departments of northern France, for example, women experienced bombardment of their family homes, requisitioning of essential supplies, and in some cases deportation to Germany of family members. Because German authorities prohibited all communication between men fighting in the French Army and their womenfolk living under enemy occupation, mothers and wives sometimes went for years with no word from their sons and husbands, no knowledge of their fate.[10] Not surprisingly, such material and emotional hardship could lead to sometimes profound psychological distress. Even though French psychiatrists were notoriously loath to trace psychological or psychiatric illness to the circumstances of war, preferring to believe that such distress was rooted in genetic susceptibility, they at least acknowledged that some women – in wartime Lille, for instance – did suffer from war-induced trauma.[11] The fragmentary evidence we have for women in central Europe and the Ottoman Empire is equally suggestive. Women in the Habsburg lands sometimes contemplated suicide when they could not secure the necessities of life for themselves and their children.[12] But, however desperate their circumstances, these war wives were spared the horrors inflicted on young Armenian women who were uprooted from their homes, forced to leave their newborn babies to die at the side of the road for want of food, and subjected to brutal assault. As one sympathetic observer recalled, they "suffered indescribably, and some lost their minds."[13]

It is surely understandable that women subjected to such material and emotional distress would suffer the effects of shattered nerves. But women who didn't live in the direct shadow of war or face famine and ethnic cleansing also experienced chronic psychological distress. Even though (as Stéphanie Petit has so rightly observed) historians have paid little attention to the psychological effects of wartime separation on women whose husbands were in uniform, she is surely correct that they lived with anxiety and its physiological consequences from the moment of their husband's mobilization.[14] Insomnia was commonplace, as was nervous exhaustion. Indeed, a prominent French physician, writing in 1914, had eerily anticipated the psychological and physiological effects of wartime separation. Francis Heckel appropriated and adapted Freud's concept of "anxiety neurosis" to argue that excessive anxiety could become manifest in physical malaise. When his work was published in 1917 in France, a nation upended by war, his argument appeared tragically apposite.[15] Women whose husbands (or sons) were in direct danger often experienced serious digestive, respiratory, and circulatory problems. Canadian war wives knew this all too well. A close reading of the available evidence reveals that persistent anxiety undermined the physical health and psychological stamina of many a Canadian war wife as well.

❧

Anxiety disrupted May Rogers's sleep, plagued her with persistent head-aches, and – she feared – robbed her of her youthful looks. Although only in her mid-thirties, she ruefully admitted to Laurie that her hair was turning grey. Laurie reassured her: "[You don't] need to worry about looking old for I will look pretty nearly as old when I get back. My hair is getting very grey and I am getting wrinkles in my face."[16] Nor could Maggie Ormsby disguise her anxiety or tame her deepest fears. After she sent George a family photograph in the summer of 1916, he noted the "worried expression" on her face. Two months later, while waiting for word that he had survived his critical wounding at the Somme, she suffered a recurrence of fainting fits.[17] Jennie Hillyer also found her nerves strained almost to the breaking point. Having struggled to maintain her duplex and cope with her drunken tenant (see chapter 3), she decided in December 1916 to vacate the duplex and relocate to an apartment nearer her sisters. Her respite from anxiety was short-lived, however, for the uncommonly cold winter wreaked havoc on her duplex, causing the pipes to burst, flood one of the apartments, and seriously inconvenience her new tenants. "I don't know how much longer my nerves can stand the strain," she confessed, consoling herself that "wars like all things must end and nothing really matters if I get you back safe and sound."[18] In the short term, she realized how much she benefited from being closer to family: "I feel far more contented over here than I did in Ville Emard. I would have lost my reason I think if I had stayed there any longer; everyone says I am looking better now. I have less work, more company."[19]

Laurie Rogers was equally certain that less work and more company would alleviate May's anxiety. Years before psychologists formally identified stress as a psychological condition with physiological consequences, he understood all too well the nature of "nervous strain," for he saw its effects on himself, his comrades-in-arms, and his wife: "You are not the only one that is getting old ... Some of the fellows have turned quite white out here owing to the constant strain on the nerves I guess."[20] Recognizing that May was not sleeping well, was losing weight, and was constantly worrying about his well-being, he recommended that she move from the small and rather inhospitable community of East Farnham into Montreal where, he was sure, she would benefit from being close to friends, family, and the counsel of their family doctor. Once she was settled in her city apartment, he urged her more than once to "go to Dr. Pat and let him give you the once over and give you a tonic or something and then just loaf around for this winter and get strong and fat."[21] He also hoped that, once free of the burdens of running the family farm, she would find time to exercise: "My you don't know how glad I am that you are taking up skating again and getting about it will do you the world of good and help you keep from worrying."[22] Long before physiologists and psychologists formally recognized that exercise could help alleviate stress, Laurie Rogers intuited its advantages.

Modern-day neuroscientists recommend a variety of strategies for managing stress: regular exercise, meditation, religious or spiritual practices, and the cultivation of social networks.[23] Some of these strategies would have been completely alien to the women of early twentieth-century Canada: they could not join a gym or go to a spa; they had probably never heard about the merits of yoga and meditation. They made effective use, however, of whatever coping measures were available to them. Women who lived with or moved close to parents and siblings benefited from their comfort and companionship. Prayer offered spiritual consolation to many war wives and, not incidentally, their husbands, for in a world over which they had so little control, prayer allowed them to envision the benevolent intercession of a compassionate deity. It is not surprising that Betty Mayse, the wife of a Baptist minister, would have "sent up many prayers for [his] safety, and speedy return." But so, too, did May Rogers, Angeline Maheux, and Jennie Hillyer. In November 1915, Laurie Rogers reassured his beloved May: "[I am] always thinking of you and know you are praying for me that is all we can do and leave the rest in the hands of a loving and higher power than our own then everything will come out all right." Frank Maheux urged Angeline to make a pilgrimage to Ste Anne de Beaupré and was comforted to know that she and the children remembered him in their prayers: "You say you pray for us, I tell you we need it to, a person can['t] believe all what we pass true." And Jennie Hillyer made sure that her two-year-old son included his father in his evening prayers: "He has said his prayers for his Daddy, I do hope the Good God will see fit to answer them as we desire." George Eastman also appreciated the prayers his wife and daughter dedicated to his safekeeping and believed that they alone had protected him while saving his companions from a grenade attack: "I believe that my Girls prayers helped me to do it as it saved my own life as well."[24]

Whether inclined to prayer or not, war wives might well have found a more prosaic antidote to stress in the ubiquitous enterprise of knitting. That women during the Great War spent many hours knitting socks and scarves for their men in uniform is well known. Canadian women, like their European counterparts, certainly engaged in knitting, sometimes in their own homes, sometimes in knitting circles organized by the Red Cross or the Imperial Order Daughters of Empire (IODE). Groups of women, from the Six Nations Indian Reserve outside Brantford, Ontario, to the several hundred war wives hosted by the Khaki Home in South Vancouver, devoted many an hour to knitting socks.[25] Although a very ordinary craft with under-appreciated benefits, knitting was recognized as a patriotic undertaking, dedicated to the well-being of men overseas: dry socks were the best protection against trench foot. And although some soldiers questioned the honesty of brokers responsible for shipping knitwear across the ocean, everyone who received them appreciated the socks, sweaters, and scarves made by their mothers or wives, sisters or daughters.[26] As May Rogers poignantly observed when preparing Laurie's Christmas parcel in 1917, the sweater Aileen made for her father might have had "some rather uneven places in knitting," but "there is a lot of love and devotion knit into it."[27] Knitting circles like the one arranged for war wives in Vancouver also gave war wives companionship, allowing them to "become acquainted with each other & prevent[ing] them from becoming lonely."[28] Equally important, knitting had therapeutic benefits whose physiological nature was unknown at the time, although likely experienced. As Katie Pickles has noted, the IODE championed knitting as a balm to the bereaved.[29] It is doubtful that these good matrons of imperial patriotism understood precisely why this was so – only many years later would physiologists discover that "knitting and crocheting can lower heart rate and blood pressure and reduce harmful blood levels of the stress hormone cortisol"[30] – but observation and experience would no doubt have made the therapeutic effects of this common practice evident.

The company of family, the consolation of faith, and the companionship of friends were a help, but for some of the most overburdened war wives these were not enough. Case files from the Manitoba Patriotic Fund reveal that women far removed from their extended families, women who had no access to the social amenities and support groups of towns and cities, and women who experienced exceptional emotional duress sometimes succumbed to physical and psychological breakdown. One especially unfortunate soul had known nothing but misery for as long as she had been married. Beaten and verbally abused by her husband, who on at least one occasion had tried to force her into prostitution, she had resisted his most malevolent inclinations and worked conscientiously to support herself, her daughter, and her aging and infirm mother. When her husband enlisted in 1915, identifying himself as an unmarried man and thus denying her access to either a Separation Allowance or his Assigned Pay, she had to turn to the Patriotic Fund for help. Even if her life was less stressful following her brutal husband's departure for war, she continued to suffer the accumulated effects of abuse, economic insecurity, and family dysfunction. Plagued by persistent headaches, poor eyesight, and undiagnosed hearing problems, she requested and received funds from the Patriotic Fund to seek treatment at the Mayo Clinic in Rochester, Minnesota. Her headaches were real enough, but her consulting physician could isolate no somatic cause: he stated that he could find "nothing of a serious nature, and her complaint was largely of a nervous character." Her problems persisted, however, and by April 1919 she was confined to bed, "suffering from nervous breakdown."[31]

Less dramatic but poignant nonetheless were the cases of two Manitoba war wives whose physical health deteriorated under the strain of wartime separation and family misfortune. One woman, apparently happily married since 1908 and the mother of two young boys, had been in poor health since at least 1914. Hospitalized in 1916, she had had to arrange for a neighbour to care for her children; a year later she was "knocked down and severely hurt by an auto." Battered by ill-health and unable to give her children the care she knew they deserved, she requested that her husband be sent home from France. As she explained to the Patriotic Fund: "My health has been indifferent and I have had severe nervous attacks due to the worry of his absence Now I feel I must have my husband home if I am to recover at all as I have two little boys age 7 and 9 who are requiring more attention than I feel able to give them." The wife of a discharged soldier incapacitated by war wounds was equally overwhelmed by "constant financial strain and worry." Although she had "supplemented her war income through dressmaking and knitting," she was by 1919 unable to continue: she was "not now in a fit condition through nervous strain."[32] For these two women the war had caused them severe, occasionally debilitating nervous strain, but they had persevered. Gustie Miller's fate was more tragic still. Jonathan Vance tells of how, following her husband's enlistment and a miscarriage she suffered shortly thereafter, she succumbed to a "downward spiral" from which her health never fully recovered. When her husband returned to Canada, she became convinced that her suffering and his were too great to endure; she shot her husband and then drowned herself.[33]

However fervently they prayed, war wives knew that prayer would not always result in the protection that they craved for their husbands. All (except, presumably, the most unhappily married) lived in dread of the telegram announcing their husband's death. And when that telegram arrived, the bereavement that ensued added immeasurably to a war wife's distress. Psychologists tell us that the emotional trauma experienced by war widows is distinctive: when young (or youngish) men are cut down in the prime of life; when death is sudden, violent, and unexpected; when there is no body to bury and no ritual of bereavement to offer comfort, war widows, most of whom are also young, only recently married and with children to care for, often lack the psychological capacity to prepare themselves for their loss or, indeed, to accept its reality when thrust upon them. Although a war wife whose husband was on active service would certainly have known that his death was possible and might have feared that it was probable, only rarely would she have accepted that it was inevitable. Unable to steel herself fully for this dreaded eventuality, she would have been denied the opportunity for the "anticipatory grieving" that precedes the death of a loved one felled by lingering disease or old age.[34] In the most extreme cases, a bereaved war widow might deny that death ever happened.

Recognizing that their wives lived in a limbo between hope and dread, husbands tried to reassure them that they would be informed promptly and properly of their death overseas. European soldiers often arranged to have their loved ones informed by a close comrade, knowing that a personal letter would usually arrive well in advance of any official notification. This consideration was not an option for Canadian troops compelled to rely on a slow and irregular mail service. They had to place their faith in the capacity of military authorities to notify next of kin in a timely manner. When May Rogers confessed her fear that she might first learn of Laurie's death by reading of it in the local newspaper, thus depriving her of the opportunity to compose herself in private before facing the well-meaning but often inapposite words of friends and neighbours, he repeatedly assured her that this would never happen: "If anything should by chanse happen to me you will hear all about it before it would come out in the paper as the Government would notify you first."[35] Yet there was always room for error. Frank Maheux knew, and Laurie Rogers probably did, too, that in a war in which many men had identical or similar names – in which uncorroborated accounts of men killed in action abounded – mistakes were almost inevitable. After the Battle of the Somme, Maheux met up with his brother-in-law, Holonger, who had heard a rumour that Frank had been killed: "[There] was a fellow name F. Mayhew he was killed at the Somme so when we came out of the Somme, Holonger saw some fellows of the 21st and they both told him I was killed so theirs so many here that the names get mix up."[36]

If an unfounded account of death in action remained confined to the front lines, it would not cause unnecessary distress at home, but if a mistaken rumour or an erroneous official report made its way home to a waiting wife, the psychological effects of a simple bureaucratic misstep could be devastating. On 30 January 1916 Frances Clarke received a telegram informing her that her husband, Edward, had been killed ten days earlier. It was probably several weeks before she realized that the telegram had been sent in error. The man killed on 20 January 1916 was, in fact, not Edward but Ernest Clarke. Both men had enlisted in Toronto in November 1914; both served in the 20th Battalion and were assigned consecutive regimental service numbers: 57381 and 57382. The unintended effects of this simple clerical error were incalculable.

While Frances Clarke mourned the death of her husband, while she worried about how she would support her children and succumbed to the temporary stupor of grief, Ernest Clarke's mother in London surely wondered why she heard nothing from her son for more than a month. It was only in early March, six weeks after he had been killed in action, that she was officially notified of his death.[37] Who suffered greater anguish: the wife who believed she was now a widow or the mother who wondered what had become of her son? Seven months later Frances Clarke received a second telegram. This time there was no room for doubt: on 2 October 1916, her husband had been killed at the Somme, one of more than a hundred Canadian soldiers who died on that day.

Telegrams like the one Frances Clarke received in error were by nature terse; their contents, terrifying. Much more comforting, and occasionally more informative, were the personal letters of condolence sent from a soldier's commanding officer. However formulaic the letter and however anodyne its contents – it would never describe an agonizing death or so much as hint that the man in question had been anything but heroic – it nonetheless offered a widow both consolation and confirmation. Thousands of miles from the fighting front, deprived of the ordinary rituals of burial and bereavement, a newly widowed wife would have cherished the carefully chosen words of her husband's superior. This, at least, is what we can glean from the moving letter Ellen Ewen wrote Arthur Leighton following the death of her husband, Bert, in January 1917. She first confessed that he had been "more than husband to me, he was, chum & son as well." Indeed, like many a war wife, she had hesitated to "let him go away in the first place" but, resigned to his resolve to serve, she had at first been consoled by the knowledge that she "had his lovely letters to look for." "But," she added, "now there is nothing." However deep her grief, she expressed her gratitude to "the boys, of the battery for their kindness in burying my boy properly." And she had a request: "if possible, could you let me know the name of the Cemetry or town. My brother is not so far from where Bert was and I should like him to see the grave. If ever this cruel war ends and I am able, I want to visit France & the grave." She wondered, too, about the precise time of her husband's death, for she had had a strange premonition: "On tuesday evening Jan. 23rd at about 8:30 I had a terribly frightened feeling for about an hour. Was in a picture show & could not move to come home." Her anxiety abated over the following days, until she "received the fatal telegram." But it was only when she "received a very nice letter from Lieut. Pedly [and] a few personal things of my boys" that she accepted the truth: her husband had indeed been killed in action.[38]

Ellen Ewen's poignant letter tells us a great deal about a wife's anxiety and a widow's initial reaction to her husband's death: of her unsettling premonition that something dreadful had befallen him; of her refusal, at first, to believe what the telegram had so tersely conveyed; of her thirst for assurance that her husband had been given a decent burial. The belief that a wife could be so spiritually attuned to her husband's well-being – or, as was more common, a mother to her son's – that she would be aware of the moment of his death was not to be scorned. An unnerving experience similar to that described by Ellen Ewen over-whelmed Mrs Laura Gillard of Montreal, whose husband died in France at 10:30 a.m. on 16 April 1916. At 2 a.m. on that very day, unable to sleep and while reading in her bedroom, she heard her husband call out three times to her. According to family witnesses, "her nerves, strung by many sleepless nights of worry, gave way completely [and] the other members of the family found her calling out wildly to her husband." She did not receive official notice of his death for another eleven days.[39] Ethel Cove, a housewife in Harrow, England, also recalled how she and her young daughter had been overcome by eerie dread on the day her husband died of wounds in France: "The first intimation that he was wounded reached me March 5th but I did not worry overmuch. On March 7th, however, I had an awful restlessness, and distinctly remember kneeling on the floor to write to a friend. Next morning, my little girl, who was then nearly six, said 'Mummy, I had such a funny dream last night. Daddy came to the bedroom window and beckoned. He was dressed all in black, and the bandage on his wounded head was black too.' You may imagine my feelings!"[40] As Brady Brower has demonstrated, hundreds of comparable accounts – formally identified as instances of "veridical hallucination" – filled the pages of *Les Annales des Sciences Psychiques* in wartime France.[41]

Ellen Ewen was by no means the only war wife to believe that she directly sensed the moment of her husband's death. Nor was she the only widow to take refuge in doubt and denial when first informed of it. It was only the return of her husband's personal effects and the compassionate words of his brothers-in-arms that finally convinced her. Other widows took months – and in some instances, years – to accept the awful truth. In France, where 250,000 French soldiers were still listed as missing in action at the end of the war, countless widows (and parents) held out hope until all prisoners of war had been repatriated. A tenacious few continued to insist well into the interwar years that their loved one was still alive. The heart-rending psychosis of persistent denial, especially acute in France, where the early weeks of the war had caused massive casualties and thousands of unconfirmed deaths, was also evident in

Canada. A family in Saskatchewan heard tell in the early 1920s of an amnesiac soldier confined to an asylum in central France, and hoped against hope that the "living unknown soldier" might be their son.[42] A widow from Grimsby, Ontario, whose husband was killed in October 1916, was persuaded by an unscrupulous teenage schemer, who produced a series of letters purportedly in her husband's hand, that he was still alive but held in a prisoner-of-war camp in Germany. His life would be so much more comfortable and his diet so much more enriching if only she were to send him regular sums of money. And thus the con artist in training extracted more than $700 from a widow who for the duration of the war refused to believe that her husband was in fact dead.[43] Like so many of her counterparts in France, Reba Dibble only came to terms with her loss when the war ended, the prisoners had returned home, and her husband was not among them.

When denial was no longer an option – when Ellen Ewen received the box of her husband's personal effects; when May Rogers discovered, tucked into Laurie's uniform pocket, the tiny teddy bear Aileen had sent her father as a good luck token – widows no doubt drew upon the means of coping that had sustained them from the moment of their husband's mobilization. Many continued to find that the emotional sustenance and economic support of family were invaluable; and so, too, was the consolation of faith. In this regard, Canadian war widows were much like the bereaved of wartime Europe, who, as Jay Winter clearly established in *Sites of Memory, Sites of Mourning*, also relied on faith and networks of kinship and community when coping with devastating grief: "most people realized that if they were to find solace ... it was from their families, their friends, their neighbors, sometimes their churches that hope came."[44] Canadian war widows whose immediate family still lived overseas often opted to return to Britain. Others, having relocated to Britain during the war, remained there after the Armistice, resigned to the fact that Canada no longer offered the comfort of family or the economic opportunities they and their husbands had confidently sought in the years before 1914.

Jennie Hillyer never left Montreal, for her family was close at hand and always ready to offer companionship in her bereavement. Her deep religious faith also shaped her postwar life and clearly informed her son's upbringing, for Norman would grow up to become an ordained minister and chaplain of a Boy Scout troop.[45] When in 1930, following the formal identification of her husband's remains, Jennie had the opportunity to choose the words to be inscribed on his grave, her choice was both simple and significant: "For God, For Truth, For Liberty."[46] More than a decade after the war had ended, Jennie Hillyer's faith in the justice of the cause for which Harry had died was as firm as her faith in God. In this, she gave voice to the confidence and conviction of many Canadians of the postwar era who continued to believe that the war, for all its horrors, had been a noble and, indeed, sanctified cause.[47] Not every war widow had the option to choose an epitaph: there was no space on the Menin Gate or the Vimy Memorial to inscribe anything beyond the names of the men memorialized there. We have no way of knowing, therefore, how Laurie Rogers (whose name appears on the Menin Gate) or Ted Clarke (one of the 11,285 names inscribed on the Vimy Memorial) might have been memorialized, had their widows had the chance.

Eric McGeer, in his rich and moving analysis of Canadian epitaphs, calculates that only a small fraction of bereaved Canadians chose a personal inscription for their loved one's grave.[48] Among those who did, however, many chose from the abundant scriptural texts that spoke of Christian redemption, the resurrection of the body, and the reunion of loved ones after death. Passages from the Old Testament that affirmed the protective love of a benevolent God – "I the Lord Have Called Thee and I will Hold thy Hand Isaiah XLII.6," is the inscription on Percy Knight's grave – offered consolation.[49] Passages from the New Testament or from Protestant hymnals, which saw in the sacrifices of the fallen echoes of the redemptive sacrifice of Christ, were especially comforting. Matilda Henry chose "Greater Love Hath No Man" as the epitaph for her husband, William; and Lizzie Dunn drew upon lines from a Presbyterian hymn, "By His Death Our Life Revealing He For Us the Ransom Paid."[50] Although a skeptic might insist that nothing would undermine faith in a loving deity as effectively as the wanton destruction of war, such a dismissive attitude fails to appreciate how these war widows, as well as parents and close relatives of men killed, maimed, or psychologically shattered by the war, drew upon their faith to assuage their suffering and make sense of their loss.[51]

When Mary Harrison pondered how best to memorialize her beloved husband in his epitaph, she turned instead to Tennyson, whose poetry proved a rich vein of reassurance: "Oh For the Touch of a Vanished Hand the Sound of a Voice that is Still."[52] Mary Harrison identified herself and her children (at least to the census takers) as members of the Church of England, but her tender lament for a lost husband captures the longing for physical communion characteristic of postwar spiritualism. Spiritualism, which traced its origins to mid-nineteenth-century America, had established a presence in Canada long before 1914. The war and the ensuing flu epidemic dramatically expanded its appeal in Europe and in North America. Whether a bereaved parent or wife had lost a child or a husband on the battlefields of France or in the hospital wards of urban Canada, many longed for direct verbal and visual connection with those who had "passed over" into the realm of spirits and they turned to mediums, whose séances held out the promise of such communion. By 1921 there were 1,558 self-identified spiritualists in Canada and many more who were occasionally drawn to its practices.[53] When Sir Arthur Conan Doyle, the most famous proponent of spiritualism, visited North America on a lecture tour in 1923, almost two thousand Winnipeggers flocked to hear him at the Walker Theatre (where only a few years earlier they had watched movies about the dastardly intentions of the demonic Hun).[54]

Representatives of Canada's major Christian religions found this not-quite-Christian search for assurance of life after death anathema, and sermons abounded on the danger spiritualism posed to the faithful. A Methodist prelate, addressing an assembly of co-religionists at Massey Hall in January 1920, denounced spiritualism as a "doctrine of the devil."[55] An Anglican minister two years later condemned it as a "long series of frauds" which led only to insanity. It was, Dr Cody insisted, "utterly unthinkable that the dead would return at the beck and call of any 'medium' to tilt tables and produce all the other ridiculous phenomena generally associated with Spiritualism."[56] However "ridiculous" these phenomena may have been in the eyes of the pious orthodox, they clearly spoke to a persistent yearning in nations devastated by the unprecedented losses of the Great War. It is impossible to know how many Canadian war widows turned to spiritualism as a way to reconnect with their fallen husbands, but the avidity with which men of the cloth deprecated "the growing inclination to communications with the dead by means of séances" seems to confirm that spiritualism – like more traditional expressions of religious faith – offered welcome consolation to those whose lives were marked by grief and mourning.

By paying close attention to the once overlooked experiences of Canada's war wives, *Anxious Days and Tearful Nights* illuminates how the Great War disrupted the lives and inevitably disturbed the psychological well-being of women thousands of miles from the battlefields of France. Just as men at the front developed ways of coping with the existential uncertainties and ubiquitous horror of war, their wives learned to cope, too.[57] They sought and often found comfort in family and solace in faith precisely because their wartime lives were so profoundly marked by day-to-day suffering and emotional anxiety. When forced to contend with inadequate budgets, the sometimes life-threatening illnesses of their children, and relentless uncertainty about the well-being and survival of husbands fighting far from home, they proved – in the main – remarkably resilient. Resilience, however, came at a cost. As Betty Mayse's experience in the spring of 1917 makes clear, even hard work, prayer, and an almost obsessive attention to the chores of everyday life were not always enough to allay the darkest fears that dominated war wives' waking hours and troubled their sleep. When the tasks of the day were done and the children asleep, Canada's war wives retreated to their lonely beds and the fears they had wrestled with all day. Having now observed them closely, we can see their tears.

Appendix

Building a Database of Manitoba War Wives

What can we know about Canadian war wives when their own voices have fallen silent? Very few of their letters survive in Canadian archives, although those that do exist – such as those held in the files of the Soldiers' Deserted Wives Fund in the Archives of Manitoba – are extremely illuminating. To create a composite profile of these mostly forgotten women – who they were, where they lived, if and where they moved during the war – I created a database of three hundred Manitoba war wives that builds upon the evidence provided in a series of official databases. Manitoba constituted a valuable case study for this project for several reasons. Manitoba had the highest enlistment rate of any province in Canada: fully 60 percent of all age-eligible men enlisted for service. Furthermore, the 1916 census of Prairie Provinces makes it possible to reconstruct family configurations at the mid-point of the war. Finally, the records of the Soldiers' Deserted Wives Fund, which include records from the Manitoba Patriotic Fund, allow for an analysis of the challenges some war wives faced during and after the war.

The database starts with the records of the Canadian Virtual War Memorial, maintained by Veterans Canada: https://www.veterans.gc.ca/eng/remembrance/memorials/canadian-virtual-war-memorial. This database commemorates all Canadian veterans who have died in, or as a result of, their military service. Using the keywords "Manitoba" and "husband," I was able to identify 1,163 men who died as a result of their military service in the First World War and who either served in the Manitoba Regiment or whose next of kin were identified as living in Manitoba. My very able research assistant, Michael Rupert, and I together cross-listed the names of these 1,163 men with their attestation records, now digitized by Library and Archives Canada (http://www.bac-lac.gc.ca/eng/discover/military-heritage/first-world-war/personnel-records/Pages/search.aspx). We were then able to identify 528 men who were residents of Manitoba and married at the time of their enlistment. (Many of those included in the original sample of 1,163 men were not residents of Manitoba at the time of their enlistment or married subsequent to their enlistment.) I then narrowed the sample of 528 married Manitoba men to a subset of 300 men whose complete service records had been digitized by the time Michael and I completed the database in 2015. Each service record provides the soldier's address at the time of his enlistment, his wife's name, and a ledger of Separation Allowance and Assigned Pay disbursements. These records provide a soldier's medical history, allowing me to assess diagnoses of venereal disease within this sample. The service records also indicate if a soldier's wife moved subsequent to his enlistment, whether she received a pension following his death, and whether she had remarried by the time war widows received the War Service Gratuity.

Because service records only occasionally provide information about a soldier's children, I consulted the 1916 census (http://www.bac-lac. gc.ca/eng/census/1916/Pages/about-census.aspx) and the Manitoba Vital Statistics database (http://vitalstats.gov.mb.ca/Query.php) to ascertain whether the soldier and his wife had children and what their ages were at the time of the 1916 census. Passenger shipping registers, available at ancestry.com, provided information about women (and children) sailing to Britain during the war and returning to Canada. The 1921 census (http://www.bac-lac.gc.ca/eng/census/1921/Pages/introduction.aspx) and the database of the Commonwealth War Graves Commission (https://www.cwgc.org/find/find-war-dead) made it possible to determine family circumstances of Manitoba's war widows and how they chose to memorialize their husbands' military sacrifice.

Notes

INTRODUCTION

1   I would like to thank Maria Clarke for sharing with me a copy of this postcard, sent by her grandfather to her grandmother.

2   Desmond Morton, *Fight or Pay: Soldiers' Families in the Great War* (Vancouver: UBC Press, 2004), 244: Table A3: Marital Condition of the Canadian Expeditionary Force, 1914–1919. 88,347 married men – officers and other ranks – served outside of Canada during the war. An additional 37,723 served in Canada.

3   Ibid., 79. Morton notes that, "with about a third of Canada's population, Ontario's three military districts sent 7,380 infantry in the first rush to Valcartier, and ultimately enlisted close to half the members of the Canadian Expeditionary Force."

4   "Earlscourt Homes Give Up Their Men," *Toronto Daily Star*, 27 April 1916.

5   Ontario contributed more men to the CEF than any other province: 241,540, which represented 45.3 percent of all men in the province eligible for service. Manitoba's contribution of 66,069 men represented the highest proportion of all age-eligible men: 61.1 percent of the eligible cohort. Chris Sharpe, "Enlistment in the Canadian Expeditionary Force, 1914–1918," *Canadian Military History* 24, 1 (2015), 55: Table VI: Male Voluntary Enlistment in Canada and Enlistment under the MSA as a Percentage of the Eligible Manpower by Province of Enlistment.

6   Desmond Morton, "A Canadian Soldier in the Great War: The Experiences of Frank Maheux," *Canadian Military History* 1, 1 (1992): 79–89.

7   Desmond Morton, *When Your Number's Up: The Canadian Soldier in the First World War* (Toronto: Random House of Canada, 1993); Tim Cook, "'My Whole Heart and Soul is in this War': The Letters and War Service of Sergeant George Ormsby," *Canadian Military History* 15, 1 (2006), 51–63; Tim Cook, *The Secret History of Soldiers: How Canadians Survived the Great War* (Toronto: Allen Lane, 2018).

8   As cited by Ninette Kelley and Michael Trebilcock, *The Making of the Mosaic: A History of Canadian Immigration Policy* (Toronto: University of Toronto Press, 1998), 174. Arthur Meighen, 12th Parliament, 7th Session, 10 September 1917, Linked Parliamentary Data, https://www.lipad.ca/full/permalink/496734/.

9   The literature on shell shock and how it was diagnosed, treated, or denied is extensive. For the Canadian case, see Mark Osborne Humphries, *A Weary Road: Shell Shock in the Canadian Expeditionary Force, 1914–1918* (Toronto: University of Toronto Press, 2018).

10 Clémentine Vidal-Naquet, *Couples dans la Grande Guerre: Le tragique et l'ordinaire du lien conjugal* (Paris: Belles Lettres, 2014), 19.

11 Colin Dyer, *Population and Society in Twentieth-Century France* (New York: Holmes and Meier, 1978), 43–4. In France, 1.4 million soldiers died in combat or as a result of injuries sustained in the war; 630,000 women received widows' pensions. This suggests that at least 45 percent of all French soldiers were married. Given that the mortality rate was highest among the youngest military classes, an extrapolation based on mortality rates alone probably underestimates the number of married soldiers in the French army. For Germany, see Benjamin Ziemann, *War Experiences in Rural Germany, 1914–1923*, trans. Alex Skinner (Oxford: Berg, 2007), 36; for Italy, Francesca Lagorio, "Italian widows of the First World War," in Frans Coetzee and Marilyn Shevin-Coetzee (eds.), *Authority, Identity and the Social History of the Great War* (Oxford: Berghahn Books, 1995), 195, n. 16. On Austria, see Maureen Healy, *Vienna and the Fall of the Habsburg Empire: Total War and Everyday Life in World War I* (Cambridge University Press, 2004), 259 and 219, n. 24. Healy notes that the Dual Monarchy suffered 1,016,200 military deaths and cites estimates to the effect that probably 400,000 Austrian women were widowed during the war.

12 Aaron B. Retish, *Russia's Peasants in Revolution and Civil War: Citizenship, Identity and the Creation of the Soviet State, 1914–1922* (Cambridge University Press, 2008), 27, 46, n. 95.

13 Juliette Pattinson, "'Shirkers,' 'Scrimjacks' and 'Scrimshanks'? British Civilian Masculinity and Reserved Occupations, 1914–45," *Gender and History* 28, 3 (November 2016): 709–27; Martha Hanna, "The Couple," *The Cambridge History of the First World War*, vol. 3: Civil Society, ed. Jay Winter (Cambridge and New York: Cambridge University Press, 2014), 7.

14 Allison Scardino Belzer, *Women and the Great War: Femininity under Fire in Italy* (New York: Palgrave Macmillan, 2010), 55.

15 T.J. Polner, *Russian Local Government during the War and the Union of the Zemstvos* (New Haven, CT: Yale University Press, 1930), 157–8, as cited by Peter Gatrell, "The Epic and the Domestic: Women and War in Russia, 1914–1917," *Evidence, History and the Great War: Historians and the Impact of*

1914–1918, ed. Gail Braybon (New York and Oxford: Berghahn Books, 2003), 201. Gatrell also cites Barbara Alpern Engel, *Between the Fields and the City: Women, Work, and Family in Russia, 1861–1914* (Cambridge and New York: Cambridge University Press, 1994) on the effects of male migration within Russia on peasant women's growing self-reliance in the decades before the war.

16 Peggy Bette, "Women's Mobilization for War (France)," *1914–1918-online. International Encyclopedia of the First World War*, ed. by Ute Daniel, Peter Gatrell, Oliver Janz, Heather Jones, Jennifer Keene, Alan Kramer, and Bill Nasson, issued by Freie Universität Berlin, Berlin 2014-10-08. DOI: 10.15463/ie1418.10027. Translated by Susan Emanuel.

17 Andrew Orr, *Women and the French Army during the World Wars, 1914–1940* (Bloomington, IN: Indiana University Press, 2017), chapter 1: "Weapons of Total War, 1914–1918"; Belzer, *Women and the Great War*, 56.

18 Susan R. Grayzel, "Women's Mobilization for War," *1914–1918-online. International Encyclopedia of the First World War*, DOI: 10.15463/ie1418.10348. On the history of factory-based daycare centres (*crèches*) in France, see Kaspar Burger, "A Social History of Ideas Pertaining to Childcare in France and in the United States," *Journal of Social History* 45, 4 (2012): 1005–25, especially 1013. On British and French policy differences concerning the creation of day-care facilities and nursing rooms for newborns, see Laura Lee Downs, *Manufacturing Inequality: Gender Division in the French and British Metalworking Industries, 1914–1939* (Ithaca, NY: Cornell University Press, 1995), 154–5, 168–70. In 1917 the Carnegie Foundation authorized a study of women's work in Britain that addressed (among other things) the importance of on-site childcare facilities for married women in the workforce. Janet M. Campbell, *Report on The Physical Welfare of Mothers and Children, England and Wales*, The Carnegie United Kingdom Trust, Volume Two, 1917.

19 Barbara Alpern Engel, "Not by Bread Alone: Subsistence Riots in Russia during World War I," *Journal of Modern History* 69, 4 (December 1997), 713.

20 Ute Daniel, "Women's Work in Industry and Family: Germany," *The Upheaval of War: Family, Work and Welfare in Europe, 1914–1918*, ed. Richard Wall and Jay Winter (Cambridge and New York: Cambridge University Press, 1988), 285.

21 Healy, *Vienna and the Fall of the Habsburg Empire*, 195. According to Susan R. Grayzel: "In Austria estimates suggest that nearly 1 million women entered the waged workforce during the war. One dramatic result was that in Vienna, after 1915 almost half of all metal-workers were women. Women even performed jobs that had previously been the sole province of men, such as welding or using lathes." Grayzel, "Women's Mobilization for War," *1914–1918 Online: International Encyclopedia of the First World War.*

22   Christa Hämmerle, "'You Let a Weeping Woman Call You Home?' Private
     Correspondences during the First World War in Austria and Germany,"
     Epistolary Selves: Letters and Letter-Writers, 1600–1945, ed. Rebecca Earle
     (Aldershot: Ashgate Publishing, 1999): 152–82.

23   Tara Zahra, "'Each nation only cares for its own': Empire, Nation, and Child
     Welfare Activism in the Bohemian Lands, 1900–1918," *American Historical
     Review* 111, 5 (December 2006), 1391.

24   Bernd Ulrich and Benjamin Ziemann (eds.), *German Soldiers in the Great
     War: Letters and Eyewitness Accounts*, trans. Christine Brocks, foreword Jay
     Winter (Barnsley: Pen and Sword, 2010), 100.

25   Maureen Healy, "Becoming Austrian: Women, the State, and Citizenship in
     World War I," *Central European History* 35, 1 (2002), 10.

26   Belinda Davis, *Home Fires Burning: Food, Politics, and Everyday Life in
     World War I Berlin* (Chapel Hill, NC: University of North Carolina Press,
     2000), 223–4.

27   Engel, "'Not by Bread Alone,'" 696–721.

28   Martha Hanna, "A Republic of Letters: The Epistolary Tradition in World
     War I France," *American Historical Review* 108, 5 (December 2003): 1338–61;
     Hanna, "War Letters: Communication between Front and Home Front,"
     1914–1918-online: International Encyclopedia of the First World War, DOI:
     10.15463/ie1418.10362.

29   Nancy Christie, *Engendering the State: Family, Work, and Welfare in Canada*
     (Toronto: University of Toronto Press, 2000), 62.

30   Linda Kealey, *Enlisting Women for the Cause: Women, Labour, and the Left
     in Canada, 1890–1920* (Toronto and Buffalo: University of Toronto Press,
     1998), 203.

31   Desmond Morton shows that a Canadian wife with two children received a
     minimum of $43.00 a month; a British war wife with two children received
     only the equivalent of $21 per month. *Fight or Pay*, 244: Table A2. In France,
     where separation allowances were based on need, and were not a universal
     entitlement as they were in Canada and Britain, a French wife with one
     child received a daily allowance of 1.25 francs and .50 franc per child (52.50
     francs per month) from August 1914 through November 1917, when the rate
     increased to 1.50 francs per day, with an additional 1 franc per day for each
     child. Susan Pedersen, *Family, Dependence, and the Origins of the Welfare State:
     Britain and France, 1914–1945* (Cambridge: Cambridge University Press,
     1993), 115–16; Françoise Thébaud, *La Femme au temps de la Guerre de 14*
     (Paris: Stock, 1986), 30–1.

32   Desmond Morton, *Fight or Pay*, 245: Table A4. 122,050 members of the CEF
     identified as employed in agriculture at the time of their enlistment.

33   Great War Veterans' Association of Burdett, Alberta, on behalf of Mrs. Alex
     Petrie, to the Minister of Justice, Ottawa, 11 December 1923, RG13-A-2,
     vol. 283, file 1923-2034, Library and Archives Canada (LAC), Ottawa.

34 Nellie L. McClung, *The Next of Kin: Those Who Wait and Wonder* (Boston and New York: Houghton Mifflin, 1917), 251, 253.

35 Paul Phillips and Erin Phillips, *Women and Work: Inequality in the Canadian Labour Market*, rev. ed. (Toronto: James Lorimer, 1993), 24–5.

36 Joy Parr, "Rethinking Work and Kinship in a Canadian Hosiery Town, 1919–1950," *Canadian Family History: Selected Readings*, ed. Bettina Bradbury (Toronto: Copp Clark Pitman, Ltd., 1992): 220–40. In Edmonton, when the Great Western Garment Company secured government contracts to manufacture military uniforms, it increased its payroll for the first time to include married women, but since the plant employed fewer than four hundred workers, the opportunity for married women – whether war wives or not – to find employment there was very limited. Catherine C. Cole, "The Great Western Garment Company during the First World War," *The Frontier of Patriotism: Alberta and the First World War*, ed. Adriana A. Davies and Jeff Keshen (Calgary: University of Calgary Press, 2015): 319–24.

37 Ian Hugh Maclean Miller, *Our Glory and Our Grief: Torontonians and the Great War* (Toronto: University of Toronto Press, 2002), 125–6.

38 Barbara M. Wilson, "Introduction," *Ontario and the First World War, 1914–1918: A Collection of Documents* (Toronto: The Champlain Society, 1977), xc.

39 Grayzel, "Women's Mobilization for War," *1914–1918-Online: International Encyclopedia of the First World War*.

40 Kealey, *Enlisting Women for the Cause*, 156.

41 "Conductorettes," *Canadian Women on the Move: Documents in Canadian Women's History*, vol. 2, ed. Beth Light and Joy Parr (Toronto: New Hogtown Press and the Ontario Institute for Studies in Education, 1983): 216–19. Article reprinted from the Kingston *Daily British Whig*, 24 August 1918; and Kori Street, "Bankers and Bomb Makers: Gender Ideology and Women's Paid Work in Banking and Munitions during the First World War in Canada," PhD dissertation, University of Victoria, 2001, 216–17.

42 In her dissertation, Kori Street argues persuasively that the often-repeated statistic that 35,000 women worked in Canada's munitions factories, vastly overstates the case. The higher number, cited first by the Imperial Munitions Board, was repeated in Enid Price's study of the Montreal munitions industries. Price found that 22 percent of the female workforce were married. Street's own analysis of the employment records of the McAvity munitions plant in Saint John, New Brunswick, reveals that married women constituted 24 percent of that factory's payroll. Street, "Bankers and Bomb Makers," 130. Joan Sangster also doubts that as many as 35,000 women worked in the Canadian munitions industry: "The claim by the Canadian government's Imperial Munitions Board that 35,000 women were working in munitions in 1917 is highly unlikely, compared with other Montreal and Ontario factory employment numbers." Sangster, "Mobilizing Women for War," *Canada*

and the First World War: Essays in Honour of Robert Craig Brown, ed. David MacKenzie (Toronto: University of Toronto Press, 2005), 164.

43   Sarah Glassford and Amy Shaw note: "Women still earned lower wages than did men for the same work, often lacked union support, and did not have access to day care facilities adequate to meet the needs of married women who went to work." Sarah Glassford and Amy Shaw, "Introduction: Transformation in a Time of War?" *A Sisterhood of Suffering and Service: Women and Girls of Canada and Newfoundland during the First World War* (Vancouver: UBC Press, 2012), 14. Kori Street, "Patriotic not Permanent: Attitudes about Women's Making Bombs and Being Bankers," *A Sisterhood of Suffering and Service*, 149. Ceta Ramkhalawansingh notes that "there seem to have been no government nurseries established during the First World War as there were during the Second World War; apparently the labour shortage was not serious enough to warrant the large-scale employment of married women." "Women during the Great War," *Women at Work, Ontario 1850–1930*, ed. Janice Acton, Penny Goldsmith, and Bonnie Shepard (Toronto: Canadian Women's Educational Press, 1974), 290.

44   Christie, *Engendering the State*, 83.

45   Clémentine Vidal-Naquet makes the important observation that in France war wives who applied for separation allowances – which were granted on the basis of demonstrable economic need – were expected to work, either on the family farm, maintaining the family business, or in waged employment. The separation allowances were supplements to a war wife's wartime income, not a full replacement for her husband's prewar income. Vidal-Naquet, *Couples dans la Grande Guerre*, ch. 3. La Question sociale.

46   In his summary report of the activities of the Canadian Patriotic Fund, the executive secretary noted that the CPF provided $38,199,282.62 in support (of which only $1,425.00 went to administrative costs); the Manitoba Patriotic Fund, which operated independently of the CPF, disbursed $5,835,128.12 to more than 14,000 families. *The Canadian Patriotic Fund: A Record of Its Activities from 1914 to 1919*, ed. Philip H. Morris, 325, 122, 116.

47   Morton, *Fight or Pay*. Morton provides data on these allowances and provincial costs of living in Table A5: Cost of Living and the CPF-SA benefits, 1915, page 245. Nancy Christie makes the point that working-class war wives were instrumental in demanding that soldiers be required to assign at least half of their monthly pay to their designated dependents. This became state policy in May 1915. Christie, *Engendering the State*, 62–4.

48   Kealey, *Enlisting Women for the Cause*, 203–6.

49   *The Canadian Patriotic Fund: A Record of Its Activities from 1914 to 1919*, 36.

50   Morton, *Fight or Pay*, 96.

51   Robert Rutherdale, *Hometown Horizons: Local Responses to Canada's Great War* (Vancouver: UBC Press, 2004), 112–13.

52 P189–P190, Edith Rogers Papers, Archives of Manitoba (AM). In 1919, when
    it became evident that a number of returning soldiers had deserted their
    wives and children, Edith Rogers, the first woman elected to the Manitoba
    Legislature, successfully argued for the creation of the Soldiers' Deserted Wives
    Fund. The records of this fund, now contained in the Edith Rogers papers,
    include dozens of cases carried over from the Manitoba Patriotic Fund.
53 Bettina Bradbury shows that Canadians at the turn of the twentieth century
    feared that children raised without a father in the home were especially
    susceptible to delinquency and immorality. Bettina Bradbury, "Canadian
    Children Who Lived with One Parent in 1901," *Household Counts: Canadian
    Households and Families in 1901*, ed. Eric W. Sager and Peter Baskerville
    (Toronto: University of Toronto Press, 2007): 247–301. These fears intensified
    with the onset of the war and were evident in Europe and Canada. David
    Smith, "Juvenile Delinquency in Britain in the First World War," *Criminal
    Justice History*, vol. 9 (1991): 119–45; Alexander Watson, *Ring of Steel:
    Germany and Austria-Hungary in World War I* (New York: Basic Books, 2014),
    365–6; Tamara Myers, "Embodying Delinquency: Boys' Bodies, Sexuality,
    and Juvenile Justice History in Early-Twentieth-Century Quebec," *Journal of
    the History of Sexuality* 14, 4 (October 2005): 383–414; Myers "The Voluntary
    Delinquent: Parents, Daughters, and the Montreal Juvenile Delinquents'
    Court in 1918," *Canadian Historical Review* 80, 2 (June 1999): 242–68. The
    belief that mothers who worked outside of the home, whether by choice or
    necessity, contributed to the delinquency of their children persisted well into
    the 1950s. See for example, Sheldon Glueck and Eleanor Glueck, "Working
    Mothers and Delinquency," *Mental Hygiene* 41 (July 1957): 327–50, as cited
    in Lori Chambers, *Misconceptions: Unmarried Motherhood and the Ontario
    Children of Unmarried Parents Act, 1921–1969* (Toronto: University of Toronto
    Press, 2007), 210.
54 Susan Pedersen makes a similar argument for the rationale undergirding
    the allocation of separation allowances in Britain: "in exchange for certain
    citizenship functions (defending the country), the man's status not only as
    an independent citizen but also as the 'breadwinner' for his family would
    be preserved." Pedersen, *Family, Dependence, and the Origins of the Welfare
    State*, 113.
55 Deborah Thom, "Gender and Work," *Gender and the Great War*, ed. Susan R.
    Grayzel and Tammy M. Proctor (New York: Oxford University Press, 2017),
    46, 49.
56 Sangster, "Mobilizing Women for War," 157–93.
57 Veronica Strong-Boag, *The New Day Recalled: Lives of Girls and Women in
    English Canada, 1919–1939* (Markham, ON: Penguin Books, 1988).
58 Ian Miller has challenged the long-standing belief that Canadian civilians
    had a distorted and overly rosy impression of front-line service by

demonstrating that newspapers often published letters sent home by local men in which they included quite graphic accounts of combat. Miller, *Our Glory and Our Grief*, ch. 2: "A Great Crusade."

59 In an oral interview conducted in the 1970s, Mrs Margaret Hand (an assigned pseudonym) recalled that soldiers wrote "very little" in their letters home: "You got very, very little information. Of course, all their letters were censored. We got many letters just blotted out." Hand, however, was a high school student during the First World War and it is not clear that she had access to letters that husbands sent to their wives. *The Great War and Canadian Society: An Oral History*, ed. Daphne Read, intro. Russell Hann (Toronto: New Hogtown Press, 1978), 192. Scholars of the Great War, writing in the closing decades of the twentieth century and deeply influenced by Paul Fussell's argument that soldiers' letters said little of importance about the character of the war, also contended that soldiers were reluctant to share with their families anything but the most optimistic and sanitized versions of their wartime experiences. See, for example, Jeffrey A. Keshen, *Propaganda and Censorship during Canada's Great War* (Edmonton: University of Alberta Press, 1996). More recently, scholars of European and Canadian letter-writing practices have revealed that soldiers' correspondence was in fact much more forthcoming than the Fussell paradigm led us to believe. This re-interpretation of the character of Canadian soldiers' letter writing is especially evident in Ian Miller's study of wartime Toronto.

60 George Timmins, *Kiss the Kids for Dad. Don't Forget to Write: The Wartime Letters of George Timmins, 1916–1918*, ed. Y.A. Bennett (Vancouver: UBC Press, 2009), 26. George Timmins to May Timmins, 17 November 1916.

61 See, for example, Alexander Watson, *Enduring the Great War: Combat, Morale and Collapse in the German and British Armies, 1914–1918* (Cambridge and New York: Cambridge University Press, 2008); Stéphane Audoin-Rouzeau, *Men at War: National Sentiment and Trench Journalism in France during the First World War* (Berg Publishers, 1992); and for Canada: Tim Cook, *The Secret History of Soldiers: How Canadians Survived the Great War* (Toronto: Allen Lane, 2018).

62 Françoise Noël, *Family Life and Sociability in Upper and Lower Canada, 1780–1870: A View from Diaries and Family Correspondence* (Montreal and Ithaca: McGill-Queen's University Press, 2003).

63 Gail G. Campbell, *'I wish to keep a record': Nineteenth-Century New Brunswick Women Diarists and Their World* (Toronto: University of Toronto Press, 2017), 135.

64 When discussing the life strategies of never-married women in early twentieth-century Victoria, Jenéa Tallentire makes this important observation: "What we find is that most women in the sample were neither solely dependent upon family nor living completely apart from kin or other

ties; rather, they fostered and functioned within networks of mutual support and multiple strategies of survival. We need to move beyond a simple, fixed independent (alone) versus dependent (at home) dichotomy." Jenéa Tallentire, "'The Ordinary Needs of Life': Strategies of Survival for Single Women in 1901 Victoria," *BC Studies* 159 (autumn 2008), 47. This notion that interdependence was characteristic of the lives of women who were either never married, married but temporarily separated from their husbands, or widows also informs Gail G. Campbell's analysis of "Independent Women" in nineteenth-century New Brunswick. She writes: "Embedded in a strong network of family and friends, the majority of New Brunswick-born women enjoyed security in the kinds of interdependence that makes such independence possible." Campbell, *"I wish to keep a record,"* 151.

CHAPTER ONE

1   Robert Brown and Donald Loveridge, "Unrequited Faith: Recruiting the CEF, 1914–1918," *Canadian Military History* 24, 1 (2015), 67. This article was first published in *Revue internationale d'Histoire Militaire Ancienne* 54 (1982): 53–79.

2   William John Howe to Ellen Howe, 25 September 1914, *Canadian Letters and Images Project*: http://canadianletters.ca/content/document-6848?position=0&l ist=eip6GJT1xLI3kr9HFISIT61H7NqTIFWxiX4Oc2WGh14

3   The Canadian Virtual War Memorial maintained by Veterans Affairs Canada identifies 1,374 Canadian soldiers killed between 22 April 1915 and 25 April 1915. Narrowing this group by entering the search term "husband" gives 103 names. Married men thus constituted 7.5 percent of all Canadian fatalities suffered in the immediate aftermath of the German assault. https://www. veterans.gc.ca/eng/remembrance/memorials/canadian-virtual-war-memorialr- memorial/

4   "General Instructions and Conditions of Enlistment," 11 August 1914, RG24-C-8, vol. 4496, file MD4-54-1-5, Library and Archives Canada (LAC), Ottawa.

5   Desmond Morton, *Fight or Pay: Soldiers' Families in the Great War* (Vancouver: UBC Press, 2004), 30.

6   Robert Brown and Donald Loveridge have analyzed the effects of the depression and widespread unemployment on Canadian enlistment in 1914. See Brown and Loveridge, "Unrequited Faith," 61–87. They emphasize in particular that, of the men who volunteered in the First Contingent, "more than sixty percent were raised in urban areas and almost half of the men, 48.4%, came from western Canada where the effects of the depression were most severe. Another 31.3% came from heavily industrialized Ontario. Many of these soldiers were among the tens of thousands of unemployed men who had been looking for work in the summer of 1914" (p. 67).

7   Morton, *Fight or Pay*, 243. "Table A1: Rates of Pay, Canadian Expeditionary
    Force, 1914–1918."

8   P190/18, Edith Rogers Papers, Archives of Manitoba (AM), Winnipeg.

9   William John Howe to Ellen Howe, 25 September 1914, *Canadian Letters and
    Images Project*, http://canadianletters.ca/content/document-6848?position=0&l
    ist=yaVRiG7Z76hk1-JPfj02s4GLK-JixrXI7MgafJviSEI

10 Morton, *Fight or Pay*, 245. Table A5: Cost of Living and the CPF-SA
    benefits, 1915.

11 http://www.veterans.gc.ca/eng/remembrance/memorials/canadian-virtual-war-
    memorial/detail/1593155?William%20John%20Howe

12 Ninette Kelley and Michael Trebilcock, *The Making of the Mosaic: A History
    of Canadian Immigration Policy* (Toronto: University of Toronto Press, 1998),
    121, 137. Terms were even more prohibitive for would-be immigrants from
    India, who had to demonstrate that they had at least $200 in personal
    funds when arriving at a Canadian port of entry. Mabel F. Timlin, "Canada's
    Immigration Policy, 1896–1910," *The Canadian Journal of Economics and
    Political Science / Revue canadienne d'Economique et de Science politique* 26,
    4 (November 1960), 529.

13 Military Service records of Ernest Hawley: http://central.bac-lac.gc.ca/.
    item/?op=pdf&app=CEF&id=B4171-S034; John Larkin: http://central.bac-lac.
    gc.ca/.item/?op=pdf&app=CEF&id=B5405-S038; Edward Lawlor: http://
    central.bac-lac.gc.ca/.item/?op=pdf&app=CEF&id=B5456-S018.

14 Pte. C.A. Graham, #6220, No. 2 Company, 1st Battalion, CEF, 5 July 1916;
    response from Superintendent of Immigration, Ottawa, to General Fiset,
    Deputy Minister, Department of Militia and Defence, 2nd August 1916,
    Migration of Soldiers' Wives and Families, Quarter-Master General, RG 9
    III-B-1, vol. 3320, file no. M-2-43, LAC.

15 Nic Clarke, *Unwanted Warriors: The Rejected Volunteers of the Canadian
    Expeditionary Force* (Vancouver: UBC Press, 2015), 11. Clarke reviewed the
    files of 3,050 men who volunteered at Valcartier and were deemed medically
    unfit. He notes that these 3,050 men constituted "approximately 60 percent
    of the total number of men rejected at Valcartier."

16 Frank Maheux to Angeline Maheux, October 1914 and 14 November 1914,
    Francis-Xavier Maheux fonds, R5156-0-4-E, LAC.

17 George Ormsby to Margaret Ormsby, 20 April 1915, Letters of George
    Ormsby, 58 A 1 153, Canadian War Museum-Military History Research
    Centre (CWM-MHRC), Ottawa.

18 Frank Maheux to Angeline Maheux, 8 November 1914, Francis-Xavier
    Maheux fonds, R5156-0-4-E, LAC.

19 James Evans to Edith Evans, 24 March 1915, *Canadian Letters and Images
    Project*, http://canadianletters.ca/content/document-3154?position=10&list=N
    bIc2ln9mK6AGSMhhheBTpppaIL_F4960C0YIusf_TA.

20 Laurie Rogers to May Rogers, 24 June 1915, Letters of Lt. Lawrence
    Browning Rogers, Textual Records 58A 1 207.1–5, CWM-MHRC.
21 William John Howe to Ellen Howe, 22 April 1915, *Canadian Letters
    and Images Project*, http://canadianletters.ca/content/document-
    6851?position=3&list=mZseZa5iP-aXLzpzox7moQLUpkI1sBAp-xySO3QozTw.
22 Frank Maheux to Angeline Maheux, 16 May [1915], Francis-Xavier Maheux
    fonds, R5156-0-4-E, LAC.
23 Laurie Rogers to May Rogers, 26 August 1916, Letters of Lt. Lawrence
    Browning Rogers, Textual Records 58A 1 207.1-5, CWM-MHRC.
24 Frank Maheux to Angeline Maheux, 16 May [1915], Francis-Xavier Maheux
    fonds, R5156-0-4-E, LAC.
25 George Ormsby to Maggie Ormsby, 10 May 1915, Letters of George Ormsby,
    58 A 1 153 CWM-MHRC.
26 Frank Maheux to Angeline Maheux, 19 May [1915], Francis-Xavier Maheux
    fonds, R5156-0-4-E, LAC. Tim Cook has explored in depth the "politics
    of surrender" and the role of Canadian soldiers in the killing of German
    prisoners of war. See Cook, "The Politics of Surrender: Canadian Soldiers
    and the Killing of Prisoners in the Great War," *Journal of Military History*
    (1 July 2006): 637–65.
27 "Lusitania is Torpedoed -- 100 Toronto Passengers," *Toronto Daily Star*,
    7 May 1915.
28 "Men Gave their Lifebelts to Women on Liner – Fifty Babies Were among
    the Lost," *Toronto Daily Star*, 10 May 1915.
29 Robert Rutherdale notes that on the day after the *Lusitania* went down,
    the editor of Guelph's local newspaper expostulated: "Today the world
    stands aghast at the latest horror of the hellish German system of warfare."
    Rutherdale, *Hometown Horizons: Local Responses to Canada's Great War*
    (Vancouver: UBC Press, 2004), 229. Suzanne Evans notes that anti-German
    rioting in Victoria "produced property damage estimated at $20,000." "Marks
    of Grief: Black Attire, Medals, and Service Flags," *A Sisterhood of Suffering and
    Service: Women and Girls of Canada and Newfoundland during the First World
    War*, ed. Sarah Glassford and Amy Shaw (Vancouver: UBC Press, 2012), 225.
30 "Canadian was Crucified, Clamped to Tree," *Toronto Daily Star*, 11 May 1915.
31 "Confirms Story of German Barbarism: Captain Rogers says Canadian
    wounded were murdered and two crucified," *Manitoba Free Press*, 15 June
    1915; "Canadians Got full Revenge for Atrocities," *Toronto Daily Star*,
    15 May 1915.
32 The definitive analysis of atrocities committed against French and Belgian
    civilians, and of the exaggerated legends that emerged from these events, is
    John Horne and Alan Kramer, *German Atrocities, 1914: A History of Denial*
    (New Haven: Yale University Press, 2001).
33 "Bryce Report Convicts Germany," *Toronto Daily Star*, 12 May 1915.

34 "Toronto Pulpits on Teutonic Savagery," *Toronto Daily Star*, 10 May 1915.
35 "The Lusitania Horror and the German Mind," *Manitoba Free Press*,
    17 June 1915.
36 "Return Showing the Number of Recruits Obtained in the Several Divisions
    and Districts of the Canadian Expeditionary Forces in Canada, October 2,
    1915," Contingents: Recruiting Headquarters Instructions, RG24-C-8, vol.
    4427, file no. MD3-26-5-64-3, LAC.
37 "Monthly Statistical Report of the Manitoba Patriotic Fund," *The Canadian
    Patriotic Fund: A Record of its Activities from 1914 to 1919*, 117.
38 "Volunteers go to Y to Develop Physique," *Toronto Daily Star*,
    15 September 1915.
39 The *Manitoba Free Press* reported on 18 June 1915 in an article entitled
    (somewhat optimistically) that "Canada Enlistment [Was] Simply
    Wonderful": "The response has been particularly good from Toronto ...
    10,000 men ... very satisfactory in Montreal ... in the west no apparent
    abatement in the rush to the colours."
40 Brown and Loveridge note that in this second phase of recruitment, the
    western provinces continued to raise the largest number of volunteers:
    "the largest number came from western Canada, 41.4% of the total, closely
    followed by Ontario's contribution of 38.3% ... Seventy percent of the men
    raised in Quebec and sixty percent in the western provinces were enrolled in
    battalions which recruited exclusively in urban areas." Brown and Loveridge,
    "Unrequited Faith," 68.
41 "Britain's Big Need Now is Munitions, More than Men," *Toronto Daily Star*,
    4 June 1915.
42 Circular from the Adjutant-General, Ottawa, to Officer Commanding,
    3rd Division, 5 October 1915, Contingents: Recruiting Headquarters
    Instructions, RG24-C-8, vol. 4427, file MD3-26-5-64-3, LAC.
43 Re: Recruiting Meeting August 4th New Glasgow, Nova Scotia, 5 August
    1915, Stimulating of Recruiting, Maritime Provinces, RG24-C-8, vol 4551,
    file MD6-125-1-6, LAC.
44 Report from Officer Commanding, 3rd Division to the Secretary, Militia
    Council, Ottawa, 29 October 1915, Contingents: Recruiting Headquarters
    Instructions, RG24-C-8, vol. 4427, file MD3-26-5-64-3, LAC.
45 O[fficer] C[ommanding], 5th Division, Quebec to Secretary of the Militia
    Council, Ottawa, 6 October 1915, RG24-C-8, vol. 4507, file MD5-17-1-49, LAC.
46 Office of the President, Dalhousie University to Major-General R.W.
    Rutherford, OC 6th Division, Halifax, NS, 28 June 1915, Stimulating of
    Recruiting, Maritime Provinces, RG24-C-8, vol. 4551, file MD6-125-1-6, LAC.
47 Report from the OC, 5th Division, Quebec to the Secretary, Militia Council,
    Ottawa, 6 August 1915, RG24-C-8, vol. 4507, file MD5-17-1-49 (vol. 1), LAC.
    Voluntary enlistment in Britain had declined noticeably by the summer of

1915, consistently falling short of Kitchener's projections of the number of men needed. When only 10,000 men a month were voluntarily enlisting in the summer of 1915, Britain began to consider the need to introduce conscription.

48 Citizens' Recruiting Association [Montreal], "The Questions of a Hesitating Canadian and the Answers of a Canadian who Believes that this is 'Our War,'" RG24-C-8, vol. 4479, file MD4-25-1-20, LAC.

49 "The Prime Minister's Advice to the Young Unmarried Men and Pledge to Married Men," Imperial War Museum (IWM), Poster: http://www.iwm.org.uk/ collections/item/object/28375. Accessed 10 June 2017.

50 Roy Douglas, "Voluntary Enlistment in the First World War and the Work of the Parliamentary Recruiting Committee," *Journal of Modern History* 42, 4 (December 1970), 580–2.

51 This reluctance to compel the military service of married men became evident when Canada introduced conscription in 1917: the National Service Act specified that married men were to be drafted only after all single men and widowers with no dependents had been called up. In Australia, where referenda to introduce conscription failed on two separate occasions, a similar presumption prevailed. Torn between their patriotic duty and their obvious commitments to their families, many married men in Australia also insisted that the obligation to enlist should fall first and foremost on unmarried men: Bart Ziino, "Eligible men: men, families and masculine duty in Great War Australia," *History Australia* 14, 2 (2017): 202–17.

52 Citizens' Recruiting Association [Montreal], "The Questions of a Hesitating Canadian and the Answers of a Canadian who Believes that this is 'Our War,'" RG24-C-8, vol. 4479, file number: MD4-25-1-20, LAC.

53 "Would Draft Unmarried Men by the Ballot," *Toronto Daily Star*, 11 January 1916.

54 "Listing of York's Young Men Planned," *Toronto Daily Star*, 11 March 1916.

55 George Ormsby to Maggie Ormsby, 20 April 1915, Letters of George Ormsby, 58 A 1 153, CWM-MHRC.

56 "Wives are Cautioned," *Toronto Daily Star*, 15 September 1915.

57 Memorandum from Paymaster, 3rd Division to A[ssistant] A[djutant] G[eneral], 3rd Division, 13 October 1915, Contingents: Recruiting Headquarters Instructions, RG24-C-8, vol. 4427, file MD3-26-5-64-3, LAC.

58 "Sustenance Pay to Soldiers is Reduced," *Toronto Daily Star*, 29 October 1915.

59 "Returned Soldiers Tell of Search for Employment," *Toronto Daily Star*, 5 October 1915.

60 OC 34th Battery CEF, Barriefield Camp to Assistant Adjutant-General, 3rd Division, 12 October 1915, Contingents: Recruiting Headquarters Instructions, RG24-C-8, vol. 4427, file MD3-26-5-64-3, LAC.

61 "Totally Disabled, but Gets $192 to live on for a year," *Toronto Daily Star*, 16 November 1915; "Wife Sick, Babe in Hospital and All Pay Stopped,"

Toronto Daily Star, 7 December 1915; "Mother Dies of Grief, Son Killed at Front," *Toronto Daily Star*, 21 February 1916.

62 "A Plea for More Generous Pensions, Patriotic Association's Report," *Toronto Daily Star*, 22 December 1915.

63 "Low Pensions Barrier to Many Enlistments," *Toronto Daily Star*, 22 December 1915.

64 George Timmins to May Timmins, 17 March 1917. George Timmins, *Kiss the Kids for Dad. Don't Forget to Write: The Wartime Letters of George Timmins, 1916–1918*, ed. Y.A. Bennett (Vancouver: UBC Press, 2009), 52.

65 Ibid., Introduction; 116. George Timmins to May Timmins, 21 July [1918].

66 Britain had used each of these tactics, starting as early as 1914. For example, a survey of households to identify men of appropriate age who had not yet enlisted but were willing to do so took place in much of England between 12 November and 12 December 1914. See Douglas, "Voluntary Enlistment in the First World War," 572. A more extensive canvass of the civilian population went into effect under the "Derby Scheme" in October 1915. For a comprehensive analysis of this new approach to recruitment, as experienced in rural southern Ontario, see Jonathan F. Vance, *A Township at War* (Waterloo, ON: Wilfrid Laurier University Press, 2018), 104–10.

67 Report, 5 August 1915, Stimulating of Recruiting, Maritime Provinces, RG24-C-8, vol. 4551, file MD6-125-1-6, LAC.

68 Report from Officer Commanding, 14th Regiment PWOR Guard, Kingston to Assistant Adjutant-General, 3rd Division, 13 October 1915, Contingents: Recruiting Headquarters Instructions, RG24-C-8, vol. 4427, file MD3-26-5-64-3, LAC.

69 "Recruiting Methods Fail in Churches," *Toronto Daily Star*, 31 January 1916; "Want Recruiting Methods Changed," *Manitoba Free Press*, 7 March 1916.

70 "100 Girl Employees Jeer Fellow Canadian Slackers," *Toronto Daily Star*, 4 February 1916; "Appealed to 200 Men, only one Responded," *Toronto Daily Star*, 4 February 1916; "Fifty Heard Speeches but All Held Back," *Toronto Daily Star*, 5 February 1916.

71 "Sunday Meetings Defended by Military Men; 15 Recruits Secured at Loews Rally," *Toronto Daily Star*, 31 January 1916.

72 "Men are Urged to Sign on at Once," *Manitoba Free Press*, 6 March 1916; "Khaki Films are Shown at Walker," *Manitoba Free Press*, 14 March 1916.

73 Memorandum from OC, NB Command, St John, NB, to DAA and QMG, MD No. 6, Halifax, 18 April 1916, Stimulating of Recruiting, Maritime Provinces, RG24-C-8, vol. 4551, file MD6-125-1-6, LAC.

74 "Travelogue Gives New Glimpse of War," *Toronto Daily Star*, 22 February 1916.

75 "Khaki Films are Shown at Walker," *Manitoba Free Press*, 14 March 1916.

76 On the reception in the United States of *Battle Cry of Peace*, see: "Battle Cry of Peace (1915)," http://web.stanford.edu/~gdegroat/NT/oldreviews/bcop.htm;

and Peter Conolly-Smith, "Casting Teutonic Types from the Nineteenth Century to World War I: German Ethnic Stereotypes in Print, on Stage, and Screen," *Columbia Journal of American Studies*, http://www.columbia.edu/cu/cjas/conolly-smith-1.html.

77 "Battle Cry of Peace," advertisement, *Manitoba Free Press*, 1 April 1916.

78 "Another Big War Picture," *Toronto Daily Star*, 4 March 1916.

79 "'Battle Cry' at Strand," *Toronto Daily Star*, 13 March 1916; "'Battle Cry' at Strand," 20 March 1916.

80 "Battle Cry of Peace" advertisement, *Toronto Daily Star*, 29 March 1916.

81 "100 Girl Employees Jeer Fellow Canadian Slackers," *Toronto Daily Star*, 4 February 1916.

82 "German Agent Tells of Plot against Canada," *Toronto Daily Star*, 29 March 1916. See also, Brock Millman, *Polarity, Patriotism, and Dissent in Great War Canada, 1914–1919* (Toronto: University of Toronto Press, 2016), 76–8.

83 James M. Pitsula, *For All We Have and Are: Regina and the Experience of the Great War* (Winnipeg: University of Manitoba Press, 2008), 148.

84 "Battle Cry of Peace," *Toronto Daily Star*, 4 May 1916; "Battle Cry of Peace," *Toronto Daily Star*, 13 March 1916.

85 Roy Douglas notes that by March 1915, there were two million copies of recruitment posters in circulation in Britain. Douglas, "Voluntary Enlistment in the First World War," 568.

86 Recruitment Posters, RG24-C-8, vol. 4507, file MD5-17-1-49 (vol. 1), and RG24-C-8, vol. 4551, file MD6-125-1-7, vol. 1, LAC.

87 Andrew Iarocci provides a detailed description of Canadian participation in the Second Battle of Ypres, which at the time was often spoken of as the Battle of St Julien, and notes that commemoration of "St Julien Day" continued to figure prominently in Canadian memory of the war until the 1960s. In 1918 a fundraising drive in Toronto to mark St Julien's Day raised the significant sum of almost $20,000. Iarocci, *Shoestring Soldiers: The First Canadian Division at War, 1914–1915* (Toronto: University of Toronto Press, 2008), 190–1.

88 "Mothers, Wives, and Sweethearts," https://www.loc.gov/item/2005696919/, Library of Congress.

89 "Canadians, it's time to take action. Don't wait until the Germans come and lay waste to Canada. Canadians, be men! Don't hang back, enlist in our French-Canadian regiments. Apply to the French-Canadian Recruitment Committee," PST 12448, http://www.iwm.org.uk/collections/item/object/5944, Imperial War Museum (IWM).

90 The Essex County Recruiting committee used the execution of Edith Cavell to spur enlistment: "Murdered by the Huns" called upon the men of Essex County, Ontario to "ENLIST IN THE 99TH AND HELP STOP SUCH ATROCITIES," PST 12217, https://www.iwm.org.uk/collections/item/object/30888, iwm.

91 Citizens' Recruiting Association [Montreal], "Mothers, Wives, and Sweethearts: Reasons Why you Should Encourage your Menfolk to Enlist," November 1915, RG24-C-8, vol. 4479, file MD4-25-1-20, LAC. For more on the significance of recruiting efforts directed at women, see Jeffrey Keshen, *Propaganda and Censorship during Canada's Great War* (Edmonton: University of Alberta Press, 1996) and Suzanne Evans, *Mothers of Heroes, Mothers of Martyrs: World War I and the Politics of Grief* (Montreal and Kingston: McGill-Queen's University Press, 2007).

92 "Call to Women, not in Dainty, Soft Language," *Toronto Daily Star*, 7 December 1915.

93 Ian Miller, *Our Glory and Our Grief: Torontonians and the Great War* (Toronto: University of Toronto Press, 2002), 123.

94 "Twelve at Hippodrome," *Toronto Daily Star*, 21 February 1916.

95 "To the Women of Canada," http://www.archives.gov.on.ca/en/explore/online/posters/big/big_30_war_poster.aspx; "Aux Femmes du Canada" http://www.iwm.org.uk/collections/item/object/31023, IWM. On the ways in which enlistment posters juxtaposed images of family – especially, innocent young girls – with references to atrocities committed against Belgian civilians, see Kristine Alexander, "An Honour and a Burden: Canadian Girls and the Great War," *A Sisterhood of Suffering and Service*, 175–6.

96 Patriotic Fund full-page advertisement, *Toronto Daily Star*, 18 January 1916.

97 Circular Letter from Department of Militia and Defence, Ottawa, to General Officers Commanding, Military Divisions, dated 4 February 1916, Recruiting Posters, RG24-C-8, vol. 4551, file MD6-125-1-7, LAC. The Chief Recruiting Officer in Nova Scotia recommended a series of substantive changes to the "Enlist Today" pamphlet distributed across the province. Whereas the original pamphlet had suggested very strongly that the Patriotic Fund would provide an "additional allowance … of $10.00 per month for wife, with from $3.00 to $7.50 per month for additional children," the revised text simply made mention of the Fund and identified it as "a fund for assistance of Soldiers' families, maintained by Voluntary Subscription." Memorandum from the Chief Recruiting Officer, 6th Division to DAA and QMG, 6th Division, 18 February 1916, Recruiting Posters, vol. 2, RG24-C-8, vol. 4551, file MD6-125-1-7, LAC.

98 "G'Bye Mary – the Patriotic Fund Will Care for You," PST 12488, http://www.iwm.org.uk/collections/item/object/31055, IWM.

99 "Triumphant Close to Big Campaign; $2,302,829 Raised in City and County," *Toronto Daily Star*, 29 January 1916.

100 Paul Maroney, "'The Great Adventure': The Context and Ideology of Recruiting in Ontario, 1914–1917," *Canadian Historical Review* 77, 1; Pitsula, *For All We Have and Are*, 147.

101 "Registration of Eligibles Starts," *Manitoba Free Press*, 10 March 1916.

102 Patriotic Fund appeal advertisement, *Manitoba Free Press*, 6 April 1916.
103 Col. G.W.L. Nicholson, *Canadian Expeditionary Force, 1914–1919: The Official History of the Canadian Army in the First World War* (Ottawa: Queen's Printer and Controller of Stationery, 1962): "Appendix C: Appointments, Enlistments, Strength and Casualties – Canadian Expeditionary Force. Table 1: Appointments and Enlistments by Months, 1914–1920," 546.
104 On 18 January 1916 the *Toronto Daily Star* noted that by the end of December 1915, 207,568 men had enlisted in the CEF; 44,442 of them were Toronto men. "Ontario Increases its Lead," *Toronto Daily Star*, 18 January 1916. On Toronto enlistments in March and April 1916, see: Attesting Officers. Records dated 6 March 1916 and 3 April 1916 submitted by Capt. T.A.E. World, RG24-C-8, vol. 4317, file MD2-34-1-76, LAC. Capt. World had been employed since December 1914 as assistant to Lt. Col. J.R. Duamere and was responsible for attesting all men who enlisted in Toronto.
105 "All Recruiting Records Broken," *Manitoba Free Press*, 17 March 1916.
106 "127 Recruits Enlist, Makes 637 for Week," *Toronto Daily Star*, 7 January 1916. "Canadians Still Ahead," *Toronto Daily Star*, 14 March 1916.
107 "Earlscourt Homes Give up Their Men," *Toronto Daily Star*, 27 April 1916. See also, Nancy Byers and Barbara Myrvold, *St. Clair West in Pictures: A History of the Communities of Carlton, Davenport, Earlscourt, and Oakwood*, 2nd edition, Local History Handbook No. 8 (Toronto: Toronto Public Library Board, 1999), 46.
108 "Monthly Statistical Report of the Manitoba Patriotic Fund," *The Canadian Patriotic Fund: A Record of its Activities from 1914 to 1919*, 117–18.
109 Correspondence between the National Manufacturing Company, Brockville, Ont., and Col. G. Hunter Ogilvie, the Assistant Adjutant General, District #3, Kingston, 8 March 1916, 21 March 1916, 22 March 1916, 6 May 1916, 15 May 1916, Contingents: Recruiting Headquarters Instructions, RG24-C-8, vol. 4427, file MD3-26-5-64-3, LAC.
110 On the significant number of men who tried to enlist but were rejected as medically unfit, see Nic Clarke, *Unwanted Warriors: The Rejected Volunteers of the Canadian Expeditionary Force* (Vancouver: UBC Press, 2015).

CHAPTER TWO

1 Laurie Rogers to May Rogers, 21 August 1917, Letters of Lt. Lawrence Browning Rogers, Textual Records 58A 1 207.1–5, CWM-MHRC.
2 The 1911 census notes that 89 percent of the population over the age of five could read and write. Literacy was especially high among British-born Canadians: 96 percent of all British-born Canadian males and females over the age of five could read and write; and 97 percent of all British-born Canadian men over the age of twenty-one were literate. The census does not

give data on literacy for women over the age of twenty-one. *Fifth Census of Canada 1911*, vol. II (Ottawa: Printer to the King's Most Excellent Majesty, 1913), xii, 477, 482, 502.

3 David Vincent, *Literacy and Popular Culture: England 1750–1914* (Cambridge: Cambridge University Press, 1989), 89.

4 Marina Dossena, "'As this leaves me at present': Formulaic Usage, Politeness, and Social Proximity in Nineteenth-Century Scottish Emigrants' Letters," *Germanic Language Histories 'from Below' (1700–2000)*, ed. Stephan Elspass, et al. (Berlin; New York: Walter de Gruyter, 2007): 13–30.

5 On the significance of correspondence in immigrant societies, see David A. Gerber, *Authors of Their Lives: The Personal Correspondence of British Immigrants to North America in the Nineteenth Century* (New York: New York University Press, 2006); Martyn Lyons, *The Writing Culture of Ordinary People in Europe, c. 1860–1920* (Cambridge and New York: Cambridge University Press, 2013); and Stephan Elspass, "Between linguistic creativity and formulaic restriction," in Marina Dossena and Gabriella Del Lungo Camiciotti, eds., *Letter Writing in Late Modern Europe* (Bergamo and Florence: John Benjamins Publishing, 2012): 45–64.

6 John S. Whitlock, Saskatoon to Department of Militia and Defence, 24 January 1919; Sergeant John Farmer, Vancouver BC, to Department of Militia and Defence, 7 April 1918, "Transportation of Soldiers' Wives and Families from Overseas to Canada," RG24-C-1-a, vol. 744 – 747, file HQ-54-21-6-85, LAC.

7 Marie-Monique Huss, *Histoires de famille: Cartes postales et culture de guerre* (Paris: Noesis, 2000), 29.

8 As quoted by Vincent in *Literacy and Popular Culture*, 51.

9 Bianca Gendreau, "Putting Pen to Paper," *Special Delivery: Canada's Postal Heritage*, ed. Francine Brousseau, Canadian Museum of Civilization (Fredericton, NB: Goose Lane Editions, 2000), 27–9.

10 Chantal Amyot and John Willis, *Country Post: Rural Postal Service in Canada, 1880–1945* (Gatineau, PQ: Canadian Museum of Civilization, 2003), 35.

11 Françoise Noël, *Family Life and Sociability in Upper and Lower Canada, 1780–1870: A View from Diaries and Family Correspondence* (Montreal and Kingston: McGill-Queen's University Press, 2003).

12 On the character of the Canadian postal service prior to the First World War, and the people who used it, see: Amyot and Willis, *Country Post*; Randy William Widdis, *With Scarcely a Ripple: Anglo-Canadian Migration into the United States and Western Canada, 1880–1920* (Montreal and Kingston: McGill-Queen's University Press, 1998); Nicholas Van Allen and Don Lafrenière, "Rebuilding the Landscape of the Rural Post Office: A Geo-Spatial Analysis of 19th-century Postal Spaces and Networks," *Rural Landscapes: Society, Environment, History* https://www.rurallandscapesjournal.com/articles/10.16993/rl.23/.

13 Amyot and Willis, *Country Post*, 113–14.

14 William Edgar Lawrence Coleman to his wife, Della, 3 October 1916, Letters of Capt. William Edgar Lawrence Coleman, Textual Records 58A 1 14.1, CWM-MHRC.

15 Ministère de la Guerre, État-Major de l'Armée – Service Historique, *Les Armées Françaises dans la Grande Guerre*, volume 11: La Direction de l'Arrière (Paris: Imprimerie Nationale, 1937), 395.

16 Michael Roper, *The Secret Battle: Emotional Survival in the Great War* (Manchester and New York: Manchester University Press, 2009), 9, 93.

17 Norma Hillyer Shephard (ed.), *Dear Harry: The Firsthand Account of a World War I Infantryman* (n.p.: Brigham Press, 2003), 123. Harry Hillyer to Jennie Hillyer, 30 August 1916.

18 Frank Maheux to Angeline Maheux, undated letter, Francis-Xavier Maheux fonds, MG30-E297, R5156-0-4-E, LAC.

19 Frank Maheux to Angeline Maheux, 6 January 1916, Francis-Xavier Maheux fonds, MG30-E297, R5156-0-4-E, LAC.

20 Laurie Rogers to May Rogers, 8 April 1916, 18 April 1916, Letters of Lt. Lawrence Browning Rogers, Textual Records 58A 1 207.1–5, CWM-MHRC.

21 R.A.L., *Letters of a Canadian Stretcher-Bearer*, ed. Anna Chapin Ray (Boston: Little, Brown, and Company, 1918), 90.

22 Laurie Rogers to May Rogers, 10 October 1917, Letters of Lt. Lawrence Browning Rogers, Textual Records 58A 1 207.1–5, CWM-MHRC.

23 Frank Maheux to Angeline Maheux, 6 November 1916, Francis-Xavier Maheux fonds, MG30-E297, R5156-0-4-E, LAC.

24 William Coleman to Della Coleman, 21 March 1916, Letters of Capt. William Edgar Lawrence Coleman, Textual Records 58A 1 14.1, CWM-MHRC.

25 Laurie Rogers to May Rogers, 2 April 1916, Letters of Lt. Lawrence Browning Rogers, Textual Records 58A 1 207.1–5, CWM-MHRC.

26 Michael B. Miller, "Sea Transport and Supply," *1914–1918 Online: International Encyclopedia of the First World War*, http://encyclopedia.1914-1918-online.net/article/sea_transport_and_supply, accessed 13 February 2017.

27 "Battle for the Treasure Chest that changed the course of the Great War," *The Independent*, 17 March 2009, http://www.independent.co.uk/news/uk/this-britain/battle-for-the-treasure-chest-that-changed-the-course-of-the-great-war-1646524.html, accessed 13 February 2017. On the loss of Canadian mail, Ruth Antliff to her son, William, 5 March 1917, Letters Sent to Private William Shaw Antliff, Textual Records 58A 1 241.3–16, CWM-MHRC.

28 David McLean to Lettie McLean, 5 March 1917 and 25 March 1917, *Canadian Letters and Images Project*, https://canadianletters.ca/content/document-1885?position=50&list=PcVfWfSnodaW7liuo5lxpUMreI-rxoBii4EgUAQ60Zg; https://canadianletters.ca/content/document-1886?position=51&list=PcVfWfSnodaW7liuo5lxpUMreI-rxoBii4EgUAQ60Zg.

29   Laurie Rogers to May Rogers, 22 March 1917, Letters of Lt. Lawrence
     Browning Rogers, Textual Records 58A 1 207.1–5, CWM-MHRC.
30   William Coleman to Della Coleman, 25 April 1916, Letters of Capt. William
     Edgar Lawrence Coleman, Textual Records 58A 1 14.1, CWM-MHRC.
31   David McLean to Lettie McLean, 25 March 1917, *Canadian Letters and Images
     Project*, https://canadianletters.ca/content/document-1886?position=51&list=P
     cVfWfSnodaW7liuo5lxpUMreI-rxoBii4EgUAQ6oZg.
32   Amos William Mayse to Betty Mayse, 12 February 1917, *Canadian Letters and
     Images Project*, https://canadianletters.ca/content/document-9744?position=58
     &list=uionBZE8G8bESplokwBsVwgh6_JyejgRFWgsRQMdfJ8.
33   George Ormsby to Maggie Ormsby, 3 June 1915, 3 November 1916, Fonds of
     Sgt. Ormsby, Textual Records 58A 1 153.1–5, CWM-MHRC.
34   Will Mayse to Betty Mayse, 22 March 1917, *Canadian Letters and Images
     Project*, https://canadianletters.ca/content/document-9799?position=69&list=u
     ionBZE8G8bESplokwBsVwgh6_JyejgRFWgsRQMdfJ8.
35   Stuart Ramsay Tompkins, *A Canadian's Road to Russia: Letters from the Great
     War Decade*, ed. Doris H. Pieroth (Edmonton: University of Alberta Press,
     1989), 160. Stuart Ramsay Tompkins to Edna Tompkins, 6 November 1916.
36   Ibid., 187. Stuart Tompkins to Edna Tompkins, 2 December 1916.
37   Laurie Rogers to May Rogers, 2 April 1916, Letters of Lt. Lawrence Browning
     Rogers, Textual Records 58A 1 207.1–5, CWM-MHRC.
38   Laurie Rogers to May Rogers, 31 May 1916, Letters of Lt. Lawrence
     Browning Rogers, Textual Records 58A 1 207.1–5, CWM-MHRC.
39   Hillyer Shephard (ed.), *Dear Harry*, 150–1. Harry Hillyer to Jennie Hillyer,
     5 November 1916.
40   Agar Adamson to Mabel Adamson, 6 April 1917, Agar Stewart Allan
     Masterton Adamson fonds: vol. 7, MG30-E149, R2538-0-9-E, LAC.
41   Laurie Rogers to May Rogers, 2 April 1916, 31 May 1916, Letters of Lt.
     Lawrence Browning Rogers, Textual Records 58A 1 207.1–5, CWM-MHRC.
42   Laurie Rogers to May Rogers, 31 May 1916, Letters of Lt. Lawrence
     Browning Rogers, Textual Records 58A 1 207.1–5, CWM-MHRC.
43   Tim Cook, *Shock Troops: Canadians Fighting the Great War, 1917–1918*, Vol. 2.
     (Toronto: Viking Canada, 2008), 181–2.
44   When Captain James Evans wrote to his wife, Edith, shortly after arriving
     in France, he noted: "Of course I dare not tell you the front we occupy. You
     might puzzle out the word some place in this letter but it will not have a
     capital letter." James Evans to Edith Evans, 23 March 1918, *Canadian Letters
     and Images Project*, http://www.canadianletters.ca/content/document-3179?pos
     ition=38&list=z5Y99PXPSGvm8xOPn_1iPC-HRUIlLQPGCBkB-MgUzZ4.
45   George Ormsby to Maggie Ormsby, 1 June 1916, Fonds of Sgt. Ormsby,
     Textual Records 58A 1 153.1–5, CWM-MHRC.

46 Tompkins, *A Canadian's Road to Russia*, 98, 106, 160–1. Stuart Tompkins to Edna Tompkins, 31 May 1916, 6 June 1916, 6 November 1916.

47 Hillyer Shephard (ed.), *Dear Harry*, 110, 125, 134. Harry Hillyer to Jennie Hillyer, 11 August 1916, 8 September 1916, 27 September 1916.

48 Desmond Morton, *When Your Number's Up: The Canadian Soldier in the First World War* (Toronto: Random House of Canada, 1993), 238.

49 Frederick Corfield to Mary Corfield, 3 April 1915, 10 April 1915, Correspondence of Frederick and Mary Corfield, Liddle Collection, University of Leeds.

50 George Ormsby to Maggie Ormsby, 16 June 1915, Fonds of Sgt. Ormsby, Textual Records 58A 1 153.1–5, CWM-MHRC.

51 George Eastman to Henrietta Eastman, 2 August 1915, 25 August 1915, 9 September 1915, 3 November 1915, 16 November 1915, Letters from Corporal George Lewis Eastman to his wife and daughter, Textual Records 58A 1 226.14, CWM-MHRC.

52 George Ormsby wrote one week after the opening of the Battle of the Somme: "During the offensive very few letters will be sent out from the front, so don't worry if you do not hear from me very often … No green envelopes are being issued just now but when I get one I will reply to yours of June 13th." George Ormsby to Maggie Ormsby, 8 July 1916, Fonds of Sgt. Ormsby, Textual Records 58A 1 153.1–5, CWM-MHRC. Harry Hillyer complained on 1 October 1916 that "the envelopes you spoke of as being issued weekly have been discontinued. I suppose some body abused the privilege as usual." Hillyer Shephard (ed.), *Dear Harry: The Firsthand Account of a World War I Infantryman*, 137.

53 George Ormsby to Maggie Ormsby, 6 September 1915, Fonds of Sgt. Ormsby, Textual Records 58A 1 153.1–5, CWM-MHRC.

54 George Ormsby to Maggie Ormsby, 1 June 1916, Fonds of Sgt. Ormsby, Textual Records 58A 1 153.1–5, CWM-MHRC.

55 Martha Hanna, *Your Death Would Be Mine: Paul and Marie Pireaud in the Great War* (Cambridge: Harvard University Press, 2006), 121. Marie Pireaud to Paul Pireaud, 19 May 1916.

56 Jean-Pol Dumont Le Douarec, ed., *Armandine: Lettres d'amour. De Binic au front (1914 – 1918)* (Keltia Graphic, 2008), 22, 29. Letters dated 15 February 1916, and [March] 1916.

57 George Eastman to Henrietta Eastman, 2 August 1915, 25 August 1915, 9 September 1915, Letters from Corporal George Lewis Eastman to his wife and daughter, Textual Records 58A 1 226.14, CWM-MHRC.

58 George Eastman to Henrietta Eastman, 3 November 1915, Letters from Corporal George Lewis Eastman to his wife and daughter, Textual Records 58A 1 226.14, CWM-MHRC.

59   George Timmins, *Kiss the Kids for Dad. Don't Forget to Write: The Wartime Letters of George Timmins, 1916–1918*, ed. Y.A. Bennett (Vancouver: UBC Press, 2009), 28. George Timmins to May Timmins, [23 Nov. 1916].

60   Tim Cook, *The Secret History of Soldiers: How Canadians Survived the Great War* (Toronto: Allen Lane, 2018), 109–17.

61   Laurie Rogers to May Rogers, 9 February 1916, Letters of Lt. Lawrence Browning Rogers, Textual Records 58A 1 207.1-5, CWM-MHRC.

62   Cook, *The Secret History of Soldiers*, ch. 2: "Death Culture."

63   George Eastman to Henrietta Eastman, 25 August 1915, Letters from Corporal George Lewis Eastman to his wife and daughter, Textual Records 58A 1 226.14, CWM-MHRC.

64   George Eastman to Henrietta Eastman, 3 November 1915, Letters from Corporal George Lewis Eastman to his wife and daughter, Textual Records 58A 1 226.14, CWM-MHRC.

65   George Eastman to Henrietta Eastman, 16 November 1915, Letters from Corporal George Lewis Eastman to his wife and daughter, Textual Records 58A 1 226.14, CWM-MHRC. Eastman's Military Service record is available at: http://central.bac-lac.gc.ca/.item/?op=pdf&app=CEF&id=B2808-S051.

66   George Ormsby to Maggie Ormsby, 7 June 1916, Fonds of Sgt. Ormsby, Textual Records 58A 1 153.1-5, CWM-MHRC.

67   Laurie Rogers to May Rogers, 9 June 1916, Letters of Lt. Lawrence Browning Rogers, Textual Records 58A 1 207.1–5, CWM-MHRC.

68   Frank Maheux to Angeline Maheux, 20 June 1916, Francis-Xavier Maheux fonds, MG30-E297, R5156-0-4-E.

69   Robert Rutherdale notes, for example, that the Trois-Rivières *Newcomer* described the Battle of Mount Sorrel in "terms of spiritual revival, battles for freedom, or taking up arms in a righteous cause." Rutherdale, *Hometown Horizons: Local Responses to Canada's Great War* (Vancouver: UBC Press, 2004), 230.

70   Stuart Cloete, *A Victorian Son: An Autobiography, 1897-1922* (New York: J. Day Co., 1973), 233.

71   Frank Maheux to Angeline Maheux, 3 November 1916, Francis-Xavier Maheux fonds, MG30-E297, R5156-0-4-E, LAC. Tim Cook argues that "the tanks played a role in shocking the Germans, as evidenced by one bewildered German prisoner who blurted 'What in hell was the meaning of waging war in such fashion?'" Cook, *At the Sharp End: Canadians Fighting the Great War, 1914–1916*, vol. 1 (Toronto: Penguin Canada, 2007), 455.

72   Frank Maheux to Angeline Maheux, 20 September 1916, Francis-Xavier Maheux fonds, MG30-E297, R5156-0-4-E, LAC.

73   Frank Maheux to Angeline Maheux, 23 September 1916, Francis-Xavier Maheux fonds, MG30-E297, R5156-0-4-E, LAC.

74 Laurie Rogers to May Rogers, 24 May 1916, Letters of Lt. Lawrence Browning Rogers, Textual Records 58A 1 207.1–5, CWM-MHRC.

75 Laurie Rogers to May Rogers, 18 September 1916, Letters of Lt. Lawrence Browning Rogers, Textual Records 58A 1 207.1–5, CWM-MHRC.

76 Laurie Rogers to May Rogers, 18 October 1916, Letters of Lt. Lawrence Browning Rogers, Textual Records 58A 1 207.1–5, CWM-MHRC.

77 Laurie Rogers to May Rogers, 5 October 1916, Letters of Lt. Lawrence Browning Rogers, Textual Records 58A 1 207.1–5, CWM-MHRC.

78 Laurie Rogers to May Roger, 13 October 1916, Letters of Lt. Lawrence Browning Rogers, Textual Records 58A 1 207.1–5, CWM-MHRC.

79 Frank Maheux to Angeline Maheux, 26 October 1916, Francis-Xavier Maheux fonds, MG30-E297, R5156-0-4-E, LAC.

80 Frank Maheux to Angeline Maheux, 26 November 1916, Francis-Xavier Maheux fonds, MG30-E297, R5156-0-4-E, LAC.

81 R.A.L., *Letters of a Canadian Stretcher-Bearer*, 99–101. 4 December 1916.

82 Laurie Rogers to May Rogers, 17 November 1916 and 1 December 1916, Letters of Lt. Lawrence Browning Rogers, Textual Records 58A 1 207.1–5, CWM-MHRC.

83 Timmins, *Kiss the Kids for Dad*, 28. George Timmins to May Timmins, 23 November 1916.

84 Ibid., 33–4, 43. George Timmins to May Timmins, 10 December 1916, 29 December 1916.

85 George Ormsby to Maggie Ormsby, 24 December 1916, Fonds of Sgt. Ormsby, Textual Records 58A 1 153.1–5, CWM-MHRC.

86 Laurie Rogers to May Rogers, 23 December 1916 and 16 January 1917, Letters of Lt. Lawrence Browning Rogers, Textual Records 58A 1 207.1–5, CWM-MHRC.

87 Will Mayse to Betty Mayse, 26 February 1917, *Canadian Letters and Images Project*, https://www.canadianletters.ca/content/document-10282?position =60&list=E_aQgwrdEurcJ7TDBsDBFHBd7F8mzIrJfa2j_1_2wS0.

88 Laurie Rogers to May Rogers, 21 March 1917, Letters of Lt. Lawrence Browning Rogers, Textual Records 58A 1 207.1–5, CWM-MHRC.

89 R.A.L., *Letters of a Canadian Stretcher-Bearer*, 149. Letter dated 29 March 1917.

90 Ibid., 139–40. Letter dated 3 March 1917.

91 Ibid., 159–60. Letter dated "Just before Easter."

92 Frank Maheux to Angeline Maheux, 2 April 1917, Francis-Xavier Maheux fonds, MG30-E297, R5156-0-4-E, LAC.

93 Laurie Rogers to May Rogers, 15 April 1917, Letters of Lt. Lawrence Browning Rogers, Textual Records 58A 1 207.1–5, CWM-MHRC.

94 R.A.L., *Letters of a Canadian Stretcher-Bearer*, 164–7. Letter dated "Right after Easter Sunday, 1917."

95 Agar Adamson to Mabel Adamson, 10 April 1917, Letters of Agar Adamson: vol. 7 Agar Stewart Allan Masterton Adamson fonds, MG30-E149, R2538-0-9-E, LAC.

96 Laurie Rogers to May Rogers, 15 April 1917, Letters of Lt. Lawrence Browning Rogers, Textual Records 58A 1 207.1–5, CWM-MHRC.

97 R.A.L., *Letters from a Canadian Stretcher-Bearer*, 96. Letter dated 9 May 1917.

98 Agar Adamson to Mabel Adamson, 15 June 1917, Letters of Agar Adamson, vol. 7, Agar Stewart Allan Masterton Adamson fonds, MG30-E149, R2538-0-9-E, LAC. Adamson wrote: "we found no signs of the German demoralization but rather the reverse, and they are holding with the greatest determination."

99 Robert Rutherdale, *Hometown Horizons*, 230. Ian Miller stresses, however, the willingness of newspapers to publish letters sent home by front-line soldiers. These letters offered civilians a more disturbing (and more realistic) portrait of combat than that conveyed by the congratulatory prose of headline stories. Civilians thus understood more about the war than scholars once believed. Ian Hugh Maclean Miller, *Our Glory and Our Grief: Torontonians and the Great War* (Toronto: University of Toronto Press, 2002).

CHAPTER THREE

1 During the winter of 1914–15, the Manitoba Patriotic Fund spent $70,023.91 "in assisting unemployed civilians." *The Canadian Patriotic Fund: A Record of Its Activities from 1914 to 1919*, ed. Philip H. Morris (n.p., n.d.), 109.

2 P190/9, Edith Rogers papers, Archives of Manitoba (AM). All cases documented in the Edith Rogers papers must remain anonymous.

3 Brock Millman, *Polarity, Patriotism, and Dissent in Great War Canada, 1914–1919* (Toronto: University of Toronto Press, 2016), 95, 100–1.

4 George Timmins, *Kiss the Kids for Dad. Don't Forget to Write: The Wartime Letters of George Timmins, 1916–1918*, ed. Y.A. Bennett (Vancouver: UBC Press, 2009), 87. George to May Timmins, 7 January 1918.

5 Laurie Rogers to May Rogers, 26 August 1915, Letters of Lt. Lawrence Browning Rogers, Textual Records 58A 1 207.1-5, CWM-MHRC.

6 Laurie Rogers to May Rogers, 20 November 1915, 9 January 1916, Letters of Lt. Lawrence Browning Rogers, Textual Records 58A 1 207.1–5, CWM-MHRC.

7 Frank Maheux to Angeline Maheux, 26 June 1915, Francis-Xavier Maheux fonds, MG30-E297 R5156-0-4-E, LAC.

8 Frank Maheux to Angeline Maheux, 1 August 1915, Francis-Xavier Maheux fonds, MG30-E297 R5156-0-4-E, LAC.

9 Frank Maheux to Angeline Maheux, undated [February 1916], Francis-Xavier Maheux fonds, MG30-E297 R5156-0-4-E, LAC.

10 Hand-written statement, 11 October 1917 from Baskatong, Que: "I here authorize Mrs. F. Maheux to keep half the potatoes she will get this year on

Mrs. Midlige [unclear if this is the correct spelling] farm. J. Midlige." Frank
Maheux to Angeline Maheux, 19 December 1916, Francis-Xavier Maheux
fonds, MG30-E297 R5156-0-4-E, LAC.

11 Frank Maheux to Angeline Maheux, undated [late summer/September 1917],
Francis-Xavier Maheux fonds, MG30-E297 R5156-0-4-E, LAC.

12 Frank Maheux to Angeline Maheux, 29 July 1917, Francis-Xavier Maheux
fonds, MG30-E297 R5156-0-4-E, LAC.

13 Frank Maheux to Angeline Maheux, undated [late summer/September 1917],
Francis-Xavier Maheux fonds, MG30-E297 R5156-0-4-E, LAC.

14 Norma Hillyer Shephard (ed.), *Dear Harry: The Firsthand Account of a World
War I infantryman* (Brigham Press, 2003), 73. Harry Hillyer to Jennie Hillyer,
26 June 1916.

15 Ibid., 80. Harry Hillyer to Jennie Hillyer, 2 July 1916.

16 Ibid., 129. Harry Hillyer to Jennie Hillyer, 20 September 1916.

17 Betty Mayse to Will Mayse, 29 April 1917, *Canadian Letters and Images Project*,
https://www.canadianletters.ca/content/document-9676?position=76&list=pz-
1mKc76GCF7hnW6IV69u5Uj3SBT2prKeimVVr2_kk.

18 Ibid.

19 Ibid.

20 Laurie Rogers to May Rogers, 14 February 1916, Letters of Lt. Lawrence
Browning Rogers, Textual Records 58A 1 207.1–5, CWM-MHRC.

21 Hillyer Shephard, *Dear Harry*, 141. Harry Hillyer to Jennie Hillyer,
18 October 1916.

22 Will Mayse to Betty Mayse, 29 June 1916, 5 July 1916, *Canadian Letters
and Images Project*, https://www.canadianletters.ca/content/document-
9767?position=18&list=pz-1mKc76GCF7hnW6IV69u5Uj3SBT2prKeimV
Vr2_kk; http://canadianletters.ca/content/document-9774?position=21&list=
TNFcn4lIPFVQkzWcYvC1YyeCaPd22FGlX7w6-JKo2bc.

23 Linda Kealey, *Enlisting Women for the Cause: Women, Labour, and the Left
in Canada, 1890–1920* (Toronto and Buffalo: University of Toronto Press,
1998), 203.

24 P190/15, P190/11, P189/19, Edith Rogers Papers, AM.

25 Kealey, *Enlisting Women for the Cause*, 204.

26 "High Rents Forcing People to Quit Housekeeping and Take up Quarters in
Rooms," Toronto *Globe*, 25 September 1920: the article noted: "shortly after
the outbreak of the war, rents of apartment suites were dropped by 35 to 40
per cent."

27 Private G. Ross – C.F.A., France – Action of landlord in raising his wife's rent,
9 October 1917, RG13-A-2, vol. 216, file 1917-1831, LAC.

28 *Manitoba Free Press*, 6 March 1916. Classified advertisements for unfurnished
apartments.

29 P190/18, Edith Rogers Papers, AM.

30　Military Service record of Ezra Cooper: http://central.bac-lac.gc.ca/.
item/?op=pdf&app=CEF&id=B1969-S025.

31　Ruth Antliff to William Antliff, 4 February 1917, Letters Sent to Private
William Shaw Antliff, Textual Records 58A 1 241.3-16, CWM-MHRC.

32　"Worst Storm of Year Grips City," *Manitoba Free Press*, 17 February 1917.

33　*Toronto Daily Star*, 8 May 1915 and *Toronto Daily Star*, 12 February 1916.

34　"Potent Cause of High Coal Prices," *Manitoba Free Press*, 1 January 1917;
"Danger of Coal Strike is Grave," *Manitoba Free Press*, 18 January 1917; "Says
Canada Faces a Coal Famine," *Manitoba Free Press*, 7 February 1917.

35　Advertisement for "David Bowman Coal and Supply Co." indicated that
"Peerless Egg coal" was $8.75/ton; and Lethbridge Imperial Lump coal was
$10/ton, *Manitoba Free Press*, 24 February 1917. Ruth Antliff noted that,
"Since the break between Germany and the US there is almost a coal famine
in Canada – the price went up $2.00 a ton and is now $10.50 besides which
anyone wanting it has to go for it, as the coal companies will not deliver –
which adds another $2.00 a ton to the cost." Ruth Antliff to William Antliff,
8 February 1917, Letters Sent to Private William Shaw Antliff, Textual
Records 58A 1 241.3–16, CWM-MHRC.

36　Ian Miller, *Our Glory and Our Grief: Torontonians and the Great War* (Toronto:
University of Toronto Press, 2002), 51.

37　Timmins, *Kiss the Kids for Dad*, 47. George Timmins to May Timmins,
4 February 1917.

38　George Davidson to Jeanie Davidson, 12 September 1917, Letters written
by Sergeant George Neilson Davidson, Textual Records 58A 1 259.11,
CWM-MHRC.

39　Ruth Antliff to William Antliff, 25 June 1917, Letters Sent to Private William
Shaw Antliff, Textual Records 58A 1 241.3–16, CWM-MHRC.

40　P190/7, Edith Rogers Papers, AM.

41　Magda Fahrni and Esyllt W. Jones, "Introduction," *Epidemic Encounters:
Influenza, Society, and Culture in Canada, 1918–20* (Vancouver: UBC Press,
2012), 4.

42　Miller, *Our Glory and our Grief*, 187–8.

43　Ruth Antliff to William Antliff, 17 October 1918, Letters Sent to Private
William Shaw Antliff, Textual Records 58A 1 241.3–16, CWM-MHRC.

44　Mark Osborne Humphries demonstrates that "the administration of the
Military Service Act in Quebec during the pandemic period contributed to
the spread of influenza." Humphries, "The Limits of Necessity: Public Health,
Dissent, and the War Effort during the 1918 Influenza Pandemic," *Epidemic
Encounters*, 35.

45　Ruth Antliff to William Antliff, 3 October 1918, Letters Sent to Private
William Shaw Antliff, Textual Records 58A 1 241.3–16, CWM-MHRC.

46　Esyllt W. Jones, *Influenza, 1918: Disease, Death, and Struggle in Winnipeg*
(Toronto: University of Toronto Press, 2007), 47.

47 Ruth Antliff to William Antliff, 17 October 1918, Letters Sent to Private
    William Shaw Antliff, Textual Records 58A 1 241.3–16, CWM-MHRC.

48 P189/12, Edith Rogers Papers, AM.

49 Jones, *Influenza, 1918*, 62.

50 Military Service record of Albert Eardley: http://central.bac-lac.gc.ca/.
    item/?op=pdf&app=CEF&id=B2801-S014; and of Abraham Harris, http://
    central.bac-lac.gc.ca/.item/?op=pdf&app=CEF&id=B4080-S047.

51 George Ormsby to Maggie Ormsby, 10 May 1915, Letters of George Ormsby,
    58 A 1 153, CWM-MHRC.

52 Timmins, *Kiss the Kids for Dad*, 115. George Timmins to May Timmins,
    13 July [1918].

53 Edward Archibald to Agnes Archibald, 14 June 1915, P88: Edward Archibald
    Fonds, Osler Library, McGill University, Montreal.

54 Edward Archibald to Agnes Archibald, 29 August 1915, P88: Edward
    Archibald Fonds, Osler Library, McGill University, Montreal.

55 Edward Archibald to Agnes Archibald, 7 September 1915, P88: Edward
    Archibald Fonds, Osler Library, McGill University, Montreal.

56 Edward Archibald to Agnes Archibald, 29 August 1915, P88: Edward
    Archibald Fonds, Osler Library, McGill University, Montreal.

57 Laurie Rogers to May Rogers, 9 August 1915, Letters of Lt. Lawrence
    Browning Rogers, Textual Records 58A 1 207.1–5, CWM-MHRC.

58 Laurie Rogers to May Rogers, 12 December 1915, Letters of Lt. Lawrence
    Browning Rogers, Textual Records 58A 1 207.1–5, CWM-MHRC.

59 Laurie Rogers to May Rogers, 20 January 1916, Letters of Lt. Lawrence
    Browning Rogers, Textual Records 58A 1 207.1–5, CWM-MHRC.

60 "Bad Slump in Health throughout Ontario," Toronto *Globe*, 8 January 1915;
    "Ontario Not Too Healthy," Toronto *Globe*, 5 January 1918; "March Heavy
    Disease Month: Nearly 350 Cases of Diphtheria in Province, with 23 Deaths,"
    Toronto *Globe*, 3 April 1918.

61 Bill Parenteau and Stephen Dutcher (eds.), *War on the Home Front: The Farm
    Diaries of Daniel MacMillan, 1914–1927*, New Brunswick Military Heritage
    Series, Vol. 7 (Fredericton, NB: Goose Lane Editions, 2006), 35.

62 "Measles Are Spreading Fast among the People," Toronto *Globe*, 7 April
    1916; "Measles Epidemic Shows Abatement," Toronto *Globe*, 8 May 1916;
    "Epidemic of Measles Still on in Province," Toronto *Globe*, 3 June 1916.
    Measles appeared in rural France, too, causing French war wives the anxiety,
    apprehension and, in the worst cases, debilitating grief known to Canadian
    war wives. One woman, in a village in the Somme where a "veritable
    epidemic" raged, was overcome by grief: "my dear little one has died," she
    wrote, "after two days of atrocious suffering; he had measles, but not a bad
    case; I can't tell you what happened to him after that." Another woman from
    the same village was somewhat more fortunate: each of her three children
    contracted the disease, but all had survived. Report of 17 January 1917,

GQG, 2ème Bureau, Contrôle postal créé de Abbeville, Amiens, 1916–1918, 16 N 1448, Section Historique de la Défense (Paris). In Brittany, one war wife noted that both of her twin boys fell ill in February 1917, and although one recovered without incident, the second twin continued to suffer for three weeks or more: measles gave way to bronchitis and then to scarlet fever. *Armandine: Lettres d'amour, de Binic au front (1914–1918)*, assembled by Jean-Pol Dumont Le Douarec (Spézet, France: Keltia Graphic, 2008), 95 and 99. "Armandine" to her husband, 18 February 1917 and 9 March 1917.

63 "Infantile Paralysis Shows Big Decrease," Toronto *Globe*, 8 November 1916; "Infantile Paralysis Almost Vanishes," Toronto *Globe*, 4 January 1917.

64 "Few Smallpox Cases outside Kent County," Toronto *Globe*, 4 July 1916.

65 "There is a small sized smallpox scare in Montreal just now, Goodwin's employees have to be vaccinated unless they can show a good mark." Ruth Antliff to William Antliff, 16 July 1917, Letters Sent to Private William Shaw Antliff, Textual Records 58A 1 241.3–16, CWM-MHRC. In December 1917, smallpox was "prevalent" in Ontario, with 65 cases in 15 municipalities, "Ontario Not Too Healthy," Toronto *Globe*, 5 January 1918.

66 William Coleman to Della Coleman, 3 October 1916, Letters of Capt. William Edgar Lawrence Coleman, Textual Records 58A 1 14.1, CWM-MHRC.

67 Ruth Antliff to William Antliff, 16 November 1916, Letters Sent to Private William Shaw Antliff, Textual Records 58A 1 241.3–16, CWM-MHRC.

68 Laurie Rogers to May Rogers, 13 November 1916, Letters of Lt. Lawrence Browning Rogers, Textual Records 58A 1 207.1–5, CWM-MHRC.

69 William Coleman to Della Coleman, 12 October 1916, Letters of Capt. William Edgar Lawrence Coleman, Textual Records 58A 1 14.1, CWM-MHRC.

70 Betty Mayse to Will Mayse, 14 June 1917, *Canadian Letters and Images Project*, http://www.canadianletters.ca/content/document-9794?position =94&list=yOcy-ISxDWLyVLj9oOPv-jmxBBW68_EgacUGUgPbVP8.

71 Hillyer Shephard, *Dear Harry*, 184–5. Jennie Hillyer to Harry Hillyer, 29 January 1917.

72 Betty Mayse to Will Mayse, 14 June 1917, *Canadian Letters and Images Project*, http://www.canadianletters.ca/content/document-9794?position=94&list= yOcy-ISxDWLyVLj9oOPv-jmxBBW68_EgacUGUgPbVP8.

73 P189/11, Edith Rogers Papers, AM.

74 P190/11, Edith Rogers Papers, AM.

75 P189/12, Edith Rogers Papers, AM.

76 P190/19, Edith Rogers Papers, AM.

77 Cynthia R. Comacchio, *Nations Are Built of Babies: Saving Ontario's Mothers and Children, 1900-1940* (Montreal: McGill-Queen's University Press, 1993), 31.

78 The information on these families is derived by cross-referencing three sets of digitized records: the soldier's Military Service record, the 1916 Prairie census, and birth and/or death records from the Manitoba Vital Statistics Agency database: https://vitalstats.gov.mb.ca/Query.php.

79   Peggy Bette, "Veuves et veuvages de la première guerre mondiale Lyon
      (1914–1924)," *Vingtième Siècle. Revue d'histoire*, No. 98 (April–June 2008), 198.

80   Clémentine Vidal-Naquet, *Couples dans la Grande guerre: Le tragique et
      l'ordinaire du lien conjugal* (Paris: Belles Lettres, 2014), 167.

81   Herbert Oates to Beatie Oates, letter #25, undated, Letters of Private Herbert
      Oates, Liddle Collection, Special Collections Library, University of Leeds.

82   Military Service record of Stafford Beaumont: http://central.bac-lac.
      gc.ca/.item/?op=pdf&app=CEF&id=B0564-S013; Census of Manitoba,
      Saskatchewan, and Alberta, 1916. http://data2.collectionscanada.ca
      /006003/t-21934/jpg/31228_4363963-00599.jpg. Military Service record for
      William Lyle: http://central.bac-lac.gc.ca/.item/?op=pdf&app=CEF&id=
      B5805-S054; Census of Manitoba, Saskatchewan, and Alberta, 1916. http://
      data2.collectionscanada.ca/006003/t-21933/jpg/31228_4363962-00400.jpg.

83   P189/11, Edith Rogers Papers, AM.

84   Military Service record of Thomas Hatcher: http://central.bac-lac.gc.ca/.
      item/?op=pdf&app=CEF&id=B4152-S005 and 1916 Census: http://data2.
      collectionscanada.ca/006003/t-21928/jpg/31228_4363957-01058.jpg;
      Military Service record of Ralph R.J. Brown: http://central.bac-lac.gc.ca/.
      item/?op=pdf&app=CEF&id=B1172-S046 and 1916 Census: http://data2.
      collectionscanada.ca/006003/t-21933/jpg/31228_4363962-00882.jpg.

85   Military Service Record of David Hilland: http://central.bac-lac.gc.ca/.
      item/?op=pdf&app=CEF&id=B4364-S041. 1916 Census of Manitoba,
      Saskatchewan, and Alberta: http://data2.collectionscanada.ca/006003/t-21933/
      jpg/31228_4363962-00403.jpg.

86   "Mother Dies of Grief, Son Killed at Front," *Toronto Daily Star*, 21 February
      1916. The death certificate for Ida Harries reveals that she lived at 328 Main
      Street, East Toronto; Harries's Military Service record shows that his wife
      moved from their home address, on Coleman Street, to 330 Main Street.
      Military Service record of John S. Harries: http://central.bac-lac.gc.ca/.
      item/?op=pdf&app=CEF&id=B4076-S022.

87   1916 census data for Jessie Beker: http://data2.collectionscanada.
      ca/006003/t-21933/jpg/31228_4363962-00956.jpg; for Elsie Bottomley:
      http://data2.collectionscanada.ca/006003/t-21932/jpg/31228_4363961-
      01043.jpg; and for Hazel Jackson: http://data2.collectionscanada.
      ca/006003/t-21932/jpg/31228_4363961-00003.jpg. Linda Kealey provides
      details of women's wages in wartime Winnipeg in *Enlisting Women for the
      Cause*, 165–8.

88   Hillyer Shephard, *Dear Harry*, 183. Jennie Hillyer to Harry Hillyer,
      29 January 1917.

89   Katharine McGowan, "'A Question of Caste and Colour': The Displacement
      of James Bay Native Soldiers' Wives During the First World War, Soldiers'
      Family Support, and the Maintenance of Pre-War Canadian Society," *Native
      Studies Review* 21, 1 (2012): 103–23.

90   Headquarters, Military District No. 6, Halifax to Secretary, Militia Council, Ottawa, March 22, 1919, Transportation of Soldiers' Wives and Families from Overseas to Canada, RG24-C-1-a, vol. 744 – 747, file HQ-54-21-6–85, LAC.

91   George Davidson to Jeanie Davidson, 12 September 1917, Letters written by Sergeant George Neilson Davidson, Textual Records 58A 1 259.11, CWM-MHRC.

92   Laurie Rogers to May Rogers, 20 January 1916, 18 September 1916, 25 September 1916, 1 February 1917, Letters of Lt. Lawrence Browning Rogers, Textual Records 58A 1 207.1-5, CWM-MHRC.

93   Tim Cook, "'My Whole Heart and Soul is in this War': The Letters and War Service of Sergeant G.L. Ormsby," *Canadian Military History* 15, 1 (2012): 53.

94   George Ormsby to Maggie Ormsby, 3 October 1915, 5 December 1915, Letters of George Ormsby, 58 A 1 153, CWM-MHRC.

95   Frank Maheux to Angeline Maheux, 17 July 1915, 5 October 1915, 11 December 1917, Francis-Xavier Maheux fonds, MG30-E297, R5156-0-4-E, LAC.

96   Military service record of William Whitford Benny: http://central.bac-lac. gc.ca/.item/?op=pdf&app=CEF&id=B0657-S030; and Harry Floyd: http://central.bac-lac.gc.ca/.item/?op=pdf&app=CEF&id=B3159-S021.

97   Frank Maheux to Angeline Maheux, 17 February 1918, Francis-Xavier Maheux fonds, MG30-E297, R5156-0-4-E, LAC.

98   Mrs Dorothy Yates, Oakland, CA, April 15–22, 1918: Complaint of legislation affecting the rights of her husband (private in the CEF), RG13-A-2, vol. 222, file number: 1918-886, LAC.

99   I am familiar with only one example of such a move: shortly after Henri Fauconnier returned to France from his rubber plantation in south-east Asia, his mother, sisters, and fiancée returned to France, too. Henri Fauconnier, *Lettres à Madeleine, 1914–1919* (Paris: Éditions Stock, 1998).

100   P189/4, Edith Rogers Papers, AM.

101   Archival records are not sufficiently complete to allow for an accurate count, but the numbers were significant. In 1919, a Canadian newspaper announced that "fifty thousand dependents of Canadian soldiers overseas [remained] in the British Isles … in addition to some 22,000 already returned to Canada." Even if half of the dependents still awaiting passage to Canada were war brides, this would still mean that at least 35,000 and perhaps as many as 50,000 Canadian wives and children had temporarily returned to Britain during the war. Newspaper clipping: "Twenty-two Thousand Dependents of Soldiers to be Brought to Canada Free," Migration of Soldiers' Wives and Families, Quarter-Master General, RG 9 III-B-1, vol. 3320, file M-2-43, LAC.

CHAPTER FOUR

1   *Canadian Letters and Images Project*, Alice and Arthur Leighton correspondence: https://www.canadianletters.ca/collections/all/

collection/20512; Details of Alice and Arthur's life before his enlistment are drawn from the Nanaimo Archives: http://www.nanaimoarchives.ca/online-resources/finding-aids/arthur-and-alice-leighton-fonds/.

2 UK Incoming Passenger Lists, October 1914, Montreal to Liverpool, Ancestry.com.

3 To Brig. General A.D. McRae, Argyll House, London, 10 February 1917, Migration of Soldiers' Wives and Families, Quarter-Master General, RG 9 III-B-1, vol. 3320, file M-2-43, LAC. "Women and children leaving Canada to go to England (Soldiers' dependents)," Microfilm C-10434, LAC.

4 Desmond Morton, *When Your Number's Up: The Canadian Soldier in the First World War* (Toronto: Random House, 1993), 279.

5 Alice Leighton to Arthur Leighton, 29 September 1916, *Canadian Letters and Images Project*, https://www.canadianletters.ca/content/document-6482?position=20&list=4r5zpBVhAi13tWsKG9YGzldNXqYyGZHOuJ9xkCRN6So.

6 James Evans to Edith Evans, 10 May 1915, *Canadian Letters and Images Project*, https://www.canadianletters.ca/content/document-3157.

7 James Evans to Edith Evans, 15 September 1915, *Canadian Letters and Images Project*, https://www.canadianletters.ca/content/document-3165.

8 James Evans to Edith Evans, 15 October 1915, *Canadian Letters and Images Project*, https://www.canadianletters.ca/content/document-3169.

9 James Evans to Edith Evans, 9 November 1915, *Canadian Letters and Images Project*, https://www.canadianletters.ca/content/document-3170.

10 James Evans to Edith Evans, 15 October 1915, *Canadian Letters and Images Project*, https://www.canadianletters.ca/content/document-3169.

11 Mrs W.L. Grant Correspondence: letters from William L. Grant 1910–1916 (vol. 35) and 1916–1932 (vol. 36), William Lawson Grant and Maude Grant fonds, MG30 D59, R11505-0-3-E, vol. 35 and vol. 36, LAC.

12 Stuart Ramsay Tompkins, *A Canadian's Road to Russia: Letters from the Great War Decade*, ed. Doris H. Pieroth (Edmonton: University of Alberta Press, 1989), 94. Stuart Tompkins to Edna Tompkins, 30 May 1916.

13 Ibid., 117. Stuart Tompkins to Edna Tompkins, 13 June 1916.

14 William Grant to Maude Grant, 30 May 1916, William Lawson Grant and Maude Grant fonds, MG30 D59, R11505-0-3-E, vol. 35 and vol. 36, LAC.

15 Private Alan Hodnett to Edith Evans, 22 February 1917, *Canadian Letters and Images Project*, https://www.canadianletters.ca/content/document-3173.

16 Georgina Lee, *Home Fires Burning: The Great War Diaries of Georgina Lee*, ed. Gavin Roynon, foreword by Hew Strachan (Stroud, Gloucestershire: History Press, 2009), 218–19. Diary entry of 31 May 1917.

17 Jerry White, *Zeppelin Nights: London in the First World War* (London: Random House, 2014), 178.

18 Military Service Records of Maj. William Yeates Hunter, http://central.bac-lac.gc.ca/.item/?op=pdf&app=CEF&id=B4637-S034; Capt. John Geddes,

http://central.bac-lac.gc.ca/.item/?op=pdf&app=CEF&id=B3460-S044; Capt. Douglas Upton Cameron, http://central.bac-lac.gc.ca/.item/?op=pdf& app=CEF&id=B1404-S004.

19 Agar Adamson to Mabel Adamson, 14 August 1916, *Letters of Agar Adamson, 1914–1918*, ed. N.M. Christie (Nepean, ON: CEF Books, 1997), 209.

20 Frederick Corfield, a career officer in the British Army whose family was accustomed to the lifestyle of the British gentry, insisted in December 1916 that his rather spendthrift wife should be able to manage easily on the £360 per annum he allocated for the family's upkeep. "When I gave you £360 a year I thought if anything considering our means and the certainty of never again getting as much as £360 again after the war, and the heavy expenses we are bound to have at first that you were being done fairly well especially as we have never had more than £300 to live on before. There's no good discussing it Darling. I thought we had thrashed it all out time after time when I was on leave. The suggestion that you sh'd work as the £360 is not sufficient when we've got to live on £300 the moment the war ends plus anything we can save now makes me feel very bitterly that you don't think I give you enough to live on." Frederick Corfield to Mary Corfield, 17 December 1916, Letters of Frederick Alleyne Corfield to his wife, Mary Corfield, Liddle Collection, Special Collections Library, University of Leeds. In 1920, the Family Endowment Committee observed that only 6 percent of British households had incomes of more than £300 per year. *The Endowment of Motherhood*, ed. Katharine Anthony (New York: B.W. Huebsch, 1920), 33.

21 Alice Leighton to Arthur Leighton, 29 September 1916, *Canadian Letters and Images Project*, https://www.canadianletters.ca/content/document-6482?positio n=20&list=90JyXBFODZmDRDuOcOz9ZuBNfasuaxJMwExS2Z_HqZk.

22 Alice Leighton to Arthur Leighton, 25 September 1916, *Canadian Letters and Images Project*, https://www.canadianletters.ca/content/document-6480?position=18&list=w_kZxIMFGlj9L4R-FAJNWqHg1IulRqr 51shMQN6xIZA.

23 On the social and cultural enterprise of the IODE, see: Katie Pickles, *Female Imperialism and National Identity: The Imperial Order Daughters of the Empire* (Manchester; New York: Manchester University Press, 2002).

24 Agar Adamson to Mabel Adamson, 2 January 1916, *Letters of Agar Adamson*, 123.

25 Peter Grant, *Philanthropy and Voluntary Action in the First World War* (New York: Routledge, 2014), 99.

26 Tompkins, *A Canadian's Road to Russia*, 132. Stuart Tompkins to Edna Tompkins, 1 October 1916.

27 Jerry White, *Zeppelin Nights*, 178. White quotes an article, dated 24 February 1917, from *The Times* to the effect that Horseferry Road had become by early 1917 a "hotbed of immorality, undisguised and unchecked."

28 Desmond Morton, *Fight or Pay: Soldiers' Families in the Great War* (Vancouver: UBC Press, 2004), 34.
29 Tompkins, *A Canadian's Road to Russia*, 132–3. Stuart Tompkins to Edna Tompkins, 1 October 1916.
30 Ibid., 184. Stuart Tompkins to Edna Tompkins, 28 November 1916.
31 Alice Leighton to Arthur Leighton, 13 May 1918, *Canadian Letters and Images Project*, http://www.canadianletters.ca/content/document-1726?position=53&list=_wpPcl9Y9aOiQae8zKPeAfw93oMkIK_IjMd6SbHnLZA.
32 Tompkins, *A Canadian's Road to Russia*, 184. Stuart Tompkins to Edna Tompkins, 29 November 1916.
33 Ibid., 232. Stuart Tompkins to Edna Tompkins, 12 January 1917.
34 Ibid.
35 May Rogers to Laurie Rogers, 17 October 1917, Letters of Lt. Lawrence Browning Rogers, Textual Records 58A 1 207.1-5, CWM-MHRC.
36 Morton, *When Your Number's Up*, 106.
37 Agar Adamson to Mabel Adamson, 4 July 1917, *Letters of Agar Adamson*, 293.
38 Alice Leighton to Arthur Leighton, 3 October 1916, *Canadian Letters and Images Project*, https://www.canadianletters.ca/content/document-1701?position=23&list=w_kZxIMFGlj9L4R-FAJNWqHg1IulRqr51shMQN6xIZA.
39 Frederick Corfield to Mary Corfield, 31 December 1916, Letters of Frederick Alleyne Corfield to his wife, Mary, Liddle Collection, Special Collections Library, University of Leeds.
40 Alice Leighton to Arthur Leighton, 22 March 1917, *Canadian Letters and Images Project*, https://www.canadianletters.ca/content/document-1720?position=42&list=w_kZxIMFGlj9L4R-FAJNWqHg1IulRqr51shMQN6xIZA.
41 Alice Leighton to Arthur Leighton, 1 October 1916, *Canadian Letters and Images Project*, https://www.canadianletters.ca/content/document-1700?position=22&list=w_kZxIMFGlj9L4R-FAJNWqHg1IulRqr51shMQN6xIZA.
42 Alice Leighton to Arthur Leighton, 18 March 1917, *Canadian Letters and Images Project*, https://www.canadianletters.ca/content/document-1716?position=38&list=w_kZxIMFGlj9L4R-FAJNWqHg1IulRqr51shMQN6xIZA.
43 *Letters of Agar Adamson*, 239. Agar Adamson to Mabel Adamson, 26 November 1916.
44 Tompkins, *A Canadian's Road to Russia*, 161. Stuart Tompkins to Edna Tompkins, 6 November 1916.
45 *Letters of Agar Adamson, 1914–1919*, 43. Agar Adamson to Mabel Adamson, 17 March 1915.
46 *Letters of Agar Adamson*, 178. Agar Adamson to Mabel Adamson, 15 May 1916.
47 William Grant to Maude Grant, 17 August 1916, William Lawson Grant and Maude Grant fonds, MG30 D59, R11505-0-3-E, vol. 35 and vol. 36, LAC.
48 Alice Leighton to Arthur Leighton, 23–25 March 1917 (postscript added to a letter started on 23 March 1917), *Canadian Letters and Images Project*, https://

www.canadianletters.ca/content/document-1721?position=43&list=w_
kZxIMFGlj9L4R-FAJNWqHg1IulRqr51shMQN6xIZA.

49 Tompkins, *A Canadian's Road to Russia*, 319. Stuart Tompkins to Edna
Tompkins, 21 April 1917. Stuart Tompkins' digitized service file: http://
central.bac-lac.gc.ca/.item/?op=pdf&app=CEF&id=B9729-S006.

50 Alice Leighton to Arthur Leighton, 15 November 1918, *Canadian Letters and
Images Project*, https://www.canadianletters.ca/content/document-1730?
position=58&list=w_kZxIMFGlj9L4R-FAJNWqHg1IulRqr51shMQN6xIZA.

51 UK Outward Passenger Lists, 1890–1960: *The Victorian* departed Liverpool, 30
August 1912, Ancestry.com. Manitoba Vital Statistics Agency database: http://
vitalstats.gov.mb.ca/Query.php.

52 Canadian Passenger Lists, 1865–1935: October 1910, Ancestry.com. Manitoba
Vital Statistics Agency database: http://vitalstats.gov.mb.ca/Query.php.

53 Canadian Passenger Lists, 1865–1935: Quebec, August 1912, Ancestry.com;
UK Incoming Passenger Lists, 5 January 1916; Canadian Passenger Lists,
1865–1935: Arrival in New York, December 1917, Ancestry.com; Manitoba
Vital Statistics Agency database: http://vitalstats.gov.mb.ca/Query.php.

54 Canadian Passenger Lists, 1865–1935: Arrival in Quebec, June 1903;
US, Records of Aliens Pre-Registered in Canada: "Alien Certificate"
issued to Ernest Andrews in Winnipeg, 10 April 1914, Ancestry.com.
Military Service record for Ernest E. Andrews: http://central.bac-lac.gc.ca/.
item/?op=pdf&app=CEF&id=B0178-S043.

55 P190/12, Edith Rogers Paper, AM.

56 Maud Pember Reeves, *Round About a Pound a Week*, intro. Sally Alexander
(London: Virago Press, 1979), first published 1913 by G. Bell and Sons Ltd.

57 Military Service record of Archibald Galbraith, http://central.bac-lac.gc.ca/.
item/?op=pdf&app=CEF&id=B0295-S011. Shipping registers show that an
Anna Bella Lowe, age nineteen, arrived in Canada from Liverpool in June
1913, she identified herself as a domestic. Ancestry.com. Manitoba Vital
Statistics Agency documents the marriage of Anna Bella Lowe to Archibald
Galbraith in February 1914, and the birth of their daughter, Jessica, in
August 1914.

58 Military Service records of Walter Bealey, http://central.bac-lac.gc.ca/.
item/?op=pdf&app=CEF&id=B0534-S050; and William Atton, http://central.
bac-lac.gc.ca/.item/?op=pdf&app=CEF&id=B0295-S011.

59 V. de Vesselitsky, *Expenditure and Waste: A Study in Wartime* (London: G. Bell
and Sons, 1917), 14, 16, 21, 58–60.

60 Jack Ellis to Kitty Ellis, 12 February 1917, 23 March 1917, 6 April 1917, 7 May
1917; from Kitty Ellis to Jack Ellis, 29 April 1917, *Canadian Letters and Images
Project*, https://www.canadianletters.ca/collections/war/468/collection/20499/
doc/221.

61 Military Service record of James McDowell, http://central.bac-lac.gc.ca/.
    item/?op=pdf&app=CEF&id=B6793-S017.

62 Military Service record of Ernest Winsor Blyth, http://central.bac-lac.gc.ca/.
    item/?op=pdf&app=CEF&id=B0833-S046.

63 Director of Pay and Records, CEF (W.R. Ward, Col., Director of Pay and
    Records, CEF) to High Commissioner for Canada, 18 October 1915,
    Repatriation of Widows and Wives of men in CEF, RG24-C-1-a, vol. 736,
    file HQ-54-21-6-50, LAC.

64 Cablegram, received at Ottawa, 29 June 1915, from London, Repatriation
    of Widows and Wives of men in CEF, RG24-C-1-a, vol. 736, file HQ-54-21-6-
    50, LAC.

65 Director of Pay and Records, CEF (W.R. Ward, Col., Director of Pay and
    Records, CEF) to High Commissioner for Canada, 18 October 1915,
    Repatriation of Widows and Wives of men in CEF, RG24-C-1-a, vol. 736,
    file HQ-54-21-6-50, LAC.

66 William Frederick Workman was unmarried when he enlisted at Valcartier in
    September 1914. Born in Gloucester, England, in 1890, he had left England
    in 1901 and appeared in the 1906 Canadian census as a hired hand on a
    farm in Alberta. It's very likely that he was the ten-year-old Fred Workman
    who arrived in Canada as a Barnado Boy in 1901; in 1912 a Fred Workman
    appears in the inbound passenger lists from Sydney to Vancouver, indicating
    that he had left Canada six months previously and had lived in Canada for
    nine years prior to sailing for Australia. In 1922 he returned to Canada from
    visiting his wife in England and indicated on his re-entry papers that he had
    first arrived in Canada in 1901.

67 H.W. Hart, Hon. Secretary, Returned Soldiers' Association, Victoria, BC, to the
    Secretary, Militia Council, Ottawa, 18 July 1916, Transportation of Soldiers'
    Wives and Families from Overseas to Canada, RG24-C-1-a, vol. 744 -747, file
    number: HQ-54-21-6-85, LAC.

68 Office of the A/Adjutant General, CEF, London, to Colonel F.A. Reid,
    A/Adjutant General, CEF, 18 October 1916, Migration of Soldiers' Wives and
    Families, RG 9 III-B-1, vol. 3320, file M-2-43, LAC.

69 Order in Council No. 760: re: repatriation of Canadian families from UK, 1
    April 1916, Repatriation of Widows and Wives of men in CEF, RG24-C-1-a,
    vol. 736, file HQ-54-21-6-50, LAC.

70 Memorandum from Major General, Quartermaster General, to Col. Reid,
    Director of Recruiting and Organization, Folkestone, Kent, August 9, 1916,
    Transportation of Soldiers' Wives and Families from Overseas to Canada,
    RG24-C-1-a, vol. 744 – 747, file HQ-54-21-6-85, LAC.

71 Memorandum from The Deputy Minister, Militia and Defence, to
    Sir Geo. H. Perley, Minister of Militia and Defence Overseas, London,

27 December 1916, Migration of Soldiers' Wives and Families, Quarter-Master General, RG 9 III-B-1, vol. 3320, file M-2-43, LAC.

72   Paymaster, Military District 6, Halifax, NS to Mr. R.P. Brown A/A and P.M.G., Ottawa, 23 April 1917; response from Ottawa, 30 April 1917, Advances to Soldiers' Returned Wives, RG24-C-1-a, vol. 998, file HQ-54-21-23-86, LAC.

73   Memo re: Mrs Simons' inquiry, from Department of Militia and Defence, Ottawa, 15 January 1917, Repatriation of Widows and Wives of men in CEF, RG24-C-1-a, vol. 736, file HQ-54-21-6-50, LAC.

74   Military Service record of Percy Hale: http://central.bac-lac.gc.ca/. item/?op=pdf&app=CEF&id=B3931-S009.

75   Memorandum to Secretary of Militia Council, Ottawa, from Militia and Defence, Halifax, regarding Transportation of Women and Children returning to Canada, 20 March 1918, Transportation of Soldiers' Wives and Families from Overseas to Canada, RG24-C-1-a, vol. 744–747, file HQ-54-21-6-85, LAC.

76   Letter from Sapper A. Senier, Toronto, 12 September 1917, Transportation of Soldiers' Wives and Families from Overseas to Canada, RG24-C-1-a, vol. 744–747, file HQ-54-21-6-85, LAC.

77   For example, of 99 soldiers enumerated in a memorandum dated 4 March 1918, 47 were unmarried at the time of enlistment; 11 were married at enlistment, and their families still resided in the United Kingdom; the remainder were married with wives residing in Canada at the time of enlistment. Assigned Pay and Separation Allowance NCOs and Men Discharged to Canada Dependents in British Isles, RG24-C-1-a, vol. 998, file HQ-54-21-23-89, LAC.

78   Black-bordered letter from Elizabeth Simons, 98 Cambusnetham St, Wishaw, Scotland, to Lieutenant-General, Minister of Militia and Defense, 22 December [1916]. Repatriation of Widows and Wives of men in CEF, RG24-C-1-a, vol. 736, file HQ-54-21-6-50, LAC.

79   Letter from Mrs Florence M. Smith, Lethbridge Alberta, 13 January 1919, Migration of Soldiers' Wives and Families, QuarterMaster General, RG 9 III-B-1, vol. 3320, file M-2-43, LAC.

80   Ethel Cove to Wilfrid Cove, 31 January 1917, Letters of Gunner W[ilfrid]. J. Cove, Royal Garrison Artillery, Liddle Collection, Special Collections Library, University of Leeds.

81   Tompkins, *A Canadian's Road to Russia*, 228–9. Stuart Tompkins to Edna Tompkins, 11 January 1917.

82   Jack Ellis to Kitty Ellis, 17 March 1917, *Canadian Letters and Images Project*, http://www.canadianletters.ca/content/document-1216?position=31&list=fW JALlneJoDoECC9xfbX3TLvLp6AGMbmHBQl9_oOwOs.

83   Emma McGill sent her husband, Harold McGill, a copy of the enclosure urging Canadian wives in Britain to return to Canada; in his letter of

30 March 1918 he returned it to her. Harold McGill's First World War letters, December 25, 1917–April 30, 1918, Harold and Emma McGill fonds, M-742-8, Glenbow Archives. https://www.glenbow.org/collections/search/findingAids/archhtm/extras/mcgill/m-742-8-transcript.pdf.

84 Memorandum from The Deputy Minister, Militia and Defence, to Sir Geo. H. Perley, Minister of Militia and Defence Overseas, London, 27 December 1916; Telegram from London to Ottawa, 20 April 1917: "Passenger list transport thirty men six hundred and eleven women one hundred and eighty eight children one hundred and sixty nine infants"; Memorandum, Dept. of Militia and Defence, indicating that a cable had been received from the High Commission in London to the effect that "918 [women and children] had embarked for Canada on the 13th Sept.," 20 September 1917, Transportation of Soldiers' Wives and Families from Overseas to Canada, RG24-C-1-a, vol. 744–747, file HQ-54-21-6-85, LAC.

85 Letter from Margaret Dickinson, Janefield Cottages, Broxburn, Linlithgoushire, Scotland, 7 August 1916, Transportation of Soldiers' Wives and Families from Overseas to Canada," RG24-C-1-a, vol. 744–747, file HQ-54-21-6-85, LAC.

86 Charles Bunch Military Service record, http://central.bac-lac.gc.ca/.item/?op=pdf&app=CEF&id=B1260-S033.

87 Mrs Emma Piper, 55 Priory St., Bowden, Cheshire, England [to Ministry of Militia and Defence] 31 January 1917, Transportation of Soldiers' Wives and Families from Overseas to Canada, RG24-C-1-a, vol. 744–747, file HQ-54-21-6-85. Military Service record of William Piper: http://central.bac-lac.gc.ca/.item/?op=pdf&app=CEF&id=B7848-S021.

88 Mrs Hector MacKenzie, Kitsilano, Vancouver [to Ministry of Militia and Defence], 14 January 1919, Migration of Soldiers' Wives and Families, QuarterMaster General, RG 9 III-B-1, vol. 3320, file M-2-43, LAC.

89 Mrs E. Smallman, Souris, Manitoba [to Ministry of Militia and Defence], 22 January 1919, Transportation of Soldiers' Wives and Families from Overseas to Canada, RG24-C-1-a, vol. 744–747, file HQ-54-21-6-85, LAC.

90 Mrs M. McLuskie, 3417 Carolina St, Vancouver, BC [to Ministry of Militia and Defence], 13 January 1919, Repatriation of Widows and Wives of men in CEF, RG24-C-1-a, vol. 736, file HQ-54-21-6-50, LAC.

91 Superintendent of Immigration, Ottawa to Major W.R. Creighton, Private Secretary to the Minister of Militia and Defense, Ottawa, 30 March 1918, Transportation of Soldiers' Wives and Families from Overseas to Canada, RG24-C-1-a, vol. 744–747, file HQ-54-21-6-85, LAC.

92 Mrs Isabella Christie, Toronto [Dec. 1917] [to Ministry of Militia and Defence], Transportation of Soldiers' Wives and Families from Overseas to Canada, RG24-C-1-a, vol. 744 – 747, file HQ-54-21-6-85, LAC.

93 Estimates of precisely how many Canadian civilians awaited repatriation in November 1918 vary. A telegram from Quebec to Militia Council,

Ottawa, indicated that the "[immigration] department negotiating for return to Canada within six weeks of upwards of thirty thousand women and children from England." Telegram from Quebec to Militia Council, Ottawa, 22 November 1918, Repatriation of Widows and Wives of men in CEF, RG24-C-1-a, vol. 736, file HQ-54-21-6-50, LAC. An undated newspaper clipping, submitted in January 1919 by Mrs Ada Varley of Regina in support of her request for compensation, stated: "Under the government's policy as announced today, these 50000 will be brought to Canada at public expense. The number includes wives, children and other dependents of all officers, non-commissioned officers and men of the Canadian Expeditionary Force still serving overseas." Transportation of Soldiers' Wives and Families from Overseas to Canada, RG24-C-1-a, vol. 763, file HQ-54-21-6-116, LAC.

94 Mrs Dorothy Morris, 384 Wood Ave, Westmount, Montreal [to Ministry of Militia and Defence], 20 January 1919, Migration of Soldiers' Wives and Families, Quartermaster General, RG 9 III-B-1, vol. 3320, file M-2-43, LAC.

95 Lt. Col. H.B. Tremain to Lt. Col. G.W. Marriott, 14 January 1919, Migration of Soldiers' Wives and Families, Quarter-Master General, RG 9 III-B-1, vol. 3320, file M-2-43, LAC.

96 Miss Helen Rintoul, Executive Committee of the Dominion Council of the Young Women's Christian Association, Toronto, to Hon. S. Calder, Minister of Immigration and Colonization, Ottawa, undated [April 1919], Soldiers' Dependents Returning to Canada, Microfilm C-10435, LAC.

97 Department of Immigration and Colonization, Government of Canada, London Office to W.W. Cory, Acting Deputy Minister, Immigration and Colonization, Ottawa, 29 March 1919, Soldiers' Dependents Returning to Canada, Microfilm C-10435, LAC.

98 W.D. Scott, Superintendent of Immigration to L.S. Tobin, White Star Dominion Line, Montreal, 18 April 1919, Soldiers' Dependents Returning to Canada, Microfilm C-10435, LAC.

99 Report of Hon. Captain and Chaplain Robert Howie, "Conditions of Travelling," 19 May 1919, Soldiers' Dependents Returning to Canada, Microfilm C-10435, LAC.

100 Report for the Repatriation Committee on the Comfort and Welfare Work of the Dominion Council YWCA for Soldiers' Dependents: Report of Miss Elizabeth Helm, YWCA Secretary on Board the *Metagama*, 22 April–3 May 1919, Soldiers' Dependents Returning to Canada, Microfilm C-10435, LAC.

101 Philip Morris, Executive Secretary, Canadian Patriotic Fund to Hon. J.A. Calder, Minister of Immigration and Colonization, 6 May 1919; Canadian Patriotic Fund, Brantford, Ontario to S. Herbert Ames, Hon. Secretary, Canadian Patriotic Fund, Ottawa, 7 May 1919, Soldiers' Dependents Returning to Canada, Microfilm C-10435, LAC.

102 W.F. Nickle, Member of Parliament to Hon. J.A. Calder, Minister of Militia
and Defence, Ottawa, 9 May 1919; response from W.D. Scott, Superintendent
of Immigration, 22 May 1919, Soldiers' Dependents Returning to Canada,
Microfilm C-10435, LAC.

103 Memorandum from Immigration Inspectors, Department of Immigration
and Colonization, 9 April 1919; Quebec office of Department of
Immigration and Colonization to Commissioner, Department of
Immigration and Colonization, Ottawa, 27 May 1919; Superintendent
of Immigration to Walter Maughan, Assistant General Passenger Agent,
CPR, Montreal, 30 May 1919, Soldiers' Dependents Returning to Canada,
Microfilm C-10435, LAC.

CHAPTER FIVE

1 George Timmins, *Kiss the Kids for Dad. Don't Forget to Write: The Wartime
Letters of George Timmins, 1916–1918*, ed. Y.A. Bennett (Vancouver, BC:
UBC Press, 2009) 45. George Timmins to May Timmins, 2 January 1917.

2 6th Census of Canada, 1921. http://central.bac-lac.gc.ca/.item/?app=
Census1921&op=img&id=e002948144.

3 Timmins, *Kiss the Kids for Dad*, 35. George Timmins to May Timmins,
10 December 1916.

4 As cited by Manon Pignon, "1918-1919: Retour des hommes et invention
des pères?" *Retour à l'intime: au sortir de la guerre*, ed. Bruno Cabanes et
Guillaume Piketty (Paris: Tallandier, 2009), 45.

5 "Preface," Stuart Ramsay Tompkins, *A Canadian's Road to Russia: Letters from
the Great War Decade*, ed. Doris H. Pieroth (Edmonton: University of Alberta
Press, 1989), viii.

6 Arthur and Alice Leighton Fonds, Nanaimo Archives, http://www.
nanaimoarchives.ca/online-resources/finding-aids/arthur-and-alice-leighton-
fonds/.

7 Arthur Mayse, *My Father My Friend*, edited and with an afterword by Susan
Mayse (Madeira Park, BC: Harbour Publishing, 1993).

8 Desmond Morton, *Fight or Pay: Soldiers' Families in the Great War* (Vancouver
and Toronto: UBC Press, 2004), 217.

9 Frank Maheux to Angeline Maheux, 17 January 1916. Francis-Xavier Maheux
fonds, MG30-E297, R5156-0-4-E, LAC.

10 On the character and challenges of the Soldier Settlement Act, see: E.C.
Morgan, "Soldier Settlement in the Prairie Provinces," *Saskatchewan History
Magazine* 21, 2 (June 1968): 42–55; Andrew Iarocci and Jeffrey A. Keshen, *A
Nation in Conflict: Canada and the Two World Wars* (Toronto: University of
Toronto Press, 2015), 192; and Allan Rowe, "Soldier Settlement in Alberta,
1917–1931," *The Frontier of Patriotism: Alberta and the First World War,*

ed. Adriana A. Davies and Jeff Keshen (Calgary: University of Calgary Press, 2015): 517–26.

11 Tim Cook, "'My Whole Heart and Soul Is in This War': The Letters and War Service of Sergeant G.L. Ormsby," *Canadian Military History* 15, 1 (winter 2006): 5–63.

12 Michael Piva observes that in 1921 Toronto had "the fifth lowest level of real annual earnings. Rent explains this result. Incomes in Toronto were not low relative to most other centres, but the cost of living was very high." Michael Piva, "Urban Working-Class Incomes and Real Incomes in 1921: A Comparative Analysis," *Social History/Histoire sociale* 16, 31 (May 1983), 164.

13 Report and cover letter from Chaplain Al. L. Burch of the Department of Soldiers' Civil Re-establishment, Spadina Ave., Toronto, 24 November 1921, Federal War Service Commission of the Churches of Canada, MG 17 F 2, LAC.

14 William Beattie, Department of Militia and Defence, to Rev. Dr. W.T. Gunn, Secretary Federal Council of Churches, Toronto, 4 January 1921. Federal War Service Commission of the Churches of Canada, MG 17 F2, LAC.

15 Military Service record of Albert Valentine Jesson, http://central.bac-lac. gc.ca/.item/?op=pdf&app=CEF&id=B4832-S024.

16 Jonathan F. Vance, *A Township at War* (Waterloo, ON: Wilfrid Laurier University Press, 2018), 250.

17 As cited by Veronica Strong-Boag, *The New Day Recalled: Lives of Girls and Women in English Canada, 1919–1939* (Markham, ON.: Penguin Books, 1988), 93.

18 On 11 December 1923, the Great War Veterans' Association of Burdett, Alberta, wrote on behalf of Mrs Petrie to the Minister of Justice, Ottawa. Case of Mrs. Petrie, wife of Alex Petrie, of Burdett, Alberta, re: non-support. RG13-A-2, vol. 283, file 1923-2034, LAC.

19 Military Service record of Alexander Petrie, http://central.bac-lac.gc.ca/. item/?op=pdf&app=CEF&id=B7772-S026.

20 Jay Cassel, *The Secret Plague: Venereal Disease in Canada* (Toronto: University of Toronto Press, 1987), 123, 124.

21 Antje Kampf cites the following infection rates for Dominion troops in 1917: "In Britain in 1917 New Zealanders had a rate of 183 infected servicemen per 1,000, Australians had 184, and Canadians had 104." Kampf, "Controlling Male Sexuality: Combating Venereal Disease in the New Zealand Military during Two World Wars," *Journal of the History of Sexuality* 17, 2 (May 2008), 239fn16. Cassel cites slightly lower figures: 13–14.5 percent for Australian troops and 13 percent for New Zealanders. By contrast, the venereal infection rate in the French Army during the last two years of the war was approximately 8 percent and that of the BEF, 5 percent. For France: Jean-Yves LeNaour, "Sur le front intérieur du péril vénérien (1914–1918)," *Annales de démographie historique* 1 (2002), 109; for Britain, Australia, and New Zealand: Cassel, *The Secret Plague*, 123.

22 On anxieties about a venereal epidemic in Austria, see Nancy M. Wingfield, "The Enemy Within: Regulating Prostitution and Controlling Venereal Disease in Cisleithanian Austria during the Great War," *Central European History* 46 (2013): 568–98. For Australia, see Judith Smart, "Sex, the State and the 'scarlet scourge': Gender, Citizenship and Venereal Diseases Regulation in Australia during the Great War," *Women's History Review* 7, 1 (1998): 5–36.

23 Brent Brenyo, "'Whatsoever a Man Soweth': Sex Education about Venereal Disease, Racial Health, and Social Hygiene during the First World War," *Canadian Military History* 27, 2 (2018): 1–35.

24 Iarocci and Keshen, *A Nation in Conflict*, 184.

25 Michelle K. Rhoades, "Renegotiating French Masculinity: Medicine and Venereal Disease during the Great War," *French Historical Studies* 29, 2 (spring 2006), 310–11.

26 Brenyo, "'Whatsoever a Man Soweth,'" 8.

27 K. Craig Gibson, "Sex and Soldiering in France and Flanders: The British Expeditionary Force along the Western Front, 1914–1919," *International History Review* 23, 3 (2001), 549.

28 Clare Makepeace, "Male Heterosexuality and Prostitution during the Great War: British Soldiers' Encounters with *Maisons Tolérées*," *Cultural and Social History* 9, 1 (2012), 70–1. Evidence of, and anxiety about, venereal infection among married soldiers also figured in the military deliberations of the Habsburg army. Nancy M. Wingfield notes that "in the years before World War I, the Habsburg Ministry of War had been sufficiently concerned about the spread of sexually transmitted infections among its married soldiers that it had Eugène Brieux's play *Les Avariés* [*Damaged Goods*; *Die Schiffbrüchigen* in German], which addressed the issue of syphilis in marriage, performed at all of the monarchy's military schools." Wingfield, "The Enemy Within," 580fn46.

29 Rhoades, "Renegotiating French Masculinity," 304.

30 "Must Help Shell-Shocked," *Toronto Daily Star*, 6 December 1918; Mark Osborne Humphries, "War's Long Shadow: Masculinity, Medicine, and the Gendered Politics of Trauma, 1914–1939," *Canadian Historical Review* 91, 3 (September 2010): 503–31; and Humphries, *A Weary Road: Shell Shock in the Canadian Expeditionary Force, 1914–1918* (Toronto: University of Toronto Press, 2018).

31 Desmond Morton and Glenn Wright, *Winning the Second Battle: Canadian Veterans and the Return to Civilian Life, 1915–1930* (Toronto: University of Toronto Press, 1987), 77.

32 P190/12, Edith Rogers Papers, AM.

33 Humphries, "War's Long Shadow," 521.

34 R. Dekel and Z. Solomon, "Secondary Traumatization among Wives of War Veterans with PTSD," in C.R. Figley and W.P. Nash (eds.), Routledge Psychosocial Stress Series. *Combat Stress Injury: Theory, Research, and*

Management (New York, NY: Routledge/Taylor & Francis Group, 2007):
137–57. D. Michael Glenn, Jean C. Beckham, Michelle E. Feldman, Angela
C. Kirby, Michael A. Hertzberg, Scott D. Moore, "Violence and Hostility
among Families of Vietnam Veterans with Combat-Related Posttraumatic
Stress Disorder," *Violence and Victims* 17, 4 (August 2002): 473–89. Casey
T. Taft, Robin P. Weatherill, Halley E. Woodward, Lavinia A. Pinto, Laura
E. Watkins, Mark W. Miller, and Rachel Dekel, "Intimate Partner and
General Aggression Perpetration among Combat Veterans Presenting to a
Posttraumatic Stress Disorder Clinic," *American Journal of Orthopsychiatry* 79,
4 (2009): 461–8: "PTSD has consistently been shown to represent a robust
correlate of aggression. Higher levels of intimate partner aggression are
consistently found among veterans with PTSD compared to those without the
disorder." https://www.ncbi.nlm.nih.gov/pmc/articles/PMC3561901/; April
A. Gerlock, Jackie Grimesey, George Sayre, "Military–Related Posttraumatic
Stress Disorder and Intimate Relationship Behaviors: A Developing Dyadic
Relationship," *Journal of Marital and Family Therapy* 40, 3 (July 2014): 344–56.
Gerlock et al. note that "Veterans with PTSD have consistently been found to
have a higher incidence of IPV [intimate partner violence] perpetration than
veterans without PTSD" (345).

35 "The King vs. John Buchanan Pirie, October 9, 1924," microfilm reel MS 8438.
RG 22-392-0-987, Criminal Assize Clerk Criminal Indictment Files, Carleton
County (Files 548–1001), 1859–1929, Archives of Ontario. "Pirie Reprieved
from Gallows; Will be Further Inspected," Toronto *Globe*, 21 March 1925.
On the testimony of Dr Harvey Clare on Pirie's mental state, see Elizabeth
M. Elliott, "The Seventh Circle of Hell: The Social Responses to Murder in
Canada," PhD dissertation, Simon Fraser University, 1996.

36 Suzanne Evans, "Marks of Grief: Black Attire, Medals and Service Flags,"
*A Sisterhood of Suffering and Service: Women and Girls of Canada and
Newfoundland during the First World War*, ed. Sarah Glassford and Amy Shaw
(Vancouver: UBC Press, 2012), 219–40.

37 Military Service records of John Kell, Arthur Jones, and Walter Atha:
http://central.bac-lac.gc.ca/.item/?op=pdf&app=CEF&id=B5040-S021;
http://central.bac-lac.gc.ca/.item/?op=pdf&app=CEF&id=B4923-S003;
http://central.bac-lac.gc.ca/.item/?op=pdf&app=CEF&id=B0280-S002.

38 P190/12, Edith Rogers Papers, AM.

39 The *Toronto Daily Star*'s extensive coverage of the Tarrington case includes:
"Wife and Nine Children are without Pension," 22 April 1918; "Widow and
Nine Children in Danger from Want," 27 April 1918; "Soldier's Widow and
Family Who Are Pensionless," 2 May 1918; "Widow and 9 Kiddies Hoping
for a Pension," 2 May 1918; "Pension for Widow Is Almost Assured," 11
May 1918; "Widow Still Waits on Veteran's Pension," 10 June 1918; "Won't
Pay Pension to Mrs. Tarrington," 29 June 1918; "Ask for Reopening of
Tarrington Case," 3 July 1918; "Was Very Sick Man after Coming Home," 4

July 1918; "Says Husband Wrote That He Was Gassed," 5 July 1918; "$300 for Mrs. Tarrington," 31 July 1918; "Raise $200 for Widow," 1 August 1918; "War Widow Forced to Part with Kiddies," *Toronto Daily Star*, 30 December 1918. "The Tarrington Case," Toronto *Globe*, 2 July 1918.

40 "No Pension to Widow," *Toronto Daily Star*, 23 August 1918.

41 "Board to Reopen Tarrington Case," *Toronto Daily Star*, 11 January 1919; "Tarrington Family to Receive Pension," *Toronto Daily Star*, 25 January 1919.

42 "Plea for Pensions Outside the Rules," *Toronto Daily Star*, 29 January 1919.

43 "Wife Follows Husband to the Tomb in Year," *Toronto Daily Star*, 6 September 1919.

44 From the Veterans of France and Comrades, Hamilton, Ont., to Sir Robert Borden, 16 August 1919, RG13-A-2, vol. 240, file 1919-2153. LAC.

45 Letter from Widows, Wives and Mothers of Great Britain's Heroes' Association, Vancouver, BC, 8 March 1920, RG13-A-2, vol. 247, file 1920-715, LAC.

46 Desmond Morton, "Resisting the Pension Evil: Bureaucracy, Democracy, and Canada's Board of Pension Commissioners, 1916–33," *Canadian Historical Review* 18, 2 (1987), 209.

47 6th Census of Canada, 1921. http://central.bac-lac.gc.ca/. item/?app=Census1921&op=img&id=e003082692.

48 Margaret E. McCallum, "Keeping Women in Their Place: The Minimum Wage in Canada, 1910–25," *Labour/Le Travail* (spring 1986): 29–56. The Ontario Minimum Wage Board, "Budget for a Saleswoman in a Retail Store, 1921," appears on page 45.

49 "High Rents Forcing People to Quit Housekeeping and Take Up Quarters in Rooms," Toronto *Globe*, 25 September 1920. The *Toronto Daily Star* reported on 13 January 1921 the case of a war widow who had ordered four tons of coal even though she had funds in her checking account sufficient to pay for only half the order. The coal merchant then took her to court, charging her with fraud.

50 6th Census of Canada, 1921. Census data for Alice Gorringe: http://central. bac-lac.gc.ca/.item/?app=Census1921&op=img&id=e002889698; Military Service record of Thomas Gorringe: http://central.bac-lac.gc.ca/.item/?op= pdf&app=CEF&id=B3661-S023. 1921 Census data for Mabel Huggins: http:// central.bac-lac.gc.ca/.item/?app=Census1921&op=img&id=e002889625; Military Service record of William Huggins: http://central.bac-lac.gc.ca/. item/?op=pdf&app=CEF&id=B4585-S024.

51 6th Census of Canada, 1921. Census data for Elizabeth Beckett: http://central. bac-lac.gc.ca/.item/?app=Census1921&op=img&id=e002893209; for Eleanor Benny: http://central.bac-lac.gc.ca/.item/?app=Census1921&op=img&id= e002882775; for Ellen Ewen: http://central.bac-lac.gc.ca/.item/?app= Census1921&op=img&id=e002892394.

52 6th Census of Canada, 1921. Census data for Alice Adderly: http://central. bac-lac.gc.ca/.item/?app=Census1921&op=img&id=e002891741; for

Charlotte Adams: http://central.bac-lac.gc.ca/.item/?app=Census1921&op
=img&id=e002890876; for Janet Gardiner: http://central.bac-lac.gc.ca/.
item/?app=Census1921&op=img&id=e002889673.

53 Military Service record of William Henry Collum: http://central.bac-lac.
gc.ca/.item/?op=pdf&app=CEF&id=B1887-S045.

54 Military Service record of William Grant Lindsay: http://central.bac-lac.
gc.ca/.item/?op=pdf&app=CEF&id=B5657-S029; Manitoba Vital Statistics
Agency, marriage records: https://vitalstats.gov.mb.ca/Query.php.

55 Mrs Muriel Birkett, widow of Pte. Harold W. Birkett [to Ministry of Militia
and Defence], 16 January 1919, Transportation of Soldiers' Wives and
Families from Overseas to Canada, RG24-C-1-a, vol. 744 -747, file HQ-54-21-6-
85. LAC. 6th Census of Canada, 1921. Census data for Muriel Birkett:
http://central.bac-lac.gc.ca/.item/?app=Census1921&op=img&id=e002876681.

56 Military Service record of Ernest Andrews: http://central.bac-lac.gc.ca/.
item/?op=pdf&app=CEF&id=B0178-S043.

57 Mrs H. Pell, Brantford Ontario to the Department of the Militia, 20 February
1919, Transportation of Soldiers' Wives and Families from Overseas to
Canada, RG24-C-1-a, vol. 744 -747, file HQ-54-21-6-85, LAC.

58 Military Service record of Ernest Blyth: http://central.bac-lac.gc.ca/.
item/?op=pdf&app=CEF&id=B0833-S046.

59 Jonathan F. Vance, *Death So Noble: Memory, Meaning, and the First World War*
(Vancouver: UBC Press, 1997), 150.

60 Erika Kuhlman, *Of Little Comfort: War Widows, Fallen Soldiers, and the
Remaking of Nation after the Great War* (New York: New York University Press,
2012), 141; Janis Lomas, "'So I Married Again': Letters from British Widows
of the First and Second World Wars," *History Workshop* 38 (1994): 218–27;
Stéphanie Petit, "Les Veuves de la Grande guerre ou le mythe de la veuve
éternelle," *Guerres mondiales et conflits contemporains* 197 (March 2000): 65–72.

61 "Girls Take a Green Glance: Secret in Widows' Veils. Sam Weller's Advice,
'Beware of Vidders' Not Heeded in Canada – 3,251 out of 13,000 War Widows
Remarry – Is Pension the Reason?" *Toronto Daily Star*, 21 October 1922.

62 "What Press Agents Say about Coming Events," *Toronto Daily Star*, 5 February
1920. This Hollywood film, starring Marguerite Clark, was an adaptation
of a Broadway play that predated the war; presumably the plot device of a
husband apparently killed in the war (until he returned home, fit as a fiddle)
was added to the script when the film was produced after the war.

63 The article, "Girls Take a Green Glance: Secret in Widows' Veils," asserted:
"most of the war widows … rue the second venture." *Toronto Daily Star*,
21 October 1922; "War Widow Married: Husband a Bigamist," *Toronto Daily
Star*, 7 September 1922; "Two Erring Husbands Given Castigation," *Toronto
Daily Star*, 17 October 1922.

64 The military service records of their first husbands reveal that a substantial majority (40 of 70) of these war wives stayed in Manitoba during the war, remarried and, as best can be determined, continued to live there after the war. An additional twelve women remained in Manitoba during the war and then moved away, settling either in another province or in the United States: British Columbia and southern California were favoured sites of resettlement. Of the seventeen women who had moved to Britain during the war and then remarried, three remained in Britain, twelve returned to Canada, and two settled in the United States. One woman had moved to Ontario during the war and then returned to Manitoba in 1918, where she remarried.

65 Military Service record of Thomas Little: http://central.bac-lac.gc.ca/. item/?op=pdf&app=CEF&id=B5679-S020 and Manitoba Vital Statistics Agency online database: https://vitalstats.gov.mb.ca/Query.php.

66 Manitoba Vital Statistics Agency database (in which the marriage record for Lillian Atha is listed as Lillian Atka: https://vitalstats.gov.mb.ca/Query.php; LAC, 6th Census of Canada 1921: http://central.bac-lac.gc.ca/. item/?app=Census1921&op=img&id=e002892603.

67 Canadian Passenger Lists, Ancestry.com. https://www.ancestry.com/interactive/1263/IMCANQC1865_T14700-00048?pid=6560451&backurl=https://search.ancestry.com/cgi-bin/sse.dll?dbid%3D1263%26h%3D6560451%26indiv%3Dtry%260_vc%3DRecord:OtherRecord%26rhSource%3D1263&treeid=&personid=&hintid=&usePUB=true&usePUBJs=true&_ga=2.30216767.1438268665.1575071992-838869748.1575071992.

68 Suzanne Evans analyzes the etiquette of mourning in early twentieth-century Canada in "Marks of Grief: Black Attire, Medals, and Service Flags," 221–6. Millie Cockriell (née Hill) married Joseph Cockriell in Winnipeg, December 1902; he died in April 1917. In June 1917 she married Ralph Smith in Winnipeg. Athalie Clemis's first husband died of wounds on 25 August 1917; she married Benjamin Hobbs on 15 September 1917. All data taken from the online database of the Manitoba Vital Statistics Agency: https://vitalstats.gov.mb.ca/Query.php.

69 Military Service record of George Wilkin Kaslake: http://central.bac-lac.gc.ca/.item/?op=pdf&app=CEF&id=B5004-S071; 6th Census of Canada, 1921. Census data for Violet Andrews: http://central.bac-lac.gc.ca/.item/?app=Census1921&op=img&id=e002889490. Although the military service records list George Kaslake, the Manitoba Vital statistics records, the Ontario birth records for their daughter, and the 1921 census spell the name Caslake.

70 Isabelle Dawn applied for US citizenship in 1941. Her naturalization application indicated that her previous names were Isabelle Bunch and, before that, Isabelle Shiells, born in Dundee in 1890. She had

three children, Mildred born in 1913 in Kenora, Doris born in 1920 (in Los Angeles), and Phyllis born in 1921 in Los Angeles. "United States of America Petition for Naturalization," number 84806. https://www.ancestry.com/interactive/3998/40735_1220701439_0031-01786?pid=2001424&backurl=https://search.ancestry.com/cgi-bin/sse.dll?indiv%3D1%26dbid%3D3998%26h%3D2001424%26tid%3D%26pid%3D%26usePUB%3Dtrue%26_phsrc%3DjGn10%26_phstart%3Dsuccess Source&treeid=&personid=&hintid=&usePUB=true&_phsrc=jGn10&_phstart=successSource&usePUBJs=true&_ga=2.30693695.1438268665.1575071992-838869748.1575071992.

71　Isabel Mary Monro's "Declaration of Intention" to apply for U.S. citizenship; application number 103641, dated 11 January 1941. Ancestry.com: https://www.ancestry.com/interactive/3998/40735_1220706418_0052-00482?pid=1890082&backurl=https://search.ancestry.com/cgi-bin/sse.dll?dbid%3D3998%26h%3D1890082%26indiv%3Dtry%260_vc%3DRecord:OtherRecord%26rhSource%3D2442&treeid=&personid=&hintid=&usePUB=true&usePUBJs=true&_ga=2.2448048.1438268665.1575071992-838869748.1575071992.

72　Military Service record of George Greenwood: http://central.bac-lac.gc.ca/.item/?op=pdf&app=CEF&id=B3800-S020; Sixth Census of Canada 1921. Census data for Kate Greenwood: http://central.bac-lac.gc.ca/.item/?app=Census1921&op=img&id=e002874025; Military Service record of John Diplock: http://central.bac-lac.gc.ca/.item/?op=pdf&app=CEF&id=B2531-S032; Sixth Census of Canada 1921. Census data for Fanny Gent (Diplock): http://central.bac-lac.gc.ca/.item/?app=Census1921&op=img&id=e002872225.

73　George A. Bonanno, "Loss, Trauma, and Human Resilience: Have We Underestimated the Human Capacity to Thrive after Extremely Aversive Events?" *American Psychology* 59, 1 (January 2004): 20–8.

74　Commonwealth War Graves Commission website: Arthur Beasant: https://www.cwgc.org/find-war-dead/casualty/522219/beasant,-arthur-william/; Andrew Dorman: https://www.cwgc.org/find-war-dead/casualty/59580/dorman,-andrew-arthur/; Fred East: https://www.cwgc.org/find-war-dead/casualty/234741/east,-fred/.

75　Veronica Strong-Boag, *The New Day Recalled: Lives of Girls and Women in English Canada, 1919-1939* (Markham, ON: Penguin Books, 1988), 2.

76　6th Census of Canada, 1921. Census data for Harriet Brown: http://central.bac-lac.gc.ca/.item/?app=Census1921&op=img&id=e002891365. The biography of Ralph Brown and his marriage to Harriet in 1913 is given at: https://www.ypres-salient.com/canada-br.html.

77　The 1921 census reveals the following instances of war widows renting rooms to lodgers: Lily Cliffe and her two daughters lived in a house in central

Winnipeg, and rented rooms to four adult male lodgers; Janette Gardiner and her four children lived at 510 Langside Avenue in Winnipeg and rented a room to a male lodger; and Jane Geere lived at 737 Simcoe Street with four of her children and a lodger. In one instance at least, these arrangements led to remarriage; in 1921 Ethel May Foster lived in a house with her mother, her daughter, and three male lodgers, one of whom was listed as Edward Rainey. Manitoba marriage records show that in May 1926 Ethel Foster married Edward John Rainey in Winnipeg. War widows who took positions as housekeepers in rural Manitoba included Mabel Guest, Jessie Holmes, and Kate Figgures. Mabel Guest had lived with her mother in Winnipeg during the war, but in 1921 she and her two daughters lived in the municipality of Victoria, Manitoba, where she was employed as a housekeeper. Jessie Holmes, mother of a four-year-old son, was the housekeeper for a farmer, Phillip Batten, in Woodlands; and Kate Figgures and her three children were living in the municipality of Langford, near Neepawa, where she was a domestic servant/housekeeper for Frederick Hall (widowed) and his two sons.

78 Bettina Bradbury, *Wife to Widow: Lives, Laws, and Politics in Nineteenth-Century Montreal* (Vancouver: UBC Press, 2011), ch. 11: "Patchworks of the Possible: Widows' Wealth, Work, and Children."

CHAPTER SIX

1 "Call First Jury on Divorce Case: Officer is Plaintiff and Baptist Minister Co-Respondent," Toronto *Globe*, 3 July 1919; "Reverend W.N. Stackhouse Makes No Defense," Toronto *Globe*, 10 July 1919. Newspaper reports identify the plaintiff as Ralph S. Holmes; his military service record identifies him as Ray Sherman Holmes. He had enlisted in March 1916. They had three children at the time of his enlistment.

2 Sarah Carter, *The Importance of Being Monogamous: Marriage and Nation Building in Western Canada to 1915* (Edmonton: University of Alberta Press, 2008), 4.

3 Mary Ellen Palmer, 66 McGill Street, Toronto, Ontario to the Minister of Justice, Ottawa, Canada, 23 July 1921, RG13-A-2, vol. 260, file 1921-1559, LAC.

4 In Belgium, a nation comparable in population size to Canada and predominantly Catholic, "the number of divorces increased from 1,207 in 1913 to 2,195 in 1920, and 3,665 in 1921." Chantal Kesteloot, "Post-war Societies (Belgium)," in: *1914–1918-online. International Encyclopedia of the First World War*, ed. by Ute Daniel, Peter Gatrell, Oliver Janz, Heather Jones, Jennifer Keene, Alan Kramer, and Bill Nasson (Berlin: Freie Universität Berlin, 2017), DOI: 10.15463/ie1418.11208. Richard Bessel points out that 15,633 German couples filed for divorce in 1913; 39,216 did so in 1921. The divorce rate in 1913 Germany was 26.6 divorces per 100,000 inhabitants;

by 1920 it was 59.1 per 100,000 and would remain well over 50 per 100,000 inhabitants through the mid-1920s. Bessel, *Germany after the First World War* (Oxford: Oxford University Press, 1993), 231.

5 For data on divorce in postwar France, see "Divorces et séparations de corps: Année 1919," *Annuaire statistique*, vol. 37 (Paris: Imprimerie nationale, 1922), 107. See also Colin Dyer, *Population and Society in Twentieth Century France* (New York: Holmes & Meier Publishers, 1978), 53; Jules Maurin, "Effets de la Mobilisation française sur la population (1914-1918)," *Revue internationale d'histoire militaire* 63, 11 (1985), 86. For a discussion of the cultural anxiety this generated, see Mary Louise Roberts, *Civilization without Sexes: Reconstructing Gender in Postwar France* (Chicago: University of Chicago Press, 1994), 138; Martha Hanna, *Your Death Would Be Mine: Paul and Marie Pireaud in the Great War* (Cambridge: Harvard University Press, 1996), 290–1; and Clémentine Vidal-Naquet, *Couples dans la Grande Guerre: Le tragique et l'ordinaire du lien conjugal* (Paris: Belles Lettres, 2014): ch. 2.

6 Griselda Rowntree and Norman H. Carrier, "The Resort to Divorce in England and Wales, 1858–1957," *Population Studies* 11, 3 (March 1958), 201.

7 "Faithless Wives: The Soldiers' Homecoming," *The Times*, 6 January 1919.

8 James G. Snell, *In the Shadow of the Law: Divorce in Canada, 1900–1940* (Toronto and Buffalo: University of Toronto Press, 1991), 49–50.

9 Snell provides statistics on divorce from 1900 to 1920 in "Table 1: Divorces by Process and Province, 1900–1940." Snell, *In the Shadow of the Law*, 10–11.

10 "Several Hundred Will Seek Divorce: If Manitoba Courts Have Power to Grant It, by Privy Council Ruling," Toronto *Globe*, 20 March 1919; "Over 1,100 Divorces Sought in Manitoba: The Majority of Applicants are Returned Soldiers," Toronto *Globe*, 22 August 1919.

11 "'The Blindness of Divorce,'" Toronto *Globe*, 20 August 1918.

12 "Spirit of the Press: Divorce," Toronto *Globe*, citing the *Edmonton Journal*, 2 September 1919.

13 "Uniform Law for Divorce: Discussed with Animation at Meeting of Canadian Bar Association," Toronto *Globe*, 5 September 1918.

14 "Program for the Soldiers: Hon. Mr. Rowell Reviews the Achievements of the Union Government," Toronto *Globe*, 20 January 1919.

15 Great War Veterans' Association – Ottawa – That fees for divorces be remitted for soldiers. The Great War Veterans' Association, Ottawa, to the Minister of Justice, Ottawa, 23 October 1917, RG13-A-2, vol. 216, file 1917-1780, LAC.

16 Pte. R.F. Stratfull, #152688, Brandon Man. to the Minister of Justice, Ottawa, 1 Nov. 1917: Desiring a divorce, RG13-A-2, vol. 216, file 1917-1917, LAC.

17 J.H.S. Coyne (114016, Fort Garry Horse), Saskatoon to the Minister of Justice, Ottawa, 11 June 1917: Steps to be taken to procure a divorce, RG13-A-2, vol. 213, file 1917-1009, LAC.

18 R. Meysonnier, Radville, Sask. to the Minister of Justice, Ottawa, 25 June
    1917: Advocating legislation granting divorce to returned soldiers whose
    wives have been unfaithful, RG13-A-2, vol. 213, file 1917-1115, LAC.

19 "The King versus Grace Laverne Henderson," MS 8567 RG 22-392-0-9138,
    Archives of Ontario. "Grace Henderson Freed on Suspended Sentence,"
    Toronto *Globe*, 13 November 1919.

20 Cpl. John Weaver (142022), London Ont., to the Minister of Justice,
    Ottawa, 12 February 1918: How to obtain a divorce, RG13-A-2, vol. 220,
    file 1918-315, LAC.

21 Albert Adams, Woodstock, Ontario to the Minister of Justice, Ottawa,
    26 February 1918: For advice on divorce, RG13-A-2, vol. 220, file 1918-
    466, LAC. Albert Adams married nineteen-year-old Elsie Fennell (born in
    Birmingham) on 31 August 1916; he was twenty-four years old. In October
    1928 she remarried and identified herself on the marriage certificate as
    a divorcee.

22 A lawyer with three cases before the Senate in 1919 observed that the average
    price was $600 and could rise to as much as $895. "Calls Ottawa Canada's
    Reno," Toronto *Globe*, 24 May 1919.

23 "Facilitate Divorce for Wronged Soldiers," Toronto *Globe*, 5 February 1918.

24 Response to A.S. Wright, Saskatoon, from the Ministry of Justice, 21 March
    1918, RG13-A-2, vol. 220, file 1918-475, LAC.

25 "Hot Criticism for the YMCA: Provincial Great War Veterans Declare Their
    Lack of Confidence," Toronto *Globe*, 27 May 1918.

26 "Veterans Want Help in Getting Divorces," Toronto *Globe*, 3 October 1918.

27 "Hamilton News," Toronto *Globe*, 28 February 1918.

28 Albert Adams, Woodstock, Ontario, to the Minister of Justice, Ottawa,
    26 February 1918: For advice on divorce, RG13-A-2, vol. 220, file
    1918-466, LAC.

29 "Veterans May Be Neutral," Toronto *Globe*, 15 May 1919.

30 Snell, *In the Shadow of the Law*, 10. "Divorces by process and province,
    1900–1940."

31 Anonymous – London – Moral conditions in Canadian Army. Letter from "A
    London West Mother," 5 August 1919, RG13-A-2, vol. 240, file 1919-2113, LAC.

32 Robert Pike, "Legal Access and the Incidence of Divorce in Canada: A
    Socio-historical Analysis," *Canadian Review of Sociology and Anthropology*,
    12, 2 (1975), 121. Snell, *In the Shadow of the Law*, ch. 9: "Divorce Outside
    the System."

33 Snell, *In the Shadow of the Law*, ch. 9: "Divorce Outside the System."

34 Fr. J. Ledger, 128 Battalion, Moose Jaw, Sask., to Attorney General, 25 May
    1916, RG13-A-2, vol. 203, file 1916-897, LAC.

35 P189/19, Edith Rogers Papers, AM.

36 Susan Pedersen shows that between 1916 and 1920, when approximately 1.5 million British women were in receipt of separation allowances, caseworkers launched 40,000 investigations of infidelity, resulting in 13,000 wives being deprived of their separation allowances. Pedersen, "Gender, Welfare, and Citizenship in Britain during the Great War," *American Historical Review* 5, 4 (October 1990), 999. She subsequently revised these numbers slightly to suggest investigations into 50,000 cases of misconduct, resulting in the cancellation of separation allowances to 16,000 British war wives. Pedersen, *Family, Dependence, and the Origins of the Welfare State: Britain and France, 1914–1945* (Cambridge: Cambridge University Press, 1993), 112.

37 "Statistics of Divorces Granted in Canada, 1868–1921," *Canada Yearbook* (1921): 825.

38 A.S. Wright, Canadian Patriotic Fund, Saskatoon, to the Minister of Justice, 27 February 1918: Inquiry re: divorce regulations, RG13-A-2, vol. 220, file 1918-475, LAC.

39 Pike, "Legal Access and the Incidence of Divorce in Canada," 117–18.

40 "Spirit of the Press: Divorce," Toronto *Globe*, 2 September 1919; "First Lethbridge Divorce," Toronto *Globe*, 24 November 1919.

41 A list of all Divorce Bills considered by the Senate in 1920 appears in the index of *The Journals of the Senate of Canada*, 4th Session, 13th Parliament, vol. LVII (1920), 14–25. *The Journals of the Senate* are now digitized at the Canadian Parliamentary Historical Resources website: http://parl.canadiana.ca/.

42 "Wanted to Bring Lady with Him to Canada," Toronto *Globe*, 3 July 1918.

43 Military Service record of William Harvey: http://central.bac-lac.gc.ca/.item/?op=pdf&app=CEF&id=B4139-S040.

44 "An Army Officer's Divorce Suit: Saunders vs. Saunders and Inglis," *The Times*, 28 April 1920; "An Army Officer's Divorce Suit: Saunders vs. Saunders and Inglis," *The Times*, 29 April 1920.

45 "'The Lovelight in my eyes tonight': Decree and £400 Damages for Tank Corps Sergeant," *Daily Mirror*, 22 January 1920.

46 "Bigamy among Soldiers," *The Times*, 19 January 1918.

47 "War Marriages," *The Times*, 9 January 1918; "War Marriages," *The Times*, 30 January 1918.

48 "Soldiers' Bigamous Marriages," *The Times*, 18 April 1918.

49 Miss Ella R. Caddey, London, England, to the Minister of Justice, Ottawa, 13 January 1918: Inquiry re divorce between H.A. Lee and wife; response dated 6 February 1918, RG13-A-2, vol. 219, file 1918-182, LAC.

50 "Officer Charged with Bigamy," *The Times*, 2 August 1916.

51 "War Marriages," *The Times*, 9 January 1918.

52 "War Marriages and Bigamy," *The Times*, 10 January 1919.

53 "Major Stewart Gets Four Years for Bigamy," Toronto *Globe*, 29 March 1918;
    "Guilty of Bigamy, Goes to the Penitentiary," Toronto *Globe*, 27 July 1918;
    "Caught in Dragnet of Toronto Police," Toronto *Globe*, 20 November 1922.

54 "Divorce Too Costly," Toronto *Globe*, 17 January 1920.

55 In 1921, there were 56 convictions for bigamy (out of 72 cases tried) but only
    10 charges and 8 successful convictions for wife desertion; in 1922, there were
    92 charges and 74 convictions for bigamy vs. 14 charges and 11 convictions for
    wife desertion. Canada Dominion Bureau of Statistics, Judicial Branch, *Forty-
    Seventh Annual Report of Criminal Statistics for the Year Ended September 30, 1922*
    (Ottawa: F.A. Acland, 1924), vii.

56 James Snell, "The White Life for Two: The Defence of Marriage and
    Sexual Morality in Canada, 1890–1914," *Social History/Histoire sociale* 16, 31
    (1983), 122,

57 As cited by Annalee E. Lepp, "Dis/Membering the Family: Marital
    Breakdown, Domestic Conflict, and Family Violence in Ontario, 1830–1920"
    (PhD diss., Queen's University, January 2001), 369.

58 "Runaway Husbands Create Big Problems for Social Forces," Toronto *Globe*,
    31 March 1923.

59 "War Romance Is Shattered: Canadian Soldier Says Wife Flees with
    American Veteran," Toronto *Globe*, 10 August 1922.

60 On the challenges working class women, designated as "heads of household,"
    confronted in the 1920s, see Suzanne Morton, "Women on their Own: Single
    Mothers in Working-Class Halifax in the 1920s," *Acadiensis* 21, 2 (spring
    1992): 99–107.

61 As cited in "Canada's Provision for Returned Soldiers: Bulletin of The
    Council for Social Service of the Church of England in Canada" 33, February
    1920. Federal War Service Commission of the Churches of Canada, MG17-F2,
    LAC.

62 Margaret Jane Hillyard Little, *'No Car, No Radio, No Liquor Permit': The
    Moral Regulation of Single Mothers in Ontario, 1920–1997* (Toronto: Oxford
    University Press, 1998), 57. Little notes that deserted wives constituted only
    3 percent of all Mothers' Allowance recipients in 1922–23, and 5 percent in
    1925–26.

63 Province of Nova Scotia, *Report of Commission on Mothers' Allowances*
    (Halifax: King's Printer, 1921), 5.

64 "Runaway Husbands Create Big Problems for Social Forces," Toronto *Globe*,
    31 March 1923.

65 "Weal of War Widow and her Little Ones Concerns Veterans," Toronto *Globe*,
    5 September 1923.

66 "Sick Woman Deserted in Shack in Woods," Toronto *Globe*, 12 March 1923;
    "No Order Is Made about Mrs Lambert," Toronto *Globe*, 2 April 1923;

"Mrs Lambert and Family Leave Canada Next Month," Toronto *Globe*, 18 April 1923.

67 Lepp, "Dis/Membering the Family," 375, 380. A survey of deserted wives living in rural Manitoba and not supported by the Soldiers' Deserted Wives Fund suggests that the reluctance or inability of extended families to support deserted wives and their children continued through the 1920s. Conducted in early 1930 (and thus before the effects of the Depression intensified the economic hardships of extended families), the survey revealed that of 62 deserted wives included in the survey, only 3 were fully supported by their family and another 22 received some family support. More were reliant on municipal relief than on family assistance. Welfare Supervision Board, Manitoba, *Report on the Problem of Family Desertion in Manitoba*, report no. 7 of the Department of Health and Public Welfare (Winnipeg, Manitoba, April 1931), 15.

68 Mary Ellen Palmer, 66 McGill Street, Toronto, Ontario to the Minister of Justice, Ottawa, Canada, 23 July 1921: How to get marriage annulled, RG13-A-2, vol. 260, file 1921-1559, LAC.

69 Ceta Ramkhalawansingh, "Women During the Great War," *Women at Work: Ontario, 1850–1930* (Toronto: Canadian Women's Educational Press, 1974), 290–1. In 1918, the city of Toronto provided small grants, totalling $2,700, to five daycare centres in the city: the Creche, East End Day Nursery, West End Creche, Danforth Day Nursery, Queen Street East Day Nursery. Ontario Government Department of Labour, *Mothers' Allowances: An Investigation* (Toronto: 1920), 124. In 1927, when the East End Day Nursery in Toronto surveyed its clients, 125 were married, 4 were widowed, 6 were single, 17 were separated, and 12 were deserted.

70 Mrs Hilda McQueen, Churchbridge, Saskatchewan, to Minister of Justice, 6 March 1922, RG13-A-2, vol. 266, file 1922-495, LAC.

71 "Charge of Desertion and also of Bigamy," Toronto *Globe*, 2 August 1919.

72 "South Norwich Farmer Sentenced for Bigamy," Toronto *Globe*, 15 July 1921.

73 P190/9, Edith Rogers Papers, AM.

74 P190/17, Edith Rogers Papers, AM.

75 P189/17, Edith Rogers Papers, AM.

76 Case of Mrs Petrie, wife of Alex Petrie, of Burdett, Alberta, re: non-support. On 11 December 1923, the Great War Veterans' Association of Burdett, Alberta wrote on behalf of Mrs Petrie to the Minister of Justice, Ottawa, RG13-A-2, vol. 283, file 1923-2034, LAC.

77 P190/9, Edith Rogers Papers, AM.

78 P190/8, Edith Rogers Papers, AM.

79 P190/18, Edith Rogers Papers, AM.

80 Linda Kealey, *Enlisting Women for the Cause: Women, Labour, and the Left in Canada, 1890–1920* (Toronto and Buffalo: University of Toronto Press, 1998), 172–3.

81 P189/12, P189/19, P189/11, Edith Rogers Papers, AM.

82 P189/12, P189/9, Edith Rogers Papers, AM.

83 P190/15, Edith Rogers Papers, AM.

84 P190/6, Edith Rogers Papers, AM.

85 P189/17, Edith Rogers Papers, AM.

86 P190/9, Edith Rogers Papers, AM.

87 P190/6, Edith Rogers Papers, AM.

88 P190/18, P190/6, P190/7, Edith Rogers Papers, AM.

89 P190/17, Edith Rogers Papers, AM.

90 P190/19, Edith Rogers Papers, AM.

91 P189/6, Edith Rogers Papers, AM.

92 P189/9, Edith Rogers Papers, AM.

93 P189/19, Edith Rogers Papers, AM.

94 P189/19, Edith Rogers Papers, AM.

95 As cited in Welfare Supervision Board, Manitoba, *Report on the Problem of Family Desertion in Manitoba*, report no. 7 of the Department of Health and Public Welfare (Winnipeg, Manitoba, April 1931), 21.

96 Morton, "Women on Their Own," 95, 99, 102. A review of children admitted to institutional care in Winnipeg between 1926 and 1929 reveals that 278 children were placed in institutional care: 148 due to the desertion of their father, 82 due to the desertion of their mother, and 48 due to abandonment by both parents. Welfare Supervision Board, Manitoba, *Report on the Problem of Family Desertion in Manitoba*, report no. 7 of the Department of Health and Public Welfare (Winnipeg, Manitoba, April 1931), 23.

97 Mrs Hilda McQueen, Churchbridge, Saskatchewan, to Minister of Justice, 6 March 1922, RG13-A-2, vol. 266, file 1922-495, LAC.

98 Mrs Grace Pelton, 55 Richmond Street, Saint John, New Brunswick, to the Minister of Justice, Ottawa, 31 May 1922: Claim for support by her husband, RG13-A-2, vol. 269, file 1922-1120, LAC.

CONCLUSION

1 Betty Mayse to Will Mayse, 27 April 1917 and 29 April 1917. *Canadian Letters and Images Project*, https://www.canadianletters.ca/content/document-10196?position=74&list=Uto30d6NBSTJzRiO1cKKEJKOtmgd1eHmAa4f30_M66w; https://www.canadianletters.ca/content/document-9676?position=76&list=Uto30d6NBSTJzRiO1cKKEJKOtmgd1eHmAa4f30_M66w.

2 As quoted in Christa Hämmerle, "'You Let a Weeping Woman Call You Home?': Private Correspondences during the First World War in Austria and Germany," in *Epistolary Selves: Letter and Letter-writers, 1600–1945*, ed. Rebecca Earle (Aldershot: Ashgate Publishing Company, 1999), 160.

3 Martha Hanna, *Your Death Would Be Mine: Paul and Marie Pireaud in the Great War* (Cambridge, MA: Harvard University Press, 2006); Frederick Alleyne

Corfield to Mary Corfield, 22 November 1916, Letters of Frederick
Alleyne Corfield to his wife, Liddle Collection, Special Collections Library,
University of Leeds.

4 *Armandine: Lettres d'amour. De Binic au front (1914–1918)*, ed. Jean-Pol
Dumont le Douarec (Spézet, Finistère: Keltia Graphic, 2008).

5 Alexander Watson, *Ring of Steel: Germany and Austria-Hungary in World War I*
(New York: Basic Books, 2014), ch. 8: "Deprivation."

6 Belinda Davis, *Home Fires Burning: Food, Politics, and Everyday Life in World
War I Berlin* (Chapel Hill: University of North Carolina Press, 2000); Maureen
Healy, *Vienna and the Fall of the Habsburg Empire: Total War and Everyday
Life in World War I* (Cambridge and New York: Cambridge University Press,
2004); Yiğit Akin, *When the War Came Home: The Ottomans' Great War and the
Devastation of an Empire* (Stanford, CA: Stanford University Press, 2018).

7 V. de Vesselitsky, *Expenditure and Waste: A Study in Wartime* (London: G. Bell
and Sons, 1917), 14, 16, 21, 58–60.

8 Susan Pedersen, *Family, Dependence, and the Origins of the Welfare State:
Britain and France, 1914–1945* (New York and Cambridge: Cambridge
University Press, 1993), 115–16; Clémentine Vidal-Naquet, *Couples dans la
Grande guerre* (Paris: Belles Lettres, 2014), 193.

9 On the effects of the war on the civilian population of northern France,
see Annette Becker, *Oubliés de la Grande Guerre. Humanitaire et culture de
guerre 1914-1918. Populations occupées, déportés civils, prisonniers de guerre*
(Paris: Éditions Noêsis, 1998); on Belgium, Sophie de Schaepdrijver, *Bastion:
Occupied Bruges in the First World War* (Bruges: Hannibal Publishing, 2014);
on the Eastern Front, Joshua A. Sanborn, *Imperial Apocalypse: The Great War
and the Destruction of the Russian Empire* (Oxford and New York: Oxford
University Press, 2014), chapter 2: "The Front Migrates"; and on civilian
populations in the Ottoman Empire, Akin, *When the War Came Home.*

10 Mémoire rédigé par Alexandre Lefebvre concernant les lettres écrites par son
père. T682. Service Historique de la Défense (France).

11 Becker, *Oubliés de la Grande Guerre*, 339–41.

12 Maureen Healy, "Becoming Austrian: Women, the State, and Citizenship in
World War I," *Central European History* 35, 1 (2002), 10. Tara Zahra, "'Each
nation only cares for its own': Empire, Nation, and Child Welfare Activism
in the Bohemian Lands, 1900–1918," *American Historical Review* 111, 5
(2006), 1391.

13 Akin, *When the War Came Home*, 169. The quotation is from Henry H. Riggs,
Days of Tragedy in Armenia: Personal Experiences in Harpoot, 1915–1917 (Ann
Arbor, MI: Gomidas Institute, 1997), 98–9.

14 Stéphanie Petit, "Le Deuil des veuves de la Grande Guerre: un deuil
spécifique?" *Guerres mondiales et conflits contemporains* 198, Dossier: Les
femmes et la guerre (Juin 2000), 54.

15 Marc-Antoine Crocq, MD, "The History of Generalized Anxiety Disorder as a Diagnostic Category," *Dialogues in Clinical Neuroscience* 19, 2 (June 2017): 107–16. https://www.ncbi.nlm.nih.gov/pmc/articles/PMC5573555/. In "Les Veuves de la Grande Guerre ou le mythe de la veuve éternelle," *Guerres mondiales et conflits contemporains*, No. 197, Dossier: Images civiles de la France en guerre (March 2000): 65–72, Petit cites Gabriel Perreux who referred to the influential impact of Dr Francis Heckel's work on a "new disease": "anxiety neurosis." Perreux, *La Vie quotidienne des civils pendant la Grande Guerre* (Monaco: Hachette, 1966), 122–3. Both Perreux and Petit incorrectly refer to Heckel as Herckel. The full citation to Heckel's work is *La Névrose d'Angoisse et les États d'Émotivité Anxieuse: Clinique, Pathogénie, Traitement* (Paris: Masson et cie., 1917).

16 Laurie Rogers to May Rogers, 2 April 1916, Letters of Lt. Lawrence Browning Rogers, Textual Records 58A 1 207.1-5, CWM-MHRC.

17 George Ormsby to Maggie Ormsby, 24 August 1916, 14 November 1916, Letters of George Ormsby, 58 A 1 153, CWM-MHRC. George Ormsby was wounded on 26 September 1916 and admitted to hospital in England three days later. Maggie wrote of her fainting fits in a letter dated 16 October 1916.

18 Norma Hillyer Shephard (ed.), *Dear Harry: The Firsthand Account of a World War I infantryman* (Brigham Press, 2003), 206, 213–14. Jennie Hillyer to Harry Hillyer, 19 February 1917, 23 February 191[7].

19 Hillyer Shephard, *Dear Harry*, 213–14. Jennie Hillyer to Harry Hillyer, 23 February 1916 [*sic*].

20 Laurie Rogers to May Rogers, 2 April 1916, Letters of Lt. Lawrence Browning Rogers, Textual Records 58A 1 207.1-5, CWM-MHRC.

21 Laurie Rogers to May Rogers, 18 October 1916, 22 November 1916, Letters of Lt. Lawrence Browning Rogers, Textual Records 58A 1 207.1-5, CWM-MHRC.

22 Laurie Rogers to May Rogers, 16 February 1917, Letters of Lt. Lawrence Browning Rogers, Textual Records 58A 1 207.1-5, CWM-MHRC.

23 Robert M. Sapolsky, *Why Zebras Don't Get Ulcers*, 3rd ed. (New York: St Martin's Griffin, 2004): ch. 18: "Managing Stress."

24 Betty Mayse to Will Mayse, 19 June 1917, *Canadian Letters and Images Project*, https://www.canadianletters.ca/content/document-9833. Laurie Rogers to May Rogers, 20 November 1915, Letters of Lt. Lawrence Browning Rogers, Textual Records 58A 1 207.1-5, CWM-MHRC. Frank Maheux to Angeline Maheux, 26 June 1915, 7 May 1916, Francis-Xavier Maheux fonds, MG30-E297, R5156-0-4-E, LAC. Hillyer Shephard (ed.), *Dear Harry*, 216, Jennie Hillyer to Harry Hillyer, 26 February 1917. George Eastman to Henrietta Eastman, 24 November 1915, Letters from Corporal George Lewis Eastman to his wife and daughter, Textual Records 58A 1 226.14, CWM-MHRC.

25 Alison Norman, "'In Defense of the Empire': The Six Nations of the Grand River and the Great War," *A Sisterhood of Suffering and Service: Women and Girls*

of Canada and Newfoundland during the First World War, ed. Sarah Glassford
and Amy Shaw (Vancouver: UBC Press, 2012), 37–9. See also Margot I. Duley,
"The Unquiet Knitters of Newfoundland: From Mothers of the Regiment to
Mothers of the Nation," *A Sisterhood of Suffering and Service*, 51–74.

26 Some soldiers wondered what happened to all the socks produced by
    women organized under the auspices of the Red Cross or the IODE. Sydney
    Winterbottom, recently arrived in England in the fall of 1916, wrote his
    mother in Kamloops, BC: "By the way Mum I am very much in need of all
    the good strong socks you could make if you feel like knitting in your spare
    moments. If I was you I wouldn't knit one more darned pair at the Red Cross
    or what ever it is. I haven't yet met a single fellow who told me they issue
    them in France. You must remember old girl that the socks the women knit
    for the 'brave soldier lads' are very often sold by some vile scoundrel who is
    getting rich by your willing labour. Don't think I am writing rot because Im
    darned sure that it isn't." Sydney Winterbottom to his mother, 18 September
    1916, *Canadian Letters and Images Project*, https://www.canadianletters.ca/
    content/document-11730.

27 May Rogers to Laurie Rogers, 17 October 1917, Letters of Lt. Lawrence
    Browning Rogers, Textual Records 58A 1 207.1-5, CWM-MHRC.

28 Ellen E. Herald to Alice Leighton, 16 April 1917, *Canadian Letters and Images
    Project*, https://www.canadianletters.ca/content/document-1746?position=45
    &list=ChtCHaXMjJCUnZZyC2XdMWbDi7YvavT8Xkaacj7YX2s.

29 Katie Pickles, *Female Imperialism and National Identity: The Imperial Order
    Daughters of the Empire* (Manchester; New York: Manchester University Press,
    2002), 45.

30 Jane E. Brody, "The Health Benefits of Knitting," *New York Times*, 25 January
    2016. Brody cites "Dr. Herbert Benson, a pioneer in mind/body medicine
    and author of 'The Relaxation Response,' [who] says that the repetitive action
    of needlework can induce a relaxed state like that associated with meditation
    and yoga. Once you get beyond the initial learning curve, knitting and
    crocheting can lower heart rate and blood pressure and reduce harmful
    blood levels of the stress hormone cortisol."

31 P190/2, Edith Rogers Papers, AM.

32 P189/17, P190/5, Edith Rogers Papers, AM.

33 Jonathan F. Vance, *A Township at War* (Waterloo, ON: Wilfrid Laurier
    University Press, 2018), 236–7.

34 On the significance of "anticipatory grief" and its absence in the bereavement
    of war widows, see Tami J. Frye, "Military Spouses: A Study of the Shared
    Experiences of Those Who Lost a Mate due to a War Casualty," A Dissertation
    Presented in Partial Fulfillment of the Requirements for the Degree Doctor
    of Philosophy, Capella University, January 2012.

35 Laurie Rogers to May Rogers, Friday 28 January 1916, 5 March 1916, Letters of Lt. Lawrence Browning Rogers, Textual Records 58A 1 207.1-5, CWM-MHRC.

36 Frank Maheux to Angeline Maheux, 29 December [1916], Francis-Xavier Maheux fonds, MG30-E297, R5156-0-4-E, LAC.

37 Military Service record of Ernest Clarke: http://central.bac-lac.gc.ca/. item/?op=pdf&app=CEF&id=B1733-S022; Military Service record of Edward Clarke: http://central.bac-lac.gc.ca/.item/?op=pdf&app=CEF&id=B1732-S010. I would like to thank my aunt, Maria Clarke, for sharing with me a copy of the telegram Frances Clarke received in error in January 1916. Frances Clarke was my maternal great-grandmother.

38 Ellen Ewen to Arthur Leighton, 2 March 1917, Canadian Letters and Images Project: http://www.canadianletters.ca/content/document-1706?position=28& list=LB1vAwaQoa9.

39 "Heard Husband Call across the Ocean," Toronto Daily Star, 28 April 1916.

40 Hand-written document, "'Weird' war story: Private record of circumstances surrounding my husband's death." Correspondence of Gunner W[ilfrid] J. Cove, Royal Garrison Artillery, Liddle Collection, Special Collections Library, University of Leeds.

41 Brady Brower, Unruly Spirits: The Science of Psychic Phenomena in Modern France (Urbana-Champaign: University of Illinois Press, 2010), 100.

42 Jean-Yves Le Naour, The Living Unknown Soldier: A Story of Grief and the Great War, trans. Penny Allen (New York: Metropolitan Books, 2004).

43 "Boy Swindled War Widow out of $700," Toronto Daily Star, 21 March 1919.

44 Jay Winter, Sites of Memory, Sites of Mourning: The Great War in European Cultural History (Cambridge: Cambridge University Press, 1995), 34.

45 Jennie Hillyer's granddaughter recalls how Jennie lived for many years with her two sisters. Norma Hillyer Shephard, Dear Harry, 238.

46 Commonwealth War Graves Commission: https://www.cwgc.org/find-war-dead/casualty/2954664/hillyer,-henry-james/.

47 Jonathan Vance, Death So Noble: Memory, Meaning and the First World War (Vancouver: UBC Press, 1997); and Mark David Sheftall, Altered Memories of the Great War: Divergent Narratives of Britain, Australia, New Zealand and Canada (London: I.B. Tauris, 2009).

48 Eric McGeer and Steve Douglas, Canada's Dream Shall Be of Them: Canadian Epitaphs of the Great War (Waterloo, ON: Wilfrid Laurier University Press, 2017), 59.

49 Commonwealth War Graves Commission: https://www.cwgc.org/find-war-dead/casualty/136974/knight,-percy-joseph/.

50 Commonwealth War Graves Commission: https://www.cwgc.org/find-war-dead/casualty/596138/henry,-william-john/; https://www.cwgc.org/find-war-dead/casualty/469901/dunn,-/.

51 Jonathan F. Vance observes: "The figure of Jesus Christ and the notion of
    redemption through sacrifice ... offered real solace ... The soldier gave his
    leg, the woman her husband, and the parents their son's mind, all to save
    the world. By offering what was most precious to them, these people had
    partaken of Christ's sacrifice." Vance, *Death So Noble*, 36.
52 Commonwealth War Graves Commission: https://www.cwgc.org/find-war-
    dead/casualty/74461/harrison,-thomas/.
53 Lynne Marks notes that before the war, "Spiritualists comprised one of the
    largest metaphysical religious groups in British Columbia," and the number
    of self-identified spiritualists in Canada grew from 674 in 1911 to 1,558 in
    1921. Marks, *Infidels and the Damn Churches: Irreligion and Religion in Settler
    British Columbia* (Vancouver: UBC Press, 2017), 189, 233. On spiritualism in
    central Canada, see Stan McMullin, *Anatomy of a Séance: A History of Spirit
    Communication in Central Canada* (Montreal: McGill-Queen's University
    Press, 2004). On the significance of spiritualism in postwar Europe, see Jay
    Winter, *Sites of Memory, Sites of Mourning: The Great War in European Cultural
    History* (Cambridge: Cambridge University Press, 1995), ch. 3: "Spiritualism
    and the 'Lost Generation.'"
54 Esyllt Jones, "Spectral Influenza: Winnipeg's Hamilton Family, Interwar
    Spiritualism, and Pandemic Disease," *Epidemic Encounters: Influenza, Society,
    and Culture in Canada, 1918–1920*, ed. Magda Fahrni and Esyllt W. Jones
    (Vancouver: UBC Press, 2012), 202.
55 "Would Judge All Religions by the Cross," Toronto *Globe*, 19 January 1920.
56 "Says History of 'Spiritism' One of Fraud," Toronto *Globe*, 15 May 1922.
57 Tim Cook analyzes in careful detail the various coping strategies Canadian
    soldiers developed to manage the stress and horror of front-line service.
    Cook, *The Secret History of Soldiers: How Canadians Survived the Great War*
    (Toronto: Allen Lane, 2018).

Index

soldiers' convalescence in, 21, 64, 80, 130, 125, 135, 138; Canadian soldiers' training in, 35, 79, 81, 101, 102, 118, 121, 122–3, 134, 160; cost of living in, 107, 138; divorce in, 174–5, 182, 183–4; Folkestone, 118, 121, 123, 124, 129, 154; Harrow, 139, 211; Hastings, 129; Hythe, 118, 121–3, 129; Liverpool, 3, 63, 143, 166, 169, 190, 194; letter-writing practices, 58; material hardship, 131, 138, 139–40; postal service, 58, 59, 62–3, 134; Seaford, 64; Shorncliffe, 101, 118, 121, 122, 123, 160, 168; war widows' remarriage, 166–7; wartime bigamy, 173, 184–5, 191; Witley, 123; Yorkshire, 129, 131, 132, 135, 138, 166. *See also* London (UK); wives' relocation

enlistment in CEF: British-born volunteers, 27, 30, 39, 47, 48, 54–5, 88; Canadian-born volunteers, 4–5, 39–40, 41, 49, 54; economic factors encouraging, 13, 15–16, 27, 28–30, 33–4, 43; First Contingent, 31, 35, 72, 109, 155, 227n6; married men's motivations, 32–5, 36, 38–9, 47, 48–51, 52–3, 170; impediments to married men's, 27–8, 31, 33, 41–4; Second Contingent, 35; statistics, 27, 32, 54, 55. *See also* conscription

Evans, Edith and James, 34, 120–1, 123

farming, 7–8, 12, 13, 34–5, 90, 91–2, 112, 132, 136, 152, 154, 177, 190, 195, 198, 205

Festubert, Battle of, 50, 154

films: *Battle Cry of Peace* (1915), 49–50, 54; *The Blindness of Divorce* (1918), 176; *Whatsoever a Man Soweth* (1917), 156; *A Widow by Proxy* (1919), 167

First Nations, 110; Maniwaki Reserve, 5, 111, 113, 114; Odawa, 5; Six Nations Indian Reserve, 206

food packages, 59–61, 81, 129, 129–30, 134, 203

food shortages, 36, 88, 116, 139, 188, 203, 204; in Europe, 7–8, 9–10, 202. *See also* hunger

France: bereavement, 204, 211; Canadian soldiers' attitudes towards, 77, 79–80; conscription, 7, 12, 162; divorce, 174, 175; letter-writing practices, 5–6, 19, 70, 202; occupied regions, 203; Paris, 8, 107; postal service, 59; psychological stress of civilians, 203–4, 211–12; refugee families in, 99–100; remarriage of war widows, 166; separation allowances, 203; venereal disease, 155; women's war work, 8, 9, 12, 14, 88, 107, 202

fuel supplies: coal, 5, 12, 16, 40, 55, 79, 83, 88, 92, 96–8, 139, 152, 163, 194, 203; wood, 91–3, 97–8, 113

Gallipoli, 184, 185

German atrocities, 35–9, 48, 50; aerial bombardment of cities, 41, 120, 123, 132; Belgian refugees, 35–6; the Bryce Report, 37–8; "crucified Canadians," 36–8; execution of Edith Cavell, 39, 48; sinking of the *Lusitania*, 36–8